Foucault and the *Kamasutra*

Foucault and the Kamasutra

The Courtesan, the Dandy, and the Birth of *Ars Erotica* as Theater in India

SANJAY K. GAUTAM

The University of Chicago Press
Chicago and London

Sanjay K. Gautam is associate professor of history at the University of Colorado, Boulder.

The University of Chicago Press, Chicago 60637
The University of Chicago Press, Ltd., London

Printed in the United States of America

25 24 23 22 21 20 19 18 17 16   1 2 3 4 5

ISBN-13: 978-0-226-34830-8 (cloth)
ISBN-13: 978-0-226-34844-5 (paper)
ISBN-13: 978-0-226-34858-2 (e-book)
DOI: 10.7208/chicago/9780226348582.001.0001

Library of Congress Cataloging-in-Publication Data

Names: Gautam, Sanjay K. (Sanjay Kumar), author.
Title: Foucault and the Kamasutra : the courtesan, the dandy, and the birth of ars erotica as theater in India / Sanjay K. Gautam.
Description: Chicago ; London : The University of Chicago Press, 2016. | Includes bibliographical references and index.
Identifiers: LCCN 2015038333 | ISBN 9780226348308 (cloth : alk. paper) | ISBN 9780226348445 (pbk. : alk. paper) | ISBN 9780226348582 (e-book)
Subjects: LCSH: Erotic literature, Indic—History and criticism. | Vātsyāyana. Kāmasūtra. | Courtesans in literature. | Dandies in literature. |Theater—Influence. | Bharata Muni. Nāṭyaśāstra. | Aesthetics, Indic. | Pleasure—Philosophy. | Sex—Philosophy. | Sex—India—History. | Foucault, Michel, 1926–1984.
Classification: LCC PK2907.E7 G38 2016 | DDC 891/.2093538—dc23 LC record available at http://lccn.loc.gov/2015038333

♾ This paper meets the requirements of ANSI/NISO Z39.48-1992 (Permanence of Paper).

To my father, Radhakrishna Singh, and my mother, Shanti Singh

Contents

Preface ix
Acknowledgments xiii
Introduction 1

1 Foucault and the Notion of *Ars Erotica*: Pleasure as Desubjectivation 20

2 Pleasure and Patriarchy: The Discourse of *Dharma* and the Figure of the Wife 50

3 The Courtesan and the Birth of *Ars Erotica* as Theater 87

4 The Courtesan and the Origins of the *Nāṭyaśāstra*: From *Ars Erotica* to *Ars Theatrica* 113

5 The Dandy-Guru and the Birth of the Discourses of Erotics and Theater 153

6 The City Dandy and the Vision of the City Based on Art 181

7 Foucault and the *Kāmasūtra*: Parting Ways 204

Notes 211
Bibliography 251
Index 273

Preface

This book is a historical exploration into three inglorious characters in ancient India: the courtesan and her two closest male companions, her patron the dandy-consort and her teacher and adviser the dandy-guru. Cast aside by history and disinherited by those bearing false witness from their rightful place among the founders of Indian culture, these three were nevertheless at the very origins of the texts universally recognized as two of the mainsprings of classical Indian culture: the *Kāmasūtra*, a treatise on sexual-erotic pleasure, and the *Nāṭyaśāstra*, a treatise on theater, music, dance, and aesthetic pleasure. The courtesan, more than her two male associates, embodied in her singular persona the highest and grandest symbols of both sexual-erotic and aesthetic pleasure. She holds the historical key to the secrets of how erotics and aesthetics came to be so deeply and abidingly intertwined in ancient India.

As a scholar of the cultural-intellectual history of ancient India, my encounter with the *Kāmasūtra* preceded my acquaintance with Michel Foucault's works on the history of sexuality. What struck me in my reading of the *Kāmasūtra* was its use of the words *nāyaka* and *nāyikā,* or actor and actress, as technical terms to designate the male and female partners in a sexual-erotic affair. Left completely unexplained, this intriguing choice of words in the *Kāmasūtra* raised a fundamental question: Why did the *Kāmasūtra* as a text on erotics borrow its critical vocabulary from theater to designate partners in a sexual-erotic affair, when the words "man" and "woman" or "lover" and "beloved" could have easily served its purpose? This choice of words seemed to carry traces of historical and conceptual affinities between erotics and theater, between the world of art and culture and that of sexual-erotic affairs, that demanded an investigation.

The *Kāmasūtra* has proved elusive to scholars seeking access to the secrets of its origins. With its catalog of male and female sexual types based on dimensions of sexual anatomies—such as "horse men" and "elephant women"—and graphic instructions on the ways of sexual-erotic pleasure, the arrival of the *Kāmasūtra* in the West after its translations into English and many other European languages in the last quarter of the nineteenth century came as a major intellectual and cultural scandal. Even as it acquired a near-universal recognition as the most iconic text in its field, perhaps the most recognized Indian text outside of India, it was greeted by an intellectual and academic silence that has largely remained in force until today, with only occasional interruptions. The *Kāmasūtra* did not seem accessible to intellectual reflection, not because it held its secrets too tightly, but because it seemed to have none. It was as if the meaning of this text was exhausted in its reading, leaving nothing for reflection. Not surprisingly, it became part of the furtive world of pornography, its appearance often inviting censors.

It was not until I came in contact with Foucault's works on the history of sexuality that my initial curiosity about the nature and origins of the *Kāmasūtra* turned into a research project. The contrast between *ars erotica*, or erotic arts, and *scientia sexualis*, or the science of sexuality, that Foucault placed at the center of his first volume of the *History of Sexuality* opened up a new intellectual horizon within which one could now locate the *Kāmasūtra*. In this contrast Foucault positioned *ars erotica* as a counter to *scientia sexualis* as best exemplified in Sigmund Freud's psychoanalysis. In doing so he recognized *ars erotica* as an independent intellectual tradition in its own right and thus relativized the discourse of sexuality as science, shattering its self-evident claims to truth and universality. It now became possible to bring the *Kāmasūtra* out of its shadowy existence and open it up to scholarly investigations. If Foucault stands before the *Kāmasūtra* in the title of this book, then that is because it was he who offered an access into it.

It is not without significance that the appearance of the *Kāmasūtra* as the most iconic text of *ars erotica* in the West coincided with the advent of psychoanalysis in the early years of the twentieth century as the exemplary school of *scientia sexualis*. Even as the world hailed psychoanalysis as a major intellectual achievement, the *Kāmasūtra* merely invited embarrassed curiosity. It is striking that even as Freud placed sexuality at the origin of civilization, he nevertheless saw no need to even comment on the *Kāmasūtra* as a treatise on sexual-erotic pleasure. This was not a matter of simple oversight; it reflected Freud's understanding of sexual-erotic pleasure and its adversarial relationship with culture and civilization. After all, psychoanalysis is founded on the assumed opposition between sexual-erotic pleasure as the domain of sensuality and culture as the domain of thought, art, aesthetics, and, indeed, love. Not surprisingly, in the grand narrative of psychoanalysis, it is through the twin mechanisms of repression and sublimation that culture and love enforce their sovereignty over sexual-erotic pleasure.

In a dramatic contrast that reveals the social-historical origins of psychoanalysis, there is no conflict between sensuality and love in the *Kāmasūtra*. Indeed, the courtesan in the *Kāmasūtra* was the most celebrated symbol of continuity between the world of sexual-erotic pleasure, on the one hand, and the world of love, aesthetics, and culture, on the other. The *Kāmasūtra*, notwithstanding its popular perception as a manual of the uninhibited celebration of sensuality, makes love an indispensable precondition for sexual-erotic pleasure. In a remarkable and revealing contrast, in the course of his investigations into the erotic lives of his patients in the *Three Essays on Love*, Freud identifies the figure of the courtesan as a symbol of sexual-erotic pleasure and sensuality without love. For Freud, the greatest allure of the courtesan as the most "debased" figure of sensual pleasure lay precisely in the fact that she did not ask for love. The contrast that the *Kāmasūtra* offers suggests that Freud's reduction of sexual pleasure to pure sensuality is a historical legacy of patriarchy—a gendered discourse of power—that gave man access to woman's body without a discourse of love. In Freud's philosophical-scientific sounding opposition between sensual-sexual pleasure and culture-love, therefore, it was the nature and history of gender relations that was really at stake. It is not surprising then that Foucault pitched *ars erotica* grounded in sexual-erotic pleasure as a counter-discourse to *scientia sexualis* grounded in power.

In the end, I have a suggestion for those readers who are unfamiliar with Foucault's works. They might want to start with chapter 2 and come back to the chapter on Foucault at the end. The book lends itself to two ways of reading: while for some readers Foucault may open a door to the *Kāmasūtra*, for others, the *Kāmasūtra* may offer a pathway into Foucault's writings on sexuality.

Acknowledgments

It is with great pleasure that I acknowledge the many friends and colleagues who have helped and supported me in the course of researching and writing this book. I owe the deepest debt of gratitude to Marjorie McIntosh and Fred Anderson for their support and their exceptional kindness and generosity over my years at the University of Colorado at Boulder. I would like to thank my colleagues in the Junior Faculty Reading Group who read initial drafts of chapters: Francisco Barbosa, Brian Delay, Matthew Gerber, Myles Osborne, Richard Reitan, and John Willis. I also thank my friends and colleagues at the University of Colorado who have encouraged and supported me through the years: Virginia Anderson, Peter Boag, Robert Ferry, Jane Garrity, Donna Goldstein, David Gross, Kira Hall, Martha Hanna, Karen Jacobs, Carla Jones, Dennis McGilvray, Carole McGranahan, Mark Pittenger, Timothy Weston, and Marcia Yonemoto.

I am deeply grateful to Patrick Olivelle for his immensely helpful comments and suggestions at the early stages of this project and for his extraordinary kindness and encouragement through the years. I also thank Partha Chatterjee and Tapati Guha Thakurta for their encouraging comments when I presented my work at the Center for Studies in Social Sciences in Kolkata. I am deeply grateful to the late Tarapada Maity, who generously shared his unpublished research on courtesans with me. I am greatly indebted to R. Champaklakshmi for her exceptional kindness, generosity, and support of my academic career during my years at Jawaharlal Nehru University in India, and for arousing in me an abiding interest in ancient Indian history. I owe a debt of gratitude to Dilip Simeon and Salim Kidwai, my favorite history professors in college, who have always been a source of inspiration. I also thank Ruth Vanita for her friendship and support.

The University of Colorado provided me with invaluable time off from teaching to work on this manuscript in its initial stages. I would like to acknowledge the IMPART grant program for providing me with travel funds for this project. For their many acts of assistance I thank the staff of the Regenstein Library at the University of Chicago, the Norlin Library at the University of Colorado, the National Archives of India, the Nehru Memorial Library in New Delhi, and the National Library in Calcutta.

Material contained in chapter 3 appeared earlier in an article in the January 2014 issue of the *Journal of the History of Sexuality*. A part of chapter 1 appeared in the December 2013 issue of *South Asian Review*. I thank the editors and publishers of the two journals for permission to reproduce the material here.

It has been a real pleasure to work with the University of Chicago Press. I am very grateful to the outside readers for their suggestions for improving the manuscript. I owe a special debt of gratitude to Douglas Mitchell, my editor at the University of Chicago Press, for his kindness and enthusiastic support of this project. I also thank Tim McGovern and Kyle Wagner for their immense patience and care with the manuscript.

Finally, I would like to thank friends and family whose support and encouragement have been invaluable: Shailendra Dhar, Pradeep Kant Chaudhari, Kundan Gautam, Rajeev Gautam, Balasubramanian Krishnan, Sharad Kumar, Poonam and Shankar Sharan, Radha Sreenivasan, and Iris Elron. I would like to acknowledge in particular Arun Kumar and Bharati for their love and hospitality during my many trips to Delhi. I am deeply indebted to Amalendu Mukherjee, Krishna Dutta, Kamalendu Dutta, and Tamanash Dutta for my home in Kolkata and for their unfailing support of this project. This book would not have been possible without the love and support of my father, Radha Krishna Singh, and my mother, Shanti Singh. Finally, I would like to thank Mithi Mukherjee for countless discussions on all aspects of this book from its very inception. I owe some of my most valuable insights to these discussions. This book would not even have been conceived without her unwavering confidence in the project. My eight-year-old twin daughters, Avanti and Yosha, have been a source of great joy and inspiration throughout the writing of this book. Their good-natured prodding played no small role in its completion.

Boulder, Colorado

Introduction

This book is a historical exploration into the nature and origins of *ars erotica,* or the erotic arts, as theater in the *Kāmasūtra* in critical engagement with Michel Foucault's works on the history of sexuality.[1] Since its translation into European languages, including English, in the late nineteenth and early twentieth centuries, the *Kāmasūtra*, the foundational text on erotics in ancient India (third century CE), has acquired an iconic status worldwide in the domain of erotics. Indeed, there are few texts from the ancient world, certainly no others from Indian culture, that enjoy the kind of world recognition that the *Kāmasūtra* does. Given its significance, it is remarkable, therefore, that there is no single book-length work in English focused on the nature and origin of the *Kāmasūtra.*[2]

Since the history of erotics in ancient Indian culture is intimately intertwined with the history of theater-aesthetics, a historical investigation into the nature and origin of the *Kāmasūtra* inevitably extends into the nature and origin of the *Nāṭyaśāstra,* or "A Treatise on Theater" (second century CE), as the founding text of theater and aesthetics in ancient India. This book, therefore, brings together four domains of historical enquiry—the nature of knowledge formation, erotics, gender relations, and theater in ancient Indian society and culture—as they converged on the historical figures of the courtesan and her male counterpart, the dandy, who together stood at the origins of both the *Kāmasūtra* and the *Nāṭyaśāstra*.

The contrast of *ars erotica,* or the erotic arts anchored in pleasure, with its origin in nonwestern cultures, including India, and *scientia sexualis,* or the science of sexuality, anchored in truth and self, as characteristic of western culture, played a central role in Foucault's problematization of his project on the history of sexuality.[3] Indeed, *ars erotica* functioned as the critical ground to Foucault's history of *scientia sexualis*.[4] Given that Foucault's volumes on the history of sexuality have been decisive in setting the agenda for a history of sexuality and sexual practices not only in the West, but for much of the rest of the world, a thorough understanding of this contrast between *ars erotica* and *scientia sexualis* by way of an exploration into the *Kāmasūtra* acquires enormous significance. A more precise understanding of the nature and history of *ars erotica*, therefore, has implications for the general contemporary debates on the history of sexuality, erotics, gender relations, and knowledge formation in different cultures.

Despite the centrality of this contrast in Foucault's project on the history of sexuality, in the years since the publication of the first of his six projected volumes of the history of sexuality, much of the academic discourse on the subject has evolved largely unmindful of its significance, as if it were nothing more than a minor point in an otherwise vast and ambitious project that pursued its subject through the entire length of western history.[5] The lack of attention that the discourse of *ars erotica* grounded in sexual-erotic pleasure has received may be due to the fact that Foucault's comments on these subjects, illuminating as they are, are scattered and often all too brief.[6] Foucault did not do for the discourse and practice of pleasure what he did so well for the discourse and practice of power, particularly in *Discipline and Punish*.[7] Not surprisingly, Foucault acknowledged that his notion of pleasure did not yet have enough content and was rather sketchy.[8] By lack of content Foucault meant that pleasure as reflected in *ars erotica* was still an unexplored domain of experience and discourse. While an understanding of *ars erotica* anchored in pleasure is vital, the fact that it was not directly the focus of Foucault's research means that his comments and observations on the subject appear enigmatic since they leave a number of insights unelaborated and largely assumed.

By way of an exploration into the *Kāmasūtra*, this book is also an attempt to engage with Foucault's brief comments on pleasure, to explore their meaning, and to give content to the notion of *ars erotica* that was vital to Foucault's project on the history of sexuality. The *Kāmasūtra*, or "A Treatise on Pleasure"—more than most other historical archives in the field—offers itself as an ideal interlocutor to Foucault and helps us understand his approach and insights, because it reveals the nature and constitution of the discursive universe that gave birth to *ars erotica* comprehensively and vividly. Since Foucault grounds *ars erotica* in the notion of pleasure, its continuity with the *Kāmasūtra* as "a treatise on pleasure" is immediately evident.[9] What also makes the *Kāmasūtra* such a useful interlocutor to Foucault is that it problematizes its own nature and origin very self-consciously as the founding text of the discourse and practice of sexual-erotic pleasure. What remains hidden, or only partially developed, in Foucault's own insightful but brief comments on *ars erotica* becomes fully evident in the *Kāmasūtra*.

Central Arguments

According to Foucault, whereas *scientia sexualis* is grounded in the notions of truth and self, or identity, *ars erotica* is grounded in sexual-erotic pleasure as the sovereign legislative category to which the notions of truth and identity are subordinated.[10] Foucault claimed that *ars erotica* did not exist in the West because pleasure could not win for itself discursive and legislative autonomy that would have allowed it to speak and make rules for itself; it always lived a furtive existence in the shadows of other discourses, such as philosophy, morality, religion, law, and science. In other words, pleasure was always subordinated to a system of knowledge and truth that was exterior to it.

In the contrast that Foucault made between *ars erotica* and *scientia sexualis*, what was, therefore, at stake was also the contrast between the nature and history of knowledge formations in the non-West and the West. Even as it offered a critical insight into the nature of *ars erotica*, Foucault's study also opened up a rare window of opportunity to problematize and study the nature and origin of knowledge formations in nonwestern cultures, such as ancient India, in all their specificity and difference.[11] It is because the *Kāmasūtra* has generally been seen, since its translations into European languages, from the perspective of the dominant tradition of western knowledge systems that its meaning and origin have proved so elusive. In the absence of an approach in tune with the logic of knowledge formation in premodern India, in its specificity and difference, the *Kāmasūtra* has hung like a scandal in the universe of western knowledge systems, producing immense curiosity but not much analysis. In other words, if we follow Foucault's logic, the *Kāmasūtra* was not accessible to western knowledge systems for the same reason that *ars erotica* did not come into being in the West in the first place. If Foucault opened a door on the *Kāmasūtra,* then that is because in the process of his search for an exteriority to truth and self as the ground of knowledge evident in *scientia sexualis*, he stumbled upon *ars erotica* in nonwestern cultures.

The questions that this book pursues relate to the precise nature and origin of the legislative sovereignty that pleasure came to acquire in ancient India as reflected in the *Kāmasūtra*. I develop this enquiry along two intersecting lines, intellectual and historical. If the *Kāmasūtra* was at all possible as *ars erotica* as a separate and autonomous domain of discourse in ancient India, that is because it found in this culture a different discursive universe, in which the rules of discourse formation differed fundamentally from the West as described in Foucault's works. Intellectually, the *Kāmasūtra* self-consciously problematized its own origin as the inaugural text of a new domain of sexual-erotic knowledge and pedagogy by locating itself within what it called the *trivarga,* or the trilogy, as a complex of three competing and conflicting ontological domains and imperatives of history and life: *dharma,* or Brahmanical law; *artha,* or political power; *kāma,* or sexual-erotic pleasure.[12] Later the trilogy came to be popularly known as *puruṣārthas,* or the ends of man. In the notion of *puruṣārthas* the trilogy was expanded to accommodate *mokṣa,* or spiritual liberation, as the fourth member, hence also the name *caturavarga,* or tetralogy.

The notion of *puruṣārthas* as the four primary ends of man, however, may be misleading because it appears to subordinate the otherwise ontological domains and imperatives to a certain assumed notion of man. This may give the impression that the trilogy-tetralogy is a psychological complex. In contrast, the numerical nomenclature of the trilogy and tetralogy suggests that there was a reluctance to subsume their constituents under a higher category because they themselves were seen as the highest categories. Depending on the context, the trilogy-tetralogy could mean the broadest ontological domains of human activity, knowledge, and history or the ontological imperatives that constitute man without being constituted by him. While the *Kāmasūtra* uses the notion of trilogy, the *Nāṭyaśāstra* deploys the term tetralogy. The most important thing to keep in mind is that the notions of trilogy and tetralogy are more ontological than moral or psychological in nature. Also note that in premodern Indian intellectual traditions multiple competing and conflicting ontologies were acknowledged and accepted almost as a matter of common sense.

The notions of the trilogy and tetralogy are of immense significance because they came to determine the nature, origin, and evolution of major discursive formations in ancient Indian history.[13] In time it was around these four constituents of the tetralogy that much of the intellectual tradition in ancient India came to be organized, giving rise to four distinct domains of knowledge, as four discursive formations: the discourse of Brahmanical law (*dharma-śāstra*), the discourse of political power (*artha-śāstra*), the discourse of sexual-erotic pleasure (*kāma-śāstra*), and the discourse of spiritual liberation (*mokṣa-śāstra*). Though these discursive formations have complex histories, each of them has what could be called a founding text: the *Mānava Dharmaśāstra* (first century BCE–first century CE), or a discourse on Brahmanical law; the *Arthaśāstra* (first century BCE), or a discourse on political power; the *Kāmasūtra* (third century CE), or a discourse on sexual-erotic pleasure; and the *Brahmasūtra,* in the domain of *mokṣa-śāstra* or a discourse on spiritual liberation.[14] Seen in this light the trilogy-tetralogy are better understood as a complex of competing and conflicting discursive formations. Reduced to the basics, trilogy-tetralogy are simply a dynamic historical-ontological complex of three or four (tri-tetra) discourses. They could also be seen as multiple competing and conflicting ontological imperatives operating on man at the same time.

In the very naming of the major genres of discourse much of the ancient Indian understanding of knowledge—that is, its origin and end—is revealed. In light of the dominant intellectual tradition in the West, as brought out by Foucault, what comes as a surprise is that, let alone being the sole sovereign ground of knowledge as such, truth is altogether absent as the ground of any of these discourses. Instead of rising above these discursive domains as a sovereign principle, truth belonged to them as a subordinate category. In this tradition, all knowledge and truth had their origin and end in the four ontological imperatives—law, power, pleasure, and spiritual liberation. There would be no truth or knowledge if these imperatives did not open up the horizon of intelligibility for it in advance. Nor would this knowledge have any purpose other than to serve those imperatives in turn. In other words, in Indian intellectual traditions truth was an ontic—not ontological—category, to use a Heideggerian distinction.[15] Given that a broad framework of the trilogy-tetralogy preceded it by a few centuries, a separate place for a discourse on *kāma,* or pleasure, had already been marked out long before the *Kāmasūtra* came to be written, and as such constituted a very important intellectual condition for its possibility.

That, however, is not to say that the *Kāmasūtra*'s existence was either inevitable or the precise nature of pleasure at stake thereby already determined. The autonomy theoretically assumed for the discursive domains could not be taken for granted; it had to be claimed and fought for. Given that they bear down on the same individual and the same society, the relationship between the discourses is marked by competition and conflict over issues of their relative legislative sovereignty and, whenever possible, hegemony.[16] Legislative sovereignty means the ability of a discourse to make its own rules and to determine what is true and false. Hegemony means the ability of a discourse to claim the right to make rules for another discourse. I locate the birth of the *Kāmasūtra* itself in an effort to win legislative autonomy for sexual-erotic pleasure (*kāma*) from the discourse of Brahmanical law (*dharma*). The *Kāmasūtra* justified the need for a discourse of *ars erotica* because it claimed that sexual-erotic pleasure (*kāma*) had come under the hegemonic influence of Brahmanical law (*dharma*).[17] Clearly, in this justification the *Kāmasūtra* directly problematizes its own origin as a founding text: it is for the sake of the legislative sovereignty of the discourse of sexual-erotic pleasure that the *Kāmasūtra* must come into being.

Through a reading of the *Kāmasūtra* I show that in the upper classes of the society at the time sexual-erotic pleasure had come to be subordinated to *dharma*, a hegemonic discourse of Brahmanical law based on the division and hierarchy of castes—Brahmin, Kṣatriya, Vaiśya, and Śudra—as articulated in the *Mānava Dharmaśāstra*, written about two centuries before the *Kāmasūtra*.[18] Together with maintaining the powers and privileges of the higher castes, the other major concern of the discourse of *dharma* was to enforce caste identity and maintain its purity and authenticity. It was thus that the discourse of *dharma* came to focus on the institution of the family and lay the ground for patriarchy. If caste and patriarchal identity were to become the basis of society, a law of identity had to be imposed on sexual practices. Complete freedom in sexual practices, after all, would have threatened these identities. Thus sex, or sexual practices, came to be subordinated to the sovereign discourse of *dharma* as a discourse of identity. The subordination of sex and sexual pleasure to *dharma* in effect was its subordination to identity.

Under this discourse of Brahmanical law women were reduced to nothing more than instruments to reproduce their husbands' identities by bearing them sons.[19] If the purity and authenticity of patriarchal identity had to be maintained, women had to be completely subordinated to their husbands. It was for the purpose of subjugating the wife that the *Mānava Dharmaśāstra* invented a whole new form of power: power that operated by constructing subjectivity, and not through coercive force. The figure of the wife had to be constructed as a new subjectivity under the discourse of Brahmanical law (*dharma*) in such a way that she would subordinate herself to her husband. The *Mānava Dharmaśāstra* thus invented an altogether new philosophy—Brahmanical philosophy—and mechanics of power that were very different from the discourse of power constructed in the *Arthaśāstra*, which was based on political and military power.

In contrast to Foucault's writings on the subject that, by and large, have overlooked the issues of gender relations in the problematization of the questions of sexuality and erotics, I argue that the question of gender was at the heart of the origin of the *Kāmasūtra* as the founding text of *ars erotica*.[20] In the discourse of *dharma* the subordination of pleasure to Brahmanical law went hand in hand with the subordination of women to men.[21] The two processes came to be so inextricably linked that they appear to be two aspects of the same historical and intellectual phenomenon. Given this discursive context in which sexual practices were caught in a web of identity anchored in relations of power, for the *Kāmasūtra* to claim autonomy for sexual pleasure as a theoretical exercise would have been nothing more than a pyrrhic victory. The real challenge for the *Kāmasūtra*, therefore, was to find a form of life located outside the circle of identity in which both women and pleasure could in fact attain and exercise their autonomy.[22]

I argue that it was in its search for that form of life outside the circle of identity that the *Kāmasūtra* stumbled upon the figure of the courtesan.[23] Neither the rules of caste nor that of patriarchal family applied to her.[24] Sex with courtesans, after all, created no confusion of identity, because the children born of courtesans continued to live outside the circle of patriarchal and caste identity. It was thus that pleasure came to acquire its historical autonomy as a sovereign legislative discourse in the figure and the institution of the courtesan. Not surprisingly, according to the *Kāmasūtra*, the courtesan was in the field of erotics what the king was in politics: the exceptional and sovereign figure.

There are of course other female figures in the *Kāmasūtra*, such as the wife, the young girl (*kanyā*), another man's wife as the adulteress (*paradāra*), and the remarried woman (*punarbhū*). But these figures either did not embody the discourse of erotic pleasure (*kāma*) in its legislative autonomy from the discourse of *dharma* as Brahmanical law or did so only partially, not fully as the courtesan did. Since the most fundamental notions and features of the discourse of erotics are revealed only in its moment of autonomy, the courtesan is the primary focus of my book. It is in the courtesan that the historical part of my inquiry into the nature and origin of the *Kāmasūtra* takes its start. As the measure and model in the domain of erotics, the courtesan was at the historical origin of the discourse of erotics as reflected in the *Kāmasūtra*, just as the notion of trilogy was at its intellectual origin. It was the courtesan and the set of practices that developed around her that constituted not only the ever-present historical and cultural context of the *Kāmasūtra* but also one of its most important sources of ideas. Insofar as the issues of pleasure, truth, and identity—the concerns that Foucault placed at the heart of *ars erotica*—wove a complex web in the courtesan's life, it was in her that the discourse and practice, the thought and history of *ars erotica* encountered each other. As a historical exploration into the nature and origin of *ars erotica*, this book thus follows the footprints of the courtesan in the *Kāmasūtra*.

Even as the courtesan constituted a sovereign figure in the domain of erotics, she could not constitute the entire field of erotics by herself—she needed an erotic counterpart. It was as the male counterpart and mirror image of the courtesan that the dandy emerged as one of the most significant—though little studied—figures in ancient Indian history. The Sanskrit term for the dandy was *vaiśika* or patron-consort of the courtesan.[25] This figure came into being because over time the relationship between the courtesan and her patron was no longer simply about a chance sexual encounter in which sexual pleasure was had in exchange for money; it reflected the historical transition of the courtesan's patron from being a customer to a lover-consort. Like Baudelaire's dandy, the figure of the dandy in ancient India was also grounded in the pursuit of beauty, love, and happiness.[26] He was a man of cultivated taste and bearing who took a great deal of interest in his personal appearance, manners, and speech. Moreover, just like Baudelaire's dandy, he too was a man of the city, a product of urban culture, and he needed to be wealthy to afford a lifestyle of leisurely pursuit. Indeed, such was the dandy's connection with the city that the *Kāmasūtra* renamed *vaiśika* as the *nāgaraka* or the city dandy.

I argue in this book that the figure of the dandy appeared in three configurations in ancient Indian culture: the young dandy as the patron-consort of the courtesan (*vaiśika*), the older dandy as the teacher-adviser or guru to the courtesan (*viṭa*), and the city dandy (*nāgaraka*), the primary male figure in the *Kāmasūtra*. Once the patron-consort of the courtesan grew old and lost much of his wealth and passion for sexual pleasure, he became the teacher-adviser to the courtesan, now more interested in the discursive aspects of the domain of erotics. What makes this figure of the dandy-guru critical to the history of erotics in India is that it was primarily in him that erotics emerged as a discourse. It was as if the courtesan came to find her self-consciousness in the dandy as her teacher-adviser. The third figure of the *nāgaraka,* or city dandy, was none other than the same patron-consort of the courtesan, only renamed by the *Kāmasūtra* to anchor its vision of the city based on art and aesthetics. *Ars erotica*, therefore, was no more possible without the dandy than it was without the courtesan.

The other line of historical inquiry that this book pursues is a subtle, but critical, affinity between erotics and theater, an affinity that holds the key to the nature of pleasure and the mode of its pursuit in the *Kāmasūtra*. One of the most revealing, albeit unproblematized, details in the *Kāmasūtra* is its intriguing choice of the terms *nāyaka,* or actor, and *nāyikā,* or actress, to designate the partners in an erotic affair.[27] This raises two primary questions: What was the precise historical genealogy of these critical but undefined words in the *Kāmasūtra*? And what was it about the nature of erotics that prompted the *Kāmasūtra* to use the language of theater to designate its central characters? I argue that if the *Kāmasūtra* left its choice of the vocabulary of theater undefined and unproblematized, that was because it found those words self-evident in the relationship between the courtesan—the sovereign figure in the domain of erotics—and the dandy as her patron-consort.

The courtesan carried a conflict at the very heart of her existence: even as she frequently played the role of the beloved—and indeed the wife—to her patron-consorts, she also knew that it was a profession for her; she knew that she must never become the wife, the real wife, even if she had to play one.[28] On the other hand, the dandy too could only play a husband, never be one in reality. In this relationship between the courtesan and the dandy, the figures of the wife and the husband were reduced to nothing more than instruments of pleasure. I argue that erotics as theater was born directly out of the imperative to reconcile this existential conflict in the lives of both the courtesan and her patron-consort. It was from the need to invent new identities in the pursuit of sexual-erotic pleasure that erotics in the *Kāmasūtra* morphed into a form of theater and art—*ars erotica* as *ars theatrica*. Anchored as it was in invented narratives and identities, this language of theater also reveals, exactly as Foucault had argued, that *ars erotica* as the pursuit of pleasure exceeded the framework of truth and identity as the twin foundations of the discourse of sexuality.

This transformation of erotics into theater was an important historical event because it also constituted the historical origin of theater as reflected in the *Nāṭyaśāstra*, the founding text on the discourse and practice of theater that came into being in India in the second century CE, a century earlier than the *Kāmasūtra*.[29] Not surprisingly then, the historical figures of the courtesan and the dandy played a major role in the origin of theater and stood as the bridge between the two foundational texts—the *Kāmasūtra* and the *Nāṭyaśāstra*—of classical Indian culture. Indeed, I demonstrate that the three primary figures of the actress, the actor, and the director that together constituted the classical Indian theater as reflected in the *Nāṭyaśāstra* were grounded in the three historical figures of the courtesan, the dandy as her patron-consort (*vaiśika*), and the dandy-guru as her teacher-adviser (*viṭa*), respectively. It was in this historical context that the courtesan and the dandy emerged as the figures of both sexual-erotic and aesthetic pleasure.

Also, the intellectual kinship between the two texts is reflected in that the *Nāṭyaśāstra* determined *rasa* or aesthetic pleasure—parallel to the *Kāmasūtra*'s sexual-erotic pleasure—to be the ultimate goal of theater.[30] What is more, the *Nāṭyaśāstra* directly grounded itself in the broader field of erotic pleasure (*kāma*) and declared it to be the highest of the four ontological-discursive domains, something even the *Kāmasūtra* was reluctant to claim.[31] It is quite evident, therefore, that just as in the *Kāmasūtra*, in the *Nāṭyaśāstra* too it was the legislative primacy of pleasure that was at stake. Indeed, the continuities and kinship between the two texts are so deep and diverse that the *Nāṭyaśāstra* and the *Kāmasūtra* appear to be embedded in—and assumed by—each other, as if they were extensions of each other; as if erotics and theater as twin discourses were determined by the same historical and intellectual necessity in their nature and origin.

Just as erotic practices gave birth to theater, the discourse of theater, in turn, played a critical role in the history of erotics. Given the nature of its historical origin, theater, as reflected in the *Nāṭyaśāstra*, was synonymous with the theater of love. The public discourse of theater-aesthetics as a discourse of love emerged as a major medium of popular pedagogy in the art of erotics. It is impossible to exaggerate the pedagogical value of this theater of love for the erotic relations between men and women. In the historical context of the period under the hegemony of the discourse of *dharma* based on the *Mānava Dharmaśāstra*, women were excluded from the discourses of both political-economic power (*artha*) and Brahmanical law (*dharma*). Without a discourse of love to anchor their relationship with men, women were reduced to nothing more than bodies, giving rise to the popular perception of sex as a purely sensual experience.[32] This perception, widespread at the time of the *Kāmasūtra*, reflects the history of man's access to the woman's body without a discourse of love. Under these historical and discursive circumstances, the only discourse that could function as a medium of communication between men and women was the erotic-aesthetic discourse of love that anchored theater. In the form of art and aesthetics, love functioned as a counter-discourse to Brahmanical law (*dharma*). As I argue, in art and aesthetics as a discourse of love, it was the nature and fate of gender relations that hung in the balance.

Indeed, in the *Kāmasūtra*, the pursuit of erotic and aesthetic pleasure appeared to be the private and public ends of the same historical and discursive continuum. This affinity and continuity between erotics and aesthetics also reveals that they were complementary to each other, as if the private pursuit of sexual-erotic pleasure was not possible in the absence of the public discourse of aesthetic pleasure grounded in love. Instead of being a sublimation of sexual-erotic pleasure, as Sigmund Freud would have us believe, in the *Kāmasūtra* aesthetic pleasure emerged as the ontological discursive precondition for sexual-erotic pleasure. Just as Foucault in his study of *scientia sexualis* found sex to be subordinated to the discourse of sexuality grounded in truth and self, in the *Kāmasūtra* one finds sex subordinated to art and aesthetics grounded in the discourse of love. Not surprisingly, art and aesthetics emerge as a medium of erotic relationship in the *Kāmasūtra*. The real question, therefore, ought not to be the nature of aestheticization of sex in the *Kāmasūtra*, but rather the history of how it came to be de-aestheticized in the world outside it.

It is in this historical context that I locate a larger vision embedded in the *Kāmasūtra* of the city grounded in art and aesthetics as a discourse of love. As an agent of its vision of the city based in art and aesthetics the *Kāmasūtra* discursively renamed—or reconfigured—the already existing historical figure of the patron-consort of the courtesan (*vaiśika*) as city dandy (*nāgaraka*). In the city dandy as the patron, connoisseur, and master of arts, the *Kāmasūtra* sought to create a public figure of aesthetic pleasure. If the *Kāmasūtra*, as the founding text of erotics, decided to anchor one of its two principal figures—the other being the courtesan—in aesthetic pleasure, then that was because in its view the discourse of erotic pleasure was not possible in its absence. In anchoring the city dandy in aesthetic pleasure, the *Kāmasūtra* assumed a whole new vision of the city based in art. In the *Kāmasūtra*'s view, for *ars erotica* to be possible, sexual-erotic practices needed to be anchored in a broader form of ethos and socialization grounded in art. Both the *Kāmasūtra* and the *Nāṭyaśāstra* offered this larger vision as a counter to the other two major visions proposed by the *Arthaśāstra*, of a society anchored in the institution of the state and the figure of the king, and the *Mānava Dharmaśāstra*, of a society anchored in the institutions of caste and patriarchy and the figure of the Brahmin. In their vision of the city anchored in art and aesthetics, the *Kāmasūtra* and the *Nāṭyaśāstra* sought to re-envision society and culture as a whole from the central perspective of gender relations.

Problems of Writing Histories of Ancient Indian Culture: A Theoretical and Methodological Approach

This book falls in the genre of cultural and intellectual history and contributes to contemporary debates relating to issues of sexuality, sexual practices, erotics, and gender relations.[33] There are many different approaches that could be deployed profitably to draw out the meanings of the *Kāmasūtra* and the *Nāṭyaśāstra*: literary, hermeneutical, philosophical, sociological, political, or scientific. None of these approaches singly can claim to exhaust the meaning of either of the two texts. In my approach as a historian, the questions relating to the nature and meaning of the two major texts of erotics and theater from ancient India are inextricably tied to their historical origins. There is an aspect of the meaning of these two texts that would remain inaccessible in the absence of a historical investigation into their origins in ancient India.

However, any investigation into the intellectual and cultural history of ancient India brings with it certain inherent and well-known methodological challenges. Perhaps the most difficult of these challenges is locating historical events, texts, and authors in a precise space-time grid with the exactitude that a historical work requires. It is not rare to see a text assigned a period of several centuries for its composition and compilation. In fact all the major texts under study in this book—the *Kāmasūtra*, the *Nāṭyaśāstra*, and the *Mānava Dharmaśāstra*—fall within that category in varying degrees. It therefore becomes imperative to make certain methodological adjustments to overcome this serious handicap.

In this regard Foucault's methodological innovations, particularly the one relating to the nature and origins of discursive formations in the historical context of relations of power, are very useful.[34] Building on Foucault's insight, this book looks at the domain of erotics and theater as two historically constructed, broad discursive formations within which both the *Kāmasūtra* and the *Nāṭyaśāstra* as texts came to be. One of the reasons that the *Kāmasūtra* and the *Nāṭyaśāstra* have eluded an investigation into their historical origins is that they have been approached and problematized as texts, rather than as discourses. The notion of discursive formation helps break the textual autonomy and isolation of works like the *Kāmasūtra* and the *Nāṭyaśāstra* as great works of thought and locates them within the context of broader history.

When approached as texts, both the *Nāṭyaśāstra* and the *Kāmasūtra* appear as singular creations of individual authors like Vātsyāyana or Bharata; knowledge in this context appears as an ahistorical and theoretical construction of an author who himself seems to stand above history. What is most characteristic of discourse in contrast to a text is that it is directly grounded in a set of historical figures, not in an individual author. In a discourse, knowledge or thoughts have not yet parted ways from the speaking subjects—they are directly grounded in the subjects that enunciate them in the course of their daily lives. As I show in this book, the discourses of both erotics and theater in ancient India were directly grounded in a set of three historical figures: the courtesan, the dandy-consort of the courtesan (*vaiśika* and *nāgaraka*), and the dandy-guru (*viṭa*)—not in an individual author. Even as the relationship between the courtesan and her patron-consort constituted the content of both the discourses of erotics and theater, it was in the figure of the dandy-guru that this content came to be the subject of reflection and took the form of a discourse.

The significance of the question about the identity of the author of the *Nāṭyaśāstra* and the *Kāmasūtra*, therefore, lies not so much in the question of whether Bharata and Vātsyāyana were real individuals, but rather in the historical figures that stood at the origins of the discourses of both erotics and theater. From this perspective, the problem relating to the exact identity of the individual authors of the two texts is thus rendered marginal, if not altogether insignificant. The nature and historical origins of both the *Nāṭyaśāstra* and the *Kāmasūtra* could be revealed through a precise determination of the identity of the historical figures behind them. Insofar as a figure is a product of history, the discursive approach allows me to pursue not only the history of a discourse but also the figures—historical figures as the enunciators of a discourse—in whom this discourse comes into being.

There is another advantage to this discursive approach: it allows one to see that what may superficially appear to be a category of thought is often in fact a mode of being evident in a historical figure. As I show in this book, the *Kāmasūtra* found autonomy for sexual-erotic pleasure in the figure of the courtesan, not solely in a category of thought. Not surprisingly, as the sovereign figure in the domain of erotics the courtesan also became a source of categories. For example, I show in this book that the *Kāmasūtra's* choice of the terms *nāyaka* and *nāyikā* to designate the male and female partners in an erotic affair was historically grounded in the relationship between the courtesan and her patron-consort (*vaiśika* or *nāgaraka*). Indeed, the entire conceptual edifice of both the *Kāmasūtra* and the *Nāṭyaśāstra* operated on the basis of the historical figures of the courtesan and the dandy. Unlike concepts, figures are grounded in history directly and unmistakably. By way of an enquiry into the figures, one is thus able to ground even an abstract-sounding category in history.

This focus on discourse allows me to trace the history of erotics and theater in ancient India by following in the footsteps of historical figures—such as the courtesan and the dandy—rather than focusing exclusively on events, chronology, or "real individuals." Thus, dates, places, and names of the individuals may not be the only—or even the best—way to approach the history of erotics and theater in ancient India. Also, methodologically, the notion of discursive formation allows one to follow the logic of discursive continuity, not chronology alone. So for example, even though the *Kāmasūtra*, the *Nāṭyaśāstra*, and the *bhāṇas* are separated in time, the three figures of the courtesan, her patron-consort, and the dandy-guru are common to these three texts, thus revealing that the content of the texts are in discursive continuity.[35] There are certain advantages in this approach: ancient Indian texts abound in historical figures that are presented with as much vividness as if they were real individuals. What is more, focus on historical figures makes literary sources, available in such abundance, accessible as an archive for historical research. However, because of the general focus in historical works on real individuals, places, events, and years, such figures may easily get overlooked. It is not surprising, therefore, that the figures such as the *viṭa*, the *vaiśika*, and the *nāgaraka* have failed to draw the attention they deserve.

Since the book is centered on the origin of the discourse of erotics, I primarily focus on the courtesan as a discursive figure, and only secondarily as a historical figure. This distinction is made necessary because not all historical figures rise to become discursive figures, let alone to become founding figures of a discourse, as the courtesan did. Indeed, just as the scholarship on the text of the *Kāmasūtra* failed to see the founding role of the courtesan, scholarship on courtesans has also overlooked her role in the birth of the discourse of erotics and theater. The discursive approach thus cuts a middle path between the purely textual approach to the *Kāmasūtra* and the *Nāṭyaśāstra* and a purely historical approach to the courtesan. My focus therefore is exclusively on those moments in which the life of the courtesan comes to intersect with the birth of a discourse of erotics and theater. Precisely for that reason, unless otherwise specified, by courtesan I mean the *gaṇika*, the highest ranked courtesans known for their accomplishments in erotics as well as in fine arts, such as theater, music, singing, and dance.

To come back to Foucault, there has been a concern among some scholars that in locating *ars erotica* anchored in pleasure in Eastern cultures Foucault was merely repeating an old gesture, that of Orientalism with its roots in colonialism.[36] The great irony in this criticism of Foucault as an Orientalist is that we perhaps owe the very notion of "Orientalism" as we know it today to him. In the preface to *History of Madness*, first published in 1962—sixteen years before Edward Said's *Orientalism* was published—Foucault says:

> *In the universality of the Western ratio, there is this division which is the Orient*: the Orient, thought of as the origin, dreamt of as the vertiginous point from which nostalgia and promises of return are born, *the Orient offered to the colonizing reason of the Occident*, but indefinitely inaccessible, for it always remains the limit: the night of the beginning, in which the Occident was formed, but in which it traced a dividing line, the Orient is for the Occident everything that it is not, while remaining the place in which its primitive truth must be sought. *What is required is a history of this great divide, all along this occidental becoming*, following it in its tragic continuity and its exchanges, while also allowing it to appear in its tragic hieratism [emphasis mine].[37]

As is evident in this passage, Foucault does not use the notion of the "Orient" as a self-evident category of academic analysis, as if there was a hidden essence that tied all the cultures that fell under that category. Foucault uses the term "Orient" in the same way as Edward Said did—as a zone of exclusion and domination. Indeed, Foucault was perhaps the first scholar to have seen the colonial politics of what we have come to know as Orientalism embedded in the self-evident notion of the orient. He saw the notion of the "Orient" to be a colonial construction that played a major role in the history of colonialism.

Book Overview

In the first chapter of the book, by way of an exploration into Foucault's thoughts on *ars erotica,* I set up some of the main themes of inquiry I later pursue in my discussion of the *Kāmasūtra.* I locate the meaning and significance of the notion of pleasure in its relationship with two of the most important notions in Foucault's works, truth and the self, as they obtain in contrasting ways in *ars erotica* and *scientia sexualis.* My main focus in this chapter is to explore the nature and process of the event and experience of pleasure as desubjectivation. In the absence of a ready historical archive of *ars erotica,* Foucault's own experiences often functioned as a personal archive for his reflections on the nature and process of the event and experience of pleasure. I focus on a number of such experiences as described by Foucault himself or reported by others. My main purpose is to determine the nature of the event and experience of pleasure as desubjectivation, as well as the precise mechanics and process of its production. I also link this notion of desubjectivation with major Indian intellectual traditions.

In chapter 2 I locate the birth of the discourse of *ars erotica* in the historical-discursive context of two far-reaching developments: subordination of the discourse of sexual-erotic pleasure to the discourse of Brahmanical law and the subordination of women to men under patriarchy. I argue that the origin of erotics as reflected in the *Kāmasūtra* in ancient India must be seen as a historical response to the growth of patriarchy and the subordination of women in the family. Through a reading of the *Mānava Dharmaśāstra* I show that the discourse of *dharma* as Brahmanical law was a new discourse of power—very different from the discourse of political power first expounded in the *Arthaśāstra*—that operated by constructing subjectivity, for example, the subjectivity of the wife. The *Kāmasūtra* built its case for a discourse of sexual-erotic pleasure as a way to overcome the hegemony of the discourse of Brahmanical law. In this chapter, I supplement the brief comments of the *Kāmasūtra* on the question of gender and patriarchy by placing it in conversation with the *Mānava Dharmaśāstra* and the *Mahābhārata,* the longest epic, of encyclopedic range in its coverage of significant themes and topics. I particularly focus on the vision buried in the *Mahābhārata* of a utopian past without patriarchy, when women were completely free—a time when erotic pedagogy was not necessary.

Chapter 3 explores the significance of the courtesan for the nature and origin of *ars erotica* in the *Kāmasūtra*. I locate the historical figure of the courtesan along two lines: the courtesan as a figure existing outside the circle of caste and patriarchal identity, and the courtesan as an actress in the theater of love. Given the general hegemony of the discourse of Brahmanical law (*dharma*), the *Kāmasūtra* projected the figure of the courtesan as an exception to this hegemony, a figure in whom the discourse of sexual-erotic pleasure came to acquire legislative autonomy. The courtesan stood outside the circle of caste and patriarchal identity that anchored the larger society. In the figure of the courtesan, the autonomy of women and pleasure went hand in hand, just as the autonomy of pleasure and women was lost in the figure of the wife. I then problematize the *Kāmasūtra*'s use of the words *nāyaka,* or actor, and *nāyikā,* or actress, to characterize the partners in an erotic affair. Even as this intriguing choice of words points to something crucial at the very foundation of the discourse of sexual-erotic pleasure—its essential connection to the domain of theater—I question why the *Kāmasūtra* left this choice unexplained, as if the terms were self-evident and needed no further elaboration. I go on to determine that the figure of the courtesan in relationship with the dandy as her erotic partner was at the source of this choice of words in the *Kāmasūtra*. The reason the *Kāmasūtra* left these crucial words unexplained was because it found them to be self-evident in the life of the courtesan as an exemplary figure in the domain of erotics. In the figure of the courtesan *ars erotica* morphed into *ars theatrica*. Through a detailed analysis of the life of the courtesan as reflected in the *Kāmasūtra*, particularly in her role as a wife to her patron, I explore what it was about her life that transformed erotics into a form of theater, an art that went beyond the logic of identity and truth. On the other hand, the use of theater terms shows that it was as theater that *ars erotica* came into being in the *Kāmasūtra* and won autonomy for itself from the discourse of Brahmanical law based on identity and truth.

The assumed but unproblematized language of theater at the center of erotics having been brought to the surface, chapter 4 pursues the affinity between theater and erotics to its logical—and historical—end by bringing out the deep and complex continuities between the *Kāmasūtra* and the *Nāṭyaśāstra*, the foundational text on theater written about a century earlier. These continuities have remained largely unnoticed and unexplored in existing scholarship. In contrast to much of the scholarship that locates the birth of theater in religion and rituals, I locate the birth of theater in the figures of the courtesan and the dandy. I show that the three figures of the actress, the actor, and the director that together constituted the theater were historically anchored in, and derivative of, the three figures of the courtesan, the dandy-consort of the courtesan (*vaiśika*), and the dandy-guru as teacher-adviser of the courtesan (*viṭa*), respectively. Given that the two male figures of the dandy were historically derivative of the figure of the courtesan, the courtesan was at the heart of the theater as it came into being in Indian culture. If erotics and aesthetics in Indian culture seemed in complete continuity with each other that was because both of them had their origin in the same figure of the courtesan. I also note numerous intellectual continuities, including the notion of *rasa,* or aesthetic pleasure, in the *Nāṭyaśāstra*—analogous to sexual-erotic pleasure in the *Kāmasūtra*—as an experience and event of desubjectivation. I argue that if the *Kāmasūtra* and the *Nāṭyaśāstra* seemed to share their origins, that was because both of them pursued erotic and aesthetic pleasure beyond the confines of identity and truth.

In chapter 5, I show the construction of the two discourses of *ars erotica* and *ars theatrica* in and through the historical figure of the *viṭa,* or dandy-guru. The *viṭa* is a complex and pivotal historical character in ancient Indian culture that has failed to draw the attention of the scholars of ancient Indian culture and history. I argue that it was in the figure of the dandy-guru that the existence of courtesan and the nature of her sexual-erotic relations with her patron-consort (*vaiśika*) became a subject of intellectual reflection, a question of thought. Even though the discourses of both erotics as reflected in the *Kāmasūtra* and theater as in the *Nāṭyaśāstra* were grounded in the being of the courtesan, the discourse of pleasure did not come to be articulated by her; she did not leave any treatises on either theater or erotics. It was in the life of the dandy-guru that the courtesan's being came to be an object of thought. I explore the figure of the dandy-guru through a study of one of the most important historical-literary sources in ancient India, the four oldest extant *bhāṇas*—collectively referred to as the *Caturbhāṇis,* or "the Quartet of *Bhāṇas*"—which were one-act plays in which the dandy-guru appeared as the sole character on stage. It is in these *bhāṇas* that the precise historical context of the discourses of erotics and theater become vividly evident. Together they constitute an archive that encompasses nothing short of the entire consciousness or subjectivity of the dandy-guru—a consciousness grounded in the figure of the courtesan. The *bhāṇas* reveal in great detail and vividness what the *Kāmasūtra* meant in elevating the figure of the courtesan to sovereign position in the domain of erotics. What appears like a theoretical exposition by a great author in the *Kāmasūtra* is evident in its historical-discursive form in the *bhāṇas.* I begin the chapter with an exploration of the figure of the *viṭa* in the *Nāṭyaśāstra* and show how the discourse of theater and erotics came to converge on the figure of the dandy-guru as theater director. I then show through an analysis of the *bhāṇas* that it was the dandy-guru's quotidian relationship with the courtesan and his insatiable curiosity and love for her that transformed him into an archivist of her life, an advocate of the discourse of sexual-erotic pleasure against that of power and Brahmanical law, and inevitably the ideal director in the theater of love that the *Nāṭyaśāstra* is grounded on.

In chapter 6, I focus on the figure of the *nāgaraka*, or the city dandy, as an agent that bore the *Kāmasūtra*'s vision of the city based on art and aesthetics. Even as I show that the city dandy is none other than the dandy-consort of the courtesan, I also pursue the reasons the *Kāmasūtra* reconfigured the historical figure of the dandy as the patron-consort of the courtesan (*vaiśika*) by renaming him as "city dandy" (*nāgaraka*). It was as if the *Kāmasūtra* sought to deterritorialize the dandy from the courtesan and reterritorialize him on the city. It is often assumed that, unlike the discourses of Brahmanical law (*dharma*) and political power (*artha*), erotic-aesthetic pleasure (*kāma*) failed to give birth to a larger vision of society, caught as it was in petty personal pursuits. On the contrary, as I show, in the *Kāmasūtra* a larger vision of a city based on erotic-aesthetic pleasure existed. In the city dandy as the patron, connoisseur, and master of arts, the *Kāmasūtra* sought to construct an agent for its vision of the society anchored in art and aesthetics as a discourse of love. Art in the *Kāmasūtra* was less about creating great works of poetry or drama and more about a medium of socialization in a city that otherwise found itself caught in the logic of commerce and exchange. Art and aesthetics as a discourse of love also functioned as a form of public pedagogy in erotics. It functioned as a tool to devirilize masculine sexuality, which reduced women to objects of sexual pleasure and sex to a purely sensual experience without a discourse of love. There is a sense in the *Kāmasūtra* that unless a society is able to construct art and aesthetics as a public discourse of love, it would be difficult, if not impossible, to maintain *ars erotica* as a viable discourse. I conclude chapter 6 by showing, on the basis of a reading of the *Nāṭyaśāstra*'s sense of its own purpose, how the discourse of *kāma* also sought to claim for itself a hegemonic position in its relationship with the discourses of *dharma* and *artha*.

The book ends with a brief critical evaluation of Foucault's turn in the last years of his life to notions of truth and self as his major concerns, even as he abandoned the concept of *ars erotica* anchored in sexual-erotic pleasure. Surprisingly, however, this well-known and much-discussed turn in Foucault's work has not been approached by Foucauldian scholars from the perspective of the fate of the concepts of pleasure and *ars erotica*. I point out that the notions of *ars erotica* and pleasure, which Foucault had so painstakingly developed in the early years of his work on sexuality, did not survive their contact with Greek philosophy, the primary archive and source of categories for Foucault's research in his last years. After all, it was Greek philosophy, grounded in truth and self, that had claimed to have overcome pleasure—and thus aborted the very possibility of *ars erotica* in the West.

1

Foucault and the Notion of *Ars Erotica*: Pleasure as Desubjectivation

Well over a century after its publication, even today the *Kāmasūtra* still carries a sense of scandal around it. Remarkably, there is no evidence in the text itself that it meant to provoke any such scandal. The *Kāmasūtra*'s approach to its own subject is far from casual. It was written in all seriousness and earnestness in the cause of sexual-erotic pleasure as one of the ontological dimensions of human existence. Indeed, the opening chapters of the first of the six books in the *Kāmasūtra* are a theoretical exploration of immense complexity and significance that seeks to establish sexual-erotic pleasure as one of the three competing and conflicting ontological domains—the others being Brahmanical law (*dharma*) and political power (*artha*)—of history and human existence. In this regard, it is interesting that at the end of the debate about the nature of difference between how men and women relate to the activity of sex, the *Kāmasūtra* states that the debate until then had been meant for the experts of erotics; that it is now going to elaborate some of the themes in detail for lay people, literally the "dimwitted."[1] What the *Kāmasūtra* alludes to in this statement is the complexity and subtlety of the issues involved and the need for interpretation to get to the meaning of this debate. It is also a warning to the reader not quickly to assume the most obvious meaning of the sutras conforming to common sense as self-evident.

It was the inability to see the *Kāmasūtra* as a work of thought that prevented generations of scholars from seeing a network of categories—above all, the notion of sexual-erotic pleasure—that grounds the discourse of erotics in it. This inability is not surprising in a world where pleasure and thought are seen in adversarial terms, where pleasure means the absence of thought. In such an intellectual environment, the *Kāmasūtra* presented a paradox to its readers: it was a text on sexual-erotic pleasure that also claimed the status of thought. Indeed, more than a paradox, its claim to thought has really been at the root of the scandal of the *Kāmasūtra* in our age. But as the title *Kāmasūtra*, or a "treatise on pleasure," suggests, pleasure was the ground of the discourse of erotics articulated in this text. It was the notion of pleasure that opened up the horizon of intelligibility in which sexual-erotic practices came to acquire a discourse in ancient India. Yet, there has been a general lack of focus on the notion of pleasure in the *Kāmasūtra*. This has been one of the most important reasons why the work has eluded a serious investigation into its historical origins.

It is in this intellectual context that Michel Foucault's *History of Sexuality* brought about a fundamental transformation. Foucault's thoughts on the notion of pleasure as the ground of *ars erotica* as a discursive formation in stark contrast to *scientia sexualis*, or the science of sexuality, for the first time directly raised the question about the relationship between pleasure and knowledge. He also clearly and decisively stated the major issues that were at stake by locating the question of this relationship within a complex of some of his most enduring concerns, such as truth, power, self, and subjectivity. It was thus that Foucault opened a path into the *Kāmasūtra* as an intellectual tradition in its own right. By way of an exploration into how the notion of pleasure is problematized in the works of Foucault, this chapter is an attempt to problematize some of the major themes that are at the heart of this book. It is not my intention to construct a theory of pleasure out of Foucault's comments and observations on the subject. Rather, this discussion is meant to be a theoretical problematization as a preparatory exercise before the historical investigation that is carried out in the rest of the book. In this I follow Foucault's useful methodological distinction between what he calls "theoretical punctuation" and "concrete historical investigation."[2]

Ars Erotica versus *Scientia Sexualis*

The contrast between nonwestern *ars erotica*, or art of erotics, and western *scientia sexualis*, or science of sexuality, played a critical role in the way Foucault problematized and planned his project on the history of sexuality. While *ars erotica*, according to Foucault, is anchored in pleasure, *scientia sexualis* is anchored in the notions of truth and self.[3] In this contrast, Foucault had an opportunity to set the discourse of sexuality as science against another fully formed discourse on sexual relations and practices from another culture. Foucault thus relativized and shattered the self-evident nature of the discourse of sexuality as science, with claims to universality and truth. What, however, makes the place of *ars erotica* in Foucault's project on the history of sexuality critical is that he claimed the notion of pleasure to be his own intellectual ground.[4] In other words, more than just a contrast, *ars erotica* was the critical ground from which Foucault approached the nature and origin of the discourse of *scientia sexualis*. It would, therefore, be difficult to fully comprehend the nature and significance of Foucault's project on the history of sexuality in the absence of an understanding of the notion of pleasure in his writings.

Much of the academic discourse on the subject has evolved, however, largely unmindful of the significance of this category of *ars erotica*.[5] Part of the reason for this could be that, beyond a few well-thought-out lines about the nature and experience of pleasure, Foucault never clearly dwelt on the experience and event of pleasure. As insightful as they are, Foucault's brief and isolated comments assume much more than they elaborate, and as such they fall far short of offering a comprehensive view on the subject of *ars erotica* with the notion of pleasure as its sovereign ground. Given Foucault's reluctance to engage in a purely theoretical-philosophical speculation on any subject and his obvious preference, like any historian, to work with an archive, the absence of a ready archive of *ars erotica* in the West imposed severe limitations on his reflections on the subject. Indeed, Foucault acknowledged that his notion of pleasure did not yet have enough content and was rather sketchy; *ars erotica* was still an unexplored domain of experience and discourse.[6] It would be a mistake, however, to assume that Foucault thought of the notion of pleasure as being incapable of having content in the form of either experience or discourse. Indeed, it was precisely to fend off the danger of his notion of pleasure being declared empty of content that he felt compelled to bring in *ars erotica* directly. It was a way for Foucault to point toward a historical-cultural archive of *ars erotica* grounded in pleasure. Since Foucault himself never got to this archive, it was a project yet to be executed.

Under these circumstances, Foucault often brought up his personal experiences at crucial moments during interviews to elucidate specific aspects of his notion of pleasure, as if those experiences constituted a personal archive for his research. Foucault thus appeared more forthcoming on the subject of pleasure in his interviews than he was in his published works. It is well known that there was a remarkable degree of continuum between Foucault's personal experiences and engagement with contemporary issues and his academic research, nowhere more so than in his research on the history of sexuality.[7] His frequent use of his own experiences as an archive, however, also shows that Foucault did think that pleasure was capable of a content accessible to historical investigation and theoretical reflection.

My intention in this chapter is to piece together what is a rather coherent view behind Foucault's brief and widely dispersed comments on the notion of pleasure. First of all, I discuss the notion of pleasure in relation to truth as it appears in contrasting ways in the discourses of *scientia sexualis* and *ars erotica*. Second, I focus on pleasure in its relationship with self and subjectivity: pleasure as an event and experience of desubjectivation, an event of a loss of the sense of the self. I then focus on Foucault's comments and observations that offer an insight into the precise dynamics that bring about this event of desubjectivation. One often thinks of pleasure, particularly sexual pleasure, to be inaccessible to any analysis that would make it intelligible, as if it marked a limit to intelligibility as such. Yet, a close study of Foucault shows that pleasure is indeed intelligible. After all, when Foucault identifies sexual pleasure to be an event of desubjectivation, he makes it intelligible and accessible to thought. What is more, in Foucault's view, pleasure as desubjectivation can open up another horizon of intelligibility, a horizon otherwise inaccessible; indeed, the notion of pleasure as desubjectivation can function as an ontological ground for a critical discourse. I end the chapter by showing that the notion of pleasure had its roots in Foucault's first project on the history of madness. The notion of pleasure came to occupy the same position madness once did in Foucault's earliest work, *History of Madness*. Interestingly, the Orient, including Indian culture, also appears to have been part of Foucault's thinking long before his discovery of *ars erotica*. Moreover, Foucault seems well aware of certain Indian spiritual-intellectual traditions grounded in desubjectivation.

Ars Erotica and the Primacy of Pleasure over Truth

In what follows I make a very brief and schematic presentation of the nature and significance of Foucault's contrast between the discourses of *ars erotica* and *scientia sexualis*. The key to understanding the nature and significance of this contrast is to determine the precise nature in Foucault's works of the relationship between truth and identity, or self, on the one hand, and pleasure, on the other.[8] The first thing that needs to be noted is that sex is a discursive phenomenon. There is no direct access to the question of sex. It is only accessible through a discourse, for example, a discourse of *scientia sexualis* or a discourse of *ars erotica*. It is because sex is a discursive phenomenon that it finds itself caught in a web of questions relating to the notions of truth and self, and also the nature and origin of knowledge formations. As Foucault himself noted, "We must not refer a history of sexuality to the agency of sex; but rather show how 'sex' is historically subordinate to sexuality. We must not place sex on the side of reality, and sexuality on that of confused ideas and illusions; sexuality is a very real historical formation; it is what gave rise to the notion of sex, as a speculative element necessary to its operation. . . . It is the agency of sex that we must break away from."[9]

What Foucault calls the "agency of sex" is the ground of Freudian psychoanalysis and is evident in its notions such as libido, sexual instinct, sexual drive, the id, and in Freud's famous statement that 'anatomy is destiny.'[10] In Freud's narration, this "agency of sex" is locked in an adversarial relationship with culture. In this ever-raging conflict, culture deploys its twin mechanism of repression and sublimation to both subdue this "agency of sex" and use it. According to Foucault, instead of discovering it as a prediscursive force of nature, it was psychoanalysis as a discourse of sexuality that "gave rise to the notion of sex" as an agency; let alone being in conflict with culture, "the notion of sex" is a product of culture. It was because Foucault did not believe in the "agency of sex" that he also did not believe in the Freudian theory of repression; the notion of repression was just as much of a historical construction, and not simply the discovery by Freud of a long overlooked fact. It is not surprising therefore that Foucault begins his project on the history of sexuality with a critique of the "repressive hypothesis." In "subordinating" sex to sexuality, what Foucault in effect does is subordinate sex to discourse. It is because sex is a discursive phenomenon that it becomes a part of the broader history of a culture or society.[11]

What makes Foucault's discovery of *ars erotica* so significant is that in it he found not only a completely different structure and rules of knowledge formation, but also a different conception of knowledge and its origin. According to Foucault, while in the discourse of *scientia sexualis* the notions of truth and identity function as sovereign categories, in *ars erotica* it is pleasure that has primacy.

> In the erotic art, truth is drawn from pleasure itself, understood as a practice and accumulated as experience; pleasure is not considered in relation to an absolute of the permitted and the forbidden, nor by a reference to a criterion of utility, but first and foremost in relation to itself. . . . Moreover, this knowledge must be deflected back into the sexual practice itself, in order to shape it as though from within and in order to amplify its effects. . . . [The West, on the other hand, is] the only civilization to have developed over the centuries procedures for telling the truth of sex.[12]

The difference between *scientia sexualis* and *ars erotica* is articulated here in terms of the contrasting relationship between truth and pleasure in the two. Foucault problematizes the relationship between truth and pleasure as a conflict over primacy or sovereignty of one over the other. He defines *ars erotica* as a discourse in which pleasure exercises sovereignty over the notions of truth and self. In stating that in erotic art "truth is drawn from pleasure itself," what Foucault in effect argued was that truth has its origin in pleasure. Given that the notion of truth also stands for knowledge, it means that in *ars erotica* knowledge itself has its origin in pleasure. Far from being opposed to thought, pleasure, in the discourse of *ars erotica*, is the condition of thought; it is pleasure that opens up the horizon of intelligibility in which thought comes into being.

Moreover, Foucault, in the same passage, states that in *ars erotica* "this knowledge must be deflected back into the sexual practice itself, in order to shape it as though from within and in order to amplify its effects." Apart from being the origin of truth, pleasure is at the same time the end of its own truth, in that the knowledge that it generates about itself must be "deflected back" to serve it. Pleasure, therefore, is the master that truth and knowledge must serve and obey. Pleasure is at once the origin and end of truth, and, therefore, of knowledge. Thus, in *ars erotica*, the notion of truth finds itself subordinated to that of pleasure, a situation exactly the reverse of *scientia sexualis*, in which truth is the sovereign category. By elevating pleasure to the position of sovereignty, Foucault thus reversed the relationship between pleasure and truth as it obtained in *scientia sexualis*. To say that truth has its origin in pleasure is to say that truth does not have its origin in itself or thought. Because pleasure is the origin of its own truth in *ars erotica*, it [pleasure] is not judged by an external truth. In other words, it cannot be subjected to a truth that has its origin in something other than pleasure, such as science and philosophy, for example. It is because of this legislative sovereignty that in *ars erotica* pleasure claims the right to make its own rules.

A series of significant consequences follow from pleasure's claim to sovereignty over truth: pleasure in *ars erotica* contests the claims of philosophy and science—as the custodians of truth—to interpret and regulate the domain of sexual practices. In other words, science and philosophy have no legitimate legislative authority to define either what pleasure is and what it is not or how it ought to be pursued or avoided. Pleasure's claim to sovereignty also contests the legislative claims of religion under the sovereignty of god, morality under the sovereignty of the good, law under the sovereignty of the state, and medicine under the sovereignty of health or human nature. In claiming the absence of *ars erotica* in the West, then, what Foucault contends is that pleasure failed to attain legislative sovereignty in western cultures. Instead, pleasure was successfully brought under the jurisdiction of philosophy, science, religion, morality, and the state, all of which together contributed in complex ways toward the making of what Foucault called *scientia sexualis*—psychoanalysis, for example—in which truth emerged as the sovereign category.[13]

The best illustration of what Foucault meant by the conflict between pleasure and truth over sovereignty, and the nature of what is really at stake in it, is offered by his own writings on ancient Greece in the last years of his life. Antiquity, particularly Greek philosophy, was the original site where the outcome of the conflict between pleasure and truth was decided. It is not surprising that Foucault found himself drawn to that archive. Pleasure, after all, was one of the most elusive adversaries that thought—or truth—encountered in Greek philosophy.[14] The telltale signs of this conflict between pleasure and truth over sovereignty are scattered across the writings of antiquity, but nowhere more vividly and decisively than in some of the most celebrated dialogues of Plato, particularly the *Symposium* and *Phaedrus*. Plato's works came to be the primary historical archive of choice for Foucault in his last years.[15]

Foucault's brief chapter in *The Use of Pleasure,* called "True Love," elaborates on how the notion of love or eros became subordinated to the category of truth in the dialogues of Plato.[16] Even the title of this chapter, "true love," reveals that truth emerged as the measure and ground of love; truth became the real object of love.[17] It was in the dialogues of Plato that even as eros came to be dislodged from pleasure, it found its new telos in truth. Foucault refers to this new discourse of love as "Platonic and Socratic erotics."[18] Yet, what was really at stake in this erotics was the very origin of western philosophy grounded in truth. After all, Socrates, the founder of western philosophy, claimed in the *Symposium* that he "knew nothing other than *ta erotika* or erotics" (177d)! Socrates' claim shows just how comprehensive truth or philosophy's triumph over pleasure was in ancient Greece that it (philosophy)—love of wisdom—claimed itself to be the real—or indeed true—erotics![19] It was thus that the possibility of *ars erotica* in the West, grounded in the legislative sovereignty of pleasure, came to be aborted. The success of truth's claim to legislative sovereignty over pleasure sealed the fate of *ars erotica.*

In Socrates' claim it becomes vividly evident just what Foucault meant when he said that *scientia sexualis* itself operated in the West as a subtle form of *ars erotica.* That is why it is important to keep in mind that subordination of pleasure to the legislative and administrative sovereignty of truth in *scientia sexualis* in the West by no means amounted to a repression of either pleasure or sex. Pleasure continues to be produced even under the sway of *scientia sexualis.* What changes is the mode of its production; it is now produced under the sovereignty of truth. Pleasure is still being had, but it is being had as the pleasure of truth. It was this insight that led Foucault to wonder whether *scientia sexualis* may really be a subtle form of *ars erotica* peculiar to the West.

> The most important elements of erotic art linked to our knowledge about sexuality are . . . to be sought . . . in this multiplication and intensification of pleasures connected to the production of truth about sex. . . . In short, the formidable "pleasure of analysis" (in the widest sense of the latter term) which the West has clearly been fostering for several centuries: all this constitutes something like the errant fragments of an erotic art that is secretly transmitted by confession and the science of sex. Must we conclude that our *scientia sexualis* is but an extraordinarily subtle form of *ars erotica*, and that it is the Western, sublimated version of that seemingly lost tradition? Or must we suppose that all these pleasures are only the by-products of a sexual science, a bonus that compensates for its many stresses and strains?[20]

If *scientia sexualis* can be "an extraordinarily subtle form of *ars erotica*," then that is because pleasure is still being produced but as the "pleasure of analysis." In this subtle form of *ars erotica* love for sexual-erotic pleasure is transformed into love for truth. In this transformation pleasure comes to be subordinated to truth. Unlike the Freudian notion of repression that refers to the repression of the desire for sex or sexual pleasure by culture, subordination refers to a conflict between the notions of truth and pleasure over discursive autonomy or sovereignty from each other and, if and when possible, hegemony over each other. From this perspective the conflict between truth and pleasure is part of discursive history, not a history of conflict between desire for sex, on the one hand, and culture, on the other. The presence of *ars erotica* in any culture means that pleasure did manage to found a discourse in its own name and as such exercise its sovereignty. This insight constitutes the very heart of Foucault's contribution on the subject. Without this insight Foucault would not have been able to challenge the well-entrenched theory of repression that had acquired the status of common sense. It is the nature and history of this subordination—not repression—of pleasure to truth that Foucault tried to outline in the first volume.

Pleasure as an Event of Desubjectivation

Along with the question of truth, Foucault also problematized pleasure—the ground of *ars erotica*—in relation to the question of identity, or self, one of his most enduring concerns.[21] Once again, Foucault problematizes this relationship in terms of a conflict over sovereignty: either identity is made to serve pleasure or pleasure will be made to serve identity. In *scientia sexualis* it is identity that has primacy over pleasure: it is always a self that seeks, or desires, and acquires pleasure, as if pleasure were a kind of object, an object of consumption and possession. In *ars erotica*, in contrast, this relationship is reversed: it is pleasure that exercises sovereignty over identity. Foucault's own perspective, once again, happens to be that of *ars erotica*.

> If identity is only a game, if it is only a procedure to have relations, social and sexual—pleasure relationships that create new friendships, it is useful. . . . If we are asked to relate to the question of identity, it must be an identity to our unique selves. But the relationships we have to have with ourselves are not ones of identity, rather, they must be relationships of differentiation, of creation, of innovation. To be the same is really boring. We must not exclude identity if people find their pleasure through this identity, but we must not think of this identity as an ethical universal rule.[22]

Just as with the notion of truth, Foucault subordinates the notion of identity also to that of pleasure. Instead of subjecting pleasure to a discourse of identity—as is done in *scientia sexualis*, it is identity that must be made to serve pleasure. That is what Foucault means when he says that "we must not exclude identity if people find their pleasure through this identity." More than taking pleasure out of the jurisdiction of the notions of the self and identity, Foucault reverses the well-established relationship: pleasure acquires sovereignty over identity. Identity must have its origin and end in pleasure; identity must serve pleasure. This is the reason identity appears to be nothing more than a game; it is not something already there—"as an ethical universal rule"—to be discovered, but something to be invented and constructed in the pursuit of pleasure. For Foucault it was as if pleasure constituted a space akin to theater, a stage on which one could create and recreate oneself as a character. It was as if it were as an actor that one could best pursue pleasure. Interestingly, when confronted with the question that some aspects of S&M may be a reproduction of relations of power, Foucault defended it by saying that it was only an "acting out" of power relations. In other words, S&M belongs to the space of theater/stage.[23] As we will see, the notions of acting and theater are absolutely at the heart of how the *Kāmasūtra* conceives the domain and discourse of sexual-erotic pleasure. It calls the partners in a sexual-erotic affair actor and actress. Indeed, classical Indian theater had its origin in the domain of erotics.

Apart from constructing an identity exclusively for the purpose of pleasure, Foucault also offers an example of another strategy to overcome identity in the pursuit of pleasure: loss of identity altogether: "It's important for there to be places like baths where, without being imprisoned or pinned in your own identity, in your legal status, your past, your name, your face, and so on, you can meet the people who are there, and who are for you—as you are for them—nothing more than bodies, with whom the most unexpected combinations and fabrications of pleasure are possible. This is absolutely an important part of erotic experiences, and it is, I would say, politically important that sexuality can function in this way."[24]

In this example of the experience of pleasure, identity is altogether dispensed with; the two individuals who meet for the sake of pleasure are complete strangers to each other. What is immediately evident is how central the question of identity was for Foucault in the domain of sexuality and erotics. Note how strongly and vividly Foucault describes the nature of the problem identity presents in the domain of sexuality—he describes identity as a prison. The notion of self or soul as a prison was a powerful and abiding motif in Foucault's works, nowhere more so than in *Discipline and Punish*, in which he chose the prison as the primary site to tell the story of the formation of the modern subject and subjectivity. As if articulating the core principle of his philosophical and historical research, it was in that book that Foucault declared the soul to be the "prison of the body."[25] This is the reason Foucault uses subjectivity in its combined meaning of self and subjection. Going by the logic of this principle, it is not the soul or the self that has to be freed from the body—it is the body that has to be freed from the soul.

Given that identity comes in the way, it is perhaps only logical that the stranger should emerge as the primary figure of pleasure in Foucault's reflections. But it is also important to remember that the emergence of the stranger as the figure of pleasure is a historical development that is associated with the rise of the gay bathhouse. In the same interview in which Foucault offered the above example, he also offers a clue into the nature of the difference between regular sexual experience and the one in which two strangers encounter each other. "The intensities of pleasure are indeed linked to the fact that you desubjugate yourself, that you cease being a subject, an identity. It is like an affirmation of nonidentity. Not only because you leave your ID card in the changing room but because the multiplicity of possible things, of possible encounters, of possible pilings-up *[amoncellements]*, of possible connections, means that, in effect, you cannot *not* fail to be identical with yourself."[26]

Here Foucault uses one of the most crucial categories in his reflections on pleasure: "desubjugation" or desubjectivation. Since it is in the form of identity that one acquires subjectivity, Foucault describes the loss of identity, the "affirmation of nonidentity," as desubjectivation.[27] Foucault articulates the adversarial relationship between identity and pleasure very precisely. In his understanding, identity and pleasure are inversely related: as the sense of identity decreases, the intensity of pleasure rises proportionately. Pleasure in its most intense form therefore would coincide with complete loss of the sense of self—an event of complete desubjectivation.

That desubjectivation was really the heart of Foucault's notion of pleasure is clear when he states, "I'm fundamentally not attached to the notion of pleasure, but I'm quite frankly hostile to the pre-Deleuzian, non-Deleuzian notion of desire. But this is all, let's say, on the order of a methodological precaution. The main thing is this notion of an event that is not assigned, and is not assignable, to a subject."[28] One should not conclude from this statement that pleasure was not really important for Foucault. Rather, what Foucault was doing in this statement was fixing the meaning of pleasure as a phenomenon that could not be assigned to a subject; pleasure must not be assigned to a sovereign subject as its possession. Central to the notion of pleasure for Foucault is its exteriority to subjectivity; that pleasure exceeds subjectivity. To say that Foucault's critical perspective on sexuality was anchored in pleasure is to say that it was anchored in desubjectivation.

In offering the stranger as the primary figure of sexual pleasure, Foucault also assumes a contrast with the regular everyday experience of pleasure in which the partners in a sexual encounter are known and familiar to each other.[29] If one were to use Foucault's example as a measure of what sexual pleasure in its most intense form ought to be, one would have to exclude most of the events and experiences of sex that take place every day. Broadly speaking then, potentially two kinds of sexual pleasure exist: one in which an individual is able to break out of the prison of subjectivity and identity and experience pleasure as an event of desubjectivation; and the other a more regular form of sexual pleasure in which an individual experiences pleasure without losing the sovereignty of identity. That is to say, in everyday events of sexual pleasure, one pursues and experiences pleasure under the sovereignty of identity; such pleasure could be more precisely designated as subjective pleasure. In other words, there are two kinds of pleasure—subjective and nonsubjective. What precisely about the sexual pleasure experienced between two individuals stripped of their identity distinguishes it from everyday sexual encounters between two individuals known to each other?

In subjective pleasure, the subject seeks and acquires pleasure as an object, as if pleasure were an object of consumption. Foucault's later writings on the discourse and practice of sexual pleasure in ancient Greece, particularly those from his second volume of the *History of Sexuality,* called *Use of Pleasure,* offer the best example of how exactly this subjective pleasure manifests itself in history. In ancient Greece the relationship between pleasure and self was problematized in a way that was as adversarial as it was between pleasure and truth. Either the self would enforce its mastery and sovereignty over pleasure or, inversely, it would come under the sway of pleasure. Just as pleasure was subordinated to truth in ancient Greek culture, so also did it come to be subordinated to self under the discourse of what Foucault described as the "mastery of the self."[30] Even the title of the second volume, *Use of Pleasure,* suggests the primacy and lordship of the self over pleasure. Pleasure was reduced to a mere object of measured consumption for a subject. Not surprisingly then, in ancient Greece erotics was in complete continuity with dietetics. Indeed, in the second volume Foucault has a chapter called "The Diet of Pleasures."[31]

There is, however, another aspect to the reduction of pleasure to an object of consumption: the discourse that reduces pleasure—sexual pleasure—to an object of consumption also reduces the person who is the source of that pleasure to an object. In subjective sexual pleasure a relationship of pleasure is also inevitably reduced to a relationship between a subject and an object of pleasure; while they appear to be parts of the same event of sex, the partners in an everyday sexual event remain locked and separated in their own individual subjectivities, in their own subjective pleasures, even as each is reduced to an object of pleasure to the other. But a relationship of pleasure that reduces the other to an object—an object of consumption—is in effect a relationship of power. In other words, the discourse that reduces pleasure to an object also reduces the relationships of pleasure to the relationships of power. One pursues and acquires pleasure as if it were power that is being pursued and exercised. This is precisely the origin of the discourse of virility in gender and sexual relationships.

Thus, in ancient Greece, the discourse of the ethics of the mastery of self over pleasure within oneself was in complete continuity with the politics of domination over the other. Under these conditions, an act of pleasure—sexual pleasure—was barely distinguishable from an act of domination. While talking about a strong presence of virility in sexual practices in ancient Greece, Foucault commented: "The Greek ethics of pleasure is linked to a virile society, to dissymmetry, exclusion of the other, an obsession with penetration, and a kind of threat of being dispossessed of your own energy, and so on. All that is quite disgusting!"[32] This virility that was part of the general discursive economy of the practices of self in antiquity is nothing but the pursuit of pleasure under the sovereignty of power; virility was an unmistakable sign of the subordination of pleasure to power in the name of self, or the mastery of self.

In the discourse of virility, what is evident is the close correspondence between relationships of power and relationships of pleasure: a discourse that reduces pleasure to an object also reduces the source of that pleasure to an object of power as an exercise in domination. Along the lines first formulated by Foucault, David Halperin sums up vividly the discourse of virility in the way it determined sexual and gender relationships in antiquity:

> Greek and Roman men generally understood sex to be defined in terms of sexual penetration and phallic pleasure, whether the sexual partners were two males, two females, or one male and one female. The physical act of sex itself required, in their eyes, a polarization of the sexual partners into the categories of penetrator and penetrated as well as a corresponding polarization of sexual roles into "active" and "passive." Those roles in turn were correlated with superordinate and subordinate social status, with masculine and feminine gender styles, and with adulthood and adolescence. Phallic insertion functioned as a marker of male precedence; it also expressed social domination and seniority. The isomorphism of sexual, social, gender, and age roles made the distinction between "activity" and "passivity" paramount for categorizing sexual acts and actors . . . to be sexually penetrated was always potentially shaming.[33]

What appears to be a case of the subordination of pleasure to self then is also pleasure's subordination to power. It is in this context that one needs to situate Foucault's notion of pleasure as an event of desubjectivation, an event that requires identity to be either altogether dispensed with or subordinated to pleasure. Inasmuch as pleasure as an event and experience of desubjectivation constitutes an exteriority to self and subjectivity, it also constitutes an exteriority to power, because power in Foucault operates by constructing subjectivity. Given the centrality of the notion of power in Foucault's works, it is clear just how critical the discourse of *ars erotica* grounded in pleasure was in its ability to constitute a domain outside power in Foucault's project on the history of sexuality. Grounded in the sovereignty of pleasure as an event of desubjectivation, *ars erotica* functioned as a counter-discourse to *scientia sexualis* as a discourse of power.

To identify the event of pleasure—sexual pleasure—as an event of desubjectivation was a major advance in Foucault's project on the history of sexuality. What, however, is not evident is exactly what it is about the event and activity of sex that makes desubjectivation possible. To say that pleasure is an event of desubjectivation and to actually explain exactly what in pleasure—including sexual pleasure—triggers the event of desubjectivation are two different things. Without some insight into the latter process, the notion of pleasure as an event of desubjectivation truly lacks an identifiable content and, as a result, does not amount to more than a simple assertion. Even though Foucault continued to show interest in and comment on the notion of pleasure, he never focused on the precise process and mechanics that trigger pleasure as an event of desubjectivation.

Despite how little Foucault said on the actual mechanics of pleasure as an event of desubjectivation, it appears that he gave it a considerable amount of thought. While discussing the event of pleasure, Foucault once said, "Pleasure ultimately is nothing more than an event, an event that happens, I would say, outside the subject, or at the limit of the subject, or between two subjects, in this something that is neither of the body nor of the soul, neither outside nor inside."[34] In one of his most insightful comments on the mechanics of the event of pleasure Foucault observed that "pleasure is something which passes from one individual to another; it is not secreted by identity. Pleasure has no passport, no identification papers."[35] In this observation, Foucault problematizes pleasure in terms of its relation with identity, but also in terms of the relationship between two individuals in the event of sex. Given the use of the words "passport" and "identification papers," it is clear that Foucault thinks of identity as a political construction anchored in power, with clearly delineated borders and boundaries, and also mechanisms to check what or who is able to enter its domain. If pleasure is able to pass from one individual to another without any identification papers, it is because it does not recognize the boundaries of identity. In its moment of autonomy pleasure exceeds the sovereignty of identity; as a phenomenon it constitutes an exteriority to identity.

Like many of Foucault's other observations on pleasure, this statement was presented quite casually. It is, however, nothing short of Foucault's thesis on the nature and activity of pleasure as an event of desubjectivation. Here, he refers to pleasure not as a concept in a discourse, but as an event, an actual experience that passes from one individual to another. What is important about this formulation is a hidden—and rare—insight into the precise nature and mechanics of the process in the event of sex that, according to Foucault, produces this rather obscure and elusive phenomenon of desubjectivation. To say that pleasure passes from one individual to another in the context of the event and activity of sex may sound tautological and self-evident. After all, insofar as an event of sex involves two people, if pleasure did not pass from one to the other, there would be no pleasure to experience. However, there is nothing self-evident about Foucault's observation. As we have seen in the Greek example, the pleasure of the master was not meant to flow into the slave, nor the pleasure of an adult into a boy. If pleasure was simply an object of consumption or an exercise in domination, it would never circulate, which is to say that pleasure of the self would never become the pleasure of the other.

It is, therefore, critical to note at the outset that Foucault's observation about pleasure is not intended for the event of sex in general, but only that sex which produces the event of desubjectivation, thus shattering the sovereignty of identity or subjectivity. This form of experiencing pleasure is not necessarily universal and indeed not altogether common. Strikingly, while articulating what sounds like a definition of pleasure, Foucault had sex between strangers in mind. It is precisely this kind of pleasure that Foucault had also offered as an example of the most intense kind of sexual pleasure. In that example, Foucault's use of the word intensity to distinguish between degrees of pleasure is telling. If the event of everyday sex were an event of desubjectivation there would be no need for Foucault to offer sex between two strangers as an example of the pleasure in its autonomy from identity.

To appreciate the significance of Foucault's observation on the mobility and permeability of pleasure, it is important to locate it in its precise context fully. In the event of sexual pleasure, one is both a subject of one's own pleasure and an object of the pleasure of the other at the same time. Notice that Foucault says *pleasure* passes from one individual to another, not that one individual is the source of another's pleasure. It is the pleasure—which is to say the experience of pleasure—of one individual that passes into another individual. Thus the pleasure of the one becomes at the same time the pleasure of the other, and conversely, the pleasure of the other becomes at the same time one's own pleasure. The pleasure of the one mirrors the pleasure of the other, and thus sets off a pleasure-pleasure spiral of ever-increasing intensity. Foucault had talked about a pleasure-power spiral in *The History of Sexuality*.[36] What is evident here is that there was also a pleasure-pleasure spiral assumed in his understanding of pleasure as an event of desubjectivation.

As soon as one is able to receive the pleasure of the other as one's own, one can no longer distinguish between one's own pleasure and the pleasure of the other; one is no longer oneself. That is to say, one has lost one's sense of the self; one has ceased to be a self. With the abolition of the self, however, the otherness of the other is also abolished; one's being extends to the other, as if the two were merely two points in a single loop of pleasure; the self and the other collapse together to form a single loop or spiral of pleasure. Having collapsed together, the subject and the object of pleasure form a single continuum. This is the event of pleasure as desubjectivation. As I will discuss in chapter 3, the *Kāmasūtra* also captures pleasure as an event of desubjectivation in its notion of pleasure-wheel (*raticakra*). What is different about the *Kāmasūtra*, however, is that the courtesan is the primary figure of sexual-erotic pleasure, not the stranger. And unlike in the case of Foucault's stranger, the courtesan's relationship with her patron is grounded in the discourse of love.

Pleasure, Desubjectivation, and Death

For Foucault the event of sexual pleasure was not a moment to assert the sovereignty of self and subjectivity, but to lose it. Indeed, it was because Foucault saw pleasure as an event of desubjectivation or cessation of self and subjectivity that, in his thought process, pleasure came to be associated with death. The importance of the motif of death in Foucault's writings and life could be gauged from the fact that James Miller anchors his biography of Foucault directly in it.[37] For Miller the motif of death offered access into the innermost secrets of Foucault's intellectual quest; the one motif that tied all aspects of his complex and singular life into a knot. I contend in contrast that the thread that in fact ties the themes of death, pleasure, and, indeed, madness together in the works of Foucault is that of desubjectivation.

In one of his interviews Foucault makes a rather startling disclosure. He states that for him the only worthwhile pleasure was similar to the experience of death. When reminded by the interviewer that he was the only Frenchman who preferred American food, Foucault responded,

> Yes. Sure. (Laughs) A good club sandwich with a Coke. That's my pleasure. It's true. With ice cream. That's true. Actually, I think I have real difficulty in experiencing pleasure. I think pleasure is a very difficult behavior. It's not as simple as that (Laughs) to enjoy one's self. And—I must say that's my dream—I would like and hope I'll die of an overdose (Laughs) of pleasure of any kind. Because I think it's really difficult and I always have the feeling that I do not feel the pleasure, the complete total pleasure and, for me, it's related to death.[38]

Given that this piece of personal revelation was accompanied by laughter, it may appear insignificant and without any intellectual value. What Foucault was revealing, however, was an intellectual insight into the nature of pleasure as an experience. In this statement Foucault problematized the nature of pleasure as an experience of death. Given the general perception of death as a moment of pain, Foucault's association of death with pleasure may appear somewhat puzzling. However, this association appears as a consistent theme in Foucault's interviews. In another interview, Foucault narrates a near-death experience as an experience of pleasure, indeed one of his most intense experiences of pleasure.[39] While responding to a question about pleasure, he recalled an experience of an accident in which he was knocked down by a car at an intersection in Paris.

> I think that the kind of pleasure I would consider as *the* real pleasure would be so deep, so intense, so overwhelming that I couldn't survive it. I would die. I'll give you a clearer and simpler example. Once I was struck by a car in the

> street. I was walking. And for maybe two seconds I had the impression that I was dying and it was really a very, very intense pleasure. The weather was wonderful. It was 7 o'clock on a summer day. The sun was coming down. The sky was very wonderful and blue and so on. It was, it still is now, one of my best memories. (Laughs.)[40]

Although this was nothing more than a fleeting experience, it left a powerful impression on Foucault and seemed to have even become an anchor and archive for his reflections on pleasure, death, and, indeed, life. This experience brought together the two otherwise incompatible experiences of pleasure and death.

If we keep in mind Foucault's understanding of pleasure as an event of desubjectivation, the precise meaning of death becomes intelligible. Death is the same as desubjectivation or the death of the self, not simply the end of life. Conventionally, the notion of self is at least as important for human life as the living body. That is the reason Foucault's use of the word death for the death of the self ought not to be seen as the metaphorical use of the word. It was because pleasure was an event of desubjectivation or the loss of self that it also came to be associated with death.[41] In Foucault's thought, death functions as an extreme form of desubjectivation and, as such, occurs as an experience of pleasure.[42] Seen in this light, if only for a few seconds during that accident, Foucault experienced life without self or subjectivity—life as such in all its anonymity and impersonality.

Foucault makes a distinction between two kinds of pleasure: "*the* real" and "complete total" pleasure, which he associates with death and regular everyday pleasure that he calls "middle-range pleasures." "I am not able to give myself and others those middle range pleasures that make up everyday life. Such pleasures are nothing for me and I am not able to organize my life in order to make room for them."[43] What exactly is the difference between these two forms of pleasure? The everyday pleasures come from consumption of objects. Foucault himself gives the example of sandwich, Coke, and ice cream. In such pleasures, the subject is fully in command; the subject consumes pleasure as he consumes objects. The self, in other words, maintains its sovereignty in such experiences over pleasure. One could, therefore, call these everyday forms of pleasure subjective pleasure. Foucault said he was not interested in such subjective pleasures. He associates the higher, more intense forms of pleasure with death. In this experience of pleasure as death, instead of the subject consuming pleasure as an object, exactly the reverse happens: it is the subject itself that is consumed and abolished by pleasure.

However, there is such a powerful hold of the self over the body in everyday life that desubjectivation as death of self may come to be closely associated with the real physical death. It is as if only in the moment of death could one experience life in all its desubjectivated anonymity, as life without identity. Indeed, it is present in Foucault's own writing as a kind of fantasy. Writing about death in an essay called "Simplest of Pleasures," Foucault says: "One has to prepare it bit by bit, decorate it, arrange the details, find the ingredients, imagine it, choose it, get advice on it, shave it into a work without spectators, one which exists only for oneself, just for that shortest little moment of life."[44] It is as if death were not an end but a culmination and telos of life. Foucault here reverses the assumed everyday experience of death as end of life. As we have also seen in the citations above, while talking about pleasure as an experience of death, Foucault also says that it was his dream, hope, and wish. Once again, it is important to keep in mind, while interpreting such instances, that death in the works of Foucault functioned as an event and experience of desubjectivation.

Whether death was also a personal fantasy of Foucault may be a matter of concern for Foucault's biographer; it does not really concern us. What is of value to us is that Foucault made them the basis of his philosophical reflections on pleasure and thus transformed them into a question of thought. After all, Foucault's own experiences often worked as an intellectual archive for philosophical reflections. Despite its personal touch, Foucault's narration of his experience has to be read not as hiding a personal wish or fantasy that could be explained in terms of his psychology, but as a work of philosophy, a work of thought, an effort to explore connections between subjectivity, pleasure, desubjectivation, and death.

Stargazing in the Mojave Desert: Pleasure as an Event of Enlightenment

Foucault makes a crucial distinction between two separate but complementary registers of desubjectivation: desubjectivation as critique and desubjectivation as "actual experience."[45] In desubjectivation as critique Foucault seeks to "call into question the category of the subject, its supremacy, its foundational function" as the sovereign ground of both knowledge and history. He puts his entire oeuvre under this title of desubjectivation as critique or what he calls "a project of desubjection." He went on to expose the category of the subject as a function of the relations of power. It is, however, very significant that Foucault emphatically adds that limited to the realm of thought and in the absence of actual experience, desubjectivation would be "meaningless" and a mere "speculation." Pleasure is one of those "actual experiences" of desubjectivation. On the other hand, these actual limit experiences would not be "full" if left unthought, which is to say, not used as the ontological ground for a critique of the subject as the ground of knowledge and history. Each called for the other as if they were complementary experiences; as if one was incomplete without the other.

In stating that desubjectivation without actual experience is meaningless what Foucault also implied is that the question of desubjectivation exceeds the realm of thought; it extends into the realm of being, being without self. Indeed, the actual experience functions as the ontological ground of the thought of desubjectivation. Pleasure as desubjectivation, therefore, is an ontological ground. While desubjectivation as intellectual critique is carried out in Foucault's works, desubjectivation as "actual experience" directs us to Foucault's own experiences as described by him. Just as desubjectivation as critique is meaningless without the actual experience, the actual experience of desubjectivation is also wasted if it is left unthought. There is then a paramount question of the highest significance: how exactly is desubjectivation as critique related to desubjectivation as limit experience in the life and works of Foucault?[46] In the context of the primary concern of this book the question becomes: what exactly is the relationship between the actual experience of pleasure as desubjectivation and thought? If, as Foucault says, this actual experience is not full when left unthought, then that is because it also opens up a horizon of intelligibility, the possibility of a discourse. At least potentially, every event of desubjectivation is also an event of thought. Pleasure as an event of desubjectivation may not be a lapse into oblivion after all, but a ground for knowledge. Given how precious these events of desubjectivation were, it may not be too much to assume that Foucault would not have allowed any such opportunity to be wasted.

It is with this context in mind that I now turn to one of Foucault's personal experiences of pleasure—an experience extremely vivid—as a historical archive. The real content of the experience, briefly narrated in Miller's biography of Foucault, consists of a night in the Mojave Desert, which Foucault, with two other friends, spent looking at the dark sky luminous with stars.[47] Foucault is reported to have said during this experience, "The skies have exploded and the stars are raining down upon me." Realizing perhaps that such a statement coming from a philosopher known for his sharp analytical skills might have sounded a little too far-fetched and poetic, Foucault quickly volunteered to acknowledge that he knew "it was not true." He concluded by saying, however, in somewhat surprising but emphatic terms, that it was nevertheless "*the* truth." What makes this event relevant and important for us is that Foucault went on to add that he now understood his sexuality, likening this experience to sexual experience between two strangers. "Tonight I have achieved a fresh perspective on myself," he is reported to have said.[48] It was as if Foucault suddenly had a moment of intellectual lucidity that offered him a series of rare insights into himself and his sexuality. Indeed, so emphatic was Foucault in declaring this experience to be "*the* truth" that it appears almost as an event of enlightenment.[49]

This experience also involved the use of drugs.[50] My focus in analyzing this experience, however, is not on the validity or legitimacy of drugs as an intellectual aid. Rather, it is the language in which Foucault chose to describe this experience that makes it important for the subject of this chapter. If I am interested in this experience, then that is because of the obvious discursive continuities in the way Foucault describes this experience and the experience of pleasure—sexual pleasure—in its relation with truth and desubjectivation. As important as it may be for Foucault's biographer, the use of drugs is only incidental for my purposes. In any case, given that Foucault directly compares this experience with the sexual experience between two strangers, it is quite evident that the experience itself exceeds the use of drugs, which is nothing more than a means.

Coming from the most well-known historian-philosopher of sexuality, this experience and the potential insights it may carry acquire enormous significance. According to Miller, Foucault continued to refer to this experience years later, and it may indeed have changed the course of Foucault's research.[51] What was it about this experience that made it so important for Foucault? While acknowledging the insights about himself and his sexuality, Foucault did not elaborate, however, what exactly they were.[52] Since Foucault himself did not offer any elaboration of this experience, it stands as an enigma. The only way to grasp those insights is to understand the nature of the core experience of pleasure itself. What makes this episode so critical for our understanding is not the psychology of Foucault as an individual, but the fact that all the most important categories—pleasure (including sexual pleasure), self-identity, desubjectivation, and truth—that anchor Foucault's project on the history of sexuality find themselves tied together into a single knot in this episode.

Foucault's statement that he now understood his sexuality after his experience in the Mojave Desert is extremely puzzling because this experience had absolutely nothing to do with sex or sexuality. The only thing that connects this experience with sexual experience, therefore, is the experience of pleasure itself.[53] Foucault compared this experience with sexual experience between two strangers that, as I have discussed above, functioned as the most intense kind of sexual experience in Foucault's personal archive. It was in reference to this form of sexual experience that Foucault had brought up the notion of pleasure as an event of desubjectivation. In stating that he understood his sexuality in this experience, Foucault acknowledged that he finally comprehended what pleasure, including sexual pleasure, as an event of desubjectivation really was. This episode clearly reveals Foucault's precise understanding of pleasure as holding the key to an understanding of sexuality, and not the other way around. It was not the anatomical aspect of sex that was important. The domain of pleasure, therefore, is much larger than that of sex.

Looked at more closely, what we have here by way of Foucault's statements and observations during this experience fall into two different groups: the first consists of the core of the experience of pleasure itself consisting of Foucault looking at the night sky. The second consists of all the important intellectual insights he is able to draw from it. During this experience, Foucault, it appears, was moving back and forth between two alternating states—one that consisted solely of the experience of pleasure, and the other that was busy drawing intellectual conclusions from it. It was the experience of pleasure that opened up a horizon of intelligibility, allowing Foucault to gain insights into some of the most enduring intellectual problems that he had pursued, such as sexuality, subjectivity, desubjectivation, pleasure, and truth. His intellectual insights are therefore derivative of the core experience of pleasure. Even as it opened up a horizon of intelligibility, the core experience of pleasure itself consisted of nothing more than looking at the sky, as if pleasure itself were a form of visibility. Pleasure, it seems, may not be a sleep of reason, but an event of enlightenment. In contrast to the age-old view of pleasure as a form of blindness, or a mere feeling, it seems, at least in this case, pleasure is a moment of revelation. Foucault would not have been able to gain such important insights into himself and some of the most vexing intellectual problems relating to pleasure, identity, and truth had the experience of pleasure not opened up a horizon of intelligibility.

Foucault's experience of pleasure, on the one hand, and the intellectual insights he was able to draw from it, on the other, need to be related and interpreted in light of each other. As long as they remain separated, these statements seem to be nothing more than a series of claims that defy explanation. Having acknowledged that his experience of skies exploding and stars raining down on him were not in fact "true," Foucault still went ahead and claimed it to be "*the* truth." At stake in this emphatic statement is the nature of relationship between pleasure and truth, a crucial axis in Foucault's notion of *ars erotica*, and more generally in his project on the history of sexuality. The notion of truth appears in two different forms: When Foucault acknowledges that his statement—"skies have exploded and stars are raining down upon me"—is not true, he thinks of this experience from the everyday perspective.

In this perspective, stars have their fixed place and trajectory in the space and do not rain down upon someone, as if they were drops of water.

It is important to note, however, that this everyday perspective is not able to prevent one from having this experience. The everyday perspective comes into effect only when this experience becomes a subject of enunciation, that is to say, discourse. In other words, it is not the experience itself, but rather the "truth" of this experience that the everyday perspective excludes; it does not allow this experience to circulate as a discourse with a claim to truth. But the same experience would be readily accepted if it were to be enunciated as part of a literary or poetic discourse. Then, however, much of Foucault's description of his experience would fall under the literary categories of metaphor, simile, and, more generally, beauty—but not truth. Any insistence on the claim to the truth of this experience would provoke doubts about the sanity of the person making these claims and open the way for a medical and scientific discourse of psychology and psychoanalysis to take over that would approach the same experience as a symptom.

Given that this event was an event of pleasure, what Foucault in effect asserted was that pleasure is *the* truth. Foucault, in other words, subordinated the notion of truth to the experience of pleasure. Pleasure was not to be measured or judged by a discourse of truth located outside it. It did not have to correspond to some general discourse of truth. This event of pleasure carried the measure of its own truth within itself. Brushing aside the certitude of everyday discourse, when Foucault declares his experience to be "*the* truth," what he really does is give originary or ontological status to this experience. It means that this experience is the ground for its own knowledge; that this experience is capable of founding a discourse of its own. It is evident that Foucault assumes two different kinds of truth: a truth that is anchored in the experience of pleasure and the other truth that is anchored in the discourse of reason and everyday experiences. To use a Heideggerian distinction, truth functions as an ontic, not ontological, category in Foucault.

When Foucault stated that he knew what he said was not true, he was speaking from the perspectives of reason and everyday experiences. But when he went on to conclude that it was nevertheless "*the* truth," he sought to preempt precisely such attempts to deny the truth of his experience. In light of Foucault's emphatic claim, let alone approach this statement in terms of psychology or psychoanalysis, even to interpret the description of his experience in literary terms as metaphorical would be a gesture of condescension. As far as Foucault was concerned, his experience and the precise words in which he chose to describe it must be taken literally.

Foucault's experience and observations fall squarely within the tradition of what I would call psychedeliology that was quarter of a century old by then.[54] Foucault was by no means the first to associate the use of drugs with pleasure, desubjectivation, and revelation, and, as I will discuss in the next section, madness. Aldous Huxley was perhaps the first thinker to problematize the experience of drugs in terms of these categories. Huxley used the word "de-individualization" to describe the experience, but what he meant by it comes close to what Foucault meant by desubjectivation.[55] The notion of de-indivdualization was the ground of Huxley's reflections on the drug-induced experiences. Moreover, Huxley also designated this event of de-individualization as a moment of revelation or, more precisely, "doors of perception."[56] Almost two decades before Foucault, Huxley had also associated drugs with pleasure.[57]

Pleasure, Madness, and the Orient

The actual experiences of desubjectivation as events of thought can advance along two axes: thought can look in at this experience of desubjectivation and make it the subject of its reflections and determine its nature. Since the historical context in which Foucault found himself involves drugs as a major source of pleasure, we see the historical birth of these reflections in psychedeliology as a new discourse. And though the academic world has largely overlooked it, this psychedelic revolution has been just as profound and far-reaching in its implications as any in our modern world. We see the emergence of a missionary—or was it revolutionary?—ethos in individuals like Huxley, Timothy Leary, and many others.

But thought can also ontologically ground itself in this experience and look out at the world outside in its light. This dimension of desubjectivation as an event of thought would draw thought out of the domain of pleasure and psychedeliology and make it critically engage the world outside. This is the birth of desubjectivation as critique. We have evidence that Foucault was very much aware of—and perhaps grounded in—this dimension. As surprising as Foucault's comments on his experience in the Mojave Desert may appear, it was a culmination of a prolonged reflection that may have preceded the project on the history of sexuality by at least a decade. What is also noteworthy is that the issue of the nature and significance of cultural and intellectual differences between the West and the East seems to be implicated in this experience.

In the course of one of Foucault's interviews in 1967, the topic suddenly shifted to the different ways in which drugs are used in the West and the East. The interviewer, P. Caruso, asked Foucault: "Do you think, then, that drugs can take on another meaning within our very culture, that of an expansion of the horizons of our mentality to the point of including new forms of sensitivity? Do you think, for example, that it is possible to speak of an irruption of the thought and culture of certain Eastern civilizations within our Western civilization?"[58] By "another meaning" the interviewer implied other than its use as an intoxicant. Notice how the interviewer assumes an ability of drugs to open up another horizon of thought and culture to be self-evident. One needs to keep in mind the historical context in which this interview was taking place to understand the underlying ethos of this question. The year of the publication of this interview was 1967. It was during that period that drugs, sex, literature, art, and spiritual quest came to be tied together in a single knot, giving rise to a sense that a new horizon of possibilities was about to appear.[59] With the advent of what became known as the "hippie trail" bringing tens of thousands of Americans, and other westerners, to India, this was also the period when there was a sudden rise in the interest in Indian culture, religions, spirituality, and philosophies.[60] The concerns and possibilities that the interviewer brought up in this question to Foucault were by no means unique. They had emerged as major cultural and intellectual concerns, beyond the narrow confines of the academia, particularly in the United States.

The same year when this interview took place, Maharishi Mahesh Yogi, an Indian spiritual guru, was touring America. The Maharishi made meditation, better known as transcendental meditation, the center of his spiritual campaign worldwide. Wherever the Maharishi went, he exhorted his young audience, often running into the thousands, to quit drugs and take up meditation. In one such meeting, Allen Ginsberg, the leading member of the beat poets, confronted the Maharishi: "There wouldn't be all these people sitting around here listening to you if it wasn't for LSD."[61] Ginsberg wanted the Maharishi to acknowledge and appreciate the role LSD had played in opening the door to spiritual gurus like him and to Indian spiritual-intellectual traditions. But the Maharishi's exhortation was hardly a moral rejection of drugs. Rather it was a plea for its substitution by meditation. Behind this logic of substitution there is an assumed equivalence between the two: why take drugs when meditation can offer the same experience. Evidently the possibility of drugs opening a window on eastern cultures was not on Foucault's interviewer's mind alone. Indeed, such has been the role of drugs in the shaping of modern culture that Foucault himself had plans to do "a study of the cultures of drugs or drugs as culture in the West from the beginning of the nineteenth century. . . . It's so closely tied to the artistic life in the West."[62]

The history of drug use, as Foucault was well aware, went further back than the 1960s. Some of the greatest names in modern literature, such as

Baudelaire, Flaubert, De Quincey, Coleridge, and numerous other authors of great renown, were deeply associated with this history.[63] Foucault's answer to his interlocutor's question is most revealing, and goes to the heart of the subject of desubjectivation, particularly in the way it involves Indian intellectual traditions and their status in the West. My concerns are, however, limited to examining briefly the notion of desubjectivation, its association with Foucault's earlier project on the history of madness, and—just as important—the reference to Eastern cultures that evidently included Indian culture. Here is Foucault's complete answer to that question:

> No, I think on the contrary that opposite phenomenon is occurring. On the face of it, for the last one hundred and fifty years, since Schopenhauer, say, we have been orientalizing; in reality, it is precisely because the whole world is Westernizing that West is becoming relatively more permeable to Indian philosophy, to African art, to Japanese painting, to Arabic mysticism. Hindu philosophy, African art acquire a consciousness of self by virtue of those structures through which Western civilization assimilates them. Consequently, the use of drugs does not at all seem to me to be a way for the Westerner to open up to the East. It seems to me that drugs as used in the East functioned essentially to tear man away from the mad illusion that the world exists and to reveal to him another reality which was the *annihilation of the individual*; the use made of them today turns out to be an individualistic one if ever there was one; it is all about refinding in oneself the internal possibilities of madness. Not, then, about dispelling the madness of the normal in order to recover true reality, according to the Eastern use of drugs, but about reclaiming through the reason of the world an individual madness which we all involuntarily possess."[64] [Emphasis mine.]

The first thing to be noted in this citation is the phrase "annihilation of the individual": this "annihilation of the individual" is the same as the death of the individual as a self, or desubjectivation in Foucault's later terminology. Notice that Foucault ties this experience of desubjectivation discursively to madness, just as he had tied his experience in the Mojave Desert to sexual pleasure. As is evident, in 1967 Foucault's thoughts on desubjectivation were still moving within the intellectual horizon opened up by *History of Madness*, published in 1961, that was framed within the opposition of reason and madness.[65] With the start of Foucault's project on the history of sexuality, pleasure came to replace madness as the position of exteriority to the discourse of reason anchored in truth and subjectivity. There is evidence that even in the sixties there was some association of madness with a specific kind of enjoyment or pleasure in Foucault's thoughts. In 1963 Foucault said: "Every man who speaks enjoys, at least in secret, the absolute freedom of being mad."[66]

The positions of madness and pleasure in the works of Foucault, therefore, are isomorphic.[67] Pleasure occupies the same place in the history of sexuality that madness did in the history of madness. There is an unmistakable continuity, not always noted, between Foucault's first work on the history of madness and his last project on the history of sexuality. This continuity also shows just how central pleasure was to Foucault's project on the history of sexuality. In the notion of madness, therefore, there is the hidden prehistory of pleasure as desubjectivation. In the wake of the publication of his *History of Madness*, Foucault continued to probe various aspects of madness, particularly the nature of its relationship with language and literature.[68] Significantly, he discusses experiences induced by drugs under the subject of "artificially provoked madness," with Henri Michaux's writings offered as an example.[69]

Foucault also observes that drugs were used in the East "to *reveal* another reality." If one replaced the word drug with pleasure or madness as an event of desubjectivation—that is exactly how it functions in the writings of Foucault—then what Foucault in effect meant was that pleasure reveals another reality. In other words, pleasure as an event of desubjectivation is a moment of revelation or visibility, not sleep or oblivion. What is revealed is another order of reality, a reality other than the one we recognize as real in our everyday experience. According to Foucault, in the event of desubjectivation, two things are revealed at the same time as if they were two sides of one and the same experience: even as the self-evidence that the world exists is revealed to be nothing more than an "illusion," the "annihilation of the individual," or desubjectivation, is revealed to be "another reality." In this experience a reversal takes place: what appears real and self-evident in everyday life is revealed to be nothing more than an illusion, even as de-individuated and desubjectivated being appears to be real. Seen in the context of Foucault's own writings, "world as illusion" refers to its being historically contingent and constructed, not an ahistorical given. Foucault, as is evident, very directly claimed that the experience of pleasure as an event of desubjectivation has the potential to open up an ontological horizon of intelligibility otherwise inaccessible.[70]

There was a reason Caruso brought up Eastern civilizations while discussing the potential impact of drugs in western culture. There are certain sects of monks in India well known for their use of cannabis as an aid in their spiritual quest. These sects consist of renunciate monks, known as sadhus, who are no longer part of the organized society.[71] Indeed, so complete is their detachment from the world that they are in many ways dead to the society around them.[72] They live their lives in complete anonymity. In renouncing the world, what they also renounce is their identity and subjectivity that kept them tied to the world. Their lives belong to a zone exterior to that of identity and subjectivity. Not surprisingly, their discourse is also anchored in desubjectivation.[73] Pictures of these sadhus with hippies began to appear in the western media in the wake of the advent of the hippie trail to India in the 1960s. It is precisely the same group that Foucault also had in mind when he brought up the East to make his point about the different discursive context of drug use there.

Significantly, Foucault's phrase "annihilation of the individual" as desubjectivation also refers to the same group. Let me repeat once more what precisely Foucault has to say about the use of drugs amongst these sadhus: "It seems to me that drugs as used in the East functioned essentially to tear man away from the mad illusion that the world exists and to reveal to him another reality which was the *annihilation of the individual*." Here is a statement from the guru of Patrick Levy, a French national, who was initiated into an order of these sadhus in India: "He who perceives this world is as deceptive as the world he perceives. When you fix your consciousness on this principle of double illusion, you find the consciousness upon which this plays itself out."[74] One of the sadhus Levy met was called Pagal Baba, or mad saint. When asked by Levy why he was called mad, Pagal Baba replied, "In this mad world which denies its madness, there is a pleasure in being mad that only a madman knows."[75] In the title of his book *Saint Foucault*, perhaps Halperin said far more than he intended.

Huxley had already noted and explored this affinity between the experiences induced by drugs and some of the Indian spiritual and discursive traditions more than a decade earlier than Foucault. Indeed, Huxley founded a whole new discursive field of psychedeliology grounded in psychedelic experiences as an interface of philosophy and spirituality by borrowing categories somewhat eclectically but extensively from Indian spiritual-intellectual traditions of both Hinduism and Buddhism. The most important of those categories was *mokṣa*, or spiritual liberation, as an experience of the loss of the sense of self, or "de-individualization" in Huxley's own rendering of it.[76] It is not god or heaven, but spiritual liberation—*nirvāṇa* in Buddhism and *mokṣa* in Hinduism—that is the highest spiritual goal. In his novel *Island*, Huxley envisioned a whole new society based on the drug-induced experience of de-individualization and *mokṣa*.[77] In the same novel he constructs a ritual of spiritual initiation for young boys and girls that involves taking of what he calls "*mokṣa* medicine."[78] Indeed, after the invention of these drugs Huxley saw no need for extreme asceticism in pursuit of spiritual liberation: "For an aspiring mystic to revert, in the present state of knowledge, to prolonged fasting and violent self-flagellation would be as senseless as it would be for an aspiring cook to behave like Charles Lamb's Chinaman, who burned down the house to roast a pig. Knowing as he does . . . what are the chemical conditions of transcendental experience, the aspiring mystic should turn for technical help to the specialists."[79] Exactly as Foucault's interviewer had suggested, through the gateway offered by the psychedelic revolution, Huxley received a major aspect of Indian spiritual-intellectual tradition.

In what appears to be a critique, Foucault suggests that in contrast to its use in Indian culture, in the West drugs are used as part of a culture of individualism: "The use made of them [drugs] today turns out to be an individualistic one if ever there was one; it is all about re-finding in oneself the internal possibilities of madness." Foucault also matter-of-factly states that everyone involuntarily possesses "an individual madness." What Foucault calls "individual madness" is nothing but an individual's innate capacity for de-individualization, or desubjectivation, just as in the case of pleasure. Therefore, what appears to be a critique of the individualistic use of drugs in the West in fact amounts to a critique of an individualistic use of pleasure as an object of consumption. The individualistic consumption of drugs is only a symptom of a larger phenomenon of individualistic relationship with pleasure as an event of desubjectivation. Since pleasure as desubjectivation or de-individualization is reduced to an object of consumption, it cannot also function as an ontological anchor of a critical discourse against a discourse of reason grounded in truth and self. In such instances an event of desubjectivation fails to become an event of thought, and as such is a wasted opportunity.

Foucault's characterization of the relationship between Eastern cultures and the West needs to be seen in light of his understanding of the status of the event and experience of desubjectivation in western culture. For a while, the cultural context of the 1960s seemed to hold the tantalizing possibility—the possibility that the interviewer brought up in his question—that the West may be finally on the historical cusp of opening up culturally and intellectually to Eastern cultures, including Indian culture. Foucault, however, suggests that what in fact was happening was part of a broader history of assimilation of Eastern cultures, including their intellectual traditions, within the individualistic cultural-intellectual framework of the West. It is significant that Foucault considers Arthur Schopenhauer, one of the greatest German philosophers (1788–1860), to be at the origin of what superficially seems like the Orientalizing of the West. Schopenhauer came under the influence of certain Indian intellectual traditions, including the Upaniṣads, a set of earliest Sanskrit texts on spirituality and philosophy, and Buddhism.[80] Indian philosophy became assimilated in the same way as the experience of desubjectivation became assimilated in a culture grounded in individualism. What seemed like an opening up was in fact nothing more than Eastern cultures and their intellectual traditions—stripped of their critical categories—being reduced to an object of consumption, rather than the ground of another discourse. They became the artifacts of an exotic culture, as enormously interesting as alien, and in the end without any meaning. Indeed, that was how the *Kāmasūtra* also fell into the universe of western intellectual traditions. Not surprisingly, it was largely ignored by the intellectual world as a tradition of thought, even as it generated immense curiosity.

Conclusion

Soon after an American from Chicago, now known as Rampuri, had been newly initiated into an order of the sadhus in India, he discovered in his bag long-forgotten blotters of LSD and offered it to a curious fellow sadhu. After a period of complete loss of control that included "turning around in circles" in heavy traffic, when the rescued sadhu came back to his senses, he told the American "he now understood why [he] had to leave the land of my birth to come to India," as if suddenly and inadvertently a secret the American had been keeping to himself was revealed.[81] Since there were not many drugs to be found in India at the time, it was not LSD that brought the American there. What brought him to India was the search for a discourse that would help him make sense of his experiences triggered by LSD and the hope that he would find it there in ascetic and spiritual-intellectual traditions. It was the wish to turn his experiences into an ontological ground for a new discourse that brought him to India.

And though the world of sexual-erotic pleasure may appear to be at the farthest point from the world of ascetic and celibate sadhus seeking spiritual liberation, an arc—the arc of desubjectivation—joins them together as if they were two ends of a rainbow. Not surprisingly therefore, according to a legend, the eighth-century monk Śaṅkara, one of the greatest Indian philosophers and the founder of the orders into which the cannbis-smoking sadhus are still initiated, offered a discourse of his own on erotics.[82] Perhaps it was the awareness of this arc of desubjectivation that led the author-figure of the *Kāmasūtra* also to claim, admittedly defying credibility, to be a man of complete celibacy and meditation.[83] And though an infinite distance may appear to separate Foucault from Śaṅkara, perhaps the same arc joined them too.

Given that Foucault was not really a historian of nonwestern cultures, it may appear that his contrast of *scientia sexualis* and *ars erotica* was merely a coincidence. The precision and directness of Foucault's answer I discussed above, however, suggests that he knew, and had thought, a good deal about the place of nonwestern culture in the West. It was, after all, in his search for exteriority to truth and subjectivity evident in both madness and pleasure that Foucault, it appears, stumbled upon nonwestern cultures.[84] It should not come as a surprise, therefore, that the "Orient" was part of Foucault's research project ever since the publication of his first major work, *History of Madness*. Indeed, *History of Madness* was merely the first in a series of major projects that Foucault intended to execute, including one on the "Orient." In the preface to the first edition of *History of Madness* Foucault wrote, "In the universality of the Western ratio, there is this division which is the Orient. . . . What is required is a history of this great divide, all along this occidental becoming, following it in its tragic continuity and its exchanges, while also allowing it to appear in its tragic hieratism."[85] It is this "division" that shows up once more in the contrast of *ars erotica* and *scientia sexualis*.

2

Pleasure and Patriarchy: The Discourse of *Dharma* and the Figure of the Wife

In Foucault's notion of *ars erotica* some scholars have detected an unfounded search for a utopian culture of pleasure in the East.[1] This, however, suggests that Foucault, one of the greatest philosopher-historians of power, thought it possible for a culture to be without relations of power. The presence of the *Kāmasūtra* in ancient India did not mean that it was a culture in which pleasure ruled as the sovereign principle in complete absence of the discourses and relations of power. On the contrary, a society without relations of power would perhaps have no need for *ars erotica* as an intellectual-pedagogical discourse because it would be innate to that culture and people. Indeed, it was precisely because potentially erotic relations—such as marriage—grounded in pleasure and love were transformed into relations of power that there arose a need for *ars erotica* in ancient India.

Since the primary form of erotic relations that the *Kāmasūtra* focused on involved man-woman relations, the question of *ars erotica* inevitably came to intersect with the question of gender relations. Indeed, gender relations seem to have been at the very origin of the *Kāmasūtra* as one of its core concerns. The *Kāmasūtra* came to be composed in a culture in which the subordination of pleasure to power was historically anchored in the subordination of women to men.[2] The two processes became so inextricably linked that they appeared to be the two ends of the same historical and intellectual continuum. The questions of sexual-erotic pleasure therefore must necessarily involve a discussion of gender relations.[3]

It was under the ascendance of the discourse *dharma,* or Brahmanical law, with the *Mānava Dharmaśāstra* (second century CE) as its founding text that even as women came to be subordinated to men, *kāma* became subordinated to *dharma.*[4] What is significant about this discourse of *dharma* is that it discovered a whole new domain and technology of power beyond violence located in the self or subjectivity.[5] The discourse of *dharma* as Brahmanical law, invented in the *Mānava Dharmaśāstra* as a new discourse of patriarchal power, sought to subordinate women to men, not so much through coercion or violence as through the discursive construction of a new subjectivity in the figure of the wife. It was the construction of the discourse of *dharma* as a discourse of power that constituted the historical context and discursive provocation to which the *Kāmasūtra* came as a subtle and covert response.[6]

In this chapter I briefly lay out the historical-discursive context of power within which the *Kāmasūtra* came into being. I focus primarily on the discourse of Brahmanical law and show how the subordination of pleasure to the hegemonic discourse of Brahmanical law went hand in hand with the subordination of women to men. I discuss the construction of the subjectivity of the wife in the *Mānava Dharmaśāstra*—which preceded the arrival of the *Kāmasūtra*. The emergence of subjectivity in the discourse of *dharma* as a new domain of power is too vast and complex a subject—even within the single text of the *Mānava Dharmaśāstra* itself—to be dealt with comprehensively in this chapter. My aim therefore is limited to offering a broad but brief sketch of this development, particularly as it relates to women.

Subordination of Pleasure to Brahmanical Law and the Origin of the *Kāmasūtra*

The *Kāmasūtra* is a comprehensive treatise that deals with various aspects of sexual-erotic pleasure: the notion of erotic pleasure and its place in life; the event of pleasure as desubjectivation; ways of seduction and sexual-erotic acts; figures of pleasure, such as the courtesan, another man's wife, remarried woman, and the city dandy; relations of pleasure, such as premarital, marital, and extramarital; and the place of art and aesthetics in the domain of erotics. As a treatise the *Kāmasūtra* is divided into seven books of uneven lengths dedicated to different topics. The seven books are further subdivided into chapters, which contain the individual sutras or aphoristic formulations on the topics under discussion. Book 1 deals with the place of *kāma* or pleasure-love-desire in a life of multiple—and often competing and conflicting—demands. The first three chapters of this first book establishes *kāma* as a separate and relatively autonomous domain of discourse and practice.[7] It also constructs the everyday profile of the *nāgaraka*, the city dandy, to whom the *Kāmasūtra* was primarily addressed. Book 2 describes different kinds of sexual-erotic practices. Book 3 is about ways to court a girl for marriage. Book 4 focuses on the wife and provides her with strategies to win and retain the love of her husband. Book 5 elaborates on ways to win the love of another man's wife. Book 6 is about courtesans and how best they can manage their lives of inherent complexity and risks. Book 7, the last, provides instructions on esoteric sexual methods and devices.

As the very title "*Kāmasūtra*," roughly translated as a "treatise on pleasure," reveals, the notion of pleasure is at the very heart of this text of *ars erotica*. In calling itself a treatise on pleasure, the *Kāmasūtra* brings all the acts and behaviors relating to sex under the sovereign category and domain of pleasure; in other words, it was as practices of pleasure that sex was received into the discourse of erotics in the *Kāmasūtra*. The *Kāmasūtra* thus elevates the question of sex and sexual-erotic relations to a question of thought in the category of pleasure. Not surprisingly, before getting into matters of sex, in its first few chapters of the first book, the *Kāmasūtra* problematizes and elaborates its notion of pleasure and locates the entire field of *ars erotica* within it.[8]

A certain casual attitude that one encounters in any discussion on the *Kāmasūtra* is partly due to the fact that the meaning of sex and sexual pleasure is often seen as self-evident, requiring no intellectual effort. Once the meaning of sex is assumed to be self-evident, all that the *Kāmasūtra* as a text on erotics can be expected to offer is varieties of sexual positions. In reality things are far more complex. One of the most critical aspects of the notion of *kāma* in the *Kāmasūtra* is that it has four distinct but closely related meanings: sexual and erotic pleasure, desire for pleasure, and love.[9] First of all, *kāma* is not just sexual pleasure, but also includes what could be broadly identified as erotic pleasure. For example, in one of its erotic routines called "moon gazing," the *Kāmasūtra* advises couples in love to move to the terrace of their house and sit there together in the darkness of the night gazing at the moon and exchanging insights into various astral constellations.[10] Although no sex is involved in this routine, the *Kāmasūtra* adds that it is capable of offering "supreme pleasure" (*parām ratim*).[11] Also, *kāma* as desire is indistinguishable from love. Indeed, the word desire is used as a synonym for love. For example, the *Kāmasūtra* advises the newly married husband to ask his wife, "Do you desire me?" while meaning to ask if she loves him.[12] But *kāma* also at the same time means desire for sexual pleasure. The *Kāmasūtra* both assumes and insists on the inseparability of these four meanings.

All this appears inconsequential and just a matter of semantics until one realizes that the *Kāmasūtra*'s view of sexual-erotic pleasure goes as much against the common sense view of it as against Freud's "scientific" view in which desire for sexual pleasure as sensual experience is in conflict with love as a product of culture. Contrary to the *Kāmasūtra's* notion of *kāma* in which sexual-erotic pleasure, love, and desire are intimately intertwined, Freudian thought posits that a conflict between love and desire for sexual pleasure is at the heart of man's erotic life: "Where they love they do not desire, where they desire they do not love."[13] This adversarial relationship between sexual pleasure and love is the very ground of Freudian psychoanalysis. After all, civilization in Freud's narration is man's victory over sexual pleasure through the instruments of repression and sublimation.

What is at stake in the discourse of *ars erotica*, as Foucault problematized it, is a culture's relation not just to sexual pleasure, but also to truth and knowledge as such. More than just an attitude toward sexual pleasure, what the presence of *ars erotica* grounded in the notion of pleasure suggests is a culture in which the set of rules that govern the nature and origin of knowledge, or, more broadly, discursive formations, is radically different from the one that gave birth to *scientia sexualis,* or science of sexuality, grounded in truth. The distinctive nature of the discursive context in which the *Kāmasūtra* came into being is evident in its very first sutra, or the opening line—a salutation to *dharma,* or Brahmanical law; *artha,* or political power; and *kāma,* or sexual-erotic pleasure, as if the three were deities to be propitiated at the opening of a major intellectual project.[14] Yet the three were not really deities at all, but the three major topics to be dealt with in the book.[15] Later in the text, the *Kāmasūtra* also refers to the three as a *trivarga,* or trilogy.[16] It is the nature and complexity of the relationship that sexual-erotic pleasure has with the other two members of the trilogy that is the major theme in the first chapter of the *Kāmasūtra,* which lays the theoretical ground for the rest of the book. The intellectual discursive context of the origin of the *Kāmasūtra* as the founding text of *ars erotica* is thus directly addressed in the *Kāmasūtra* itself.

Although the three—*dharma, artha, and kāma*—became part of what came to be known later as *puruṣārthas,* or the ends of man, the numerical nomenclature of the trilogy—Brahmanical law, political power, and sexual-erotic pleasure—in the *Kāmasūtra* suggests that there was a reluctance to subsume the three under a higher category; it also carries an implicit acknowledgment that the three were seen as the highest categories. Depending on the context, they could mean the three broadest domains of human activity and knowledge or three primary ends. However, both as domains and as ends, the three are more ontological than moral or psychological in nature. Later *mokṣa,* or spiritual liberation, came to be added to the set as the fourth member, hence also the name *caturavarga,* or tetralogy.

The notions of the trilogy-tetralogy are of immense significance because they came to determine the nature, origin, and evolution of knowledge or discursive formations in ancient Indian history.[17] In time it was around these four ends that much of the intellectual traditions in ancient India came to be organized, giving rise to four distinct domains of knowledge, or discursive formations. Although these discursive formations have complex histories, each of them has what could be called a founding text, often named directly after an end. These are the *Mānava Dharmaśāstra* (second century CE), the founding text of the discourse of Brahmanical law; the *Arthaśāstra* (first century BCE), the founding text of the discourse of political and economic power; the *Kāmasūtra* (third century CE), the founding text of the discourse on pleasure; and the *Brahmasūtra* in the domain of *mokṣaśāstra,* or the founding text of the discourse on spiritual liberation.

What comes as a surprise in this set of ends is the absence of truth—and therefore knowledge as such—as an end in its own right, let alone as the highest end.[18] In light of the dominant intellectual tradition in the West, as brought out by Foucault, in which truth reigns as the sovereign category, this absence becomes all the more significant.[19] As the very naming of these genres of knowledge suggests, instead of rising above these domains and ends as the sovereign and legislative voice of reason and truth, as it did in the West, knowledge in the *Kāmasūtra* was seen to be subordinated to them.[20] There was no knowledge that did not have its origin and end in the domains and ends of human activity. There would be no truth or knowledge if these domains and ends did not open up the horizon of intelligibility for it in advance. Nor would this knowledge have any purpose other than to serve those domains and ends in turn. The legislative sovereignty of pleasure—or power—over truth and knowledge on the basis of which Foucault mounted his critique of *scientia sexualis* was seen in the *Kāmasūtra* as the very basis or condition of knowledge, or discursive formations.[21] The notion of a trilogy or tetralogy that had marked out a separate place for pleasure, therefore, constituted a very important intellectual condition for the possibility of the *Kāmasūtra.*

Not surprisingly, the theme of conflict between truth and pleasure that, according to Foucault, has dominated western intellectual traditions for over two millennia, is missing in the *Kāmasūtra.*[22] Instead, the conflict as evident in the *Kāmasūtra* is between the three domains and ends. Given that they bear down on the same individual and the same society, the relationship between the domains and ends, not surprisingly, is marked by competition, conflict, and compromises over issues of their relative legislative sovereignty, and, if possible, hegemony.[23] By legislative autonomy and sovereignty I mean the ability and tendency of each member of the trilogy—Brahmanical law (*dharma*), political power (*artha*), and sexual-erotic pleasure (*kāma*)—to define itself and make rules for how best it could be pursued or avoided, rather than allow the other two to do that for it. By hegemony, on the other hand, I mean the tendency in each of the three to encroach into the others' domain and impose its own concerns on them. The relationship between the members of the trilogy is therefore dynamic and unstable, and as such ever open and evolving.

However, although the notion of trilogy assumes a certain legislative autonomy for each of the domains and ends included in it, this autonomy for the ends could not be entirely taken for granted; it had to be claimed and fought for. Indeed, the *Kāmasūtra* locates its own origin in the need to win legislative autonomy for the domain of sexual-erotic pleasure from the hegemonic encroachments of the other ends. In the clearest and most decisive way, the *Kāmasūtra* made a claim for the discursive and legislative autonomy of sexual-erotic pleasure—relative though it was—within this complex of conflicting ends seeking hegemony over each other. In an answer to a hypothetical question about the need for a treatise on pleasure at all, given that sexual pleasure was just as innate in humans as it was in other creatures, the *Kāmasūtra* responds that it is "because of the subordination or subjugation (*parādhīnatva*) of sex (*samprayoga*) between a man and a woman [that] there is a need for a strategy (*upāya*) [to overcome the subordination]."[24] The word *parādhīnatva* literally means subordination, or the state of being under the rule or command of the other—in other words, not free. The word *parādhīna* is the antonym of *svādhīna*, which roughly translates as free or independent. What the *Kāmasūtra* means is that unlike animals, amongst humans sex or sexual relationship does not enjoy natural sovereignty; it has to operate in a state of subordination. Hence, the need for a strategy to overcome this subordination.

Parādhīnatva is also often translated as dependence to mean that in matters of sex one is dependent on another person. Since *samprayoga* means sex, it may seem that *parādhīnatva* refers only to the activity of sex, not pleasure. But seen in the context of the discussion, it becomes quickly evident that subordination, in fact, refers to sexual pleasure and not just to sex. While distinguishing man from animals in the way he approaches the activity of sex, the *Kāmasūtra* asserts that unlike humans, animals mate only during their mating seasons.[25] In this assertion, the *Kāmasūtra* implies that mating of animals is driven only by the species' need for reproduction; amongst animals sex functions as a biological necessity. Animals, therefore, do not mate for the sake of pleasure. Any pleasure that they may experience in mating is exhausted by their need to reproduce. Sexual pleasure, in other words, is not a separate and autonomous pursuit amongst animals. What the *Kāmasūtra* suggests in this assertion about animals is that man, in contrast, engages in sex also for the sake of pleasure. In other words, sexual pleasure amongst humans is an autonomous pursuit. The subordination (*parādhīnatva*) of sex amongst humans as claimed by the *Kāmasūtra*, therefore, comes into effect precisely at the point where sexual pleasure exceeds the need and logic of biological reproduction.

If we review the question of dependence in light of the *Kāmasūtra*'s distinction between humans and animals, things appear far more complex. After all, common sense would suggest that animals are just as dependent on other animals in matters of sex as humans. Yet the *Kāmasūtra* offers the example of animals as a contrast to the needs of humans. Dependence must therefore mean something different for humans than it does for animals. Also, if the matter of dependence was so obvious, the hypothetical question about any need for *ars erotica* at all among humans would have taken it into consideration. The reason why dependence was not considered at all in the hypothetical question was because heterosexual marriage was assumed to be the exemplary sexual relationship in which the husband had unhindered access to the wife, who was hardly in a position to refuse; there was no real dependence in this relationship.

If the *Kāmasūtra* makes this dependence the critical factor in the need for *ars erotica* then that is because it assumes an erotic context in which both men and women are free to refuse even as they strive to win each other's affections. In other words, sexual-erotic pleasure involves the ability to win another person's affection and love. The way to sexual-erotic pleasure passes through speech, that is to say, discourse, a discourse of love. Short of violence or money changing hands, there is no direct route to sexual-erotic pleasure without a discourse of love in the *Kāmasūtra*. The relations of sexual-erotic pleasure are, therefore, discursive in nature. Even as the *Kāmasūtra* is grounded in sexual-erotic pleasure, its concerns extend far beyond sexual positions and types to the discourse of love. Whenever the *Kāmasūtra* refers to pleasure, it always assumes love as its inseparable part; in the same way, the discourse of sexual-erotic pleasure always assumes the discourse of love. *Ars erotica*, therefore, has to do with managing the complexity and subtlety of the sexual-erotic relationship of love between two individuals.

Here the other meaning of *parādhīnatva* as subordination—discursive subordination—comes to the fore. The same sutra that locates the question of sexual pleasure in terms of the difference between humans and animals also states that animals engage in sex *abuddhipūrvaka* or unthinkingly.[26] Here the contrast between the nature of sexual practices among humans and animals is located decisively in the context of their respective ability and inability to think. What is implied in the *Kāmasūtra*'s contrast is that unlike animals, men and women pursue sexual pleasure "thinkingly," that is to say, discursively.

Unlike the common sense view of sex as an entirely sensual experience, in the *Kāmasūtra* the activity of sex is grounded in discourse. It is because sex is often seen as an entirely sensual experience that it is also associated with a certain sense of animality, as if sexual pleasure were originally native to animals and existed among humans only in a residual form. The *Kāmasūtra*'s view is exactly the opposite: sexual pleasure is a discursive phenomenon and as such does not belong to the world of animals.

Once again, the *Kāmasūtra* finds itself on the opposite side of Freud, who calls sex "animal love," as if in sexual pleasure there takes place a regression of humans to their prehistory as animals. It is because Freud reduces sex to a purely sensual experience that he also calls it "animal love." Animality and sensuality find themselves on the same side of the divide between sexual pleasure and love, sensuality and civilization.

> The fundamental processes which promote erotic excitation remain always the same. Excremental things are all too intimately and inseparably bound up with sexual things; the position of the genital organs—inter urinas et faeces—remains the decisive and unchangeable factor. One might say, modifying a well-known saying of the great Napoleon's, "Anatomy is destiny." The genitals themselves have not undergone the development of the rest of the human form in the direction of human beauty; they have retained their animal cast; and so even to-day love, too, is in essence as animal as it ever was. The erotic instincts are hard to mould; training of them achieves now too much, now too little. What culture tries to make out of them seems attainable only at the cost of a sensible loss of pleasure; the persistence of impulses that are not enrolled in adult sexual activity makes itself felt in an absence of satisfaction.[27]

"Even today love in its essence is as animal as it ever was"! Freud also suggests the impossibility of training the "erotic instincts" because culture and sexual pleasure as sensuality are altogether incompatible. These instincts are neither accessible nor amenable to the logic and persuasion of culture. Contrary to Freud, the *Kāmasūtra* finds no conflict between sexual pleasure and love; indeed, it grounds sexual pleasure in the discourse of love. From the perspective of the *Kāmasūtra*, therefore, all the problems and possibilities in the field of erotics stem from the fact that the pursuit of sexual pleasure is grounded in a discursive relationship of love. Before any sex between the two partners in an erotic affair, there needs to be a discursive relationship of love in place between them. Seen in light of this discussion, *parādhīnatva* as discursive subordination amounted to sexual-erotic pleasure grounded in love not enjoying the legislative sovereignty to define itself and to make rules for itself as to how it was to be pursued or avoided. What was that discourse to which sexual-erotic pleasure had come to be subordinated? The *Kāmasūtra* identifies *dharma* as Brahmanical law to be that discourse. It locates this subordination of sexual-erotic pleasure within the larger framework of the trilogy as the three competing and conflicting discursive formations: "When the trilogy of Brahmanical law (*dharma*), political power (*artha*), and sexual-erotic pleasure (*kāma*)—are considered together as a whole, between them the former has primacy over the latter. [That is to say, while Brahmanical law has primacy over both political power and pleasure, political power has primacy over sexual-erotic pleasure.]"[28]

In the citation above the *Kāmasūtra* was forced to acknowledge that there was a hierarchy amongst the three members of the trilogy with Brahmanical law at the top and sexual-erotic pleasure at the bottom. Evidently, when the *Kāmasūtra* came to be composed, both political power (*artha*) and sexual-erotic pleasure (*kāma*) had come under the general hegemony of the discourse of Brahmanical law (*dharma*) and risked losing their sovereignty to it (*dharma*). This discourse of Brahmanical law in ancient India was grounded in patriarchal and caste identity. By subordination of sex and sexual pleasure the *Kāmasūtra*, therefore, meant *kāma*'s subordination to *dharma* as the discourse of Brahmanical law based in patriarchy and caste identity. Therefore, if pleasure had to acquire legislative sovereignty, it had to found a discourse of its own and devise a strategy to overcome this subordination—hence the need for a discourse of *ars erotica* in the *Kāmasūtra*. Clearly, in this answer the *Kāmasūtra* directly problematizes its own origin as the founding text of a discourse: it is for the sake of the legislative and discursive sovereignty of sexual-erotic pleasure that the *Kāmasūtra* must come into being.

What did this hegemony of *dharma* amount to in practical terms? How precisely did it affect the behavior of men and women in pursuit of sexual-erotic pleasure? While answering the question about the need for a discourse of *ars erotica* at all, the *Kāmasūtra* points to another difference between animals and humans: unlike females among animals, which are *anāvṛt,* meaning unclothed or naked, as well as free and unfettered, females among humans are veiled and fettered.[29] The *Kāmasūtra* here refers to women's lack of freedom in the human world. Notice that while referring to the lack of freedom for women, the *Kāmasūtra* leaves men out, suggesting thereby that men perhaps did not suffer from the same disability. The *Kāmasūtra* clearly problematizes the question about the absence of autonomy for pleasure itself in the historical context of the absence of freedom for women. In the *Kāmasūtra*'s view men and women played different historical roles in, and were affected differently by, the discursive subordination of sexual-erotic pleasure. The subordination of pleasure and the lack of freedom for women, therefore, are two historically related phenomena in the *Kāmasūtra*.

This veiling does not refer to women physically wearing veils but rather to their veiled approach to sexual-erotic pleasure. In one of its sutras, the *Kāmasūtra* characterizes women to be of veiled nature (*prācchāditasvabhāva*) and of secret and mysterious ways (*gūḍhākāra*).[30] It was as if, due to some historical development, women's desire for sexual-erotic pleasure had come to hide behind a veil. This veiling of the desire for sexual-erotic pleasure and the lack of freedom for women are related to the subordination of the discourse of pleasure to Brahmanical law. The subordination of pleasure to Brahmanical law went hand in hand with the subordination of women. Indeed, the two events of subordination seemed to have been two aspects of one and the same historical phenomenon. In the same sutra the *Kāmasūtra* also states that under the sway of passion and love the same women reveal, or unveil (*vivṛṇoti*), their real nature and their desire for pleasure (*ratilālasā*).[31] Love, it seems, had the power to unveil women's desire for sexual-erotic pleasure that had come to be veiled in *dharma* as Brahmanical law. In other words, the conflict between *dharma* and *kāma* as two members of the trilogy was really a conflict between the discourse of Brahmanical law and the discourse of love.

Women, Pleasure, and a Past without Patriarchy: A View from the *Mahābhārata*

The *Kāmasūtra* seems to be advancing a line of thought regarding the veiling of desire for sexual-erotic pleasure amongst women that is in continuity with one articulated in the *Mahābhārata*, one of the two great epics in ancient Indian culture (the other being the *Rāmāyaṇa*).[32] There is hardly any important topic in ancient India that went untouched by this encyclopedic epic. It is not surprising then that it also dwells on the nature and origin of the institution of marriage and the theme of conjugal fidelity on which it came to be based.[33] My reading of the *Mahābhārata* is limited to offering a brief glimpse into the historical-discursive context of the critical term *anāvṛt* as it relates to women's status and the discourse of Brahmanical law (*dharma*). It is not my goal to pursue either the status of women or the notion of *dharma* in the *Mahābhārata* as a whole.

While discussing the nature of relationship between husband and wife, the *Mahābhārata* also uses the word *anāvṛt* (or free and unfettered) to describe the position of women in the society long past. It also explains how this relationship came to be recast, leading to women's subordination to their husbands. What is more, the *Mahābhārata* problematizes the relationship between husband and wife in terms of the relationship between *dharma* and *kāma* in such a way that the subordination of women to their husbands and the subordination of pleasure to Brahmanical law appear to be two sides of the same historical development. Discussing the true essence of *dharma* as it relates to the nature of the relationship between husbands and wives, the *Mahābhārata* states,

> In the ancient past, as is well known, women were unfettered (*anāvṛt*) . . . going the way of their desire and pleasure (*kāmācāravihārinī*), and free (*svatantra*). They lived in transgression (*vyuccaramānāḥ*) of their husbands from their years of maidenhood, but that was not a violation of law (*adharma*) but rather that was in accordance with the law (*dharma*) in the ancient times. And the same law (*dharma*) of early times is followed still today, free from love and hatred, by the beings that linger in an animal birth. . . . For this is the eternal law (*sanātana dharma*) that shows favor to women.[34]

In seeking to identify the historical moment in which women came to lose their freedom, this passage looks back to a time long gone when what the *Mahābhārata* calls eternal law (*sanātana dharma*) was in force and women were unfettered and free (*anāvṛt*).[35] The two other crucial terms in the cited passage make it clear that women's freedom characterized the society in ancient times: *kāmācāravihārinī* (the woman who follows the way of her desires and pleasure) and *svatantra* (free). Given that the three crucial terms in this passage are used to describe the state of women in the ancient past, they seem to function as synonyms meant to reinforce the central thought about the freedom of women under eternal law. Not surprisingly, the *Mahābhārata* also adds that those ancient times were favorable to women, meaning that they were free and did not have to live in subordination to men. This observation also implicitly acknowledges that the current state of affairs did not favor women; they had lost their old freedom and came under the subordination of men.

This passage problematizes women's freedom and the nature of the husband-wife relationship in terms of the relationship between two of the three ontological discourses named by the *Kāmasūtra* in its notion of trilogy: *kāma,* or pleasure, and *dharma,* or law (the third being *artha,* or political power). The word *kāma* in *kāmācāravihārinī* has two meanings, desire and pleasure. The word *kāmācāravihārinī,* therefore, means both a woman who follows her desire and a woman who follows the way of pleasure. "The woman who follows her desire" is a reference to her freedom and the freedom of her gender. She was neither bound to her husband nor confined to the house as she became later. The other meaning as "the woman who follows the way of pleasure" suggests that her being as a woman was anchored in sexual-erotic pleasure as the sovereign principle.

The *Mahābhārata* goes on to state that women in the old days lived in transgression of their husbands, having sexual relationships with other men as a matter of routine. However, let alone being against the law, this practice was entirely in accordance with it. Indeed, the *Mahābhārata* goes even further, declaring the practice to be, in fact, the eternal law (*sanātana dharma*) itself. Spouses, it would appear, did not have monopoly over each other in the matters of sex and sexual relations. Women were not bound by the laws of spousal fidelity to their husbands. For women, the pursuit of sexual-erotic pleasure took precedence over any other commitment. This was only possible if the society itself was anchored in the sovereignty of the discourse of sexual-erotic pleasure. Let alone being subordinated to law (*dharma*), pleasure itself was the law.

What is significant is that the *Mahābhārata* calls the social norms as it obtained in the old times, when women were free, *sanātana dharma,* or eternal law. In making this statement, the *Mahābhārata* of course knew it was not the form of law that was in force at its time. The form of law in force was *varṇa-dharma,* or Brahmanical law based on the division and hierarchy of castes in which women had lost their freedom. By calling the old form of law eternal (*sanātana*) what the *Mahābhārata* meant was that it was the true law, not that it was always in effect. In referring to the older form of law that was identical to the law of pleasure as eternal, it was in effect questioning and critiquing the form of law that was currently in force.[36] In the view of the *Mahābhārata,* the new form of Brahmanical law based on the division and hierarchy of castes that currently held sway was a perversion and distortion—a historical aberration—of the true law of former times.

Notice that even as the *Mahābhārata* mentions law and sexual-erotic pleasure, it does not mention the third member of the trilogy—political power. What the *Mahābhārata*'s memory of an ideal society assumes is the absence of political power as an organizing principle of society. In other words, pleasure became the sovereign principle and law in a society where power was absent. The legislative sovereignty of pleasure and the freedom of women belonged together, as if they were two aspects of the same society in which power was absent.

It is also significant that women's freedom did not mean the absence of family. The *Mahābhārata* clearly states that women did have husbands. It was just that the husband-wife relationship was not based on monogamy and the law of spousal fidelity. Pleasure had not yet been brought under the sovereignty of Brahmanical law that was exterior to it. Women and men could be husbands and wives without having to commit to exclusivity in their sexual relationship. This family was without identity, a family without patriarchy.

In a family that was not based on monogamy and spousal fidelity, the biological identity of the child could not be determined with certainty. But more importantly, in a society such as the one the *Mahābhārata* has in view, the biological identity of the child did not matter; it was not central to the idea of the family. In other words, neither the family nor the society in which it found a place was based in identity. Pleasure became the law in society because it did not have to face identity or self as its adversary. Everything changes when biological identity—that is to say, true paternity—becomes the foundation of the discourse of the family.

The Son and the Origin of the Patriarchal Law of Monogamy

Having set up this ideal period in the history of the relationship between man and woman, the *Mahābhārata* goes on to narrate how the subordination of woman to man and pleasure to Brahmanical law came about. The story that is at the origin of the new form of Brahmanical law goes back to Śvetaketu, the son of the sage Uddālaka, who is outraged to see his father consent readily to his mother's adulterous relationship.[37] When it was explained to him that this was entirely normal and in accordance with *dharma*, Uddālaka became incensed.

> The sage's son would not bear with this law, and he laid down the following moral order for woman and man, among human beings only . . . but not among other creatures; and since that time this moral rule has been in existence, and so we have heard: "If a woman is unfaithful to her husband, then, from today onwards, that is a crime leading to loss of caste, like the killing of a child in the womb, gruesome and bringing down evil. And likewise it is a crime leading to the loss of caste, if a man is unfaithful to his wife, who has walked in maidenly chastity and keeps faith with her husband. A wife lays the same burden on herself, if she be charged by her husband for the sake of a son, and does it not." With these words . . . did Śvetaketu, the son of Uddālaka, set up by force the barrier of the law.[38]

This citation gives a vivid and dramatic account of the very origin of the law of monogamy and sexual fidelity between spouses, anchored in the new discourse of Brahmanical law based in the division and hierarchy of castes. At the same time, it also explains how women came to be subordinated to their husbands, and how from being the law, sexual-erotic pleasure came to be subordinated to the discourse of Brahmanical law. It is significant that Śvetaketu's mother has her husband, sage Uddālaka, present when she accompanies another man presumably for sex. Her husband makes no effort to stop her as if what happened was entirely within the horizon of his expectations; no rules were being violated. Evidently it is the same kind of family the *Mahābhārata* had described in which women were free.

It is important to note that in the new Brahmanical law that was being instituted, sexual fidelity was not anchored in love. That sexual infidelity may lead to the loss of love and trust between the spouses was not a concern, because marriage itself was not anchored in love. It was anchored in caste and family identity. In the event of sexual relations outside marriage, both men and women risked losing their caste identity. The discourse of patriarchy thus came to be anchored in the discourse of caste. The discourse of Brahmanical law, or *dharma,* has become synonymous with the discourse of caste. Spousal fidelity in the matters of sex and sexual relations becomes the law. Also, spousal fidelity and infidelity are problematized in light of the need to enforce and maintain caste identity. The law of sexual and spousal fidelity is therefore derivative of the law of patriarchy and caste.

Together with the loss of caste, an act of adultery is also equated with an act of feticide, and as such it is problematized in terms of the woman's relationship with her child, not the husband. It was as if in an act of adultery she harmed—indeed killed—her child more than she betrayed her husband. Adultery or sex outside of marriage is, of course, not a case of feticide in actual fact; it is equated to an act of feticide. If we follow the logic of this law, adultery throws into confusion the true paternity of the child, and thus his identity. In and through this law a moral and legal equivalence is constructed between an act of feticide and an act of adultery leading to the loss of the child's identity. Identity is life, and the loss of identity is equated with the loss of life. A man who has lost his caste identity therefore has lost life itself. This new discourse of *dharma* as Brahmanical law constitutes a social economy of caste identity as life itself.

While maintaining the powers and privileges of the higher castes, the other major concern of the Brahmanical discourse of *dharma* was to enforce caste identity, and to maintain its purity and authenticity.[39] It was thus that the discourse of *dharma* came to focus on the institution of the family and laid the groundwork for patriarchy. If caste and family identity were to become the basis of society, a law of identity had to be imposed on sexual practices. Complete freedom in sexual practices, after all, would have threatened these identities. Therefore sex and sexual practices came to be subordinated to the sovereign discourse of *dharma* as a discourse of identity. Based on caste and family identity, *dharma* in effect was a discourse of identity. In the *Mānava Dharmaśāstra,* identity was offered as *dharma*. The subordination of sex and sexual pleasure to *dharma* in effect was its subordination to identity.

It is also important to keep in mind that the question about the status of sexual-erotic pleasure is directly linked with the issue of the status of women in their relationship with men. In the narrative of the *Mahābhārata,* the subjugation of pleasure was a phenomenon that ran parallel with the subjugation of women. The questions relating to pleasure and the desire for pleasure, therefore, cannot be pursued in isolation from the questions regarding the status of women.

The *Mahābhārata* states that currently the *sanātana dharma* as eternal law obtained only among animals and the people called the Northern Kurus. From the perspective of this discussion, whether the society and the family the *Mahābhārata* had in view did in fact exist historically or was merely an exercise in the construction of a utopia is not important. Even if the notion of the age of pleasure (*kāma*) were to be nothing more than a piece of fiction, what it accomplished was of immense significance. It prevented *dharma* based on caste identity and the subjugation of women from appearing like an eternal, immutable, ahistorical, and divinely ordained way of life. What really matters is that this became the historical benchmark against which the *Mahābhārata* measured the present. The *Mahābhārata*'s vision of a society and family in which women could expect freedom otherwise denied to them in patriarchal societies shattered the naturalness of the institution of family anchored in patriarchy and the subordination of women. It prevented *dharma* of caste and patriarchy from taking on the air of being either the only or the best model for good life. It introduced the temporal disjuncture that made the discourse of *dharma* appear to be a historical phenomenon.[40] The *Mahābhārata* thus casts the emergence of Brahmanical law in the narrative of the subordination of women and the loss of the sovereignty of sexual-erotic pleasure. It exposes the discourse of *dharma* to be, in reality, a discourse of power. By making the subordination of women a historical development, it opened up the possibility of a vision of their future freedom.

The *Mānava Dharmaśāstra* and *Dharma* as Discourse of Caste Identity

The discourse of *dharma,* as Brahmanical law based in caste identity, that the *Mahābhārata* had in view when elaborating the law of monogamy in the passage cited above found its foundational expression in the *Mānava Dharmaśāstra.*[41] It is possible that the *Mahābhārata* perhaps had the *Mānava Dharmaśāstra* in view as the exemplary voice of the discourse of *dharma.*[42] The *Mānava Dharmaśāstra* was composed between the first century BCE and second century CE, at least a century, perhaps more, ahead of the *Kāmasūtra,* which is dated to the third century CE.[43] It was the founding work of immense historical significance that launched the genre of *dharmaśāstra,* as the discourse on Brahmanical law.[44] It laid the foundations of a Brahmanical vision of a society based on the division and hierarchy of castes: Brahmins, or the priestly caste; Kṣatriyas, or the warrior caste; Vaiśya, or the business caste; and Śūdras, or the servant caste. The four castes were ranked in descending order, with the Brahmins at the top and the Śūdras at the bottom of the social hierarchy. While the top three castes had access to the Vedas, the sacred Sanskrit texts that made up the discursive and ritual ground of the caste system, the Śūdras were barred from having any access to them.

The notion of *dharma* as elaborated in the Brahmanical text of the *Mānava Dharmaśāstra* came to acquire such dominance in the field of Indian studies that it began to be seen as the timeless and ahistorical expression of Indian society and culture. It is often difficult to think that there were other traditions of *dharma* in which the meaning and significance of this pivotal term may have been very different.[45] Nor were those other traditions insignificant. In recent years, scholars have begun to place the origin of the Brahmanical discourse *dharma* in general and the *Mānava Dharmaśāstra* in particular in its historical-discursive context. Olivelle locates the origin of the *Mānava Dharmaśāstra* primarily in the historical context of the Mauryan Empire and its patronage and promotion of non-Brahmanical religions such as Buddhism and Jainism.[46]

For example, the understanding of *dharma* projected in the inscriptions of the Mauryan emperor Aśoka (269–232 BCE), who had converted to Buddhism, offers an altogether different perspective from the one advocated by the *Mānava Dharmaśāstra* on this issue.[47] Aśoka's *dharma* had nothing to do with the Vedas or the rituals connected with it; nor did it have anything to do with the caste system. Not grounded in specific identity, Aśoka's discourse of *dharma* was universal in its principles.[48] Aśoka sought to turn *dharma* into a popular discourse of ethics, a form of civic *dharma*. The notion of *dharma* propagated by Aśoka preceded the Brahmanical discourse of *dharma*; it preceded the *Mānava Dharmaśāstra* by at least two centuries. Indeed, Olivelle claims that "the very creation of a Brahmanical genre of literature dedicated to *dharma* was possibly due to the elevation of this word to the level of imperial ideology by Aśoka."[49]

By the time the *Mānava Dharmaśāstra* was written, *dharma* had already emerged as one of the most important categories of popular discourse, not just scholarly discourse. It becomes quite evident that the *Mānava Dharmaśāstra* was an attempt to appropriate an already existing and a very powerful discourse of *dharma* for a new vision of society based on the division and hierarchy of castes. The revolution brought about by the *Mānava Dharmaśāstra* consisted in transforming *dharma* from a largely ethical discourse anchored in the care of the other into a discourse anchored in the care of the self and identity—caste and patriarchal identity. This appropriation of *dharma* not only changed the popular meaning of *dharma*; it reversed it.

To point out the presence of other traditions of *dharma*, however, is not to underestimate the significance or the power of the Brahmanical discourse of *dharma* projected in the *Mānava Dharmaśāstra*. Indeed, when the *Kāmasūtra* refers to *dharma*, it has the *Mānava Dharmaśāstra* in view.[50] If the *Kāmasūtra* gives it that much importance it is not necessarily because it was the most important—let alone the best—notion of *dharma* at the time, but because it was this discourse of *dharma* that most came in the way of the pursuit of pleasure.

The Son and the Nature of Patriarchal Identity in the Discourse of *Dharma*

The *Mahābhārata*'s attempt to associate the discourse of Brahmanical law, or *dharma*, with the subjugation of women, and consequently the subjugation of pleasure, may have its source in the *Mānava Dharmaśāstra*. This becomes clear in its references to women, their social status, their role in the family, and their relationship with their husbands.[51] To understand the nature of women's subordination to men—particularly their husbands—it is important that we understand the nature of the patriarchal family as it came to be constructed in the *Mānava Dharmaśāstra*.[52] In this regard, one detail in the *Mahābhārata*'s account of the birth of the law of monogamy is very significant. As a son, Śvetaketu enunciated the law of monogamy; his father was not perturbed at all about his wife accompanying another man for sex. It was the son who brought an end to the society without patriarchy and identity, a society anchored in the sovereignty of pleasure without identity. In addition, the wife's extramarital relationship was equated with feticide, the killing of a fetus, and not with the betrayal of her husband. What makes the son—not the father as the husband—a legislative figure in the domain of patriarchal law? After all, women's subordination largely refers to her relationship with her husband.

The *Mānava Dharmaśāstra* holds a clue to the reason behind the emergence of the son as the legislator. This is reflected in two verses in the *Mānava Dharmaśāstra,* which have puzzled commentators and scholars. In the *Mānava Dharmaśāstra* a woman who has either been unfaithful to her husband or has even contemplated being so is asked to repeat this somewhat enigmatic statement like a *mantra* to expiate her act or wish of transgression: "'May my father keep from me the seed that my mother, roaming about unfaithful to her husband, craved.' When a woman contemplates anything harmful to her husband in her mind, this statement is said to be a thorough expiation of that infidelity."[53] This injunction is significant because the unfaithful wife is asked to repeat a statement that seems to have been made by a son to his father, wishing that he would keep the seeds, presumably from other men, from coming in contact with him. The son, it seems, wants to keep his identity from getting mixed up or contaminated with the seeds from a man other than his father. After all, a son aware of his mother's marital infidelities cannot be sure of his own paternal identity.

What puzzles scholars is why the wife is expected to repeat a statement originally enunciated by a son to his father.[54] The mother is neither the addresser nor the addressee of the statement. She is its object. The statement, which is more like a plea for help, is addressed by the son to his father. Recall that in the passage cited from the *Mahābhārata* it was the son who enunciated the law of spousal fidelity to his father. The wife is asked to do nothing but repeat the law of monogamy enunciated by the son. By repeating this law she of course reminds herself of what the law is. But what she also does is renew her vow of fidelity to her husband by reminding herself that it is her son's identity at stake in her pursuit of sexual pleasure outside the marriage. The patriarchal family is anchored more in the figure of the son than in that of the husband. The relationship between husband and wife, it seems, is mediated by the figure of the son. Marriage is not seen as a relationship between husband and wife as two individuals, but a relationship that is anchored in the son as the third figure.

The reason that a husband and a wife appear related to each other through their son lies in the peculiar notion of identity that was at the heart of the *Mānava Dharmaśāstra*. While elaborating the nature of relationship between husband and wife, it says, "The husband enters the wife, becomes a fetus, and is born in this world. This, indeed, is what gives the name to and discloses the true nature of the wife (*jāyā*)—that he is thus born (*jāyate*) again in her. For a wife bears a son resembling the man she loves; to insure the purity of his offspring, therefore, he should carefully guard his wife."[55]

These two verses offer perhaps the most precise insight into the nature of the relationship that binds the three figures—the husband, the wife, and the son—together into a single knot. The verses explain this relationship by way of interpreting the word *jāyā* for wife. In the *Mānava Dharmaśāstra*'s definition, this word *jāyā* means both wife and mother. The wife is at the same time mother to her husband, because through the wife, the husband is reborn again as the son. The son is seen as the rebirth of the father. In the son the father sees himself as if in a mirror: "From my every limb you spring; out of my heart you are born. You are my self (*ātman*) called son; live a hundred autumns."[56] It is in his second birth as the son that the father finds his real being, his identity. The father and the son together constitute a single identity or individuality.[57] A man is not born with a complete identity; it is a project. According to the *Mānava Dharmaśāstra,* the family was precisely the way to acquire that identity. In the absence of a son, one was faced with the prospect of losing his identity altogether; not having a son was tantamount to committing suicide. Since the son was the telos of the family, he was given the honor to enunciate the most important law of patriarchy—monogamy. The family as represented in the *Mānava Dharmaśāstra* was a mechanism for man to produce and reproduce himself as identity.[58]

As is evident, the most important relationship is between the father and the son—not the husband and the wife. The wife is only a means, a moment in the production and reproduction of her husband's self as identity. It was this social economy of identity embodied in the discourse of *dharma* and the social institutions of family and caste that, according to the *Mahābhārata,* robbed woman of her freedom. In this process, she was reduced to nothing more than a means, an instrument, to reproduce the identity of the family and patriarchy. She was reduced to a chattel, or a piece of farmland on which sons were grown.[59] It is not surprising, therefore, that in the *Mānava Dharmaśāstra* a husband's relationship with his wife is not problematized in terms of love. For a discourse of love to be possible, the wife has to be an end in herself, not simply a means to a son.

As a mere means of self-reproduction, the wife does not have an independent identity; her being is lost entirely in the being of her husband. As the *Mānava Dharmaśāstra* says, "The wife (*jāyā*), the self (*ātman*), and the offspring (*prajā*)—that is the full extent of man (*puruṣa*). Brahmins, likewise, proclaim this: 'The husband, tradition says, is the wife.'"[60] "Full measure" simply means that the three together constitute the being of man. They are three moments in the dialectic through which a man constitutes himself as an identity. The absence of any one of the three—the wife, the self, and the son—would jeopardize, indeed negate, man's being. Notice that the self (*ātman*) is only one of three components that together constitute a man's being; *ātman* by itself is unable to constitute the individuality of a man. A man also needs a wife and a son to constitute himself. A wife is nothing more than a moment in the dialectic through which man constitutes his being in the world. "When a wife unites with her husband according to rule, she takes on the qualities he has, like a river uniting with the ocean."[61] This is again a variation on the same theme of how the wife gives birth to a son in the likeness of her husband. Also, "the husband is the wife" does not mean that the wife is elevated to the status of her husband, but that she is absorbed in the identity of her husband; she becomes indistinguishable from her husband.

The Discourse of *Dharma*: Subordinating and Confining the Wife

Since the production and reproduction of one's own self through one's wife was the highest goal for a man, it was important that the husband make sure that there were no doubts about the identity of his offspring. Any lingering doubts in this matter would throw the defining project of his life off course. It would not only threaten his family line but also the social structure based on caste. Any signs of an extramarital sexual-erotic relationship that could result in the conception and birth of a child had to be guarded against. The *Mānava Dharmaśāstra* states: "Women in particular should be guarded (*rakṣya*) against even the slightest evil inclination, for when they are left unguarded, they bring grief to both families. Seeing that this is clearly the highest Law of all social classes, even weak husbands strive to guard (*rakṣitum*) their wives; for by carefully guarding his wife, a man guards his offspring, his character, his family, himself, and the Law specific to him."[62]

The verb *rakṣa* means both to protect and to guard. As Olivelle notes, "Women need to be protected from the outside and guarded against their own natural propensities."[63] "Evil inclination" is a euphemism for any desire for an extramarital sexual relationship on the part of the wife. "Both families" refers to her family and the family of the man she may have an extramarital relationship with. The *Mānava Dharmaśāstra* identifies guarding one's wife against any possibility of extramarital relationship as "the highest Law" for all castes. It was the highest law because the entire chain of being that connected a man to his family, ancestors, caste, and to himself, here and in the hereafter, depended on the authenticity of his offspring's parental identity. In the patriarchal logic of the *Mānava Dharmaśāstra*, the only way that authenticity could be guaranteed was if the wife could be guarded from entering into a sexual relationship outside the marriage. The woman thus becomes a prisoner to her closest male relatives in her own house. The *Mānava Dharmaśāstra* says, "Day and night men should keep their women in subordination (*asvatantra*); for, attached as they [women] are to sensual pleasures, men should keep them under their control (*vaśe*). Her father guards her in her childhood, her husband guards her in her youth, and her sons guard her in her old age; a woman is not qualified for freedom (*svātantrayam*)."[64]

This citation makes evident what exactly guarding women meant: it meant keeping women in subordination (*asvatantra*). The crucial word *asvatantra* in this passage means unfree or the state of being under someone else's power or authority.[65] As if to make sure the word *asvatantra,* or "in subordination," is understood correctly, in the latter half of the same verse the text says that men should keep women under their control (*vaśa*). For women to be kept *asvatantra* or unfree meant to be kept in man's control. And when the *Mānava Dharmaśāstra* states that a woman should be guarded throughout her life by a man—as the father, the husband, and the son—it stresses the importance of keeping her in subordination throughout her life. There is no period of her life when the woman could be allowed to be free. The term "day and night" has been added to reemphasize that women should not get even a moment of freedom, suggesting their total subordination to men.

The verse cited above ends with the words "a woman is not qualified for freedom (*svātantrayam*)." It states unequivocally that wives must not be allowed freedom. The same sentiment is repeated once again when it says, "[Women] must not enjoy freedom (*svātantrayam*)." Unlike the word *svatantra* that refers to the *fact* of someone being free, *svātantrayam* refers more to freedom as a state or *mode* of being a self, one's own self, as a privilege that women cannot enjoy; here freedom means freedom of the self or sovereignty of the self. In the language of the *Mānava Dharmaśāstra* it means the ability to produce and reproduce oneself as identity; to make others serve as a means to this pursuit of identity. Being *asvatantra* or unfree, as women were supposed to be, however meant to be without a self, an inability to produce and reproduce oneself as an identity; it meant to be forced to serve men in their pursuit of identity.

Notice also that the *Mānava Dharmaśāstra*'s advocacy for the need to keep women under the control of their male relatives is done in the name of women's natural orientation to sensual pleasures. Here, there is a contrast assumed between men and women in their relationships to sensual pleasures: while men are capable of exercising their mastery and sovereignty over sensual pleasures, women are not. Women, on the contrary, are entirely under the sway of their sensual pleasures, completely unmindful of their duty toward their families, particularly the husbands. "They pay no attention to beauty, they pay no heed to age; whether he is handsome or ugly, they make love to him with the single thought, 'He is a man.' Lechery, fickleness of mind, and hard-heartedness are innate in them; even when they are carefully guarded in this world, therefore, they become hostile towards their husbands. Recognizing thus the nature produced in them at creation by Prajapati, a man should make the utmost effort at guarding them."[66] Women's propensity for sexual pleasure becomes their most defining characteristic, indeed their nature since their creation. Since men are in control of their senses, they do not need to be guarded. In contrast, women cannot guard themselves and therefore need to be guarded by men. In other words, since women could not control their senses men had to control women.

There is a very strong suspicion of women in the *Mānava Dharmaśāstra* bordering on paranoia. This deep and pervasive suspicion of women comes from the knowledge that women did not have anything at stake in the discourse of Brahmanical law, except their subjection; that woman was reduced to an instrument in the production of her husband's identity. Women were nothing more than an instrument in the economy of identity upheld by the discourse of *dharma*. As such, women had no incentive of their own to be in conflict with the pursuit of sexual-erotic pleasure. This conflict between *dharma* grounded in self-identity and sexual-erotic pleasure (*kāma*) really belonged to men, whose family and caste identity were at stake.

This conflict between the senses and the self is the direct result of raising identity—both caste and family—to be the sovereign concern in life. In fighting the senses, what the *Mānava Dharmaśāstra* really had in view was pleasure—the senses were just a euphemism for sexual-erotic pleasure. Instead of problematizing it as a conflict between *dharma* and *kāma*, the *Mānava Dharmaśāstra* problematizes it in its own terms as a conflict between the self and the senses. The conflict was really between self and pleasure. The idea was to subordinate pleasure to the logic and needs of identity. In this logic what is actually a social-political project of patriarchy and caste hierarchy is subtly converted into a moral issue of the self's mastery of the senses. To the extent that monogamy, as a discourse and practice that arose with the rise of patriarchy, sought to control the practices of sexual-erotic pleasure, it did so in the name of controlling the senses. The fight against the senses that is often taken as a moral and ethical issue was in fact an extension of the political discourse of identity into the realm of subjectivity. This was how pleasure came to be subordinated to identity. Here it becomes quite evident how the loss of freedom for women and the loss of sovereignty for pleasure as one of the three ontological imperatives went hand in hand.

Guarding the Self: Constructing the Subjectivity of the Wife

The *Mānava Dharmaśāstra* met with two challenges in implementing its goal of subordinating women in the household: first, the doubt that no amount of guarding could ever guarantee that women would never come in contact with other men if they were determined to do so. In this context, it is important to note that the *Kāmasūtra* has one of its six books dedicated exclusively to the different ways of establishing extramarital sexual-erotic relationships.[67]

The nature of difficulties involved in physically guarding the women of the household becomes even more evident when one reads the part in the *Kāmasūtra* that deals with women in the royal harem; it gives a set of instructions to those women regarding how to get men from outside the palace to sneak in and out of the royal harem, often with the connivance of the guards who were supposed to prevent it. If it was difficult to guard the women in the royal household, one can imagine how much more difficult it was in the average household of the three higher castes. In other words, the *Mānava Dharmaśāstra* realized that there was no sure way to physically sequester women from the outside world.

Second, the physical confinement of women, as necessary as it seemed, also ran the risk of arousing their hostility toward their husbands. Notice the words—women when guarded "become hostile to their husbands." If bearing children for her husband was all she did, the woman's sequestration was an option. The wife, however, needed to nurture the children, cook, and generally take care of the household. Attempts to forcefully confine her would result in anger and resentment within the family. Securing the cooperation of the wife, her willingness, therefore became vital to the process of subordinating her.

The woman had to be physically guarded, but this method had its limits. The limit of this method was the limit of force or violence as an instrument of power. The *Mānava Dharmaśāstra* needed to address this issue if it were to go beyond invectives against women. It did indeed take up this challenge, and it was precisely in its response to the challenge that its real contributions to the discourse of power lie. Having laid out the goal of subjugating women to their husbands, the *Mānava Dharmaśāstra* turns its attention to first acknowledge and then devise the right strategy to address precisely this challenge. Efforts to guard women had to be complemented by an inducement that would encourage women to guard themselves: "No man is able to thoroughly guard women by force; but by using the following strategies [*upāya*], he will be able to guard them thoroughly. He should employ her in the collection and the disbursement of his wealth, in cleaning, in meritorious activity, in cooking food, and in looking after household goods. When they are kept confined within the house by trusted men, they are not truly guarded; only *when they guard themselves by themselves are they truly guarded.*"[68]

In this last line the *Mānava Dharmaśāstra* articulates the very heart of its Brahmanical philosophy of power, a philosophy as thorough as it is original: when the *self* is guarded by it*self* it is truly guarded. The *Mānava Dharmaśāstra* thus invented a new discourse and mechanics of power. The idea was to turn the self back on itself. The self is split into two: the one that does the watching and the other that is watched. The relationship that the wife had with her husband is transformed into her relationship with herself—she becomes her own guard. The relationship of power that she had with her husband is transformed into her relationship with herself. It is in the moment of the wife guarding herself that a new subjectivity—the wife as a subjectivity—comes into being. If it were to be executed well, there would be no need for her physical confinement. The figure of the wife had to be constructed as a new subjectivity in such a way that she would guard herself, needing little or no external intervention of force. It is quite evident that the *Mānava Dharmaśāstra* had discovered in the self a new domain of power.

Also, notice the word *upāya,* or strategy, in the citation above. While pointing out the limits of force as a tool of power, the *Mānava Dharmaśāstra* offers its insights into a better way of controlling women as part of a new strategy (*upāya*). In its use of the notion of strategy, it is clear that this book that purports to be about religion and the Vedas understands very well the real nature and significance of its own being—a treatise that would establish a new discourse of power. The discourse of *dharma* as it relates to women needs to be seen as a strategic intervention in order to secure the goal of a patriarchal and caste-based society. The *Mānava Dharmaśāstra* was therefore determined to find precise strategies to construct new subjectivities. Unlike power as force that constitutes an exteriority, this new mechanism allowed power to operate by producing new subjectivities. For the *Mānava Dharmaśāstra*, producing subjectivity was the best way of exercising power. Power needed to operate as subjectivity, not as force. The idea was to withdraw force as much as possible as an instrument of power.

One of the strategies that the *Mānava Dharmaśāstra* offers in the verses cited above is to leave it to the wife to look after collection and disbursement of wealth and perform meritorious activities such as cooking and cleaning. It was meant to make the wife feel as if she had effective control over the household, which was divided into two complementary domains: public and domestic. While the husband had control over the public and external aspects of the household, the wife exercised control over the domestic matters. What seems like an act of empowerment, however, is meant to be a strategy to confine the wife within the house and a life of domesticity. To the extent that women exercised power over domestic things, they also enjoyed a bit of freedom. However, this was the freedom of the subject, not the master. Through this strategy, the act of her confinement to domesticity without the use of force was made to appear to be an act of empowerment.

Power, Subjectivity, and Desire

In the passage cited above, the *Mānava Dharmaśāstra* directly problematizes and contrasts two different kinds of power: power that is imposed and enforced from outside and power that is enforced internally, power that has its origin and end in the self.[69] The philosophy of power that it articulated was also very different from the one that came to be expounded in the *Arthaśāstra,* or "A Treatise on Political Power," the founding text on politics in India, composed earlier than the *Mānava Dharmaśāstra.*[70] In pointing out the limit of force as a means of exercising power, the *Mānava Dharmaśāstra* also sought to expose the limit of the *Arthaśāstra*'s understanding of political power and its wish to go beyond it. The *Dharmaśāstra*'s view is that force is neither the most comprehensive nor the most efficient way of exercising power. The *Arthaśāstra* hardly knew anything about subjectivity as a domain of power, focused as it was on political, economic, and military power.[71]

In launching one of the most ambitious campaigns for power, the *Mānava Dharmaśāstra* placed a significant amount of emphasis on *ahiṃsā,* or nonviolence.[72] One of the most important aims of the *Mānava Dharmaśāstra* was to dissociate power from violence as much as possible. The Brahmins were told that they were the highest class of human beings on earth: "Because of his distinctive qualities, the eminence of his origin, his observance of restrictive practices, and the distinctive nature of his consecration, the Brahmin is the lord of all classes."[73] At the same time, they were also told to shun violence. Indeed, the Brahmin's commitment to nonviolence became one of his distinguishing traits.[74] By renouncing violence, the Brahmin renounced his direct claim to the state, yet found a way to discursively subordinate the state or political power to *dharma* as a discourse of Brahmanical law. By eschewing violence, the Brahmin was not renouncing power; he was renouncing only the form of power that required violence. In reality, however, the emergence of the notion of *ahiṃsā* in Brahmanical sources reflects the discovery of subjectivity as a domain of power beyond violence.

There is a sense in the *Mānava Dharmaśāstra* that there are two different kinds of power grounded in two different figures—the king and the Brahmin—each with its own specific way of exercising it. What is more, the power of the Brahmin carries primacy over that of the king. "A Brahmin who knows the Law shall not inform the king about any matter; solely with his own power (*svaviryena*) should he chastise men who do him harm. Between the king's power and his own, his own power is far more potent. A twice-born, therefore, should punish enemies solely with his own power. . . . Clearly, speech (*vākaśāstram*) is the Brahmin's weapon; with that a twice-born should strike down his enemies."[75] While comparing and contrasting the power of the king and that of the Brahmin, the *Mānava Dharmaśāstra* states in unambiguous terms that the power of the latter is more potent. The Brahmin is instructed to tainformingke the law into his own hands if it concerns his own person, without the king. The Brahmin's relationship with the law is not mediated by the king or the state; he has a direct unmediated relationship with the law. That is because in the discourse of Brahmanical law (*dharma*) Brahmin relates to himself.

Notice also that in these verses the contrast between the power of the king and that of the Brahmin has been defined in terms of the weapons the two wield: while the king wields a physical weapon as an instrument of violence, the Brahmin wields words as a weapon. If narrowly construed, *vākaśāstram* as word- or speech-weapon may simply refer to the Brahmin's ability to use the words of the Vedas as a mantra. However, if the entire context of the *Mānava Dharmaśāstra* is taken into account, it means discourse as a new Brahmanical weapon and instrument of power. There was no better discursive weapon in the arsenal of the Brahmin than the *Mānava Dharmaśāstra* itself: "A *kṣatriya* overcomes his adversities by the power of his arms; a *vaiśya* and a *śūdra*, by means of wealth; and a Brahmin, through soft recitation and sacrifices. A Brahmin is called the creator, the chastiser, the teacher, and the benefactor; one should never say anything unpleasant to him or use harsh words against him."[76]

It becomes evident how the discourse of *dharma* as a new discourse of power seeks primacy over the political discourse of power. *Artha* was sought to be subordinated to *dharma*. In this scheme, the Brahmins, or the priestly caste, as the custodians of the Vedas claimed a higher position than that of the warrior, or ruling, caste, which was politically and militarily dominant. This ranking of the castes assumed that *dharma,* as a discourse and system of law represented by the Brahmins, stood higher than *artha,* or political power, represented by the warrior class. Not surprisingly, in the discourse of *dharma* as Brahmanical law, the maintenance and defense of the caste system was termed the most important duty of the state. In other words, in the vision projected by the *Mānava Dharmaśāstra*, the state itself came to be subordinated to the discourse of *dharma* as Brahmanical law.[77]

If the *Mānava Dharmaśāstra* was to construct women as a new form of subjectivity, and persuade wives to guard themselves, it had to find a way into the self of woman. It was under this imperative that the *Mānava Dharmaśāstra* encountered desire as an opening into the self of a person.

> To be motivated by desire (*kāmātmatā*) is not commended, but it is impossible here to be free from desire; for it is desire that prompts vedic study and the performance of vedic rites. Intention (*saṃkalpa*) is the root of desire (*kāma*); intention is the wellspring of sacrifices; and intention triggers every religious observance and every rule of restraint—so the tradition declares. Nowhere in this world do we see any activity done by a man free from desire, for whatever at all that a man may do, it is the work of someone who desired it. By engaging in them properly, a man attains the world of the immortals and, in this world, obtains all his desires just as he intended.[78]

This passage gives us an insight into just how central the notion of desire was for the *Mānava Dharmaśāstra*. Desire is placed at the very foundation of human existence: all human activities have their origin in desire.[79] What we have in this passage is the ontology of mankind as a whole that sits at the core of the *Mānava Dharmaśāstra*. Indeed, it goes on to add unambiguously that intention as the root of desire is the source of "vedic study and vedic rites" and "every religious observance and every rule of restraint." In saying that, the *Mānava Dharmaśāstra* grounded both religion and law in its notion of desire-intention. No one would follow either religion or law unless it was grounded in desire. Since religion and law cover the entirety of *dharma*, the *Mānava Dharmaśāstra* in effect grounds *dharma* itself in desire.

The direct implication of this insight is: if one is to follow the ways and injunctions of *dharma*, one must first desire it. In the absence of this desire, *dharma* would be either not followed or followed only under the threat of violence. Here is the very first verse of the chapter that has the passage on desire cited above: "Learn the Law always adhered to by people who are erudite, virtuous, and free from love and hate, the Law (*dharma*) assented to (*abhyanujñāto*) by heart (*hṛdayena*)."[80] Notice the phrase that appears at the end of the verse as an independent clause, "*dharma* assented to by heart." The "assent of the heart" to *dharma* is the same as desire for *dharma*. In these words the *Mānava Dharmaśāstra* assumed the best way in which one could relate to *dharma*: one must desire *dharma*, not merely obey it.

Notice, once again, how the *Mānava Dharmaśāstra* defines Goodness that it considers to be a mark of *dharma:* "What a man desires (*icchati*) to know with all his heart and is not ashamed to perform, at which his self (*ātmā*) rejoices (*tuṣyati*)—that is the mark of the attribute of Goodness (*sattva*)."[81] In this citation we see the entire set of terms that together form a complex come together: desire to know, self, Goodness, and happiness. If *dharma* becomes an object of desire, its pursuit cannot but produce pleasure in one who pursues it. That was how "pleasure of the self" came to be recognized as one of the sources of *dharma* in the *Mānava Dharmaśāstra*: "The root of the Law (*dharma*) is the entire Veda; the tradition and practice of those who know the Veda; the conduct of good people; and what is pleasing to oneself (*ātmanastuṣṭireva*)."[82] In another verse in the same chapter, "pleasure of the self" is acknowledged as one of the marks or conditions of *dharma*: "Veda, tradition, the conduct of good people, and what is pleasing to oneself (*svasya ca priyamātmanaḥ*)—these, they say, are the four visible marks of the Law."[83]

Given that the pursuit of *dharma* required one to impose severe restrictions on oneself, the *Mānava Dharmaśāstra* realized that the desire for *dharma*, and the pleasure experienced in its pursuit, could not be assumed to be a given; methods had to be devised to secure them. These restrictions imposed by *dharma* were nowhere more pronounced than in the pursuit of sexual-erotic pleasure (*kāma*). There was an inherent conflict between the pursuits of *dharma* as Brahmanical law and sexual-erotic pleasure (*kāma*). Just as the *Kāmasūtra* had conceded, in the hierarchy of the three ontological imperatives in the trilogy, the *Mānava Dharmaśāstra* puts *dharma* at the top and sexual-erotic pleasure (*kāma*) at the bottom: "Pleasure (*kāma*) is said to be the mark of Darkness (*tamas*); power (*artha*), of Vigor (*rajas*); and Law (*dharma*) of Goodness (*sattva*). Each later one is superior to each preceding."[84] The *Mānava Dharmaśāstra* then goes on to mention the different rewards for the pursuit of each of the three ends: "Those who possess Goodness become gods, those who possess Vigor become humans; and those who possess Darkness always become animals."[85] Notice that for the pursuit of pleasure one is rewarded with a life as an animal in the next birth. As is evident, this is not really a reward but a punishment, suggesting that in the discourse of *dharma* the pursuit of pleasure is akin to a crime.

Not surprisingly, the *Mānava Dharmaśāstra* conjures up the most vivid and detailed punishments for those in pursuit of sensual pleasure:

> The more that people addicted to sensual pleasures indulge in sensual pleasures, the more their proclivity to them grows. By repeatedly engaging in these sinful actions, these men of little understanding undergo torments here in various births—tossing about in dreadful hells such as *Tāmisra*; the hell *Asipatravana* and the like; being tied up and cut up; various kinds of torture; being eaten by crows and owls; being burnt by hot sand-gruel; the unbearable torture of being boiled in vats; taking birth constantly in evil wombs full of suffering; being assailed by cold and heat; terrors of various kinds; repeated residence in different wombs; being born agonizingly; being wrapped up in painful ways; doing servile work for others; being separated from relatives and loved ones; having to live in the company of evil people; earning and losing wealth; winning friends and enemies; old age, against which there is no

remedy; being assailed by illness; various afflictions; and death itself, which is impossible to overcome.[86]

In other words, the desire for *dharma* or pleasure in pursuing *dharma* had to be cultivated in the face of the temptations of sexual-erotic pleasure. The *Mānava Dharmaśāstra* needed to go beyond the simple demand that one take pleasure in the pursuit of *dharma* to addressing the question of how exactly this habit was going to be acquired. If *dharma* had to become the primary object of desire and source of pleasure, the *Mānava Dharmaśāstra* had to find a way to overcome the desire for sexual pleasure (*kāma*). It is in light of this discussion that one can understand the following verses:

> As his sense organs meander amidst the alluring sense objects, a learned man should strive hard to control them, like a charioteer his horses. . . . When a man feels neither elation nor revulsion at hearing, touching, seeing, eating, or smelling anything, he should be recognized as a man who has mastered his organs. Of all these organs, however, if a single one slips away, through that his wisdom slips away, like water through the foot of a skin. By bringing the full range of his organs under control and by restraining his mind, a man will achieve all his goals without having to shrivel up his body through yoga.[87]

These verses appear in the second chapter, which deals with the life of a young Brahmin boy as a student. It is not surprising that the same chapter that puts forward desire as the ontological ground of man's existence and the expectation that one take pleasure in the pursuit of *dharma* also lays out an elaborate and complex world in which desire finds itself constantly drawn to and distracted by countless objects of the senses. There was no other way to cultivate the desire for *dharma* unless one found a way to exercise mastery over one's own sense organs. The absence of control over even a single sense organ could bring down the entire project. Notice that what the *Mānava Dharmaśāstra* called guarding or mastery of the self by the self in effect means mastery of the sense organs by the self. In exercising mastery over oneself, therefore, one exercises mastery over one's sense organs. This is at the core of the discourse of asceticism that pervades the *Mānava Dharmaśāstra*.[88]

The *Mānava Dharmaśāstra* then goes on to give a detailed breakdown and the mechanics of the eleven sense organs:

> I will explain precisely and in their proper order the eleven organs described by wise men of old: ear, skin, eyes, tongue, and the fifth, nostrils; anus, sexual organ, hands, feet, and speech, listed by tradition as the tenth. Of these, the five in order beginning with the ear are called the organs of perception; and the five beginning with the anus, the organs of action. Know that the eleventh

> is the mind, which, by virtue of its own distinctive quality, belongs to both groups. So, by mastering it, one masters both these quintets.[89]

Notice that the mind is identified as one of the sense organs. It is also the most important of all the sense organs. The mind is the most important because it "belongs" to both the sets of sense organs—the organs of perception and the organs of action—and as such is the bridge between the two sets; it is the mind that allows the two sets to communicate with each other. It is through the mind that one gains access to all the sense organs; there is, in other words, no direct access to the sense organs. It is, therefore, by controlling the mind that one can exercise mastery over one's sense organs.

The *Mānava Dharmaśāstra* then goes on to warn that one cannot bring the sensory organs in control by starving them of their objects.

> By attachment to the organs, a man undoubtedly becomes corrupted; but by bringing them under control, he achieves success. Desire is never quenched by enjoying desires; like a fire fed with ghee, it only waxes stronger. Between a man who obtains all these and a man who gives them all up—giving up all desires is far better than obtaining them all. Corrupted as these organs are by sensory objects, one cannot bring them under control (*saṃniyantum*) as effectively by abstinence (*asevaya*) as by constant insight/awareness (*jñyanena nityaśaḥ*). Vedas, gifts, sacrifices, constraints, and ascetic toils—none of these is ever successful for a man with a corrupt heart.[90]

Abstinence here simply means starving the sense organs of the objects they crave. From the perspective of the *Mānava Dharmaśāstra*, abstinence as a form of asceticism that starves the sense organs of their objects is not the most effective way of exercising mastery over them. The real source of the problem is desire and its locus, the mind. Those who prioritize abstinence as the primary method of mastering the self assume that the sense organs are autonomous and sovereign. For the *Mānava Dharmaśāstra*, in contrast, the sense organs are grounded in the mind as the locus of desire: "Action produces the human conditions . . . one should understand that the action of the embodied self . . . is set in motion by the mind."[91] Therefore, desire is overcome neither by feeding one's desire the sense objects it craves nor by depriving it of those sense objects. It is this understanding that is at the root of the *Mānava Dharmaśāstra*'s critique of the method of abstinence, and the contrast that it makes between abstinence and constant insight (*jñyān*) as the two ways of bringing sense organs under control. It emphasizes constant vigilance against the subtlest signs of a desire in one's mind and ultimate mastery of desire through knowledge and awareness. The object was to control the sense organs by controlling desire, not by shunning the objects of sense organs. Abstinence and observation of the mind are two primary forms of controlling the sense organs, with the second being the more effective means of disciplining the mind and cultivating the self.

The Wife as the Obedient Servant

Subjectivity has two components: desire and the mechanics of the mastery of the self. In its discovery of subjectivity as a new domain of power, the *Mānava Dharmaśāstra* realized two things: women needed to guard themselves if they were to be guarded truly and they would guard themselves truly only if there was a desire for that in them. In the absence of a desire to guard themselves, they could not be forced to do so. What is distinctive about desire is that it is not easily discerned or detected. The husband could keep a watch over his wife's acts, but not her desires; he had no access to her desire. Since the wife alone had such access, she alone could keep a watch over her desire. She had to learn to govern her own desires. But why would a woman control her desire for sexual-erotic pleasure, unless there was something that she desired even more? It was imperative that it appear to her that she was guarding herself for her own best interest. These following verses reveal just how the *Mānava Dharmaśāstra* sought to accomplish this: "A woman who controls (*saṃyata*) her mind, speech, and body and is never transgressive (*nābhicarati*) to her husband attains the worlds of her husband and virtuous people call her a 'good woman.' By being unfaithful to her husband (*vyabhicarattu*) on the other hand, a woman becomes disgraced in the world, takes birth in a jackal's womb, and is afflicted with evil diseases."[92]

The citation above brings together several powerful and central strands on women running through the *Mānava Dharmaśāstra*: guarding or mastering the self as "control of the mind, speech, and body"; the imperative not to transgress the husband; reward for guarding herself and nontransgression of her husband, and punishment if she failed to do so. In this passage one can see how desire is manipulated by constructing new objects of desire. Notice the rewards for women if they were to guard themselves: they would attain the "worlds of her husbands," a phrase that indirectly refers to heaven. This reward operated as an inducement to create a desire to find a place in heaven right alongside her husband. With heaven would come all the pleasures and happiness that are associated with it in religious and popular culture. Here the construction of heaven and its pleasures as an object of desire for women worked as a substitute or replacement for an unwanted object of desire, the desire for sensual-sexual pleasure in the present life. The anticipation of pleasures of heaven may help women continuously defer sexual-erotic pleasure.

Even as the *Dharmaśāstra* offered the inducement of heaven, it also let wives know what would await them if they failed to do so: they would take birth in jackals' wombs and suffer from all kinds of evil diseases. In other words, together with inducements the *Mānava Dharmaśāstra* also deployed the fear of not finding a place in heaven and being born in undesirable life-forms in the next life as a way to prevent women from engaging in activities not prescribed in the discourse of *dharma*. This fear was another way of keeping women from engaging in sexual activities outside marriage.

Notice that these rewards and punishments have nothing to do with the law that could be administered by either the state or the society and the family. Indeed, they could not even be administered in this life on earth. They are grounded in the afterlife: life after death in heaven or rebirth in another life-form. Here it is important to note that there are two sets of laws that are intricately and seamlessly woven together in the discourse of *dharma* as Brahmanical law: state and social law and the law of the afterlife. The law grounded in state and society constitutes an exteriority because it has to be administered by an external authority. Any violations of those laws are also to be witnessed and discovered by someone other than the woman herself. If her violations went undetected, there was no cause to punish her. Though it was certainly meant to be a deterrent, it could easily encourage a woman to take risks in her pursuit of sexual-erotic pleasure outside the marriage while making sure that it did not get discovered. That is to say, these laws too depended on external guarding of women.

But the law that is based in the afterlife exists only in the wife's mind; if she were to ignore this law no punishment would follow in this life; for it to work, she had to have belief in the afterlife; it could only exist as part of her belief system. Also, transgression never goes undetected, and retribution would invariably and inevitably follow any acts of violation; there is no way to keep these violations a secret; her own knowledge and acknowledgment of any violations is the proof—this is also part of her belief system. To be able to truly adhere to this law of the afterlife, there is no one other than herself who can keep an eye on her thoughts and activities. Not surprisingly, it is primarily under the gaze of this law of the afterlife that she constitutes herself in the subjectivity of the wife. Indeed, the only way this law of the afterlife could be effective is if she constitutes herself as a subjectivity by being on guard over and against herself. It is not surprising therefore that the *Mānava Dharmaśāstra* joins the theme of the guarding the self with the law of the afterlife.

Also note that in the verses cited above, the mastery of the self for the wife is directly linked with not transgressing the husband. The definition of a good woman who exercises control over her senses is someone who never transgresses her husband. And though transgression here appears to carry the special meaning of sexual transgression, it also more broadly refers to any kind of transgression that the wife may potentially commit against the authority of her husband. Her mastery of her own self and her obedience to her husband are the two sides of the same phenomenon. Here it is important to remember that the discourse of the mastery of the self is not important for the wife or women alone—it was as important for men. Yet the purpose of the control of the self changed according to whether it was meant for men or women. While a man needed to exercise control over himself for himself and as such became free, the woman exercises control over herself as part of her duty to subordinate herself to her husband. In acquiring mastery over herself, what the woman in effect does is let her husband exercise mastery over her. The self that exercises mastery is not the woman's own, but that of her husband; the self that is mastered is that of the woman.

Since the self that exercises mastery over the wife's sense organs is that of her husband, the woman herself is reduced to nothing more than sense organs without a self—that is to say, a body without a self. Since women do not have self, they cannot master the senses on their own. Indeed, women in the discourse of the *Mānava Dharmaśāstra* are nothing more than a complex of the senses and sense organs without a self. A woman, therefore, has to borrow the self of her husband to master her senses, that is, herself. That is the reason why a woman's mastery over the senses is indistinguishable from her subjection to her husband. Cultivating the control of the sense organs was nothing more than an exercise in subordinating herself to her husband as the master self. The woman is reduced to a body, a bundle of sense organs, not as an object of sexual pleasure but as an instrument for the husband to reproduce himself as an identity and thus secure immortality for himself. The subjectivity of the wife is that of a servant, while that of her husband is the subjectivity of a master.

The subjectivity that had to be constructed for the wife was that of an obedient servant to her husband as the master. Listing all the things that a husband receives from his wife, the *Mānava Dharmaśāstra* states, "Offspring, rites prescribed by Law, obedient service (*śuśrūṣā*), good sexual pleasure (*ratiruttama*), and procuring heaven for oneself and one's forefathers—all this depends on the wife."[93] What stands out in this list is obedient service (*śuśrūṣā*). The literal meaning of *śuśrūṣā* is the desire to listen, but it also means desire to take command, to obey, and to serve. In the context of the *Mānava Dharmaśāstra* it means desire to obediently serve. All the other things listed are specific objects, such as offspring and pleasure. Obedient service, on the other hand, is the mode in which these objects are to be received by a husband from his wife. Obedient service defines the nature of the relationship a wife has with her husband. The desire in *śuśrūṣā* as the desire to serve is significant. It is not enough that the wife serve her husband—she must desire to serve him if she wants to be an ideal wife. It is not just the act of service or obedience, but the desire or will to obey and serve that is offered by the *Mānava Dharmaśāstra* as the very essence of being a wife. The domain that is opened up for mastery is that of desire, not merely of the act. It is important to note that the same *Mānava Dharmaśāstra* advises the Brahmin that he must not earn his living by service (*sevā*) no matter how dire the circumstances, because a life of service is a "dog's life."[94] The paranoia of the Brahmin about a life of service reveals just how much he prized his independence.

In time the wife came to be forbidden from uttering her husband's or another man's name.[95] Calling her husband by name would assume some level of symmetry and exchange between her and her husband, signaling the possibility of dialogue and reciprocity, a possibility that would go against the discourse of obedience. No true conversation or dialogue between husband and wife could possibly occur under these circumstances. The obedient service (*śuśrūṣā*) that defined the wife's relation with her husband meant the desire to listen, not to speak to him. She did not address him directly; she talked to him in the third person.

To understand the significance of this term "obedient service" one needs to see it in contrast to love. The *Mānava Dharmaśāstra* says of the husband: "He must never eat with his wife or look at her while she is eating, sneezing, yawning, or seated at ease; nor should the Brahmin, if he wants energy, look at her while she is applying collyrium to her eyes or oil on her body, or when she is undressed or giving birth."[96] The idea was to prevent a casual and informal relationship of familiarity, dialogue, intimacy, and friendship from developing between the husband and the wife. The fear was that such a relationship would dilute the authority of the husband. It was as if the husband was to talk to his wife only in a language of command whenever needed; otherwise he was expected to stay away from her.

The rules of *dharma* were meant to convert the husband into the master of his wife. For the wife, her husband was her goal. Hers was an ethics of obedience. While the husband had his Vedic gods he made obeisance to, for the wife her husband was the only access she had to the Vedas, the rituals and gods, and, most of all, heaven.[97] Women were neither allowed nor expected to learn and recite the Vedic scriptures; they also could not have rituals performed for themselves: "No rite is performed for women with the recitation of ritual formulas—that is well-established Law. 'Without the strength or ritual formula, women are untruth'—that is the fixed rule." The *Mānava*

Dharmaśāstra calls women *amantrā*, or without access to the Vedas and without strength, as if the two belonged together.[98]

The *Mānava Dharmaśāstra* offers an inducement to the wife: in return for all her services she could attain the "worlds of her husband," a reference that includes heaven. She has no direct access to heaven. The possibility of a place in heaven adds another aspect to her relationship with her husband. Since the husband holds the key to heaven, it elevates him to the level of a deity: "For females, tradition tells us, the marriage ceremony equals the rite of vedic consecration; serving the husband equals living with the teacher; and care of the house equals the tending of the sacred fire."[99] Evidently the wife's obedient service to her husband takes on the aura and ethos of piety, as if it were a religious duty.

The disposition of obedient service that resembled piety was substituted for love that the wife may have had toward her husband. The discourse of *dharma* required the wife to subordinate the desire for pleasure to the desire to obediently serve, two concepts that are altogether incompatible. Under these circumstances the wife could engage in sex only as an act of service to her husband. Given her disposition of obedient service, the wife would feel awkward carrying any sexual-erotic feelings toward her husband. The expectation of her own pleasure and happiness that would necessarily be a part of erotic desire goes against her fundamental ethos of obedient service. She would not want to be seen to participate in sex for her own pleasure. Any overt expression of pleasure or enjoyment on the part of the wife would appear odd—or indeed, an act of transgression and disobedience—in a relationship marked by the discourse of pious obedience.

Having taken on the subjectivity constructed for her in the *Mānava Dharmaśāstra*, in time the figure of the wife came to resemble the wife in this poem by Bahina Bai, a woman saint of seventeenth-century Maharashtra:

> Keeping my proper duty in mind,
> I'll reach God by listening to the scriptures.
> I'll serve my husband—he is my god.
> My husband is the supreme Brahman itself.
> The holy water that has washed my husband's feet
> Combines all holy waters in one.
> Without that water, nothing is of worth.
> The Goal is in serving my husband,
> In my husband alone is all my aim.
> If I have any other god but my husband,
> It will be as bad as killing a Brahman.

> My husband's my guru; my husband's my way—
> This is my heart's true resolve.[100]

Conclusion

The *Mānava Dharmaśāstra* approached the issue of the man-woman relationship in general, and their sexual relationship in particular, from its fundamental concerns about the purity and authenticity of the family and caste identity. Sexual promiscuity threatened two registers of identity at the same time: family and caste. It was this concern about caste and family identity that was at the basis of the *Mānava Dharmaśāstra*'s approach to the question about women's role in the family and the society at large. If the purity of identity had to be maintained, the movement and mobility of women must be regulated. The subordination of women, therefore, was linked to the discourse of caste identity as a social and political discourse. The language deployed by the *Mānava Dharmaśāstra* to define a man's relationship with his wife is quite overtly and stridently the language of power. It deals with gender relations as if they were political relations of power. Here the discourse of *dharma* reveals itself to be a discourse of power, the underlying theme being the subjection and control of women by men.

It is interesting that in Plato's *Symposium*, when Diotima identifies love to be a desire for immortality, she also points out two ways of acquiring it: by procreating children and by procreating ideas, that is, knowledge. Needless to say, in Greek culture immortality—immortality of the self—through procreation of ideas came to be privileged over the other route to immortality, through children.[101] In his search for immortality, the Brahmin, in contrast, went the way of the son. Where the Greeks found truth, the Brahmin discovered the son. Both cultures—Greek and ancient Indian—sought to subordinate pleasure, but they did it very differently: pleasure in ancient Greece, as discussed at length by Foucault, came to be subordinated to the legislative sovereignty of truth and self, particularly in the dialogues of Plato.[102] The conflict between pleasure and truth-self, therefore, emerged as one of the most important questions, and as such became part of the origin of philosophy. In the Brahmanical culture in ancient India, however, pleasure came to be subjected to the legislative sovereignty of the son as the bearer of patriarchal and caste identity, giving birth to the discourse of *dharma* as Brahmanical law.

It was the historical-discursive context of *dharma* as Brahmanical law in ancient India that the *Kāmasūtra* had in view when it stated that it was due to the subordination (*parādhīnatva*) of sexual-erotic pleasure that there was a need for an *ars erotica* to overcome it. The *Kāmasūtra* came to be composed as a historic intervention to win autonomy for the discourse of sexual-erotic pleasure from the hegemonic discourse of *dharma* as a discourse of power. Erotics could exist at all as an autonomous domain of practice only with the help of a pedagogical discourse in the form of *ars erotica*, precisely because it was no longer part of normal and spontaneous life; erotics had to be a learned behavior that needed a pedagogical discourse. Thus, it was in the form of the *Kāmasūtra* that *ars erotica* emerged as an autonomous domain and genre of knowledge. It was in search of a figure that could embody the discourse of sexual-erotic pleasure in all its sovereignty that the *Kāmasūtra* encountered the figure of the courtesan, the subject of the next chapter.

3
The Courtesan and the Birth of *Ars Erotica* as Theater

The subordination of sexual-erotic pleasure (*kāma*) to Brahmanical law (*dharma*) and of wives to their respective husbands were two aspects of the same historical phenomenon. The discourse of Brahmanical law as a discourse of power was grounded in patriarchal and caste identity. If the discourse and practice of *kāma* had to find its legislative autonomy in the face of the hegemonic discourse of *dharma*, the *Kāmasūtra* had to find another figure—other than that of the husband and the wife—and a relationship other than marriage. It was in search of this sovereign figure of pleasure beyond identity, and thus beyond the jurisdiction of the discourse of Brahmanical law as a discourse of power, that the *Kāmasūtra* discovered the figure of the courtesan.[1] Insofar as the issues of pleasure, truth, and identity wove a complex web in the courtesan's life as she went about her daily routine, it was in her that the discourse and practice, thought and history of *ars erotica* encountered each other. The courtesan thus holds the key to both the historical origin and the nature of *ars erotica* as it took form in the *Kāmasūtra*.

The figure of the courtesan was located outside the circle of both patriarchal and caste identity. Just as the subordination of women and pleasure converged in the figure of the wife under the discourse of *dharma* as Brahmanical law, so also the autonomy of pleasure and the freedom of women converged in the figure of the courtesan. Anchored as she was in pleasure, the courtesan was the counter-figure to the figure of the wife grounded in the discourse of Brahmanical law. Just as the king was the sovereign figure in the domain of politics, the courtesan was paramount in the domain of erotics. The birth of the *Kāmasūtra* as the founding text of erotics was, therefore, no more possible without the courtesan than the *Arthaśāstra*, the founding text of politics, was without the king.

It was the courtesan and the set of practices that developed around her that constituted not only the ever-present historical and cultural context of the *Kāmasūtra*, but were also at the origin of a number of central categories in it. Two of the most important of such categories were *nāyaka,* or actor, and *nāyikā,* or actress, to designate the male and female partners in an erotic affair, as if the art of erotics was also an art of theater. It was as if men and women could be admitted into the domain of erotics only as actors and actresses, having donned a new identity exclusively for the pursuit of pleasure. Even though the *Kāmasūtra* did not quite problematize its choice of these terms directly, in deploying them it nevertheless assumed *ars erotica* to also be *ars theatrica*, the art of theater, an art in which identity is nothing more than a game, constructed exclusively for the sake of pleasure, just as Foucault had envisioned it in his notion of sexual-erotic pleasure. The notion of identity as nothing more than a game in the pursuit of pleasure is radically different from the discourse of Brahmanical law, in which the wife and the husband were altogether caught up in their identities as subjectivities. These two terms, therefore, hold the key to the nature of *ars erotica* as *ars theatrica* in the *Kāmasūtra*. If the *Kāmasūtra* did not think it necessary to problematize its choice of the terms, then that was because it found them to be self-evident in the historical figure of the courtesan. In this chapter I discuss how it was in the figure of the courtesan that *ars erotica* came to constitute itself as *ars theatrica* in ancient India.[2]

The Figure of the Courtesan and the Autonomy of Pleasure

To put our discussion of the *Kāmasūtra* in the right perspective it may be relevant to recall some of the more important dimenstions of pleasure in Foucault's understanding of *ars erotica*: pleasure in relation to truth and self, the figure of pleasure, the relationship of pleasure, and the event of pleasure. All these dimensions of pleasure are at play in the *Kāmasūtra*, but with important variations of far-reaching consequences that reflect the social, historical, and cultural context in which this text had its birth. The *Kāmasūtra* does not problematize sexual-erotic pleasure as an event of desubjectivation directly in the way Foucault did. But it does assume desubjectivation in the way it describes the event and experience of sexual pleasure.

While concluding the chapter on the art of embracing, the *Kāmasūtra* makes an intriguing observation: "The relevance of knowledge (*śāstra*) [in sexual activity] lasts only as long as there is dull pleasure (*mandarasa*) for humans. But for the one who has entered into the pleasure-wheel (*raticakra*), neither knowledge (*śāstra*) nor sequence (*krama*) matters."[3] Later in the text, the *Kāmasūtra* cites another authority on erotics on the notion of the pleasure-wheel, according to whom: "[Once one has] entered into the pleasure-wheel, one no longer knows what is a proper or improper place [on the body for nail marks]."[4] Just like Foucault, the *Kāmasūtra* also makes a clear distinction between two kinds of sexual pleasure: the more common experience of sexual pleasure it calls "dull pleasure" and the "pleasure-wheel." Unlike in dull pleasure, with the onset of the pleasure-wheel not only knowledge is rendered irrelevant, one is no longer in a position to think at all; one is unable to pursue pleasure in a sequential order (*krama*) or linear progression toward the final end of pleasure as an object of consumption by a sovereign subject. Complete spontaneity marked by a loss of the ability or the need to think and act deliberately then is both the measure and marker of the event of the pleasure-wheel. Evidently, what is at stake in this event of the pleasure-wheel is the relationship between pleasure and the self or subject.

Dāmodaragupta, an eighth-century author, narrates an event of the pleasure-wheel between two characters, a courtesan in Kashmir and a young man from a distant land, in which the two could not even tell their bodies apart, as if they had completely lost themselves into each other.[5] The author adds that it was impossible to know whether the man had entered the woman and lost himself, or whether it was the other way around.[6] In these expressions Dāmodaragupta wants to convey the loss of the sense of the self, that is to say, an event of desubjectivation. Just as the image of the wheel suggests, in the event of sexual-erotic pleasure the two partners are drawn together into a circle in which each begins to receive the pleasure of the other as if it were one's own, leading to the loss of one's subjectivity.

But unlike the stranger in Foucault, it is the courtesan that emerges as the figure of sexual-erotic pleasure in the *Kāmasūtra*. To turn the historical figure of the courtesan into a discursive figure of pleasure, the *Kāmasūtra* needed to make a philosophical detour through the trilogy of Brahmanical law, political power, and sexual-erotic pleasure. As discussed in the last chapter, the *Kāmasūtra* problematized the need for a discourse of *ars erotica* grounded in pleasure in the context of a historical-cultural contingency: the subordination of pleasure (*kāma*) to Brahmanical law (*dharma*) as a discourse of power grounded in patriarchal and caste identity. The *Kāmasūtra* thus gave itself a clear task of winning autonomy for the discourse of pleasure. There was another problem, however—the subordination of pleasure to Brahmanical law was historically grounded in the subordination of the wife to her husband. The *Kāmasūtra* was therefore confronted with a stark question: Was there any social context, erotic relation, or figure in which pleasure could attain its autonomy from the discourse of Brahmanical law and reveal its nature fully? It is in response to this implied question that the *Kāmasūtra* states:

> When the three members of the trilogy—Brahmanical law (*dharma*), political power (*artha*), and sexual-erotic pleasure (*kāma*)—are considered together as a whole, between them the former has primacy over the latter. [That is to say, while Brahmanical law has primacy over both political power and pleasure, political power has primacy over pleasure.] However, for the king political power [has primacy over both Brahmanical law and sexual-erotic pleasure,] because people's lives depend on it. Similarly for the courtesan [sexual-erotic pleasure holds primacy over both Brahmanical law and political power.] Thus the discussion of the trilogy (*trivarga*) is complete.[7]

As is evident from the last sentence in the passage, these observations come as the concluding statements on the question of the trilogy and the precise nature of relationship between its three members—Brahmanical law, political power, and sexual-erotic pleasure. The *Kāmasūtra* clearly has to acknowledge the general primacy of Brahmanical law (*dharma*) over both political power (*artha*) and pleasure (*kāma*). I have already explored the implications of this discursive subordination of sexual-erotic pleasure in the last chapter. Notice, however, that no sooner had the *Kāmasūtra* laid out the relative position of the three discourses in the descending order than it pointed out the exceptions to this general rule, exceptions in which Brahmanical law lost its general primacy, setting the discourses of political power and sexual-erotic pleasure free from its hegemony. The two exceptional instances in which power and pleasure attained their respective autonomy as two separate discourses occurred in the two historical figures and institutions of the king and the courtesan. For the *Kāmasūtra*, even as Brahmanical law held the general primacy over the other discourses, the king was an exception to it in the domain of politics, as he was guided primarily by the imperatives of power (*artha*), not Brahmanical law or pleasure. Similarly, sexual-erotic pleasure (*kāma*) found its exception, and therefore autonomy, in the figure of the courtesan. In the life of the courtesan, according to the *Kāmasūtra*, pleasure held primacy over both Brahmanical law and political power.

In effect, the *Kāmasūtra* was arguing that the courtesan was in the domain of erotics precisely what the king was in the domain of politics—an exceptional and sovereign figure.[8] The fact that pleasure as an end found its autonomy in the figure of the courtesan also suggests that pleasure as a discourse and practice found its own voice and fullest expression in her, becoming a legislative discourse with the power to define its goals and make rules for itself. The historical figure of the courtesan emerged as the lawmaker in the field of erotics, just as the son did in the discourse of Brahmanical law. It was in the figure and the institution of the courtesan that the pursuit of sexual-erotic pleasure attained its historical autonomy from the discourse of Brahmanical law anchored in caste and patriarchal identity, which also led to the subordination of women. The courtesan is at the very origin of the *Kāmasūtra* as the model and measure in the domain of erotics. Without her a legislative discourse of pleasure would not have been historically possible. The nature and origin of *ars erotica* as articulated in the *Kāmasūtra*, therefore, is not only an abstract or theoretical question—it is also a historical question anchored in the figure of the courtesan.

In addition to numerous references to *veśyā* (courtesans) throughout the text, book 6 of the *Kāmasūtra*, called *Vaiśika*, is devoted exclusively to the life of the courtesan. This book describes in great detail the lives and activities of the courtesans, their role and place in the society. It is important to note that the book is addressed to courtesans and had been written with their interests in mind. Not surprisingly, therefore, it instructs them about how best to manage a life of inherent difficulty and complexity. Written from the perspective of the courtesan and not that of her patrons, it teaches courtesans ways to seduce new patrons and discard old ones.[9] This is remarkable for a text that is otherwise primarily directed to the male elites, called *nāgarakas* (city dandies)—the likely patrons—as its primary audience.

The Courtesan in Ancient India

Although stray references to what can only be termed earliest prototypes of the courtesan figure are found in the Vedic period (1,500 BCE–900 BCE), the profession started to come into its own as a new form of social institution beginning in the seventh and sixth centuries BCE.[10] This period was marked by the beginning of a phase of rapid urbanization in India as reflected in the growth of long-distance trade networks, the emergence of large and prosperous cities, and the advent of an economy based on money.[11] Courtesans were a historical by-product of this explosion of an economy based on money, expanding urban culture, and the breakdown of tribal society.[12] In Buddhist sources going back to the fifth century BCE, references to courtesans suddenly become more frequent and vivid, suggesting that they had become a familiar feature of everyday life in the cities. Some very famous courtesans were well-known donors to Buddhist monasteries.[13] In these sources courtesans are also mentioned for other charitable public works, such as their participation in building bridges, temples, and inns.[14]

The wealth and grandeur of the courtesans' quarters in the city is vividly brought out in the *Caturbhāṇis*, written between 300 and 500 CE:

> Behold the supreme splendor of the Courtesans' Quarter where the turrets of the palaces resemble the peaks of Mount Kailaśa, where the windowsills are leaned on by the sloping breasts of the hetaeras, which is cloudy with the diffused smoke of *agaru* incense, whose side-doors laugh with flower-strings, where amorous men hope to hear the chimes of sounded girdles and musical instruments, whose halting speech is the sound of anklets, and which is the head office of *Kāma*. For here the courtesans' maids parade up and down like *Kāma's* triumphal banners, with readied glance-missiles . . . their delightful gait is unsteady with playful coquetry. One can see exquisite beauties, *petites dames* who are treasuries of coquetry, whose faces are adorned with perpetual smiles; their eyes are wide with wonder. . . .
>
> Furthermore, the rows of the mansions, thundering as it were with incessant drum-beats, alarm the pigeon couples. The gates of the mansions vie with each other, marshaling hosts of craftsmen, with their flower ornaments tossed about by bustling servants. Fragrant oils, which allay the fatigue of the battle of love, are being applied. Colored powders, to be spread on the slopes of swelling breasts, are being ground. Garland accouterments, tender as the hearts of virtuous women, are being put on. The music of lutes, which engages the ear as much as the words of one's beloved, is audible.[15]

While the term *veśyā* was used to cover all categories of courtesans, the title *gaṇikā* was usually reserved for the highest-ranked courtesans in ancient India.[16] *Gaṇikās* were known for their artistic achievements in fields such as dance, music, and theater. They were perhaps as responsible for the development and spread of the arts in ancient India as any other historical figure.[17] Each major city had a chief courtesan known as *nagaraśobhinī*, or the ornament of the city.[18] The Buddha is known to have ordained Āmrapālī, a celebrated *gaṇikā*, into the Buddhist order.[19] The *Kāmasūtra* gives a vivid portrait of the *gaṇikā* in the chapter on courtesans: "A courtesan who is well versed [in the arts mentioned above] and is also endowed with a good nature, beauty, and other qualities, earns the title of *gaṇikā*, and finds a place in public forums. She is always honored by the king and admired by good men; approached and solicited [by all] she also becomes a role model."[20]

As is clear, the common courtesan had to "obtain the title of *gaṇikā*." The title of *gaṇikā* was a mark of social recognition that could be achieved only through long and hard work in sixty-four arts and crafts that included dance, music, theater, and painting.[21] What is also significant is that the *gaṇikā* was "honored" by no less a person than the king and "admired" by the learned, the elites of society. As the *Kāmasūtra* states, the *gaṇikā* was not only "solicited" by all but also became a "role model." The *Kāmasūtra*'s use of the word "role model" ought not to be interpreted solely, or even primarily, in terms of the courtesan's sexual accomplishments. Rather, she was given the status of a role model because it was in her that erotics gained continuity with art. There was, it seems, more than a grudging admiration for the *gaṇikā*: with her artistic accomplishments and her status as a cultural icon, she came to be seen as the symbol of the glamor and the grandeur of the kingdom fortunate enough to host her. It was not surprising, therefore, that kingdoms with famous courtesans aroused envy in their rivals.[22] Although there are other kinds of courtesans noted in the *Kāmasūtra*, the *gaṇikā* has the dominant presence. When I use the term courtesan I mean the *gaṇikā* throughout this book, unless noted otherwise.

Although the denunciation of courtesans in the discourse of Brahmanical law may give the impression that the profession of courtesan was outlawed in ancient India and courtesans were reviled figures, in reality this profession remained legal throughout ancient and early medieval India. An entire chapter in the *Arthaśāstra*, written in the third century BCE, is devoted to the office of the *gaṇikā-adhyakṣa* (the government superintendent of courtesans), who was responsible for a whole part of the city that was reserved for the courtesans.[23] In describing in great detail the duties of this official, the *Arthaśāstra* has left one of the most detailed pictures of the state of courtesans and their profession in ancient India.[24] According to the *Arthaśāstra*, the state was advised to control, supervise, manage, and, indeed, run and profit from the business of courtesans.[25] What becomes evident is that by the time of the *Arthaśāstra*, the profession of the courtesan had acquired great depth and complexity in terms of both the types of courtesans (categorized, and often ranked, according to their skill and training) and the nature of their activity. The complexity and variety in the profession are reflected in the fact that, by Sternbach's estimate, there were over 250 synonyms for the word prostitute in the Sanskrit lexicon.[26]

Thus the *Kāmasūtra*'s decision to ground the discursive autonomy of the notion of pleasure in the figure of the courtesan was made possible by the tremendous significance that this figure had come to acquire historically in the life of the city in the period leading up to the third century CE. With her many accomplishments in the domain of art and aesthetics and her status as a cultural icon, the *gaṇikā* had come to embody the glamor and grandeur of the city. The *Kāmasūtra* could therefore legitimately claim that the courtesan was in the domain of pleasure what the king was in the domain of politics.

The Courtesan as an Actress of Love

It is significant that even as the *Kāmasūtra* chose to declare the courtesan to be the exceptional and sovereign figure in the domain of erotics, it did not quite elaborate on the reasons for its choice; it simply assumed the choice to be self-evident, requiring no further justification. The reason for the self-evident nature of this choice is that it was imposed on the *Kāmasūtra* by history. Insofar as the *Kāmasūtra* was not entirely a creation of thought, but also a product of history, the courtesan was the unproblematized historical figure who lay at the very core of it. In its choice of the courtesan as the sovereign figure in the domain of pleasure, the *Kāmasūtra* broke out of its seeming textual isolation as a work of thought and opened up a window on its own historical origins. After all, unlike concepts, figures, such as the courtesan, are directly and unmistakably grounded in history. The only way to get to the nature of erotics at stake and its historical origin in the *Kāmasūtra* is to problematize this choice by posing two basic questions: What was it about the courtesan and the nature and mode of her existence that made her an exceptional and exemplary figure in the domain of erotics? Conversely, what is it about the nature of erotics in the *Kāmasūtra* that found in the courtesan its most complete expression?

A clue to the deeper conceptual links between the nature of erotics at stake in the *Kāmasūtra* and the figure of the courtesan lies buried in a pair of significant terms that slipped into the text without being directly problematized: *nāyaka* (male protagonist) and *nāyikā* (female protagonist) in a play.[27] The *Kāmasūtra* uses these twin technical terms to designate the male and the female partners in a sexual-erotic relationship.[28] The two words, of course, belong to the language of theater, and if reduced to their essentials, they simply mean actor and actress. Even when a courtesan is involved in an erotic affair, she is referred to as actress (*nāyikā*), not courtesan, in the *Kāmasūtra*. Although the *Kāmasūtra* itself does not dwell on the reasons for its choice of these precise words, they do suggest something significant about its approach toward the entire domain of sexual-erotic pleasure. After all, the male and female partners in an erotic relationship could simply have been referred to as man and woman. For the *Kāmasūtra*, it was as if erotics belonged to a realm akin to theater; as if the space opened up by the discourse of erotics was more like a stage. The crucial question that arises is, what was it about erotics as a domain of discourse and practice that required this shift from the space of everyday life to the space of theater?

An actor is distinguished from a common man or woman because the actor portrays a character that he or she is not. In other words, he or she is only playing a role. The actor assumes an identity, but he is not that identity; the identity he assumes is nothing more than a mask. No matter how absorbed an actor is in the role he plays, he must still carry a sense of distance toward or difference from the character he is playing. The *Kāmasūtra*'s assumed analogy with theater suggests that one does not extend one's everyday identity or self into the space of erotics; one has to invent or construct a new identity, a new role for oneself. Erotics, it would appear, was the invention of a new mode of being—as acting or playing. Only as an "other" could one inhabit the space of erotics. Erotics, in other words, required a sense of difference with oneself. Where does this necessity of losing one's identity come from? Is there something incompatible between identity and the erotic experience? Without directly formulating the answer, the *Kāmasūtra* assumes that the domain of erotics is located outside the economy of identity; the pursuit of pleasure-love carries one beyond the circle of identity, just as Foucault had surmised.

The words "actor" (*nāyaka*) and "actress" (*nāyikā*) were reserved in the *Kāmasūtra* for those erotic relationships that were anchored in pleasure as the sovereign principle, without any interference from the discourse of Brahmanical law (*dharma*). Since the courtesan was the exceptional and sovereign figure that embodied *ars erotica* in the fullest sense, it is not surprising that she was also the historical source for the terminology of actor and actress. That the courtesan was the apparent source becomes evident when we look at the criteria the *Kāmasūtra* seems to have assumed while enumerating a list of sociohistorical figures that could potentially play the role of actress in the domain of erotics. The *Kāmasūtra* lists four possible types of *nāyikās,* or actresses: the *kanyā,* or the unmarried girl; *punarbhū,* or the remarried woman; *pākṣikī,* or another man's wife; and *veśyā,* or courtesan.[29] On the face of it, it seems that the courtesan is only one of the four types of actresses, but a close look reveals that she is assumed to be the most representative of the four types.

Studied more closely, this list of potential actresses is marked as much by the figure that it excludes as by the ones it includes. One figure that is conspicuous by its absence in this list is the wife. Given that the list of actresses was an enumeration of the female characters in the domain of erotics, it was almost as if the *Kāmasūtra* assumed that the wife did not belong in the domain of erotics at all. Yet it was as husband and wife that most men and women were likely to experience sexual-erotic pleasure. What was it about erotics that made the figure of the wife unwelcome even as the courtesan became the most exemplary figure? Conversely, what is it about the wife that made her unfit to be included in the domain of erotics? It was as if erotics and marriage were incompatible and exclusive pursuits. The *Kāmasūtra*, once again, does not ask these questions because it does not problematize the absence of the wife from this list of actresses. Yet, by excluding the wife from its list of dramatic personae, the *Kāmasūtra* assumes something very vital about the nature of erotics and its essential characters.

The *kanyā* (the unmarried girl) could be a potential wife, but is not yet one. The *Kāmasūtra* offers instructions in ways to court a girl for marriage.[30] It considers the *gandharva* form of marriage based on love, not the one arranged by the two families as recommended by the discourse of Brahmanical law, to be the best form of marriage.[31] So the phase the *Kāmasūtra* has in view when characterizing a young girl to be an actress is during the time she is still being courted by a man. It is during courtship, therefore, that a man and a woman become actor and actress. However, as soon as the courtship ends in marriage, the terminology of actor and actress is no longer applicable. With marriage their relationship had come under the discourse of *dharma* as a discourse of identity.

The other figure that is included in the list of actresses is the *pākṣikī*, or another man's wife. A whole book in the *Kāmasūtra* is devoted to the ways of establishing an erotic relationship with another man's wife.[32] It may appear that the wife has made it to the list of actresses after all. It is important to note, however, that the *pākṣikī* as a type of potential actress refers only to those wives who are in extramarital sexual-erotic relationships in violation of their marriage vow under the discourse of Brahmanical law. In other words, only in the moment of the breach of their marriage vow did wives make it into the list of actresses; it was only as an adulteress that the wife could become an actress.

Given that erotic love-pleasure was systematically removed from the relationship between the wife and the husband in the discourse of *dharma*, anyone longing for it would have had to seek it outside his or her marriage. For women, there were two escape routes from the prison house of Brahmanical law. One way was for a woman to get into a love marriage and hopefully secure a relationship of friendship and reciprocity with her husband for life. The other way was to become involved in an extramarital relationship. The husbands also had two options available to them: extramarital affairs with another man's wife and/or affairs with a courtesan. This fact is also reflected in the *Kāmasūtra*'s recommendation to men of the elite classes in the city to maintain two separate residences—the inner one to be shared with their wives, and the outer one for extramarital erotic pursuits.[33] The residence that a man shared with his wife functioned under the discourse of Brahmanical law, and the one he shared with another woman functioned under the discourse of sexual-erotic pleasure.

It is precisely in these moments of extramarital erotic pursuits that pleasure came out of its subordination to Brahmanical law. Given that women had nothing at stake in the discourse of Brahmanical law except their subordination, the *Kāmasūtra* observes that women do not really care for *dharma*; they only seek pleasure.[34] What is evident is that the *Kāmasūtra*'s valorization of extramarital affairs was in clear violation of the discourse of Brahmanical law. After all, the discourse of *dharma* was constructed precisely to ensure the purity and authenticity of family and caste identity. Extramarital erotic relationships put this identity at grave risk. If the *Kāmasūtra* was really committed to *dharma*, it would be difficult to explain why it contains an entire book on ways to establish erotic relationships with other men's wives. What is clear is that even while overtly acknowledging the hegemony of Brahmanical law as discussed earlier, the *Kāmasūtra* was quite overtly subverting its core principles. What is evident here is that the *Kāmasūtra*'s acknowledgment of the primacy of *dharma* was only for strategic purposes.

The third figure in the list of actresses is *punarbhū*, or a remarried woman, a woman who has either been left by her previous husband or, having left him, has married a new man of her choice.[35] It is possible that some of these remarried women were involved in extramarital erotic affairs and eventually ended up leaving their husbands and marrying their lovers. The remarried woman, however, was no ordinary wife. Even though the *Kāmasūtra* includes a discussion of the remarried woman in the book on the wife, she was far from being a regular wife; the nature of her second marriage was radically different from her first.[36] The *Kāmasūtra* never mentions a remarried woman to be the only wife; she invariably appears in the company of another wife, or wives if her husband had more than one. It was as if the remarried woman could not be the sole wife—she could only appear in a complementary role.

The *Kāmasūtra* clearly distinguishes the role of the remarried woman from the other wives, in terms of her duties and expectations. She is never noted as having her own children, even as she is instructed to care for the children of her husband with other wives.[37] It is possible that the remarried women never had a child. Perhaps the absence of a child set them free from their ties to the family, and indeed from *dharma*. It was also probably for that reason that she could remarry. As I discussed in the last chapter, a woman without a child, particularly a son, was not really a wife in the actual sense of the term, because it was only as the mother of a son that a woman really became a wife. Once she was not able to bear a son, she had cut herself loose from that circle of patriarchal and caste identity constituting the family. Therefore it was perhaps the absence of a child which brought autonomy to sexual-erotic pleasure in the remarried woman's life. Here we can see why the figure of the son was made the original legislator in the discourse of Brahmanical law in the last chapter. More so than the husband, it was the son to whom she was tied in the discourse of *dharma*.

The figure of the remarried woman in the *Kāmasūtra* is thought of almost exclusively in terms of sexual-erotic pleasure, not in terms of bearing children. Unlike the wife who was confined to the home, the remarried woman could accompany her husband in public and interact with her husband's friends without any inhibitions.[38] Indeed, the *Kāmasūtra* equates her with the figure of the courtesan: "[As with] the courtesan, sex with a *punarbhū* /remarried woman, even from higher caste, is not a violation of morality because she has been with many [men]."[39] The remarried woman occupied a position halfway between a wife and a courtesan. Like the courtesan she had the freedom to accompany her husband in public as a friend and an equal, and pursue with him a life of sexual-erotic pleasure outside the discourse of *dharma*. At the same time, unlike with the courtesan, no money changed hands in this relationship. Thus, in her figure one can catch a glimpse of what the *Mahābhārata* possibly meant when it spoke of an age when a type of marriage and family existed that was not anchored in monogamy and the patriarchal and caste identity of the husband. The remarried woman was part of a family, yet may not have been expected to be entirely monogamous in her sexual relationship. The typical behavior of the remarried woman that the *Kāmasūtra* describes paints a portrait of a woman who was comfortable and at home in public in the company of men—behavior that was very different from what was expected of a typical wife, who was meant to confine herself to the domestic life of the family within her home. Evidently the remarried woman's second marriage came to be anchored in sexual-erotic pleasure (*kāma*), not Brahmaical law (*dharma*).

Finally, the *veśyā* (the courtesan) as a potential actress is not only not a wife, she is the antithesis of the very idea of wife; the wife and the courtesan are mutually exclusive social figures and institutions. What is common, therefore, to all four categories of actresses is what separates them from the wife. The set of four actresses, in other words, is partly defined by what it excludes—the wife and the behavior appropriate to her. Given that the courtesan stands at the farthest point from the very notion of the wife, she, more than the others, embodies all the characteristics of an actress in its completeness.

In one of the four extant *bhāṇas*, a genre of Sanskrit plays from ancient India, the *viṭa,* or dandy-guru, who also happened to be the principal adviser and chief spokesperson of courtesans, said this of the wife: "The heart really ought not to be condemned to the prison of the chaste wife, who is born blind in matters erotic, has a dour visage, habitually mumbles, inflicts dejection even upon the cheerful, who is shrouded in a veil (*āvṛtam*) of modesty, who plainly has never seen even her own pudenda, a dumb animal in the guise of a woman."[40] This scornful indictment of the wife might give the impression that the dandy-guru was making fun of the wife figure, but it is important to remember that such wives were the construct of the discourse of Brahmanical law. This is really a critique of *dharma*, a discourse of power based in identity which set out to construct precisely such a subjectivity. If the wife appeared blind, deaf, and dumb in the matters of pleasure and love, then that was how the discourse of Brahmanical law wanted her to be. Even as she appeared to be the very antithesis of the figure of love and pleasure, in the discourse of Brahmanical law she was the ideal wife. It was under these historical and discursive circumstances that the courtesan came to be the most representative of all the actresses in the domain of erotics.

In this regard a seemingly minor detail in the *Kāmasūtra* about the courtesan and the remarried woman—two figures on the list of actresses—is highly revealing: "[Sexual intercourse] with a courtesan (*veśyā*) and a remarried woman (*punarbhū*) is neither approved nor forbidden because [after all, it is only] for pleasure (*sukhārthatvāt*)."[41] Here the *Kāmasūtra* characterizes the nature of man's erotic relationship with the courtesan and the remarried woman. If sexual intercourse with a courtesan and remarried woman was neither sanctioned nor prohibited, that was because the sexual relationship with the courtesan was solely for the purpose of pleasure. While making this characterization, the *Kāmasūtra* has in view—unstated though it is—the distinction, indeed contrast, between a man's sexual relationship with his wife, on the one hand, and the courtesan, on the other. While a man's relationship with a courtesan or remarried woman is characterized entirely by pleasure, his relationship with his wife, in contrast, is characterized by the pursuit of a child, preferably a son, to carry on the lineage and identity of the family.

For the *Kāmasūtra*, erotics as the pursuit of pleasure found its purest and most complete expression in a man's relationship with a courtesan. Given that pleasure was the overdetermining goal in erotics, the latter found its autonomy in the figure of the courtesan whose relationship with her male patron was defined exclusively in terms of pleasure. Not surprisingly, therefore, while the *Mānava Dharmaśāstra*, the treatise on Brahmanical law, focused on the husband-wife relationship, the *Kāmasūtra*, in contrast, put the courtesan at the very foundation of erotics, as an exceptional and exemplary figure. Furthermore, it becomes evident why the *Kāmasūtra* dropped the wife from the list of actresses even as it included her in the moment of transgression of her marriage vow as an adulteress. If it was only as an adulteress that the wife could become an actress, that was because in adultery the pursuit of sexual-erotic pleasure attained its autonomy from the discourse of *dharma*.

The Birth of *Ars Erotica* as Theater of Love

From the discussion of the figures of "actresses" above, it is evident that pleasure found autonomy in their sexual relationships, unencumbered as it was by the laws of family and caste identity. The autonomy of pleasure from the law of identity, however, does not explain why these figures should be characterized as actresses. The question remains: what specifically about the nature and pursuit of pleasure transformed the figure of the courtesan into an actress? What was it about erotics that transformed it into a domain of theater? It is worth repeating that for the *Kāmasūtra*, pleasure did not consist merely of sex. Far from it, the sexual act had to occur within a narrative of love; the pursuit of pleasure consisted of the pursuit of both pleasure and love, because *kāma* meant both pleasure and love. This is why the *Kāmasūtra* insists that a courtesan must first set up a narrative of love before it is followed with sex. For the courtesan, it was her skill to stage love, to make her patron believe that she was genuinely in love with him, which was often as important as sex.

Yet, to maintain the appearance of love could not have been easy for a courtesan, given that the profession was her only means of livelihood. The real challenge for the narrative of love was to survive the inevitable contact with that reality. In the very first lines of the book on courtesans, the *Kāmasūtra* addresses directly what seems like the central issue in the life of a courtesan:

> By its very nature the company of men for the courtesan is both out of love-pleasure (*rati*) as well as profession/money (*vṛtti*). When [she is] driven by love-pleasure (*rati*) it is natural (*svabhāvikam*), [but when] the purpose is money (*artha*) it is artificial (*kṛtrim*). However, [even when her love for her patron is only for the purpose of making money] she should act as if it is natural (*svabhāvika*), because only those women who appear to be driven by love (*kāmaparāsu*) are capable of [winning] a man's trust. For the purpose of proving [the truth of her love to the man], let her show complete absence of greed; and to protect her future [relationship with him] she should refrain from acquiring money from him by wrongful means.[42]

The courtesan's being as related to her patron consisted of two conflicting aspects: love-pleasure (*rati*) and profession (*vṛtti*). Love (*rati*) is a form of relationship—not a single event of pleasure like sex—between the courtesan and her patron-lover. Given that these two aspects were self-evidently incompatible, the courtesan carried a conflict at the very heart of her existence. Not only did she need to maintain the appearance of real love when it was in fact her only profession, she also had to temper her love for someone with the knowledge that it was also a profession, that it could not and must not result in marriage—she must not become a wife. The distinction between artificial (*kṛtrim*) and natural love (*svabhāvikam*) is not a real distinction. As the *Kāmasūtra* itself adds, even as artificial, love must always appear natural—the natural love of the courtesan. On the other hand, it must always be accompanied with the awareness that this love was also part of her profession.

If sexual pleasure alone constituted erotics, the courtesan would not have had to face an existential conflict because there would have been no need for cultivating a relationship of love. Evidently the *Kāmasūtra* has the *gaṇikā* in view because common courtesans were used to receiving money for sexual favors. Besides, common courtesan did not have a relationship with their patrons; pleasure was confined to sex. In the case of the *gaṇikā*, it was not just the event and activity of sex that was the source of pleasure but also the relationship of love. There is a pleasure that is derived from sex, but there is also a pleasure that is derived from being in a relationship of love with someone. The courtesan's erotic relationship with her patron, therefore, had two aspects: sexual pleasure and the pleasure of love. As closely as the two are linked, they cannot be reduced to each other. Sexual pleasure and the pleasure of love each have their relative autonomy. What this reveals is that sex is not the only source of pleasure. Pleasure, in other words, exceeds sex. This was an important moment in the historical evolution of erotic pleasure, because within the general domain of erotics another horizon of love opens up. This is also where the *Kāmasūtra* departs from Foucault's stranger as the figure of sexual pleasure. The stranger, after all, did not share a relationship of love with his partner. In general readings of the *Kāmasūtra*, attention has been so focused on the sexual aspect that the significance of love is easily missed. This distinction between sexual pleasure and pleasure of love is also reflected in the existence of two different kinds of courtesans: courtesans who offered sex to their patrons in exchange for money, and courtesans who stayed in a long sexual-erotic relationship with one patron.

In the moral denunciation of the use of money in the erotic relationship between the courtesan and her patron, what remains hidden and is really at stake is a subtle but critical difference and relationship between love and pleasure, or more precisely love as pleasure and love as "true" and "authentic" commitment to someone in particular above and beyond pleasure.

A thorough understanding of this issue is all the more important because the *Kāmasūtra*, as is evident in the last citation, also insists on a narrative of love in an erotic affair, even as we know that pleasure has primacy in the *Kāmasūtra*. Often the relationship between the notions of love and pleasure is seen as adversarial; it is a relationship of conflict and competition for primacy of the one over the other. While love is assumed to be a somber and sacred commitment, pleasure in comparison appears to be a relatively trivial matter unable to stand in the face of the majesty of love. In such narratives of love, sexual pleasure, though not excluded, is secondary. Indeed, it may be missing altogether. Love after all can bring pain. Indeed, it is the pain and suffering experienced in the course of its pursuit that brings out the majesty of love. In this assumption, pleasure is silently reduced to sex, and as such is subordinated to love.

Once again truth and identity coincide in the dominant discourse of love. This subordination of pleasure to love is, in fact, its subordination to the notions of identity and truth. In the discourse of erotics, love often operates as a proxy for identity and truth. Through the notion of love, the notions of truth and identity are subtly introduced into the discourse of erotics. After all, love represents an unshakable and undying commitment to an individual, someone in particular. It is difficult to think of love as a general phenomenon without a specific individual, a unique and singular self and identity, being an object of it. This love cannot be about what the individual possesses, but about the individual himself, stripped of all his possessions and accomplishments, his power, property, or fame. The phenomenon of love therefore is directly anchored in identity—it is an individual, a person with a specific identity that one is in love with. In other words, when pleasure is subordinated to love, it is at the same time subordinated to identity. Once pleasure is subordinated to identity, the theatrical terms "actor" (*nāyaka*) and "actress" (*nāyikā*) no longer apply to this relationship. Any association with acting would abolish the very idea of love. When it comes to real love there cannot—must not—be any hint of acting; acting, after all, would only expose the falsehood and inauthenticity of love as nothing more than an appearance.

If love and acting seem to exclude each other, then that is because the phenomenon of love also directly involves the question of truth. Together with identity, the notion of truth is also introduced into erotics by way of love. Indeed the word "true," as in the notion of "true love," is redundant because love already carries within it the notion of truth. If truth is still added to love, then that is only to distinguish it from what claims to be love but in fact is not, or is a false love—a love only in appearance. The notions of falsehood and appearance, on the one hand, and truth and reality, on the other, are an essential part of the notion of love. When it comes to love, authenticity is its most important element. The idea of acting is excluded from the idea and relationship of love. From the perspective of this discourse, what seemed like courtesan's love was nothing more than an act of deception, contrived to make as much money out of her patron as possible.

The *Kāmasūtra* reverses the commonly understood relationship between love and pleasure: it subordinates love to pleasure and thereby also reduces identity and truth to pleasure, just as Foucault had claimed. Truth and identity have no value other than being instruments of pleasure. The *Kāmasūtra* is built on the premise that pleasure stands higher than truth and identity. The narrative of love, true love, is deployed as a means to produce pleasure as an end. That is the reason the distinction between the real and the artificial does not make any sense in the theater of pleasure, because the logic of the real and the artificial, truth and appearance, is put in the service of pleasure.

Yet the courtesan's love for her patron must appear authentic to be effective. Given the public perception of courtesans, this was a major problem. The *Kāmasūtra,* therefore, invests a considerable amount of attention to devise ways to overcome this problem and make it appear that monetary compensation was not a motivating factor at all. The most important way in which this conflict was sought to be resolved was by dividing the professional and erotic aspects of the relationship between the courtesan and the courtesan's mother, biological or professional. The courtesan could maintain her amorous relationship with her patron as if it was based on true love, altogether untouched by money, while delegating the professional aspect of her relationship to her mother: "Let her [represent herself] as dependent on a mother who is of cruel character and who is after money alone; in the absence of a mother, upon someone who is like a mother. Let her [the mother], however, not be too fond of the lover, and let her try to take her daughter away [from him] by force. Let the woman (*nāyikā*) express displeasure, shame, embarrassment, and fear [at her mother's behavior], though she ought not to defy [her mother's] command."[43]

The *Kāmasūtra* is compelled to devise this mechanism as a strategy, to completely isolate the pursuit of pleasure as a culmination of a relationship of love from any contact with the pursuit of a living. With the help of her mother, the courtesan completely separates the financial and professional from the erotic, as if the two were altogether autonomous pursuits. The delegation of the financial-professional responsibility to the mother freed the daughter to become the focus of her patron's undivided love and attention. Once this separation had been successfully made, the general perception about the courtesan's relationship with her patron as based on money no longer seemed to apply. The relationship between the courtesan and her patron appeared no longer to be a matter of simple exchange of money for sexual favor. Sex was important, of course, but it came as a moment in the unfolding narrative of love.

This narrative, the core of which is starkly visible, sets up perfectly a theater of love: a greedy and cruel mother, the long-suffering and helpless daughter madly in love with a man who now must step in periodically to keep the evil mother at bay and enjoy the company of his beloved. It is apparent here how theater is being born out of the process of the courtesan trying to reconcile the two deeply conflicting, indeed, irreconcilable, sides of her existence. What, however, seems like a piece of theater is indistinguishable from the courtesan's life; life itself had been transformed into theater. Theater, in other words, was a mode of being for the courtesan. This love that is subordinated to pleasure is the origin of the courtesan's acting skills, which went on to play a founding role in the birth of the theater of love as reflected in the *Nāṭyaśāstra*, the founding text of theater in classical India, the subject of discussion in the next chapter.

For the courtesan appearance is reality. To be more precise, the dualism between appearance and reality is turned into the source of a new kind of life. It could be said that the dualism is not completely abolished; erotics assumes this dualism and puts it to productive use. Any attempt to abolish this dualism would end up with the courtesan either becoming a wife to her patron or losing her patron altogether as a lover. After all, theater would not be theater if it did not assume its difference from the real. Yet, at the same time, a theater must also create the appearance of reality. The self of the courtesan-wife is nothing but an appearance, like that of an actor on stage, even though it is effective only as long as she can make her patron take this appearance for real.

The theater of erotics, or erotics as theater, was born directly out of this existential conflict between love and profession at the heart of the courtesan's being, and the imperative, equally existential, to reconcile this conflict.[44] The courtesan was playing a role, putting on an identity. She would have had a real identity only beyond her life as a courtesan. However, being a courtesan was not a part-time profession. As a courtesan, she lived outside the circle of identity that became the subject matter of the *Mānava Dharmaśāstra*'s vision of a caste-based society, in which a woman was seen as nothing more than a means to procreate sons and perpetuate one's family and caste identity. The courtesan was a woman without identity; the question of caste and family identity made no sense in her life. Not surprisingly, Manu's *Dharmaśāstra,* which came into being a couple of centuries before the *Kāmasūtra,* has hardly much to say about the courtesan, focused as it was on the preservation and perpetuation of caste and family identity.[45]

It was the figure of the mother who made sure the courtesan never forgot the nature of her existence; that in her love for her patron she must never transgress the line that separates a courtesan from a wife. The *Kāmasūtra* says, "She [the courtesan] does not argue about money [with her patron] and she does nothing without her mother."[46] This terse piece of advice from the *Kāmasūtra* makes it clear that the courtesan must not touch the issue of money, even as she is expected to let her patron know that she is in no position to disobey her mother. When a courtesan went to her lover against the wish of her mother, the *viṭa* (the dandy as adviser to courtesans), while chiding her, also reminded her of the importance of the mother figure in the life of a courtesan: "What you have done is clearly not to your mother's liking. . . . Spurning the greed of your mother, your heart addicted to the pleasures of love, renouncing the principles of harlotry (*vaiśika-śāsanam*), which yield a good profit and cannot be foregone by courtesans, you have gone to the house of your lover, and enjoyed a delicious love-festival (*kāmotsavam*)—thus the courtesans have been trampled on by your virtues (*guṇa*). . . . You have infringed the mores of the courtesans (*veśyopacāra viruddham*)."[47]

While chiding the courtesan, the dandy reminds her of the courtesans' code of conduct (*vaiśika-śāsanam*). The figure of the mother seemed to have played the role of the enforcer of this code of conduct. What seems like the mother's greed in the face of the courtesan's love is, in fact, the essential condition to prevent the courtesan from forgetting that her love belongs to the domain of theater; that she must always maintain a sense of distance from her love. It is also a reminder that she must maintain her independence from her patron; she must always be able to walk away from her patron. She must never become a prisoner of either love or her patron. This code of conduct prevented the courtesan from getting caught in the discourse of true love and turning into a wife, and thus falling within the discourse of Brahmanical law (*dharma*). It was through this code of conduct that the sovereignty the *Kāmasūtra* bestowed on the figure of the courtesan in the domain of erotics anchored in pleasure was protected. Thus, the courtesans' code of conduct was more than just about harlotry: it was a counter-discourse to *dharma*. While *dharma* is a discourse based on the subordination of women to men and pleasure to Brahmanical law, the courtesan's code of conduct was anchored in freedom of courtesans as women, and the primacy of pleasure over truth and self. The dandy's statement that she had trampled on the ways of courtesans with her virtue (*guṇa*) was a sarcastic reference to her sense of true love and her commitment to her lover.

In this regard, it is significant that the "*sādhāraṇī,*" or the general woman, and "*sāmānyā,*" or the common woman, were two generic terms used for courtesans throughout ancient and early medieval India.[48] The words "general" and "common" are not used here entirely—or even primarily—in their positive and possessive sense to mean that a courtesan was common property or available for the sexual gratification of all. Rather, the two words were used primarily in their negative sense: the courtesan did not belong to anyone in particular; she was a woman without a husband and a family—a woman without any specificity and identity. It needs to be recalled that in the discourse of Brahmanical law (*dharma*) a woman from her childhood lived in subordination to her father, husband, or son. She had no identity of her own; hers was a derived identity. In contrast, a courtesan was a woman who had been cut loose from the structure of family and caste, the circle of identity, and thus from the discourse of Brahmanical law. *Sādhāraṇī* and *sāmānyā*, therefore, mean a woman without a self, or insofar as women acquired a self only as wife to a man, a woman who was not attached to a self. It was precisely because the courtesan was a woman without an identity that she could take on any identity and feel at home in it, as actors do in their roles. It was for this reason that courtesans were often recruited by the state in ancient India as spies and also as assassins.[49]

The Courtesan in the Role of Wife

This logic of theater that characterized the life of the courtesan and the domain of erotics is pushed to its limit in the *Kāmasūtra* when it culminates in the invention of a new form of existence that could only be called a parallel or virtual mode of existence. This limit is reached in the figure of the *ekacāriṇī,* or the courtesan as wife. The word *ekacāriṇī* means wife, but in the chapter on courtesans, it means the courtesan who stays with one patron for a variable but significant period of time, often running into years, as a devoted wife. In this figure, the courtesan takes on the self of the wife for her own pleasure and for the pleasure of her patron-husband; she takes on the subjectivity of the wife. In this transformation of the courtesan into wife, life itself is turned into a stage. As discussed earlier, the figure that comes closest to occupying the opposite end of the social spectrum to the wife is the courtesan. Yet, as an *ekcāriṇī*, it was the same courtesan that became a wife. Even as the wife failed to make it to the list of the actresses, it was as an actress that the courtesan became a wife. Indeed, in the *Kāmasūtra* pleasure found its most complete expression in the figure of the courtesan-wife. Not surprisingly, it was in this figure of the courtesan-wife that the logic of theater determining the nature of erotics in the *Kāmasūtra*, which took it beyond the twin categories of truth and identity, found its most extreme expression.

In the relationship the courtesan-wife had with her patron-husband, sex occurred as the culmination and fulfillment of the narrative of love. Every care was taken by the courtesan to give the relationship with her patron-husband the form and flare of a love affair. The *Kāmasūtra*'s advice to the potential courtesan-wife makes it clear that money in exchange for sex was not the most important thing on her mind: "Even though invited [by a patron] she should not agree in haste, because men despise what is easily acquired."[50] This advice goes against the normally assumed image of a courtesan as someone for whom money alone matters. The first thing to be noted in this instruction is that the courtesan is assumed to be looking for a relationship, not money—alone—in exchange for sexual favors. The courtesan is advised not to rush into a relationship. The wish, it is apparent, was to win the love of her patron and to not allow herself to be used merely as an object of sexual gratification; she wants, in other words, to be treated as beloved.

The *Kāmasūtra* instructs the courtesan to initiate a carefully orchestrated process made to appear as a series of coincidences to seduce the patron into a long erotic affair. The patrons often came from the highest class of the city and were usually bankers, traders, important state officials, ministers, generals, and famous artists. Courtesans maintained an elaborate network of characters—such as masseur, singer, dancer, jester, barber, washer-man, beggar, art teacher, and dandy-guru—that they were advised to mobilize for this purpose. Before initiating the affair, the courtesan is instructed to find out the true nature of her future patron: "In order to find out the state of his feelings (*bhāvajijñyāṣā*) let her appoint her masseur, singer, and jester; or in their absence let her send the libertine etc. From them let her find out his [sense of what is] pure [and what is] impure, his passions and aversions, his [emotional] attachments and non-attachments, and his generosity or lack thereof. [After determining] the possibility, let her plan love (*prītim yojayet*) under the guidance of the dandy-guru."[51] The *Kāmasūtra* suggests that having found out the relevant details about the potential patron the courtesan should work out a plan for love (*prītim yojayet*) under the guidance of the *viṭa* or dandy-guru. *Prītim yojayet* means she should prepare a plan for love. Here, the dandy-guru appears as a guide in the courtesan's pursuit of love. It was as if once the actors are identified, the dandy-guru as a director steps in to help the courtesan devise the right narrative and strategy.

After finding out the psychological profile of the potential patron through her agents, the courtesan sets up a series of moves to establish contact with him and initiate a carefully calibrated process of seduction:

> Let the dandy-guru (*viṭa*) bring the man to her house, under the pretext of witnessing the fights of quails, cocks, or rams, or of hearing a parrot or a mynah [bird] talk, or of watching a play, or some other art; or he may bring her to his house. At the arrival of the man to her house, let the woman give him something capable of arousing his love and curiosity, some gift [as a token of her] love, telling him that it was [meant] exclusively for his enjoyment. [Then] wherever it pleases him, let her call a party and entertain him there.[52]

What is remarkable is that the initiative seems to always be in the hands of the courtesan and not her patron. To extend the theater analogy, in this play the courtesan is the playwright, director, and actor, all at the same time. Having been seduced into a relationship, the patron finds himself slowly growing into a role scripted for him by the courtesan. It is a role that brings him pleasure because it was designed with his likes and dislikes in mind. Just as important, however, given the courtesan's caution and initiative at its origin, this narrative was also meant to help her realize her own fantasies of love.

Once the courtesan has successfully won her patron's love she is instructed to settle into the role of a wife.[53] She constructs for herself the self of a wife to her patron-husband. She does not wear any makeup and jewelry when he is away.[54] She offers prayers to gods and performs many rituals as a token of her gratitude at the return of her patron-husband.[55] She tells him she would have died had he not come back.[56] She trains herself into emotionally identifying with him so closely and deeply that the ebb and flow of her own emotions mimic that of her man's. The *Kāmasūtra* says: "She should hate those he hates, and like those he likes. . . . She should become happy when he is happy and sad when he is sad."[57] In her the man could confide the tales of his woes and triumphs with the assurance that it would find attentive ears and an empathetic heart. Such emotional attunement on the part of the courtesan as wife would come across to the man as a sign of her deep and abiding love.

The role of a wife, however, was not complete without a child, especially a son, because, in the period in which the *Kāmasūtra* was written, a family without a child was not yet a family. For a family to be worth its title, the devoted wife must also become the proud mother of her husband's child. The *Kāmasūtra*, not surprisingly, instructs the courtesan-wife to express to her patron-husband that "she wants to have a son with him and does not want her life to be longer than his."[58] Yet, even as she was instructed to express this wish, she knew that her patron-husband was unlikely to acknowledge publicly that he had a child with her. It is known that the children of courtesans in ancient and early medieval India were people without identity. This was particularly true of the sons, because the daughters were almost invariably trained to follow in the footsteps of their mothers.[59] Sons often drifted away from their mothers in the absence of any defined role for them in the household.[60] Given this historical reality, the courtesan's wish to have a child with the man did not carry any real meaning except as a gesture to show not only how much she loved him, but also to give her relationship with her patron the context of a complete family, virtual though it was.

In the display of her fidelity and love to her beloved patron-husband the courtesan-wife was not afraid to embrace death itself—the highest test of true love: "If her mother takes her elsewhere by force, then she yearns for poison, fasting to death, a dagger [to kill herself], or a rope [to hang herself]."[61] This tale about her evil mother forcing her to go with another man and thus provoking her into threatening suicide is made to appear all the more authentic by having one of the courtesan's hangers-on bring it to her patron, instead of enacting it in front of him: "Let her convince the man (*nāyaka*) of this [her suicidal state of mind] through her secret agents."[62] This was meant to create the impression that her love for him was not just a show—it was authentic—since she threatened to commit suicide in his absence, and did not even tell him about it herself. This tale was designed to serve two conflicting purposes. First, it demonstrated to the man how desperately she loved him and that she was willing to end her life if she were forced to lose him. Second, it helped serve notice to the patron that if he really wanted to keep her, he could not afford to forget her mother; he must keep the latter happy. In one brilliant stroke this little piece of theater accomplished two seemingly conflicting and irreconcilable goals: it brought more love to the daughter and more money to the mother without letting the two become entangled; it scrupulously maintained the narrative of pure, or true, love on the part of the daughter. It was as an actress that the courtesan became a wife, and it was as an actor that the patron became a husband. They lived their lives as if they were characters in a work of fiction or literature on stage.

What is curious about the *Kāmasūtra*'s elaboration of different types of actresses is that it does not really dwell as much on the actors. The primacy of the courtesan is brought out by the fact that when faced with the need to elaborate the potential types of male actors in the erotic field, the *Kāmasūtra* defers it, promising to come back to the subject in the *Vaiśika* chapter that deals with courtesans.[63] Interestingly, in the book on courtesans there is no direct discussion of the types of actors (*nāyakas*) at all. Instead, the book deals with the complexity and contradictions of a courtesan's life and is intended to educate her on different types of patrons she will likely come in contact with, as well as ways to forge relationships with them while making sure she makes enough money for herself. It seems what the *Kāmasūtra* means by actor (*nāyaka*) is none other than the different types of patrons with whom courtesans were likely to have relationships. If the discussion of types of potential actors belonged in the book on the courtesan, then that was precisely because it was as a patron of the courtesan that a man could become an actor in the domain of erotics. The figure of the actor (*nāyaka*), in other words, was a derivative character—his origin lay in the figure of the courtesan.

Conclusion

It is not surprising that in the age of the hegemony of *dharma*, *ars erotica* found refuge in two figures of scorn: the courtesan and the adulteress. The two of the longest books of the *Kāmasūtra* are devoted to the lives of these two figures. The *Kāmasūtra* declared the courtesan to be the very embodiment of pleasure. What was common to these two figures was that, whereas the courtesan was located outside the Brahmanical social economy of caste identity, the adulteress exceeded and thus disrupted this economy from within. If the *Kāmasūtra* elaborated ways of adultery despite strong sanctions on it in the *Mānava Dharmaśāstra*, then that was because it did not believe in its ideals. It was guided by pleasure alone as the sovereign principle in the matters concerning sexual-erotic relationships. In the age of *dharma*, adultery became the refuge of love-pleasure. The reason was not only that in adulterous relationships pleasure alone was the sole object, but also that in this relationship the woman came closest to achieving her freedom.

As is evident, the *Kāmasūtra* did not borrow the terms "actor" and "actress" from the *Nāṭyaśāstra*, as the founding ancient Indian treatise on theater. It was the figure of the courtesan that was the source of these two terms. As the *Kāmasūtra* did not elaborate on the choice of these words seemingly central to the question of the best way to pursue pleasure, one can assume that it found them self-evident in the figure of the courtesan. In other words, the *Kāmasūtra* did not need to explain these words because once it made the choice of the courtesan every aspect of her existence that appeared important for the discourse and practice of pleasure were simply incorporated without any clarification.

In the *Kāmasūtra* as the founding text of *ars erotica*, the notion of self and truth operate under the sovereignty of pleasure; self or identity and truth are nothing more than instruments that serve the need of pleasure. The real scandal of the *Kāmasūtra*, therefore, lies elsewhere than in its unassuming frankness about matters of sex: it lies in its audacity to establish a discourse that not only turned its back on but also toyed with the notions of self and truth, as if they were nothing more than technologies of pleasure. From the imperative to invent new subjectivities and identities beyond the notions of truth and authenticity, the pursuit of pleasure-love in the *Kāmasūtra* morphed into a form of theater, a form of art—*ars erotica*, with the courtesan as its historical face. It was also thus that the art of *ars erotica* turned into *ars theatrica*. If the *Kāmasūtra* ends up elaborating a mode of life that is lived as if on stage, then that is because *kāma*, as both love and pleasure, is accessible to one only as an actress or actor. The essence of this theater of erotics did not lie in the imitation of the real, but in transcending the logic of the real and the true.

The *Kāmasūtra*, however, recognized that *kāma* could not but be only one of the multiple, often competing and conflicting, pursuits—such as *dharma* and *artha*—in life. As it elaborated a system of *ars erotica* as a theater of love-pleasure, the *Kāmasūtra* conceded that not all of life could be turned into a stage: the wife could not help but be a wife even if she had to play an adulteress in pursuit of sexual-erotic pleasure. The courtesan, on the other hand, could not be a wife, even if she had to play one, once again, in pursuit of pleasure. It was only in its difference in a world based on multiple ontologies that the theater of erotics held much of its promise and allure. If, in the process, the *Kāmasūtra* could not help but appear as a scandal and its dramatic personae as an assortment of scoundrels, then that was the inevitable price it had to pay in a world of multiple ontologies at odds with each other.

Let me end by referring back to Foucault's contrast between the discourses of *ars erotica* and *scientia sexualis*. It may come as a surprise that the courtesan makes an appearance also in psychoanalysis as a discourse of *scientia sexualis* as an extreme figure of pleasure, only now with her status reversed: Freud finds the courtesan to be the most extreme but also the most debased and degraded figure of pleasure and sensuality.[64] If the courtesan is the most debased and extreme figure of pleasure for Freud, that is because she demands no love; the allure of the courtesan, after all, lay precisely in this absence of the demand for love. In contrast, the courtesan as *gaṇikā* is the sovereign figure of both pleasure and love in the *Kāmasūtra*; in it there is complete continuity between sexual-erotic pleasure and love as reflected in the historical figure of the *gaṇikā*; there is no pleasure without a discourse of love.

The contrasting status of the courtesan in the *Kāmasūtra* and Freud's works is due to their contrasting notions of love and pleasure. For Freud pleasure can come only at the cost of love; the wife could be a figure of love only at the expense of also being an object of sexual pleasure. This conflict between pleasure and love is anchored in the conflict between nature as sensuality and culture as love in psychoanalysis. For its every achievement culture must pay a price in sexual-erotic pleasure; more culture would inevitably result in less pleasure. As we saw in the last chapter, this Freudian division between sensuality and culture occurs also in the discourse of Brahmanical law (*dharma*) as the discourse of caste and patriarchal identity. Was Freud's division of sensuality and culture presented as a scientific fact rooted in the history of patriarchy, just as the discourse of *dharma* was? After all, how could the courtesan as the most debased figure of nature and sensuality at the same time rise to be the greatest artist, indeed the founder, of a whole culture of arts as rich and enduring as any in the world? It would appear that history itself stands in the way of Freud's foundational principles of psychoanalysis, or as Foucault called it, *scientia sexualis*.

4

The Courtesan and the Origins of the *Nāṭyaśāstra*: From *Ars Erotica* to *Ars Theatrica*

In the life of the courtesan, *ars erotica* slowly and subtly morphed into *ars theatrica,* as discussed in the last chapter. In this morphing, the nature and history of the relationship between erotics and theatrics-aesthetics also came to be determined. It was this event that was at the origin of theater as conceived in the *Nāṭyaśāstra,* the founding text on the discourse and practice of theater in India, dated to the second century CE, a century earlier than the *Kāmasūtra.*[1] Because theater in ancient India included music and dance as its central elements, the *Nāṭyaśāstra* was also the founding text on these two arts. The art of theater in ancient Indian culture came as the culmination—not sublimation, as Freud would have us believe—of a long and complex evolution of the art of erotics anchored in the figure of the courtesan. In this chapter I will discuss how the figure of the courtesan became the historical bridge between the two foundational texts of Indian culture, intertwining the histories of erotics and theatrics-aesthetics.

The continuities and kinship—both conceptual and historical—between the *Nāṭyaśāstra* and the *Kāmasūtra* are so wide-ranging that the two texts appear to be embedded in each other, as if erotics and theatrics-aesthetics were determined by the same historical and intellectual necessity in their nature and origin. While the *Kāmasūtra* was anchored in erotic pleasure, the *Nāṭyaśāstra* was anchored in aesthetic pleasure (*rasa*). Just as the *Kāmasūtra* understood sexual-erotic pleasure as an event of desubjectivation, so too did the *Nāṭyaśāstra* define aesthetic pleasure as an experience and event of desubjectivation, in which both truth and identity were brought under the sovereignty of pleasure as the final end.

One of the central assumptions underlying the work of historians of ancient Indian theater until now has been that theater had its origin in religious rituals, Vedic and non-Vedic.[2] What, however, has been overlooked in the existing scholarship written from this perspective is that theater in its most dominant and representative form in the *Nāṭyaśāstra* as a theater of love was, in fact, the result of a break from religious rituals and spectacles.[3] Although it is rarely noted in the scholarship on Indian theater, the figure of the courtesan was as much at the origin of *ars theatrica* as she was of *ars erotica*. It is a remarkable fact, unnoticed in existing historiography, that the three central figures that together constituted theater as articulated in the *Nāṭyaśāstra*—the actress, the actor, and the director—are anchored in the three most important historical figures in the domain of sexual-erotic pleasure—the courtesan, the young dandy as her patron-consort (*nāyaka*, *vaiśika*), and the old dandy as her guru (*viṭa*), respectively. Indeed, it was in the figure of the dandy-guru that both erotics and theatrics came to be constituted as twin discourses. Since the two figures of the dandy—dandy-consort and dandy-guru—were historically derivative of the figure of the courtesan, it was she who was the most important figure at the origin of both erotics and theater.

Because it is one of the founding texts of ancient Indian culture as a whole, the significance of the *Nāṭyaśāstra* is impossible to exaggerate. An exhaustive text on all aspects of Indian theater, including music and dance, it remains a core element of the ancient Indian understanding of art and aesthetics.[4] Until the advent of western education under the British Empire, for a millennium and a half, the philosophy of theater and aesthetics invented by the *Nāṭyaśāstra* dominated the discourse on literature and arts in Indian culture. At the turn of the second millennium, the philosophy of theater and art became associated with religious and philosophical speculation, particularly in Abhinavagupta's commentary on the *Nāṭyaśāstra*.[5] Later, during the medieval period, a branch of *bhakti*, or the devotional form of Hinduism—much of which is organized around different forms of art, such as poetry, theater, music, and dance—still dominant today, developed a theology on the basis of the *Nāṭyaśāstra*'s discourse of love and its philosophy of theater and aesthetics.[6] The *Nāṭyaśāstra*'s notions of love and aesthetic pleasure mutated into spiritual love (*bhakti*) and spiritual pleasure or joy (*rasa*), even as the figure of god came to be seen as an embodiment of love and joy. In the wake of this mutation, the old figure of the courtesan, ever the custodian of the twin discourses of erotic and aesthetic love and pleasure, reappeared once again as the *devadāsī* or humble servant of god at the temple door as a trustee of spiritual love and pleasure.[7]

The Celestial Courtesan and the Advent of Theater on Earth

The first and last chapters of the *Nāṭyaśāstra* give an account of its own origins as the founding treatise on the art of theater. This origin story is thought to be a later addition to the original text.[8] In this story, a clear attempt is made to give the art of theater an invented genealogy that would bring it social and intellectual legitimacy as a new discursive field. In this account, the *Nāṭyaśāstra* claimed a divine origin for itself, asserting that the art of theater was offered as a gift to humanity by Brahmā, the god of creation in ancient Indian culture, at the request of other gods. Brahmā created the art of theater in the *Nāṭyaśāstra* as the fifth Veda—the *Nāṭyaveda,* or the Veda of theater—by incorporating different elements of theater from the four existing Vedas.[9] Since the gods expressed their inability to either understand or make use of the art of theater, it was handed to the care of the sage Bharata, the first theater director and author of the *Nāṭyaśāstra*. Bharata, in turn, taught this art to his hundred sons, with whose help he offered to stage a play for the first time for the pleasure of Brahmā and the other gods.

Behind this story of the divine origin of theater, however, there lies buried another story bearing a vital clue to the historical origin of theater. After giving an account of how the art of theater was created by Brahmā in heaven, the *Nāṭyaśāstra* goes on to narrate how this art came to earth among humans. The credit for persuading Bharata to come down to earth and to introduce theater to the world is given to Nahuṣa, an earthly king in heaven.[10] Nahuṣa wanted celestial courtesans to come down to earth and stage plays, but that request was denied because celestial courtesans were not allowed to perform plays in the world of humans.[11] The *Nāṭyaśāstra* uses the word *apsaras* for the figure I refer to as celestial courtesan. The term *apsaras* is generally translated as nymph or celestial maiden. But the *Nāṭyaśāstra* also uses the word *divyaveśyā*, literally "celestial courtesan," for the same figure.[12] Given the historical context of the *Nāṭyaśāstra*, "celestial courtesan" seems to be a far more meaningful translation of the word than "nymph." It is important to note, however, that the celestial courtesan is different from the earthly courtesan in that the former is not shown to engage in erotic-romantic relationships in exchange for money. In classical Sanskrit literature she simply functions as the most celebrated figure of erotic-romantic love. If she is still referred to as celestial courtesan then that is simply to reflect her freedom as a single woman outside the circle of family and patriarchal identity, as a woman who is not the wife, and as such is free to strike an erotic-romantic relationship with whomever she likes.

Even though Nahuṣa's wish to have celestial courtesans bring the art of theater to earth is denied, he tells Bharata in the course of their conversation that he (Bharata) would not be the first to bring theater to earth; he reveals that theater had, in fact, been brought to earth once before by the most celebrated of celestial courtesans, Urvaśī, when she lived as a wife to his grandfather, Purūravas, the founder of the lunar dynasty, one of the two most powerful royal dynasties in ancient India. The name of Urvaśī comes up once more in another place, when the *Nāṭyaśāstra* states directly that "just as drama came to be established in heaven through Rambhā, Urvaśī [celestial courtesans], and the like, similar has been the case in the kings' harems in this world."[13]

The legend of Purūravas and Urvaśī has had a long history in ancient Indian culture.[14] It first appeared in the *Ṛgveda*—generally dated to 1,000 BCE and earlier—in the form of a dramatic dialogue between Purūravas and Urvaśī.[15] In the absence of the entire story as a context, it is difficult to determine the precise meaning of the parts of this dialogue. The core of the story, however, is clear, and it has largely remained unchanged through its several iterations: Urvaśī, the celestial courtesan, fell in love with the king Purūravas on earth and decided to live with him. However, there was a condition—the real core of the story—attached to Urvaśī's stay with King Purūravas on earth: she must leave the king and return to heaven as soon as she bore him a child.[16] And when Urvaśī did bear the king a son she decided to leave him and return to heaven. When Purūravas in utter despair entreated Urvaśī not to leave, she told him that like the wind she was difficult to capture.[17] Later in the dialogue she also added that there could not be any lasting friendship with women; women's hearts were like those of hyenas.[18] She remained unmoved even when Purūravas hinted that he might commit suicide if she left. As if looking beyond his possible imminent death, Urvaśī ended the dialogue by telling Purūravas that his sons—including the one with her—would offer oblations to gods that would secure his presence and happiness in heaven.[19]

What has puzzled poets and scholars over the intervening centuries after the story appeared in the *Ṛgveda* is the cold elusiveness of the figure of Urvaśī as evident in the dialogue. Since its appearance in the *Ṛgveda*, the story has gone through several iterations in major texts of ancient Indian culture, including the *Rāmāyaṇa*, the *Mahābhārata*, and the *Purāṇas*. In the process the story went through several minor but meaningful changes.[20] One of the most famous renderings of this story is by Kālidāsa—the most celebrated playwright of ancient India—in his *Vikramōrvaśīyam*, or *Story of Vikrama and Urvaśī*.[21] My aim here is not to approach this legend as a theme in itself, or the meaning it may have had in Vedic mythology and ritual. Rather, my approach is determined by the fact that in deploying this story the *Nāṭyaśāstra* left a clue to the origin of theater in India.

As is evident, the original story as first presented in the *Ṛgveda* had nothing to do with theater. The *Nāṭyaśāstra* wove the story of its own origin into an existing love story. According to the *Nāṭyaśāstra*, it was during her stay with the king that Urvaśī taught the art of theater to the members of the king's harem.[22] Nahuṣa tells Bharata that it was after the departure of Urvaśī that the art of theater was lost on earth. The *Nāṭyaśāstra* thus transforms Urvaśī, the elusive beloved of Purūravas, into the original founder of theater on earth. In the *Nāṭyaśāstra* the two stories get so inextricably linked that the only way to get an insight into the origin of theater is through an interpretation of this love story.

This love story needs to be seen in light of the nature of relationship between the courtesan and her patron at the center of the discourse of *ars erotica* in the *Kāmasūtra*, the subject of investigation in the last chapter. What is at stake in this love story is the nature of the relationship between a man as the head of a family, and as such under the discourse of Brahmanical law (*dharma*), and a courtesan as the sovereign figure in the domain of sexual-erotic pleasure (*kāma*). When Urvaśī refused to return to Purūravas, she, in effect, refused to be absorbed within the royal household as the king's wife. In her refusal, Urvaśī asserted her independence as a courtesan. But why did she wait until the birth of the son to assert her independence? What was it about the birth of the son that triggered Urvaśī's sense of independence? It is clear that the enduring elusiveness of Urvaśī and her love for Purūravas was anchored in the figure of the son. Unless the significance of the son in this relationship is fully understood, the figure of Urvaśī and the nature of her love would continue to elude any coherent explanation.

Urvaśī had to leave the king as soon as she bore him a child. It was as if the family could only be made of two people—not three: either the husband and the wife or the father and the son, as if the son and the mother were two exclusive figures who could not exist together. In chapter 2 I discussed the Brahmanical logic of identity that made the son the legislator of the law of monogamy in the discourse of *dharma*. In the Brahmanical discourse of law, it was in the son that the father realized his identity; in the son the father saw his own image as if in a mirror. The husband and the wife by themselves did not yet constitute a complete family—it needed the son as the third member. In the discourse of Brahmanical law, the wife was reduced to nothing more than a means to have a son. It was the relationship between the father and the son that constituted the real axis of identity and anchored the family. At the end of the dialogue in the *Ṛgveda*, Urvaśī reminds the king that he might have lost her but still had his sons, who would secure his and his ancestors' continued happiness in heaven, a statement entirely in line with the discourse of *dharma*. What Urvaśī as a courtesan seems determined to prevent is the father and son forming a circle of identity, reducing her to nothing more than an instrument in her husband's quest to secure his identity.

It is evident that Urvaśī was a courtesan who lived in the manner of a devoted wife to her patron Purūravas as discussed in the previous chapter. Recall that it was in this relationship that erotics came to be transformed into theater. It was due to this underlying logic of theater that the *Kāmasūtra* came to deploy the terms actor (*nāyaka*) and actress (*nāyikā*) to designate the two partners in an erotic affair. Recall also that the *Kāmasūtra* did not include the figure of the wife—the real wife—in the list of actresses in its theater of love, even as it chose the courtesan to be at the top of this list. If one places the story of Purūravas and Urvaśī in this perspective, the nature of the problem in their relationship becomes all too clear: as soon as the son was born, the courtesan as wife was in danger of being transformed into a real wife. From being an actress in the theater of love, Urvaśī was about to be transformed into a wife. The condition that she will leave her lover as soon as she bore him a son was put in place to make sure that Urvaśī as a courtesan did not become the king's wife—his real wife.

Had Urvaśī agreed to return as a wife, she would have come under the direct subordination of her husband and lost her freedom as a celestial courtesan. In refusing to return, she asserted her freedom. Such was the logic of the discourse of Brahmanical law (*dharma*) that it was only as a courtesan that a woman could be free. Grounded as she was in the discourse of sexual-erotic pleasure (*kāma*), what Urvaśī also rejected in the figure of the wife was the discourse of *dharma*. As the real wife to the king, Urvaśī would have immediately become subject to the discourse of *dharma* as a discourse of identity. In the refusal of Urvaśī what we have is a courtesan's refusal to be captured by the discourse of *dharma* anchored in the caste and patriarchal identity of the husband.

Furthermore, it is important to keep in mind that in Urvaśī's fate the autonomy and sovereignty of the discourse of sexual-erotic pleasure (*kāma*) was at stake. What appears to be elusive in the figure of Urvaśī is the nature of pleasure itself, which could not be captured in the discourse of Brahmanical law as a discourse of identity. Evident in Urvaśī's story is the courtesan's existential commitment to the discourse of *kāma,* or pleasure. Her absolute commitment to it shows that in her autonomy as a courtesan it was the autonomy of the discourse of pleasure from *dharma* that was at stake. It is not surprising therefore that the *Kāmasūtra* acknowledged the courtesan to be the sovereign figure in the domain of pleasure, just as the figure of the king was sovereign in the domain of political power. In Urvaśī's assertion of independence, what was also claimed was the sovereignty of pleasure as a separate domain of discourse and practice from that of political power. In Urvaśī's refusal to the king, it was pleasure that refused to shed its autonomy and subordinate itself to political power (*artha*).

This story is evidently a love story between a king and a courtesan. Numerous such stories must have been part of common experience in the period under discussion here. It is important to note that this love story is itself a theater, exactly as the *Kāmasūtra* understood it to be. When Urvaśī ruled out the possibility of the father and son coming face to face, what she had in mind was the sanctity of this theater as the theater of love; that theater must maintain its difference and separation from the real; she must not become the wife. In her commitment not to become the wife she was committed to the cardinal principle that defined the existence of the courtesan, her location outside the circle of identity. She was ready to live as wife to the king for only as long as he was ready to accept life as if it was a form of theater. The *Nāṭyaśāstra* claims that Urvaśī brought theater to the world in the form of teaching or pedagogy. It is evident, however, that theater defines her very being; theater is present in the very structure of this love story. As shown in the last chapter, the relationship Urvaśī has with the king was precisely how the discourse of theater came into being historically. This story reproduces the historical origin of theater in narrative form. This story of Urvaśī and Purūravas is the story of the origin of theater, not as something brought from heaven, as the *Nāṭyaśāstra*, claiming somewhat half-heartedly, would have us believe. Instead, it is the historical origin of theater as it came into being in the figure of the courtesan on earth.

Erotic-Romantic Style and the Birth of Theater

The story of Urvaśī as the celestial courtesan who brought theater to earth for the first time is embedded in a much longer and more involved narrative of the origin of theater in the *Nāṭyaśāstra*. It is important, therefore, to place the figure of the celestial courtesan within this larger narrative. As mentioned earlier, the *Nāṭyaśāstra* claimed a divine origin for itself, asserting that the art of theater was created by Brahmā, who handed it to the care of the sage Bharata, considered to be the first theater director and author of the *Nāṭyaśāstra*. Just when Bharata announced that he was ready to perform a play with his sons, Brahmā asked him to add another style, called *kaiśikī*, or the erotic-romantic style, to the already existing repertoire of styles. The art of theater in this origin narrative thus involved two separate steps in its construction, as if it went through two major iterations, the addition of the erotic-romantic style as theater of love constituting the second iteration. What is interesting about the second iteration is that Brahmā simply asked Bharata to add a new style to the existing one, as if he assumed Bharata to be already familiar with this genre of theater. Indeed, Brahmā asked Bharata to give him a list of things he would need to perform such a play, indicating that Brahmā himself did not know this style very well. Thus, the narrative indirectly suggests that Brahmā may not have been the author of the erotic-romantic style, which had a separate origin.

What is also significant about the *Nāṭyaśāstra*'s story of its own origin is that just as the art of theater is shown to have been constructed in two steps, the staging of plays also evolved in two steps. The first staging involved the story of battles between gods and demons, in which the latter were defeated. Since demons did not like themselves being represented as villains on stage, they were determined to create mischief to prevent such plays from being performed again. Brahmā then decided to make a fundamental change to protect the art of theater from the demons: he moved theater indoors by ordering the construction of a playhouse.[23] In this second staging theater would no longer be a spectacle performed outside in the open. Determined to win over the demons, Brahmā went further still: he reassured them that plays to be performed in the newly constructed playhouse would no longer be about the battles between gods and demons. Drama from then on would be a "representation of feelings (*bhāvanukīrtan*) in the three worlds."[24] This change introduces a revolutionary ontological shift in the very ground on which theater had stood until then. The subject of representation on stage would not be the acts and events of battle between gods and demons, but feelings. Evidently, the *kaiśikī* style was not merely a new style of play; it was a whole new form of theater.

Bharata gives a more detailed and precise insight into what this "representation of feelings" entailed when asked by Brahmā to provide a list of things he would need for the performance of a play based on the erotic-romantic style (*kaiśikī*): "Give me instruments necessary for putting the *kaiśikī* style into practice. At the time of Śiva's dance I have seen his *kaiśikī* style appropriate to the erotic sentiment (*śṛṅgārarasa*), and this requires beautiful dresses and is endowed with gentle movements of the limbs and has sentiment (*rasa*), emotions (*bhāva*), and action (*kriyā*) as its soul."[25] The *kaiśikī* style is not merely graceful; it is also erotic. Indeed, grace is only an aspect of the erotic, which is a much broader category. In chapter 22 of the *Nāṭyaśāstra*, which deals with styles of plays, *kaiśikī* is defined more precisely both in terms of form and content: "That style is called *kaiśikī* which is specially interesting on account of charming costumes worn [by dramatis personae] mostly women, and in which many kinds of dancing and singing are included, and the themes acted are practices of erotic love and are connected with (literally 'arising from') its enjoyment."[26] There are two aspects to this definition of the *kaiśikī* style: first, the characteristics of form such as colorful costumes, women, and an abundance of dancing and singing, and second, the content that is erotic pleasure or, more precisely, erotic-aesthetic pleasure (*śṛṅgārarasa*), to distinguish it from the sexual-erotic pleasure of the *Kāmasūtra*.

The *Nāṭyaśāstra* then goes on to define the "soul" of the erotic-romantic style to consist of *rasa*, or aesthetic pleasure; *bhāva*, or feelings; and *kriyā*, or actions.[27] In this definition the *Nāṭyaśāstra* lays down the ontological ground of the classical Indian theater and aesthetics. *Rasa* as aesthetic pleasure is the single most important category of the aesthetics developed in the *Nāṭyaśāstra*.[28] Although the *Nāṭyaśāstra* lists eight different kinds of *rasas* as aesthetic pleasure, the erotic-aesthetic pleasure (*śṛṅgāra rasa*) is the most important of them. As aesthetic pleasure, *śṛṅgāra rasa* in the *Nāṭyaśāstra* is the aesthetic counterpart of sexual-erotic pleasure in the *Kāmasūtra*. But the *Nāṭyaśāstra* also makes it abundantly clear that they are also in complete continuity with each other as if they are two ends of the same continuum. The *Nāṭyaśāstra* defines erotic-aesthetic pleasure as "that coming together of man and woman that results in sexual intercourse . . . to be known as *śṛṅgār*. This pleasure (*sukha*) is produced by [appropriate erotic] activity."[29] Notice also in the citation in the last parargraph, *kaiśikī* as erotic-romantic style is directly grounded in erotic-aesthetic pleasure (*śṛṅgārarasa*); erotic-aesthetic pleasure is the real content of the erotic-romantic style. In other words, the erotic-romantic style is a means to produce erotic-aesthetic pleasure. When Brahmā asks Bharata to add *kaiśikī* what he wants is an instrument that can produce erotic-aesthetic pleasure. Since a whole set of categories that came into being with the birth of the *kaiśikī* are also the ontological ground of the aesthetics developed in the *Nāṭyaśāstra*, it would not be an exaggeration to say that the question about the origin of theater in the Natyasastra is really the question of the origin of the *kaiśikī* style; there is a complete identity of the core of the *Nāṭyaśāstra* with the *kaiśikī*.

All the details associated with the birth of the *kaiśikī* style—the addition of erotic-romantic style, the shifting of theater indoors, the dropping of conflicts between gods and demons as the dominant motif, the introduction of feelings as the object of representation in plays, and erotic-aesthetic pleasure—belong together as so many aspects of one and the same phenomenon. The *Nāṭyaśāstra* seems to acknowledge that theater in its original form as created by Brahmā was primarily a reenactment of battles between gods and demons to be performed out in the open as a public spectacle. To that extent, it had its origin in Vedic rituals and mythology. The introduction of the *kaiśikī,* or erotic style, marked by the moving of the stage indoors into a playhouse and the emergence of feelings as the object of representation in plays, however, introduced a whole new set of categories that inaugurated a decisive break from this tradition. It may have appeared on the surface that *kaiśikī* as the erotic style of theater was nothing more than an afterthought, added as an addendum to the original one. Yet, the erotic-romantic style remains at the very heart of the *Nāṭyaśāstra*; it would not be an exaggeration to say that theater in the *Nāṭyaśāstra* is the theater of love.

Celestial Courtesans and the Birth of the Theater of Love

The carefully constructed narrative of the *Nāṭyaśāstra*'s origin as entirely a creation of Brahmā and therefore with roots in Vedic ritual really begins to unravel when Brahmā asks Bharata to give him a list of things he would need to stage a play in the *kaiśikī* style. In the details that follow, the *Nāṭyaśāstra* has left the telltale signs of the historical origin of the art of theater, particularly the theater of love (*kaiśikī*). One of the most important characteristics of *kaiśikī*, Bharata states, was the dominance of women in this style of theater. Plays in the erotic style, Bharata tells Brahmā, could not be performed without the participation of women, because they were based on the narrative of love.[30] In the process the *Nāṭyaśāstra* also indirectly admitted that before the birth of this erotic-romantic style of plays, women were not necessary—and so perhaps did not participate—in theater because the narrative of love was not the content of plays. Plays were about the conflict of gods and demons, for which men alone were needed. Not having directed an erotic-romantic play before, Bharata had no women—he had a hundred sons—at his disposal to help in this endeavor.

The central importance that the *Nāṭyaśāstra* gives to the fundamental division between *kaiśikī* and those plays dominated by the narrative of battles between gods and demons is clear from the fact that this division comes up for discussion once again later in the text under a slightly different nomenclature. In chapter 35, the *Nāṭyaśāstra* divides plays into two broad metagenres: *sukumāra,* or delicate (this term functioned as a euphemism for erotic-romantic), and *āviddha,* or violent.[31] It is significant that these two metagenres of plays were divided along the same lines we encountered in the origin story. In *kaiśikī* the *Nāṭyaśāstra* assumed the presence of all those types of plays that it also included under the category of the *sukumāra* genre. This division between violent and delicate plays is just another way of reproducing the original division between the theater of wars between gods and demons and the *kaiśikī* as the theater of love evident in the origin narrative of the *Nāṭyaśāstra*.

It is significant that this division of plays into two major types is occasioned in the course of a discussion on the participation of women in theatrical performances. The *Nāṭyaśāstra* makes a distinction between the two kinds of theater in terms of whether it was dominated by men or women. While the themes of war, violence, and tumult were predominant in the theater dominated by men, singing, dancing, and the discourse of love were central in the theater dominated by women.[32] The *Nāṭyaśāstra* directly states that the theater dominated by men involves wars and tumult and impersonation of gods and demons, once again a reference to the theater of battles between gods and demons.[33] One can call this theater a theater of war. It is also significant that according to the *Nāṭyaśāstra*, it was not that women were entirely absent on the stage dominated by men, but that they were silent.[34] In other words, women had a nondiscursive presence on stage in the theater grounded in the conflict between gods and demons; women were minor objects of discourse, not the subject.

The *Nāṭyaśāstra* recommends that women should be allowed to perform exclusively in plays that were of delicate nature (*sukumāra*).[35] Indeed, women seemed to have a monopoly over these plays, playing the roles of both men and women.[36] They were seen to be better than men in playing even male characters in an erotic-romantic play because they were seen as naturally gentle and playful.[37] The *Nāṭyaśāstra* says, "Generally, in temples, palaces, at the houses of generals, and other leading persons, plays are staged by women, even in men's roles."[38] Given that there were no other groups of women who were known to be as skilled in the art of theater as courtesans, the "women" in the citation most likely referred to courtesans. One is led to conclude that courtesans had near monopoly over the delicate type of plays (*sukumāra*). In the course of the discussion the *Nāṭyaśāstra* goes on to link this division to the very origin of theater, both in heaven and in the palaces of kings. According to the *Nāṭyaśāstra*, "This was how theater came to be established in heaven by Urvaśī and other celestial courtesans."[39] It has increasingly become evident that this division between men's and women's—or more precisely courtesans'—theater is in fact a division between a theater of war and a theater of love. While men had near monopoly over the theater of god-demon war, the women had a dominant presence in the theater of love. There is absolutely no continuity between these two forms of theater. Quite the opposite, they are marked by a fundamental break or division. This is yet another attempt to tell the story of theater's origin in India as a division or break. If the *Nāṭyaśāstra* can't seem to tell the story of theater's origin in India without narrating this division, that is because the story of origin is the story of this division.

To go back to the origin story, when Brahmā asked Bharata to add the *kaiśikī* style, Bharata responded that he needed women, who were absolutely essential to this style of theater. Not having performed an erotic-romantic play before, Bharata as the director had no women at his disposal. It was then that Brahmā created from his mind celestial courtesans (*apsaras*) skilled in the art of theater.[40] Brahmā needed to create women for this form of play. Instead he created celestial courtesans, an act of excess that is very revealing. In other words, when Bharata stated that the erotic-romantic style of play could not be performed without the help of women, what he really meant was that it could not be performed without the help of courtesans. Later in the *Nāṭyaśāstra*, Bharata says, "For the purpose of diversion, this discourse on theater has been established by me in heaven with the help of celestial courtesans and the sages Svātī and Nārada."[41] Notice also that in the previous citation, Bharata added that the celestial courtesans created by Brahmā were skillful in embellishing drama, without really explaining how they had acquired those skills. When Bharata received the art of theater from Brahmā for the first time, he had to train his hundred sons into this art before they could stage a play for the gods. In contrast, when referring to courtesans, the *Nāṭyaśāstra* simply assumed their theatrical skills as a given, suggesting these skills were part of their very being; they required no further training.

Strikingly, the *Nāṭyaśāstra* tells directors of erotic plays not to instruct women in playing female characters and direct them only when they are playing the roles of male characters.[42] Women do not need any extra instructions for playing female roles in erotic plays because they are naturally endowed with the qualities and skills needed for such roles. The most likely reason for this is that these women were courtesans who were well versed in the art of erotics as part of their existence. They grew up in a matriarchal environment in which they did not develop the same inhibitions that a woman in patriarchal family inevitably would. Women brought up in a patriarchal environment would carry too many inhibitions to be naturally skillful in playing erotic roles in public.

While recounting a past experience, Bharata himself acknowledged "holding the performance of a drama according to what [he] heard from celestial courtesans (*apsaras*)."[43] Here, Bharata as a director admits that he had had a play performed according to what he heard from the celestial courtesans. This statement contradicts the earlier claim in the *Nāṭyaśāstra* that it was Bharata who received the art of theater directly from Brahmā. Why should Bharata, as the author of the *Nāṭyaśāstra,* receive the rules of theater from celestial courtesans, unless courtesans were the original practitioners—indeed, inventors—of theater? This statement somewhat inadvertently admits the historical truth about courtesans being the true source of the art of theater in ancient India. Behind the mythical narrative that the author of the *Nāṭyaśāstra* self-consciously constructs, what is hidden is the real historical figure around whom both erotics and theater in ancient India simultaneously developed.

The Centrality of the Courtesan as Heroine in the Popular Romance

The centrality of the courtesan and the discourse of love in the historical origin of theater is also evident in the two most important of the ten types of plays defined and elaborated by the *Nāṭyaśāstra*—the *prakaraṇa,* or popular romance, and the *nāṭaka,* or royal romance.[44] When one thinks of classical Sanskrit theater, one has these two genres of play in mind. Both of them fall within the broader category of the erotic-romantic style (*kaiśikī vṛtti*), and as such are grounded in the discourse of love. At the moment of theater's birth when Brahmā asked Bharata to add the erotic-romantic style (*kaiśikī*) to the already existing repertoire, what he really meant were the genres of popular romance and royal romance. Indeed, the *Nāṭyaśāstra* directly states that apart from the royal romance and the popular romance none of the other eight genres of plays ought to be based on erotic-romantic style (*kaiśikī vṛtti*).[45] While in the royal romance a royal male figure is at the center of an erotic-romantic affair, in the popular romance it is a male member of the nonroyal elite classes of the city who occupies the center stage in the narrative of love.[46] The courtesan is the central female figure in both these types of plays: as *gaṇikā,* or the highest-ranked earthly courtesan, in the popular romance and as *apsaras,* or celestial courtesan, in the royal romance.

The *Nāṭyaśāstra* distinguishes the royal romance and the popular romance in terms of two different locations and figures of erotic-romantic affairs: "Erotic activity between men and women in theatrical convention are of two kinds: internal and external. While the internal is to be followed by kings in the *nāṭaka* or royal romance, the external is to be followed by courtesans in the *prakaraṇa* or popular romance."[47] The division of the theater of love between "internal" and "external" refers to the private erotic realm—particularly the harem—of the king and the public realm of the courtesan. More importantly, the *Nāṭyaśāstra* grounds the two genres of the royal romance and the popular romance in the two figures of the king and the courtesan respectively. In grounding the popular romance exclusively in the courtesan, the *Nāṭyaśāstra* simply assumes her to be the sole and sovereign figure of love in this genre. Since the choice of the courtesan as the sovereign figure of love is by no means self-evident, it is interesting that the *Nāṭyaśāstra* makes no effort to explain it. If the *Nāṭyaśāstra* did not problematize and explain its choice of the courtesan as the sovereign figure of love, that was because it was not a choice at all; it was a legacy the *Nāṭyaśāstra* inherited from history, a history it shared with the *Kāmasūtra*. As I discussed in the last chapter, it was in the courtesan that the discourse of *ars erotica* found its sovereignty. The courtesan emerged as the sovereign figure of both sexual-erotic pleasure and love because in the *Kāmasūtra* they functioned as the two complementary dimensions of the same discourse of pleasure. Of the two dimensions of *ars erotica*, even as the sexual dimension retreats into the background, the discourse of love comes to occupy the center stage in the *Nāṭyaśāstra*.

The plot of a popular romance (*prakaraṇa*) was a fictional tale woven around the romance between a courtesan and her patron-consort. The best-known example of a *prakaraṇa* is the famous Sanskrit play *Mṛcchakaṭikam* (*The Little Clay Cart*) written by the playwright Śūdraka and set in the ancient city of Avantika. The central plot is about the romance between Cārudatta, an honest but impoverished young Brahmin, and a wealthy courtesan, Vasantasenā, who is being pursued by Saṃsthānaka, the boorish brother-in-law of King Pālaka. Although happily married and the father of a small son, Cārudatta falls in love with Vasantasenā.

The *Nāṭyaśāstra* defines the popular romance as a play that is to be composed by a playwright on the basis of his personal abilities (*ātmaśaktyā*) as a work of fiction.[48] This was a way of distinguishing the popular romance as the product of an author's own imagination from the narrative of a royal romance, which was handed down by tradition in the epics. Yet this freedom that the author of the popular romance was allowed was not unlimited. It is precisely this limit that reveals the historical origin of the popular romance. "The popular romance (*prakaraṇa*) should be known as not made up with an exalted hero. And it does not contain the character of any god, has no story of the king's enjoyment [of pleasures], and it is connected with the men outside [the palace]."[49] Here the *Nāṭyaśāstra* defines the popular romance in negative terms of what it must not be. The primary concern in defining it negatively is to mark out the major differences between the royal romance and the popular romance with precision and clarity. This concern was only natural, given that in most other respects there was not much to distinguish a popular romance from a royal romance as both of them were focused on erotic-romantic affairs. It was the *Nāṭyaśāstra*'s way of making sure that the distinction between the two genres was strictly maintained; the idea was to protect the sanctity of the royal romance and prevent its contamination with the popular romance.

The *Nāṭyaśāstra* also enumerates the kind of men and women who lived outside the palace who ought to be made the primary male and female characters in a popular romance. According to the *Nāṭyaśāstra*, "The plays in the genre of popular romance (*prakaraṇa*) should include servants, the dandy-guru (*viṭa*), and head of the banker's guild, the attendance of courtesans as well as exploits of depraved women of good family."[50] Apart from the figures mentioned in this citation, the *Nāṭyaśāstra* also lists several other nonroyal figures such as the banker, the leader of trading caravans, the Brahmin, the priest, the minister, and the government officer.[51] Male protagonists of the popular romance came from this group. These figures were by no means commoners; they came from the elite classes of the society, except that they were not directly related to the royal household. As is evident, the *Nāṭyaśāstra* not only fixed the erotic-romantic affair to be the sole theme of the *prakaraṇa* grounded in the courtesan; it also set in stone the social groups from which the male protagonist was to be drawn for this affair. It thereby leaves a clue into the social-historical context in which the discourse of love as evident in the popular romance emerged. Notice the two female characters—the courtesan and "the depraved woman of good family"; we have already encountered them in the *Kāmasūtra* as actresses in the theater of love. The second character is none other than another man's wife as an adulteress to whom an entire book is dedicated in the *Kāmasūtra*. It is important to note, however, that the adulteress is not really a major figure in the popular romance; the courtesan reigned unchallenged in this genre. What this fleeting appearance of another man's wife as a potential character in the popular romance reveals, however, is the nature and social-historical context of the discourse of love that the *Nāṭyaśāstra* shared with the *Kāmasūtra*.

In placing the courtesan at the heart of the popular romance, the *Nāṭyaśāstra* was aware that it was in effect putting the theater of love outside the discourse of Brahmanical law (*dharma*). This awareness is reflected in how the *Nāṭyaśāstra* sought to keep the courtesan as the figure of love away from the wife located in the discourse of *dharma*:

> [In an act of the *prakaraṇa*] where a minister, head of bankers' guild, Brahmin, priest, minister, and leader of caravans stay in their family circle, no courtesan should be brought in there. [In the *prakaraṇa*] when a person is in the

> company of a courtesan, there should not be [at the same time] his meeting with any respectable woman, and while he is with a woman of high family no courtesan should meet him then. If out of necessity there occurs a meeting of courtesans and respectable ladies in [any scene of a *prakaraṇa*], their language and manners should be kept undistorted.[52]

"Respectable woman" and "respectable ladies" in this passage refer to the wives in the families of the potential male protagonists from the elite classes of the city in a popular romance. This passage clearly reveals the social location of theater as reflected in the popular romance and shows the inherent conflict between the discourses of sexual-erotic pleasure (*kāma*) centered on the courtesan and Brahmanical law (*dharma*) centered on the wife. The real concern is to keep the two figures—the courtesan and the wife—that represent two discursive realms of sexual-erotic pleasure-love (*kāma*) and Brahmanical law (*dharma*), respectively, apart. Any public encounter between the courtesan and the wife was fraught with danger because what was really at stake in it was the dignity of the discourses of *kāma* and *dharma*. In saying that in the unavoidable event of their encounter their "language and manners should be kept undistorted," what the *Nāṭyaśāstra* suggests is that the dignity of both the courtesan and the wife must be protected; one must not be made to appear inferior to the other. As I have discussed in the last chapter, the *Kāmasūtra* constructed its discourse of *ars erotica* as a counter-discourse to *dharma* and grounded it in the figure of the courtesan, a counter-figure to the wife. Is it just a coincidence that, just as the *Kāmasūtra* anchors its discourse of erotics in the courtesan, the *Nāṭyaśāstra* also grounds the entire genre of popular romance in the figure of the courtesan and is anxious to make sure that her dignity is upheld in the unavoidable circumstance that she comes face to face with the wife? Had the theater of love been grounded in the figure of the wife and the discourse of *dharma*, the *Nāṭyaśāstra* would have used this opportunity to denounce and denigrate the figure of the courtesan. But as we saw in chapter 2, the discourse of Brahmanical law was incompatible with the discourse of love.

In fact the history of the word *prakaraṇa* also reveals the historical-social site in which theater in India had its origin. In one of the *bhāṇas*, a genre of plays in which the dandy-guru—the teacher and adviser of the courtesan—is the sole character on stage, a maid of a courtesan tells the dandy-guru in the course of a conversation that her mistress, the courtesan, was "engaged in a love affair (*kāmatantra prakaraṇe*)" with a very important person.[53] Here the term "*prakaraṇa*" is used as a common everyday word for a "love affair" between a courtesan and her patron in the real world, not for a genre of plays.

Once more in the same *bhāṇa*, when the dandy-guru runs into a courtesan, he says to himself, "Another love affair (*śṛṅgāra prakaraṇa*) presents itself."[54] The word *śṛṅgāra*, used here to refer to a love affair involving a courtesan, is an important technical term that refers to the erotic sentiment as the most important of the eight sentiments elaborated in the *Nāṭyaśāstra*. Notice that in both these instances the word *prakaraṇa* refers to real love affairs between courtesans and their patrons, exactly as the *Nāṭyaśāstra* defines the genre of popular romance.[55] In at least two instances in the *bhāṇas* the word *prakaraṇa* also occurs in relation to the staging of plays, suggesting a seamless continuity between the world of theater and the real world of the courtesans and their patrons.[56] This is just one more aspect of the more general continuity between the discourses of theater and erotics in ancient India that link the *Nāṭyaśāstra* with the *Kāmasūtra*.

The Dandy-Consort as the Hero in the Popular Romance

Given that the *nāṭaka* as royal romance was reserved for the royal family, the *prakaraṇa* as popular romance was the only major genre of plays in which stories from the rest of the society could find a place. What made this genre so promising was the freedom it offered to the writers to create their own stories based on their experiences in the real world, altogether unshackled from the crippling duty imposed on the authors of the royal romance to improvise but also repeat the stories full of otherworldly characters handed down from tradition. Yet the only aspect of social life that could become the content of a *prakaraṇa* was the erotic-romantic affair. That is to say, it was only as part of an erotic-romantic narrative that the countless characters of a complex society could enter theater. Needless to say, a society as complex as ancient India's could have offered limitless subjects and characters to an imaginative and inventive playwright. But the *Nāṭyaśāstra* imposed a strict discursive boundary around the *prakaraṇa* that could not be violated.

It is not even asked, let alone answered, why other aspects of society could not become the subject of drama. The absence of this question reveals that what the *Nāṭyaśāstra* offered as a rule was nothing more than an inherited convention that carried the birthmarks of theater's origin in India as a theater of love. In its definition of the *prakaraṇa*, the *Nāṭyaśāstra* did not exercise its legislative sovereignty as the founding text of theater; it simply documented what it saw to be a long-standing practice that carried the signs of theater's origin in the domain of erotics as part of a larger discourse of sexual-erotic pleasure (*kāma*). In enumerating and fixing the precise social figures—the courtesan and her male patron from elite social groups in the city—that could appear in the erotic-romantic plot of a *prakaraṇa*, the *Nāṭyaśāstra*, once again, only recorded an old convention that bears the telltale sings of theater's birth in the lives of these historical characters. As I discussed in the last chapter, it was exactly amidst the same characters that the discourse of *ars erotica* as reflected in *Kāmasūtra* was also born.

Until now I have focused on the figure of the courtesan, but the *Nāṭyaśāstra* has also left the evidence of the process through which the social-historical figure of her patron, who came from the elite classes of the city, mutated into a major figure in the discourse of theater, a hero in the theater of love. A man had to go through a long erotic-aesthetic training in the company of courtesans before he emerged as a hero in the theater of love. The *Nāṭyaśāstra* uses the term *vaiśika* to implicitly refer to the male protagonist in a popular romance. Yet the word *vaiśika* literally means "related to courtesans" or "someone who deals with courtesans." The figure of the *vaiśika* in the *Nāṭyaśāstra* appears precisely in the same chapter that is also devoted to the figure of the courtesan in the popular romance. The *Nāṭyaśāstra* defines the figure of *vaiśika* in the opening verses of the twenty-fifth chapter in terms of its two primary characteristics: first, as someone who deals with courtesans.[57] Second, "a man who has learned all the fine arts (*kalā*) and is an expert in all the crafts (*śilpa*), and can captivate the heart of women is called a (*vaiśika*)."[58] Here the term "deals with" is only a euphemism for a sexual-erotic relationship with courtesans. In other words, *vaiśika* as a hero on stage in the theater of love was really the patron of the courtesan; it was as her patron that a man morphed into a hero in the popular romance.

The relationship between the courtesan and her patron-consort is at the heart of the popular romance. As I have discussed earlier, the *Nāṭyaśāstra* states that a popular romance should be based on the lives (*caritam*) of Brahmins, merchants, minsters, priests, high-ranking government officers, leaders of caravans, and the head of the bankers' guild.[59] These were the leading figures in the city who belonged to the three dominant classes: the political class made up of functionaries of the state, the commercial class made up of merchants and bankers, and the priestly and intellectual class made up of priests and Brahmins. Evidently these men had enormous financial resources at their disposal and it was their relationship with courtesans that transformed them into *vaiśikas*. Insofar as it was as a *vaiśika* that the figure of the hero in the popular romance came into being, it was as patron-consorts of the courtesans that these social characters became part of the discursive world of theater.

The second definition that the *Nāṭyaśāstra* gives of the patron-consort as an expert in the arts, crafts, and winning women's love is also related to his relationship with the courtesan. Given that the figure of the courtesan was at the center of the arts, it is not surprising that individuals who spent significant amounts of time in the company of courtesans became familiar with the arts and could even become experts in it. While enumerating a list of things one could learn from courtesans, one of the *bhāṇas* also includes painting and other such arts.[60] Nor should this come as a surprise, because art, including music and dance, often functioned as the medium of an erotic relationship between the courtesan and her patron-consort. The patron-consort (*vaiśika*), in other words, was a man who was good in dealing with courtesans and who in their company had developed expertise in both art and erotics. The courtesan's lover-consort, therefore, had two major aspects to his being: erotic and aesthetic. His erotic aspect was reflected in his relationship of love with the courtesan and his ability to "captivate the hearts of women." His aesthetic aspect was reflected in his mastery of the arts.

Recall that the *Nāṭyaśāstra* divided the theater of love into two genres of the royal romance and the popular romance while also calling them "internal and external," respectively. The "internal" referred to the erotic affairs of the king in the private realm of his harem; the "external" referred to the erotic affairs of the courtesan in public.[61] The term "external," however, has another meaning as well: it also refers to the erotic affairs of a man with women outside the family, primarily courtesans. Chapter 25 of the *Nāṭyaśāstra* is called "*bāhya-upacāra*" or "dealings with the outside world," but really means dealings with courtesans.[62] "Dealings" simply refers to ways of establishing and maintaining erotic-romantic relationships with courtesans. Therefore, what this chapter is really about is the erotic-romantic relationship between the courtesan and her patron-consort. In the last chapter I discussed how the *Kāmasūtra* recommended the elites of the city to build residences with outer and inner quarters.[63] While the outer quarters were reserved for a man's erotic relationship with women outside the family, the inner quarters were reserved for the women of the family. Even as a man's relationship with his wife, located in the inner quarters, came under the discourse of Brahmanical law (*dharma*), his relationship with the women outside, or courtesans, came under the discourse of sexual-erotic pleasure (*kāma*). What we see here in the *Nāṭyaśāstra* is exactly the same division.

The word *vaiśika* reflects the historical transition of the courtesan's patron from being a customer to being a patron-consort. The term patron-consort came into existence because of the need to convey the meaning of a relationship between the courtesan and her consort, which was no longer about a chance sexual encounter in which sexual pleasure was had in exchange for money. The real issue was to describe an erotic relationship based on love. It was as the consort of the courtesan that her patron came into being as a new historical figure. Even as the *Kāmasūtra* had made the courtesan into a sovereign figure in the domain of pleasure, she could not constitute the entire field of erotics by herself without a male counterpart.

It is significant in this context that the *Nāṭyaśāstra* makes a reference to a preexisting body of knowledge called the *vaiśikaśāstra,* or a "discourse on courtesan and her patron-consort."[64] The *Nāṭyaśāstra* cites this discourse as an authority on ten different stages of love. Evidently, the *Nāṭyaśāstra* regarded it to be its definitive source of thoughts on the subject of love. The relationship between the courtesan and the dandy-consort could not have emerged as an authoritative discourse on love unless the idea of love itself became synonymous with the relationship between a courtesan and her consort. What is also significant is that the *Nāṭyaśāstra* used the term *ars erotica* (*kāmatantra*) more frequently to refer to the same discourse of erotics, as there was no difference between the two.[65] Once again, the historical origin of *ars erotica* as a discourse in the courtesan's relation with the dandy-consort is clearly evident. Even as the use of the term *ars erotica* (*kāmatantra*) suggests that the discourse of erotics was slowly coming to be anchored in the notion of pleasure (*kāma*), the continuing use of the term *vaiśikaśāstra* reveals, nonetheless, that this discourse was still tied to the two historical figures of the courtesan and the dandy-consort. At the time of the writing of the *Nāṭyaśāstra*, the *Kāmasūtra* was about a century away into the future.

Although the figure of patron-consort has failed to draw much scholarly attention, it was one of the most fascinating and significant figures in ancient Indian history and had a significant impact on the nature and evolution of ancient Indian culture. To bring out the full historical and discursive profile of this figure and its contributions to ancient Indian culture, it needs to be seen as a lifestyle and a matter of choice, and not inherited by birth as an identity. Indeed, in one of the *bhāṇas* there appears a term, "*vaiśika vṛtti*," which literally means "the lifestyle of a patron-consort of the courtesan."[66] But in the discursive context in which the term appears, it also means an erotic and aesthetic lifestyle, a lifestyle in which pursuit of erotic-aesthetic pleasure acquired primacy. This is also confirmed by one of the *Kāmasūtra's* central notions, "*nāgaraka vṛttam*," or the "lifestyle of the city dandy."[67] As I will discuss in chapter 6, this *nāgaraka,* or city dandy, is none other than the historical figure whom the *Nāṭyaśāstra* called *vaiśika,* or the patron-consort of the courtesan. Seen in their contexts, the terms *vṛtti* of the *bhāṇa* and *vṛttam* of the *Kāmasūtra* carry exactly the same meaning: "lifestyle" grounded in the pursuit of erotic-aesthetic pleasure.

One of the reasons why this figure has escaped serious scholarly attention is because it appears in three different configurations in ancient Indian history and texts—the patron-consort of the courtesan (*vaiśika*), the city dandy (*nāgaraka*), and the teacher-adviser of the courtesan (*viṭa*)—and thus fails to appear in its consolidated profile. The English term that best captures the full historical and discursive profile of this figure of the patron-consort of the courtesan is "dandy."[68] And although there are important differences between the dandy as he appeared in various parts of the West and the dandy in ancient India, there are also enough similarities to make it the most appropriate translation in the circumstances.[69] In any case, even in the West there were important differences among the dandies appearing in different periods and cultures.[70] Indeed, Baudelaire—perhaps the most influential theoretician of this figure—himself envisioned the dandy to be a universal figure that could be found in other periods and cultures, and one that was not exhausted by the culture or the period in which it happened to be presently located.[71] Part of the reason that the dandy could transcend a specific period and culture was that dandyism was a lifestyle, exactly as it was in the *Kāmasūtra*, the *Nāṭyaśāstra*, and the *bhāṇas*, a matter of choice. In other words, it is possible to think of different variations of the figure of the dandy depending on the period and the culture.

Like Baudelaire's dandy, the figure of the *vaiśika* is also grounded in the pursuit of beauty, love, and happiness.[72] He was a man of cultivated taste and bearing, who took a great deal of interest in his personal appearance, manners, and speech.[73] Moreover, like Baudelaire's dandy, he too was a man of the city, a product of urban culture, and needed to be wealthy to afford a lifestyle of leisurely pursuit. The ancient Indian dandy, as a figure who devoted his life to a pursuit of erotic and aesthetic pleasure, was a squanderer in the midst of an urban culture of commerce and exchange, and as such bears striking similarities with the dandy in the West.[74]

Seen in this light, the three configurations of the dandy in ancient Indian culture as profiled by the *Kāmasūtra* and the *Nāṭyaśāstra* could be identified as the young dandy as the patron-consort of the courtesan (*vaiśika*), the older dandy as the guru of the courtesan (*viṭa*), and the city dandy (*nāgaraka*) who was also intimately associated with the courtesan.[75] These three characters were three stages or configurations of the same dandy historically anchored in the figure of the courtesan: the dandy-guru was none other than the same dandy-consort grown old; having left his years of pursuing sexual pleasure behind, he now worked as an adviser to courtesans and their patron-consorts. The city dandy, however, is exactly the same as the dandy-consort, except that the *Kāmasūtra* decided to rename or reconfigure him to fit its own vision of the city based on art and aesthetics. It was the courtesan and the three dandies that together anchored the entire field of erotics and the theater of love.

This figure of the dandy-consort is none other than one that the *Kāmasūtra* called actor (*nāyaka*). Having discussed various types of actresses of love, when the *Kāmasūtra* comes to the discussion of actors, it states that it will discuss the topic in another book dedicated exclusively to the affairs of courtesans called *Vaiśika,* or "about courtesans." In doing so it silently assumes that actors are the same as the dandy-consorts of courtesans; *nāyaka* and *vaiśika*, therefore, are synonymous words. That is not surprising because, as I discussed in the last chapter, it was as a patron-consort of a courtesan that a man became an actor in the domain of erotics. Recall also that the *Kāmasūtra* did not include the wife in the list of figures that could play the role of an actress in the theater of love. In other words, a man could become an actor only in a relationship with someone who was outside the family, someone other than the wife. And though the *Kāmasūtra* mentioned figures like a young girl, a remarried woman, and another man's wife as potential actresses, it was the courtesan who held the pride of place in the list.

Mṛcchakaṭikam, or *The Little Clay Cart*, as the most famous specimen of popular romance seems to have been based on an older version of the play known as *Cārudattam*, attributed to Bhāsa, dated approximately to the first century CE.[76] Just as in the *Mṛcchakaṭikam*, the plot centers on a love affair between an impoverished businessman, Carudatta, and a courtesan, Vasantasenā. In the stage directions of the play the character of Carudatta appears not by his personal name but simply as *nāyaka*, meaning the male protagonist in a play. The courtesan also does not appear in her own personal name in the stage directions, but simply as *gaṇikā*, a designation used for the highest-ranked courtesans. Of all the thirteen plays attributed to Bhāsa, this is the only one in which the male protagonist appears simply as "*nāyaka*." Is it merely a coincidence that this is also the only play that is based on a love affair between the male protagonist and a courtesan? There is another untitled play, not by Bhāsa, from the first century CE in which the male protagonist appears simply as *nāyaka* in the stage directions.[77] Although it is not possible to reconstruct the plot of this play from the surviving fragments, once again there is a courtesan (*gaṇikā*) present.[78]

If the word *nāyaka* simply meant an actor or the male protagonist, it could have been used in the other plays of Bhāsa, but it was not. It must, therefore, have meant something more specific. Given the theme of love and the presence of courtesan, the word perhaps simply meant the lover of a courtesan, exactly as in the *Kāmasūtra*. It would appear then that the word *nāyaka* referred to a social-historical figure before it came to acquire the meaning of actor and male protagonist in a play. In other words, *vaiśika* and *nāyaka* are two names for the same historical figure, the patron-consort of the courtesan.

Not surprisingly, in a chapter meant to discuss the figure of the courtesan, the *Nāṭyaśāstra* ends up elaborating the figure of the *vaiśika* as *nāyaka* and the *Kāmasūtra* promises to discuss the figure of the *nāyaka* in a book titled *Vaiśika* and devoted, once again, to the figure of the courtesan. In the *nāyaka*, a social-historical figure of love mutates almost imperceptibly into a figure of love on stage as an actor, just as his private affair of love morphs into a public spectacle on stage. This double mutation is the origin of the popular romance in particular and the classical theater of love in general.

It appears that the *Nāṭyaśāstra* found itself in a bind: it sought to give itself a divine origin by making Brahmā the creator of the art of theater. But it was also acutely aware of the historical-social context of the dominant form of theater as a theater of love and the source of its own categories—the erotic relationship between the courtesan and her male counterpart, the dandy-consort (*vaiśika*). If Brahmā had to be the creator of this erotic theater, its real origin had to be camouflaged. Thus the name *kaiśikī* perhaps came about. In terms of its real content as evident in the popular romance, what the *Nāṭyaśāstra* called *kaiśikī vṛtti* entirely coincides with what a *bhāṇa* called *vaiśika vṛtti,* centered on the relationship between the courtesan and her dandy-consort. The *kaiśikī vṛtti,* therefore, is exactly the same as *vaiśika vṛtti,* the lifestyle of a *vaiśika* as the patron-consort of the courtesan. There is a reference to the word *kaiśikī* in a *bhāṇa*, a genre of one-act play, meaning a sad song or tune expressive of a courtesan's separation from her beloved.[79] In its search for a term that would hide the historical origin of theater, the *Nāṭyaśāstra* found it convenient to invest this otherwise marginal term with a new meaning. It is very likely therefore that this use of the term *kaiśikī vṛtti* is nothing more than an attempt to mask the historical origin of theater in the figure of the courtesan.[80]

The King and the Royal Romance

Apart from the *prakaraṇa,* or popular romance, the *nāṭaka,* or royal romance, is the most important genre of play in the *Nāṭyaśāstra.* It is significant that of the ten types of plays, it is on the *nāṭaka* that the *Nāṭyaśāstra* dwells most elaborately. It would not be an exaggeration to say that in the *Nāṭyaśāstra*, the royal romance occupies the most privileged place. What is more, the *Nāṭyaśāstra* seems to have its own perspective on theater grounded in the *nāṭaka* as the theater of royal love. Recall that it locates the popular romance among the people outside the palace, the nonroyal elite classes of the city, while at the same time assuming the royal romance to be located inside the palace, indeed within the royal harem. The designation of the *prakaraṇa* as the theater of the outside is very suggestive: it could appear as the theater of the outside only if the *Nāṭyaśāstra*'s own perspective was located inside the royal palace; evidently it was out of the discursive space of the *nāṭaka* that the *Nāṭyaśāstra* approached the art of theater, particularly the theater of love. Not surprisingly, this also determined the *Nāṭyaśāstra*'s answer to the question about the origin of theater. Indeed, as we will see, it was the perspective of the *nāṭaka* that necessitated the construction of the divine origin of classical Sanskrit theater in India.

The definition of *nāṭaka* or royal romance as given in chapter 20 of the *Nāṭyaśāstra* has three primary dimensions. First, the plot of a royal romance must be based on well-known stories of the lives of great kings.[81] Second, unlike the popular romance, a royal romance had to have gods and divinities as characters in it. Third, the story had to come from the epics and the *Purāṇas* as great reservoirs of tales of gods and legendary kings. In other words, the story had to be a retelling of an already known story, not a product of an individual author's inventive imagination. By implication, a royal romance could not be based on the life of a historical king. This chapter, which includes the royal romance and the popular romance as two of the ten forms of drama, is addressed to playwrights, and it dwells mostly on the structural subtleties and complexity of constructing a good plot for the *nāṭaka* without directly addressing the question of the royal romance's narrative content.

It is chapter 24 of the *Nāṭyaśāstra* that deals specifically with the narrative content of the *nāṭaka* exclusively focused on the erotic-romantic activity (*upacāra*) of the king. It is important to note that in laying out the types of women that the king can have erotic relations with, the *Nāṭyaśāstra* clearly states that apart from the women of the interior (*ābhyantara*), meaning the royal harem, the king can have union only with a heavenly courtesan, not with an ordinary earthly one.[82] The *nāṭaka* places the king at the center of the discourse of theater. What is remarkable is that it is not as a political figure that the king becomes the hero in a royal romance. Rather it is the personal or private life of the king, particularly his erotic-romantic affairs, that becomes the central theme of the royal romance. There is virtually nothing of much significance about the political, bureaucratic, and military aspects of the king's life in the royal romance. Given that the king is a political figure, it would have been more natural for a playwright to put the affairs of the state at the center of his play. Yet, what we in fact see in the *nāṭakas* is that there is very little that deals directly and in any sustained way with the king's affairs of state. Even when wars or political affairs are brought up, they only come in an oblique way and constitute merely a background to the king's erotic-romantic adventures. It is revealing that in its list of characters best suited for the roles of male protagonists in popular romance, the *Nāṭyaśāstra* places the king's ministers and high-ranking officers under the category of "outsiders," even though they were related to the king very closely in their professional capacity and, as such, were part of the royal court. Had the plot of the *nāṭaka* been grounded in *artha,* or the discourse of political power, the ministers and the officers of the king would have undoubtedly been part of the interior.

Evidently, the framework through which the king entered or was received in the discourse of theater was determined by the discourse of sexual-erotic pleasure (*kāma*), not political power (*artha*). It was not the discourse of political power as reflected in the king's public life of managing the affairs of the state that was supposed to be the ground of the *nāṭaka*, but sexual-erotic pleasure as it was reflected in the king's personal and private life. In the domain of theater, therefore, there is a clear discursive subordination of political power (*artha*) to sexual-erotic pleasure (*kāma*). The *Nāṭyaśāstra* approaches the king more from the perspective of the *Kāmasūtra* than from that of the *Arthaśāstra* as the founding treatise of the discourse of political power: it is the king's erotic affairs that become the central aspect of his life, not his relation to the state and politics. Given the existence of a treatise like the *Arthaśāstra*, the figure of the king at the center of a state described by Kautilya would have offered innumerable themes for a gripping political narrative. It is clear from the *Arthaśāstra* that the king's household, although important, was not central in the discourse of political power (*artha*). However, there is no genre of plays enumerated in the *Nāṭyaśāstra* that covers the public-political aspect of the figure of the king. It is as if the *Nāṭyaśāstra* finds itself constrained to receive the king as an erotic figure, not as a political figure. It is clear that the *Nāṭyaśāstra* marginalizes, if not altogether excludes, the public-political aspect of the king as if it did not belong to the realm of theater.

The sovereignty of erotic pleasure over political power in the domain of theater is also reflected in how traditional stories from the epics are adopted into plays. As mentioned above, one of the distinguishing features of a royal romance (*nāṭaka*), apart from the centrality of the royal figure, is that the plot in that romance is to be adopted from a well-known story handed down from tradition, particularly from the two epics—the *Rāmāyaṇa* and the *Mahābhārata*—involving a king in the central role. However, the *nāṭaka* did not have any place for the traditional narratives with primary focus on the public-political duties of the king that would broadly fall under the discourses of political power (*artha*) and Brahmanical law (*dharma*). The traditional stories picked up from the epics in the royal romances are either already erotic-romantic or else have been transformed into erotic-romantic narratives in the process of their adaptation into *nāṭakas*. It was as if the *nāṭaka* followed a rule that its plot must be erotic-romantic. In other words, two things happen in the *nāṭaka*: the figure of the king is placed at the center of the discourse of theater; yet, the king is not received in the discourse of theater in the form in which one finds him in the discourse of political power (*artha*). The primary theme of the *nāṭaka* is neither the king's relationship with his subjects nor that with his enemies. This is where theater marks such a break from the epics: even as it remains dependent on the epics for its characters and stories, there is an eroticization of the epic narratives and characters in the theater. While the two epics themselves are centrally focused on general social and political problems, the subtle change that takes place in the process of their adaptation into theater is the primacy given to erotic pleasure (*kāma*) over Brahmanical law and political power. One cannot explain the mandatory eroticization of the epic narrative in *nāṭakas* unless that was the only form in which it could be received in theater.

It is one thing for the king to occasionally appear as a figure of love in a play, but a different thing altogether if that becomes the law of theater, as it indeed did in the *Nāṭyaśāstra*. What is the historical origin of that law? This law of eroticization of the king as a figure of love in the *Nāṭyaśāstra* is a departure from the *Kāmasūtra,* in which it was the dandy as the patron-consort of the courtesan, not the king, who was placed at the center of the discourse of erotics. The king had no significant role to play in the discourse of erotics in the *Kāmasūtra*. Recall that in the *Kāmasūtra* the king was acknowledged as an exceptional and sovereign figure in the domain of political power, not sexual-erotic pleasure; the courtesan was the sovereign figure in the discourse of erotics. Grounded as it was in the relationship of love between the courtesan and her patron-consort, the erotics elaborated in the *Kāmasūtra* corresponded entirely with the genre of popular romance (*prakaraṇa*), not the royal romance (*nāṭaka*). So if the *prakaraṇa* obeyed the law of eroticization of its characters, that was understandable because its characters were historically native to the domain of erotics (*kāma*). The same law could be enforced in the *nāṭaka* on the figure of the king as native to the domain of political power (*artha*) only by extension, as an importation. The key to the origin of theater grounded in erotics, therefore, lies in the origin of the *prakaraṇa* or popular romance, not in the *nāṭaka*. The *Nāṭyaśāstra*'s was an attempt to transform the figure of the king located in the domain of political power into a royal dandy, a figure that belonged to the domain of erotics. The *nāṭaka*, in other words, was derived from the *prakaraṇa*. The *Nāṭyaśāstra*'s projection of the king in the *nāṭaka* as the royal dandy may appear like a subtle appropriation of what by right belonged to the *prakaraṇa,* but in reality exactly the opposite happened: it was the discourse of political power (*artha*) that ceded its sovereignty over the figure of the king to the discourse of erotic pleasure (*kāma*) in the domain of theater, and more generally of art.

The King and the Celestial Courtesan in the Royal Romance

In chapter 24, the *Nāṭyaśāstra*, while placing the king at the center of the royal romance (*nāṭaka*) as hero, states that if the king were to have an erotic relationship with a courtesan, it could only be with a celestial courtesan. Two of the most celebrated and iconic *nāṭakas* of ancient India—*Vikramōrvaśīyam* and *Abhijñāna Śākuntalam*—written by the most important playwright, Kālidāsa, had the romance between a king and a celestial courtesan and again a king and the daughter of a celestial courtesan as their themes. *Vikramōrvaśīyam* is based on the story that I have already narrated earlier of the romance between King Purūravas and the celestial courtesan Urvaśī, who is credited with being the first to bring the theater of love to earth.[83] In Kālidāsa's rendering, King Purūravas falls in love with Urvaśī, but she has to return to the heavens to perform in a play. However, she is so lost in her thoughts of her lover that she forgets her words in the play. Bharata, the director, banishes Urvaśī from heaven and also curses her that she will have to return to heaven when her lover King Purūravas sets eyes on the son she bears. Ultimately, the curse is lifted and the couple comes to live together.

What is striking about *nāṭakas*, or royal romances, as described by the *Nāṭyaśāstra* and as evident in both the plays by Kālidāsa, is the presence of the celestial courtesans. The central question that arises is what imperative made the *Nāṭyaśāstra* introduce the figure of the celestial courtesan as a literary-theatrical device? If an ordinary courtesan was not acceptable as an erotic partner for a king then why did the *Nāṭyaśāstra* not abandon the figure of the courtesan altogether? The *Nāṭyaśāstra* seems compelled to do two contradictory things at the same time: on the one hand, it felt compelled to retain the figure of the courtesan, given that the theater of erotic love it advocated was historically rooted in the figure of the courtesan and the set of erotic practices and principles that was grounded in her. On the other hand, it could not show in public an ordinary courtesan to be in an erotic relationship with a king, because of the prohibitions placed on him by the discourses of Brahmanical law (*dharma*) and political power (*artha*). If the *nāṭaka* must have a courtesan as the erotic partner of a king, then the *Nāṭyaśāstra* must also find a way to camouflage her identity in such a way that even as she continues to be a courtesan she does not carry the burden of an ordinary courtesan. The solution was found in the discovery of the figure of the courtesan located in heaven—the celestial courtesan (*apsaras*). Indeed, all the major features that characterize the *nāṭaka* as a genre of play have their origin in this need to reconcile these two evidently contradictory demands.

The *Nāṭyaśāstra* could not abandon the figure of the courtesan despite the impediments because the principles and philosophy of love on which its own conception of erotic theater was based made it impossible. A clue to the imperative of having a celestial courtesan in the royal romance can be found in the *Nāṭyaśāstra*'s understanding of love and erotics that it offers in chapter 24, which is focused on the *nāṭaka* and the love affairs of the king. While discussing love, it says, "Where there is love (*snehaḥ*) there is fear, and where there is jealousy there is the god of love (*manmathaḥ*)."[84] This is a very specific understanding of love. It assumes a situation in which both the partners in an erotic affair have other potential partners who are ever present on the horizon as options, and with whom both the partners maintain various degrees of contact. It is one thing to say that the fear of losing one's beloved or jealousy is a potential emotion in a relationship of love; it is an altogether different thing to say that love can only bloom in the shadows of fear and jealousy. Jealousy, fear, anger, and malice toward rivals are essential preconditions for erotic affairs in the *Nāṭyaśāstra*.[85] Since celestial men, according to the *Nāṭyaśāstra*, do not feel these emotions, erotic affairs of the kind to be portrayed in a *nāṭaka* are not possible in heaven.[86] This erotic agonism is the ontological condition for the possibility of love and erotics in the *Nāṭyaśāstra* and as such is consistent with the erotic principles in the *bhāṇas* and the *Kāmasūtra*. In these texts, a courtesan always had more than one suitor even when she was in a long-term relationship with a patron; she was always free to leave one patron for the other. This kind of erotic relationship was possible only outside the institution of marriage in which women increasingly lived sequestered lives.

It is significant that the *Nāṭyaśāstra* makes this philosophical statement on love in the chapter that is largely dedicated to the *nāṭaka*, the royal romance. This philosophy was meant to apply to the king himself, not just to the women who were in love with him. The problem, however, was that it was difficult, if not impossible, for a king to be in a position of being either jealous or afraid in matters of love. It was unlikely that a king could have a rival in his erotic pursuits within his own kingdom, particularly if his lover happened to be a courtesan; as his subject, no courtesan would be able to refuse the king. In her relationship with the king, a courtesan completely loses her personal autonomy, which is the bedrock of her erotic affairs. An earthly courtesan could not but offer her love to him as a form of service. On the other hand, even as "entreaties towards women" is an essential element of erotic love, a king's solicitous behavior toward a courtesan would appear morally abhorrent and completely unrealistic to the audience made up of his subjects.[87] It also goes without saying that no one in his kingdom would be able to act as a rival to the king in an erotic affair. All this goes to show that if the king was shown to be in a relationship with an ordinary courtesan, the specific set of principles on which the *Nāṭyaśāstra*'s erotics was based could not be maintained. In other words, the prohibition imposed by the discourse of Brahmanical law (*dharma*) on the king having a relationship with a courtesan was not the only reason why a king could not be shown in an erotic relationship with this figure.

The *Nāṭyaśāstra*, therefore, was confronted with another set of two contradictory demands: on the one hand, the logic of its specific discourse of erotics demanded that the courtesan constitute one end of the erotic affair. On the other hand, in the absence of the courtesan's autonomy to refuse, there was no true erotic relationship possible. Once again, the figure of the celestial courtesan was introduced as a theatrical convention to reconcile these two contradictory demands. Located in the heavens, the celestial courtesan falls outside the king's earthly dominion and as such retains her autonomy. This was also the reason that well-known exalted epic heroes were made necessary as characters in the *nāṭaka*. Celestial courtesans consorting with well-known earthly figures, even if they were kings, would not appear believable, and as such, would get in the way of a play's aesthetic appreciation by the audience. One of the literary devices to bring a celestial courtesan down to earth was to have her receive a curse for some fault that would require her to spend time in this world.[88] The *Nāṭyaśāstra* states that when celestial women came in contact with human beings on earth they assume the emotions of human beings.[89] As residents of heaven, they could leave the king at will and return to heaven. Kings, though, could not enter heaven as and when they wished.

The theatrical convention of investing celestial courtesans with supernatural powers, such as the ability to become invisible, was also used as a device to embellish their autonomy by making them elusive. The *Nāṭyaśāstra* says, "While remaining invisible, she should [tempt her lover] with flowers, ornaments, and her voice, and then making herself visible for a moment, she should disappear. The hero (*nāyaka*) is driven mad with dresses, ornaments, garlands, letters, and by other similar means."[90] The *Nāṭyaśāstra* very directly states the reason for using such literary-stage devices: "That love (*kāma*) which comes out of being driven mad is more pleasing. That love which arises naturally does not produce such intense feelings."[91] What drives the king as erotic hero mad in such a situation is precisely the elusiveness of the beloved, who seems inaccessible; ever present but just beyond his reach. With the king as the erotic hero, fear of losing one's beloved is not created by the presence of rivals, but by the elusiveness of the celestial courtesan. Also, if the king were to be solicitous to an earthly courtesan, it would appear unseemly and unrealistic. But if the same king were to be solicitous to a celestial courtesan, a figure endowed with the halo of the heavenly world, it would be acceptable.

The *Nāṭyaśāstra* had to invent so many theatrical conventions for the royal romance (*nāṭaka*) precisely because it wanted to base this romance on the same erotic ethos that was found in the popular romance (*prakaraṇa*) between a courtesan and her male patron, the dandy-consort (*vaiśika*). It was an attempt to transform the king into a royal dandy on stage. The *nāṭaka* was really a *prakaraṇa* with the king as the erotic-romantic hero. The *prakaraṇa* did not need any literary device to create a realistic erotic affair, because in the relationship between a dandy-consort and a regular courtesan, jealousy and fear were natural emotions. The erotic ethos in the popular romance was in complete continuity with the historical context in which erotics itself was born. If the royal romance (*nāṭaka*) needed the invention of so many theatrical conventions then that was because the figure of the king, otherwise alien to the domain of erotics as reflected in the *Kāmasūtra* and the *bhāṇas*, had to be transformed into an erotic hero, a royal dandy, on stage. The figure of the celestial courtesan was nothing more than a theatrical ruse to introduce the figure of the courtesan into the royal romance. The story of Urvaśī offers the clearest evidence of precisely how a popular romance was transformed into a royal romance. It is the *prakaraṇa*, therefore, that carries the history of the origin of theater within it in a way the *nāṭaka* cannot.

Since the *Nāṭyaśāstra* locates itself primarily within the royal romance and the figure of the king as its erotic-romantic hero, quite naturally it reduces the question of the origin of theater to the origin of *nāṭaka* as royal romance. And, since the earthly world of the king in the epics and the celestial world of the gods and celestial courtesans form a continuum, it is not surprising that the story of theater's origin would also reflect that. This was how classical Sanskrit theater in India came to have a divine origin. Given its royal perspective, the *Nāṭyaśāstra* felt compelled to hide the popular historical origin of theater. Admittedly, it did so somewhat absentmindedly, because the signs of the courtesan being the mother of theater in classical India are scattered all over this encyclopaedic text.

The Courtesan in the Harem and the Royal Romance

The two most important things evident in the story of the celestial courtesan Urvaśī discussed earlier were, first, that she brought the art of theater to the royal harem on earth before Bharata, and second, she did so while living in the royal harem as the king's erotic companion. The identity of Urvaśī as a celestial courtesan may give these details that are of immense significance the appearance of a fiction, but both of them are based on real historical experience. The art of theater was indeed brought into the royal harem by courtesans, and kings did in fact live in close enough proximity with courtesans to have erotic relationships with them. All attempts at camouflaging her identity notwithstanding, if the *nāṭaka* could not abandon the figure of the courtesan despite all the inconveniences and awkwardness she caused, then that was also because she was a close companion to the king in real life. As is evident in the *Nāṭyaśāstra* itself, it was his intimate association with the courtesan that transformed the king into a royal dandy, the hero of the *nāṭaka* as royal romance. Just as the *prakaraṇa* was grounded in the erotic affair between the courtesan and her dandy-consort, the *nāṭaka* was also historically anchored in the king's relationship with the courtesan.

One of the most revealing details in this story of Urvaśī is that she introduced the art of theater into the royal harem as the center of the king's private realm, not the royal court as the king's public realm. Theater, in other words, was located in the private realm of the king, which was also the realm of sexual-erotic pleasure (*kāma*), not in his public realm, grounded as it was in political power (*artha*) and centered on the royal court. Notice that the location of theater in the royal harem as part of the private realm of the king is consistent with the rules regarding the narrative-plot of the *nāṭaka*: it was not the king grounded in political power, best reflected in the royal court, that was to be the subject of a *nāṭaka*, but the private erotic affairs of the king. The path from the *prakaraṇa* to the *nāṭaka*, therefore, goes through the royal harem; the institution of the royal harem is the historical bridge between the popular romance and the royal romance.

A close reading of the *Nāṭyaśāstra* reveals that the courtesan was an important figure in the royal harem. The *Nāṭyaśāstra* offers an elaborate list of women associated with the king in various capacities: "I shall now describe the classes and functions of women who have dealings with the king. They are the chief queen (*mahādevī*), other queens (*devī*), other highborn wives (*svāminī*), ordinary wives (*sthāyinī*), concubines (*bhoginī*), craftswomen (*śilpakārinī*), actresses (*nāṭakīyā*), dancers (*nartakī*), maids in constant attendance (*anucārikā*), maids of special work (*paricārikā*), maids for running errands (*preṣanacārikā*), matrons (*mahattarās*), ushers (*praharīs*), maidens (*kumārī*), old dames (*sthāvirās*), and women overseers (*āyuktikās*)."[92]

In this list of women in the royal harem, the figure of the *nāṭakīyā* is the most important for our purposes. The term *nāṭakīyā* could be simply translated as a "theater woman." The term *nāṭakīyā* is significant for another reason: it is derived from the word *nāṭaka,* or the royal romance. As derivative from the word *nāṭaka*, the term *nāṭakīyā* would mean a woman associated with the *nāṭaka* or the performance of the *nāṭaka* as a particular genre of plays. It is likely that she received this name because of her job involving staging of *nāṭakas* in the royal theater located in the harem.

The *Nāṭyaśāstra* gives a brief profile of this theater woman:

> Women who have physical beauty, good qualities, generosity, feminine charm, patience, and good manners, and who possess soft, sweet, and charming voice, and varying notes in her throat, and who are experts in the representation of passion (*helā*), and feeling (*bhāva*), know well of representation of the temperament (*sattva*), have sweetness of manners, are skilled in playing musical instruments, have a knowledge of notes, rhythm (*tāla*), and pause (*yati*), and are associated with a teacher (*ācāryaupasevikāh*), clever, skilled in acting, capable of using reasoning positive and negative (*uhāpoha*) and have youthful age with beauty, are known as actresses (*nāṭakīyā*).[93]

All the attributes of a good *nāṭakīyā* are related to her job as performer in the royal theater. It may appear from this profile that a *nāṭakīyā* could be any woman so long as she had the required skills. Moreover, the presence of the teacher (*ācārya*) may suggest that anyone with an interest in learning the art of theater could have done so and found a job in the royal theater.

However, a close reading of the text reveals that in offering this profile of the theater woman (*nāṭakīyā*) in the royal harem the figure that the *Nāṭyaśāstra* had in view was none other than the courtesan. The parallel between the *nāṭakīyā* and the *gaṇikā,* a member of the most accomplished class of courtesans, is evident in the brief portrait that the *Nāṭyaśāstra* gives of the *gaṇikā* when elaborating on how this figure should be represented on stage: "A woman who is ever attentively engaged with the teacher in connection with the performance of arts, and is endowed with graceful movements, emotion, feeling, temperament, discipline, and charm, and is possessed of the sixty-four arts, is deft in dealing with the king, free from female diseases, sweet spoken, clear in speech, dexterous, and tireless is called a courtesan (*gaṇikā*)."[94]

In interpreting this portrait, one ought to keep in mind that the *Nāṭyaśāstra* sought to draw a stereotypical profile of the courtesan as *gaṇikā* prevalent in the society at the time. After all, the purpose of this portrait was to present the *gaṇikā* in such a way that people could instantly recognize her on stage as one. The idea, therefore, was not to embellish her character or to exaggerate her accomplishments. According to the *Nāṭyaśāstra*, the courtesan as *gaṇikā* is one who is endowed with all the skills necessary to express emotions, feelings, and temperament essential for a theater actress. It is evident from this portrait that the characteristics of a good theater actress, which were attributed to the theater woman (*nāṭakīyā*), and indeed to celestial courtesans in the origin narrative of the *Nāṭyaśāstra,* were in fact the characteristics of the courtesan of the highest rank (*gaṇikā*), a well-known figure in the cities of India at the time.

It is also significant that when giving a portrait of the figure of the *gaṇikā*, the *Nāṭyaśāstra* focuses on her passion for learning different forms of arts and crafts. Just like in the portrait of the theater woman (*nāṭakīyā*), the figure of the teacher (*ācārya*) figures prominently in the profile of the courtesan (*gaṇikā*) too. The courtesan is described as a devoted student always attending on her teacher in connection with learning different arts and crafts. The courtesan's devotion to her teacher corresponds to her devotion to learning and knowledge of arts. It is striking that the *Nāṭyaśāstra* singles out the courtesan as the one who is defined by her passion to learn, especially the arts. The portrait of a courtesan emphasizing her passion for learning, rather than her sexual skills, upsets the commonsensical view of this figure. In her devotion to her teacher, the only other historical figure that comes to mind is that of a young student living at his teacher's hermitage in strict celibacy. Knowledge in ancient Indian tradition is often associated with an ascetic lifestyle and celibacy. The courtesan's case was exactly the opposite. It is also important to note that she is the only female figure who is associated with a desire to learn and a dedication to her teacher in such a central way. Why should the courtesan, anchored in sexual-erotic pleasure, be devoted to learning the fine arts, unless erotics itself had been subtly and imperceptibly transformed into a form of aesthetics in her life? It is the clearest evidence that a whole system of knowledge—primarily of the arts—had come to be formed around the figure of the courtesan. A celebrated *gaṇikā* effortlessly straddled the worlds of both the fine arts and erotics. In her life, the arts and erotics became parts of a single continuum.

Notice also the *Nāṭyaśāstra's* statement that a *gaṇikā* needs to be good at dealing with the king. It is clear that *gaṇikās* were known and expected to be closely associated with kings. If they were in fact merely professional theater artists, there would have been no need for the *Nāṭyaśāstra* to emphasize this special skill in particular. Evidently, *gaṇikās* were more than just theater artists for the king. This requirement reflects the practice of kings having erotic relationships with courtesans who were also at the same time associated with the theater in the royal harem. It is simply a euphemism for the fact that *gaṇikās* could and did have erotic relationships with kings.

These details relating to courtesans in the royal harem, including the royal theater, given in the *Nāṭyaśāstra* are confirmed by the *Arthaśāstra*, the founding text of the discourse of political power in ancient India. It has an entire chapter dedicated to matters relating to courtesans. Here is an instruction to the officer in charge of managing the affairs of courtesans: "He should provide a livelihood from the royal coffers to those who instruct courtesans, female slaves, and actresses in the following skills: singing; playing musical instruments; reciting; dancing; acting; writing; painting; playing the lute, flute, and drum; reading another's mind; preparing perfumes and garlands; conversation; shampooing; and the arts of a courtesan."[95] The *Arthaśāstra* clearly instructs the state officer to appoint teachers who will teach courtesans (*gaṇikās*) varieties of art at the expense of the state. Notice also that instruction in various arts—acting, dance, singing, playing various musical instruments, and painting—constitutes the major part of her training. Since theater in ancient India had music and dance as its essential elements, a courtesan needed to be very accomplished in them.

There were, however, some other skills, like shampooing, making garlands, and preparing perfumes, that the courtesan also needed to acquire. These skills—particularly shampooing—are not directly relevant for her job as a figure of great artistic accomplishment. However, they would have been necessary if she were also to serve the king as his personal attendant, looking after various aspects of his daily routine. If one looks at the list of women employed in the royal harem, cited at the beginning of this section, in light of this possibility, it is clear that a number of them may have been courtesans. At least seven of the functions listed there could have been fulfilled by courtesans with varieties of skills and accomplishments: concubines, craftswomen, actresses, dancers, personal maids, special maids, and maids for running errands. That was perhaps the reason why some of the figures and functions in the royal harem were interchangeable. According to the *Nāṭyaśāstra*, "Women in the royal harem who attend all the movements of the king should be employed, when they are proficient in performing all classes of dance, in the [royal] theater under the authority of the harem."[96] It appears that if a personal attendant of the king, following him closely in his daily routine, happened to know or learned dancing, she could also be employed in the royal theater as a *nāṭakīyā* or theater woman under the authority of the harem. It becomes quite evident why the *Nāṭyaśāstra* included the skill to deal with the king as one of the necessary skills of a courtesan—because she could be needed to serve the king as his personal attendant. Clearly, the courtesans were ubiquitous in the royal harem.

It appears that apart from serving the king as his personal attendant, the courtesan played two primary roles in the royal household: as the secret lover of the king and also as the primary bearer of the theater of love in the royal harem. It was in the figure of the courtesan that the king's erotic and aesthetic pleasure was grounded. Recall that these two roles were inseparably tied together in the story of Urvaśī's erotic relationship with the king Purūravas: she was both the elusive lover of the king and the one who brought theater to the royal harem. Like Urvaśī, a *gaṇikā* could not be transformed into a wife without setting off a scandal and threatening the very legitimacy of the state and kingship. There was a limit to the power of the state. Even as a courtesan could not refuse to serve the king in an erotic role, nevertheless, the fact that she could not be transformed into a wife made her elusive: she could not be made part of the king's identity and family like the wife; despite her inability to refuse, she still lived outside the circle of the king's identity. She could not be made part of the discourse of Brahmanical law (*dharma*). Since a courtesan could not refuse the king, it is not she who came in the way, but the discourse of *dharma*. In other words, the elusiveness of the courtesan in the royal harem did not reflect her personal freedom, but was derived from the discourse of *dharma*. The same elusiveness is made to appear as the courtesan's personal freedom as soon as she morphs into a celestial courtesan in the royal romance as a genre.

In light of the nature of the courtesan's presence, it is quite evident that the story of Urvaśī is a dramatization of the real, though also secret, erotic relations between the king and the courtesan within the royal harem. All the theatrical conventions that came to be attached to the *nāṭaka* as a genre were due to the existing discursive censor that prohibited the king to be shown in a relationship with a courtesan. The mutation of the *prakaraṇa* into the *nāṭaka*, thus, came in the wake and as a result of the absorption of the public figure of the courtesan into the royal harem and the transformation of popular theater into private royal theater. Just as a member of the elite class in the city was transformed into a dandy as a consort of the courtesan, the figure of the king too came to be transformed into a royal dandy in the company of the courtesan. It was not just in its plot that this theater was a theater of love, but also in its location in the royal harem. It is not surprising, therefore, that theater as the premier genre of art found its place first in the royal harem, the erotic domain of the king, not in the public domain of the royal court. It was in the figure of the courtesan and by way of erotics that art and aesthetics made their entry into the royal household, and then later into the royal court.

The *Kāmasūtra* in the *Nāṭyaśāstra*

The extent of the continuity between the *Nāṭyaśāstra* and the *Kāmasūtra* could be gauged from the fact that a brief discourse on erotics resembling the *Kāmasūtra* is included within the *Nāṭyaśāstra*. The historical origin of theater in the domain of erotics is not just reflected in the figures—the courtesan, the dandy-consort, and the dandy-guru—that are common to both the *Kāmasūtra* as the founding text of erotics and the *Nāṭyaśāstra* as the founding text of theater; it is also reflected in the approach to the notion of pleasure that is at the heart of both these texts. There are two kinds of pleasure discussed in the *Nāṭyaśāstra*: *rasa,* or aesthetic pleasure, and *kāma,* or sexual-erotic pleasure.[97] Given that it is the founding text on theater, a discussion of aesthetic pleasure (*rasa*) in the *Nāṭyaśāstra* is entirely understandable. What is intriguing, however, is its extensive and involved discussion and elaboration of erotic pleasure and ways of securing it, in precisely the two chapters that focus on the two most important types of plays, the royal romance and the popular romance.

The presence of a discourse on erotics in the *Nāṭyaśāstra* raises two questions. Why should this founding work on theater and aesthetics contain a book on erotics? What does it say about the nature and origin of theater? Also, why should that discussion on erotics be placed in the chapters on the two most important forms of plays, the royal romance and the popular romance? If the object was simply to construct an erotic narrative-plot for a play or to offer instructions for playing erotic roles, there was no need for the *Nāṭyaśāstra* to delve into the question of sexual-erotic pleasure as such. Yet the *Nāṭyaśāstra* seems very concerned about determining the nature of this pleasure and securing its rightful place in the broader scheme of life. It was as if in sexual-erotic pleasure the being of aesthetic pleasure itself hung in the balance. More than its philosophical orientation, in the affinity that it draws between the two pleasures—sexual-erotic and aesthetic—the *Nāṭyaśāstra* reveals its own origin and the origin of the theater it elaborates.

It is remarkable that the *Nāṭyaśāstra* discusses the same topics within the larger theme of erotics that one also finds in the *Kāmasūtra*. Just to mention a few important ones: the *Nāṭyaśāstra* offers a definition of erotic pleasure (*kāma*) and elaborates on it; it discusses the place of *kāma* within the trilogy (*trivarga*) that includes Brahmanical law (*dharma*) and political power (*artha*); it engages in a theoretical discussion of sexual-erotic pleasure and its relationship with the mind; it lays out different types of actresses named after various animals; it elaborates on ways of seducing a woman; it describes signs of love in women; it elaborates on ten stages of love; it offers instructions on the employment of messengers in erotic affairs. Last but not least, it also mentions and discusses the figures of the courtesan, the fallen wife, the dandy-consort, and the dandy-guru.[98]

Although, the *Nāṭyaśāstra's* discussion of pleasure does not always follow the *Kāmasūtra*, the primacy and sovereignty of erotic pleasure (*kāma*) is the foundation of theatrical discourse as much as it was of erotic discourse. As I discussed in the last chapter, for the *Kāmasūtra kāma* was in direct conflict with the discourse of Brahmanical law (*dharma*). However, rather than directly claiming the sovereignty of erotic pleasure over *dharma*, the *Kāmasūtra* had taken a subtle and indirect way: it claimed the sovereignty of the figure of the courtesan in the field of erotic pleasure. Unlike the *Kāmasūtra*, the *Nāṭyaśāstra* is bolder and more direct in claiming the sovereignty of erotic pleasure over *dharma*: "[While] ascetic practices (*tapas*) are for the sake of religious merit (*dharma*), religious merit (*dharma*) is for the sake of happiness. Happiness has its source in women with whom erotic union is desired."[99] Here happiness (*sukha*) is understood to be the final end, the end of all ends; all other ends, such as *dharma* and *artha*, are subordinated to it. And though the *Nāṭyaśāstra* uses the word happiness (*sukham*), it leaves no doubt that what it had in view was the same as erotic pleasure, because in the second half of the same verse it goes on to add that women are the source of happiness. The same thought is repeated once again in a verse that says, "In this world one always desires happiness (*sukham*). And women are the source of happiness."[100] Since women are designated to be the primary source of happiness, it is evident that the *Nāṭyaśāstra* understands happiness primarily—perhaps, even exclusively—as erotic happiness. The union of man and woman is, after all, grounded in sexual-erotic pleasure (*kāma*).[101]

The historical kinship and continuity of the *Nāṭyaśāstra* with the *Kāmasūtra* also extends beyond their common characters into the realm of categories: parallel to sexual-erotic pleasure in the *Kāmasūtra*, the *Nāṭyaśāstra* declared *rasa*, or aesthetic pleasure, to be the ground of classical theater. In the centuries to come, this notion of aesthetic pleasure became the very foundation of aesthetics in India. But the continuities extended farther still: the *Nāṭyaśāstra* went on to define aesthetic pleasure as an event of the dissolution or loss of self and identity, or, to use Foucault's phrase, an event of desubjectivation. It states that aesthetic pleasure is born when a set of emotions are "imbued with the quality of universality (*sāmānyaguṇayogena*)."[102] The key word here is "*sāmānya*," which means common or general, that is to say, not individual or personal. Aesthetic pleasure, in other words, is an event of de-individualization or depersonalization of emotions that are otherwise individual or personal, that is to say, grounded in the self. Recall that the courtesan was also called *sāmānyā*, or the one who is common, a woman who is located outside the circle of caste and patriarchal identity. It is not a coincidence that one of the most critical words in the philosophy of aesthetic pleasure is also used to designate the courtesan. In the word *sāmānya*, the theory of aesthetic pleasure carries its historical birthmark.

The *Nāṭyaśāstra*'s insistence on elevating erotic pleasure above all the other ontological domains of life should not be seen as an instance of rhetorical excess without any consequence. On the contrary, this insistence is very revealing, particularly in light of two things. First, given the inseparability of erotic and aesthetic pleasure in the *Nāṭyaśāstra*, in raising erotic pleasure to the top of the hierarchy, it also raised aesthetic pleasure above the other ontological imperatives. Second, this insistence amounts to a subtle deterritorialization of the king and the state from the discourse of political power (*artha*) and their reterritorialization on erotic-aesthetic pleasure (*kāma*). In other words, the *Nāṭyaśāstra* sought to subordinate the discourse of political power to the discourse of erotic-aesthetic pleasure. This was not a case of eroticization and aestheticization of power. On the contrary, it was an attempt to deploy power—that is to say, the king and the state—in the service of erotic-aesthetic pleasure. This is an instance of the hegemonic ambitions of the *Nāṭyaśāstra* to extend the jurisdiction of the discourse of erotic-aesthetic pleasure beyond its own confines to the other domains.

Conclusion

Contrary to the *Nāṭyaśāstra*'s presentation of its own origin, theater was neither a divine gift to humanity nor the invention of a lone genius. Rather, it was the result of a historical mutation that came to pass in the figures of the courtesan, the dandy-consort, and the dandy-guru. Even though the figure of the courtesan was known to have been an expert in as many as sixty-four arts, it was theater that remained at the heart of her existence. The notion of theater tied all aspects of her singularly complex life together into a perfect knot and gave rise simultaneously to the two traditions of theatrics-aesthetics in the *Nāṭyaśāstra* and erotics in the *Kāmasūtra*. If the *Nāṭyaśāstra* and the *Kāmasūtra* extended into each other, it was because the very being of the courtesan as a historical figure had theatrics-aesthetics and erotics as its two major aspects. Both the *Kāmasūtra* and the *Nāṭyaśāstra* pursued erotic and aesthetic pleasure in and through the figure of the courtesan beyond identity and truth. Just as Foucault asserted, truth and identity were brought under the sovereignty of pleasure as the final and only end. Even as every effort was made to make the story and characters—the identities—appear real and true on stage, it was also obvious that the story's only end was to produce pleasure in the audience.

Given the nature of its historical origins, the *Nāṭyaśāstra*, as the founding text of the discourse of theatrics, not surprisingly located itself directly within the broader domain of *kāma* as erotic-aesthetic pleasure, as if theatrics were only a branch of the larger field of erotics. Just as in the *Kāmasūtra*, in the *Nāṭyaśāstra,* too, it was the legislative primacy of erotic-aesthetic pleasure that was at stake. It was because the pursuit of sexual-erotic pleasure was already an aesthetic pursuit that it could give rise to such a powerful tradition of theater in ancient Indian culture. It is quite evident why the *Kāmasūtra* called sexual pleasure primarily a discursive phenomenon, as opposed to an entirely sensual phenomenon. What made sexual pleasure a discursive phenomenon was precisely what also made it an aesthetic phenomenon. It was because the relationship between the courtesan and her dandy-consort was as aesthetic as it was erotic that art became a medium of communication between them.

An assumed sense of evolution has prevented scholars and historians of ancient Indian theater from noticing the other—nonreligious—origin of the *Nāṭyaśāstra*. Given the centrality and dominance of the motif of love in the *Nāṭyaśāstra*, it is likely that historically the *Nāṭyaśāstra* came to be composed in the wake of the emergence of the *kaiśikī,* or erotic-romantic style. It was not the spectacle of battles between gods and demons that turned into a theater of love after a long period of evolution as a seed growing into a tree—it was the theater of love that retrospectively offered the old spectacle the status of its own prehistory.

While commenting on the status of the courtesan in classical India, E. Powys Mathers observed: "Being at once sensual and a mystic, the Hindu has always asked too much of his courtesans. He has not only required a beauty framed in every luxurious circumstance, an agitation of passion and its swooning pacification, but he also has expected sincerity and love. His too intense desire overleaps its object, and then reason proclaims that object to be illusion."[103] Mathers is correct in claiming that the courtesan in classical India was more than Freud's debased object of sexual pleasure. She was indeed a figure of love, sincere love. Mathers' observation would lead one to believe that once the courtesan's love was discovered to be nothing more than an illusion, a tragedy must inevitably follow. But what seems logically plausible was nevertheless historically not true. The classical Sanskrit theater of the *Nāṭyaśāstra* had no real notion of tragedy; nor could the *Kāmasūtra* see anything other than pleasure in the courtesan's love.

The real problem with Mathers' comments lies elsewhere: to foist the binary of reality and illusion or truth and falsehood on the courtesan's love is to impose on it a moral discourse while also losing sight of the discourses of *ars erotica* in the *Kāmasūtra* and *ars theatrica* in the *Nāṭyaśāstra* within which this love came to be understood in classical India. It is to think in terms of the ontology of truth and identity. Erotics in the *Kāmasūtra* and theatrics-aesthetics in the *Nāṭyaśāstra* were located outside the Aristotelian ontology based on the principle of noncontradiction, according to which "it is impossible for anyone to believe the same thing to be and not to be" (*Metaph* IV 3 1005b24).[104] The courtesan, contrary to this principle, was and was not the wife at the same time and to the same man. The discourses of *ars erotica* and *ars theatrica* were grounded in the ontology of pleasure. Under the sovereignty of pleasure, the notion of truth and falsehood, reality and appearance, are reduced to being strategic categories in the service of pleasure, exactly as Foucault had understood them to be in his definition of *ars erotica*. For Foucault, too, pleasure, as much as power, was an ontological category, while truth and self were strategic categories ever active in the service of power and pleasure. If tragedy is missing from the *Nāṭyaśāstra*, that is because there is no conflict in this theater of love that cannot be resolved with a deft use of its strategic categories of truth and appearance or reality and illusion, or, indeed, illusion as reality. Exactly where Mathers saw illusion, the classical India of the *Kāmasūtra* and the *Nāṭyaśāstra* built a theater of love.

5

The Dandy-Guru and the Birth of the Discourses of Erotics and Theater

The origins of erotics and theater in ancient India were historically and discursively so intimately intertwined that it is often difficult to tell these two discourses apart with respect to their beginnings. As the previous chapters have shown, just as the discourse of theater in India emerged as a branch of erotics, so too erotics was born as a theater of love. While the discourse of erotics found its most dominant and enduring form in the *Kāmasūtra*, the discourse of theater did so in the *Nāṭyaśāstra*. The courtesan, designated the sovereign figure in the domain of erotics by the *Kāmasūtra*, was just as central to the domain of theater as represented by the *Nāṭyaśāstra*. Given this shared origin, it is not surprising that the *Kāmasūtra* gave the technical designations of actor and actress to the male and female partners in an erotic affair without explaining itself, as if the logic of this otherwise puzzling choice ought to be self-evident to its readers. The history of erotics and theater is therefore best pursued together as two sides of one and the same historical phenomenon.

Until now the central question that has animated scholars with regard to the origins of the *Nāṭyaśāstra* and the *Kāmasūtra* has to do with determining the identity of the authors of the two texts, Bharata and Vātsyāyana. Were these just invented names that came to be attached to the two texts? One of the reasons that discussions relating to the origins of the *Kāmasūtra* and the *Nāṭyaśāstra* have not moved beyond the identity of the authors is that the two texts have been problematized as individual works, rather than located within broader discourses grounded in larger historical formations. The question about the origins of the *Kāmasūtra* and the *Nāṭyaśāstra* cannot be adequately problematized until erotics and theatrics are approached as two historically formed domains of discourses, of which these two texts are only a part. One, therefore, needs to make a distinction between the *Kāmasūtra* as a text and the broader discourse of pleasure, or *kāma,* as a historical phenomenon. As a text the *Kāmasūtra* may appear like the work of a great genius, but seen as a discourse, the same text is part of a historical phenomenon exceeding the genius of an individual author. The *Kāmasūtra* did not found the discourse of erotic pleasure. Rather, it came to exist in the space opened up by that discourse. The text of the *Kāmasūtra* needs to be placed within the discourse or discursive horizon which made it possible, and in which it came to be. The same applies to the *Nāṭyaśāstra* as a text within the larger discourse of theatrics.

What is most characteristic of a discourse—in contrast to a text—is that it is directly grounded in the one who speaks, in a historical subject. In it thoughts are also offered as a part of speech and in the form of speech; thoughts have not yet parted ways from the speaking subjects; thoughts are directly grounded in the subjects that enunciate them.[1] In a discourse, knowledge is directly grounded in historical figures. In contrast, when a text is seen as an individual author's singular creation, knowledge itself appears as an ahistorical and theoretical construction. The significance of the question about the identity of the authors of the *Nāṭyaśāstra* and the *Kāmasūtra* therefore lies not so much in the question of whether Bharata and Vātsyāyana were real persons, but rather in the question of the historical figures that were at the origins of the discourses of theater and erotics. In the determination of the identity of the historical figures, the nature and historical origins of both the *Nāṭyaśāstra* and the *Kāmasūtra* could be revealed.

In this chapter I show the construction of the two discourses of *ars erotica* and *ars theatrica* in and through the historical figure of the *viṭa,* or dandy-guru.[2] I argue that it was in the figure of the dandy-guru that the existence of the courtesan and the nature of her sexual-erotic relations with her patrons became a subject of intellectual reflection, a question of thought. The mere presence of courtesans and the fact that their lives resembled theater could not by themselves lead to the emergence of a discourse of erotics as theatrics in ancient Indian culture. Even though the discourses of both erotics as reflected in the *Kāmasūtra* and theater as reflected in the *Nāṭyaśāstra* were grounded in the being of the courtesan, the discourse of pleasure did not come to be articulated by her; she did not leave any treatises on either theater or erotics. Her own existence did not become an object of self-reflection for her. It was in the life of the dandy-guru that the courtesan's being came to be an object of thought. It was as if she found her self-consciousness in the figure of the dandy-guru.

The *viṭa* or dandy-guru is a complex and pivotal historical character that has failed to draw the attention of scholars of ancient Indian culture and history. Fortunately, a good many textual sources are still available that give us a vivid insight into this figure. The most important amongst such historical-literary sources are the four oldest extant *bhāṇas*—collectively referred to as the *Caturbhāṇī*, or "the Quartet of *Bhāṇas*"—one-act plays in which the dandy-guru appears as the sole character on stage.[3] It is in these *bhāṇas* that the precise historical context of the discourses of erotics and theater becomes vividly evident. The *bhāṇas* reveal in great detail and vividness what the *Kāmasūtra* meant in elevating the figure of the courtesan to the sovereign position in the domain of erotics. What appears like a theoretical exposition by a great author in the *Kāmasūtra* is evident in its historical-discursive form in the *bhāṇas*.

Given the complexity of the *viṭa* as a historical figure, the variety and depth of his intellectual interests, and the enormous amount of fascinating detail the four *bhāṇas* offer on him, a comprehensive enquiry into this figure would not be possible in a short chapter. In the context of this work, I can do no more than give a brief sketch of the *viṭa*, my essential purpose being to briefly lay out the nature of his relationship with both courtesans and the discourses of erotics and theater. I begin the chapter with an exploration of the figure of the *viṭa* in the *Nāṭyaśāstra* and show how the discourses of theater and erotics came to converge on the figure of the dandy-guru as the director of the theater of love. I then show through an analysis of the *bhāṇas* that it was the dandy-guru's quotidian relationship with the courtesan and his insatiable curiosity and love for her that transformed him into an archivist of her life, an advocate of the discourse of pleasure against that of power and Brahmanical law, and inevitably the ideal director in the theater of love that the *Nāṭyaśāstra* is grounded in.

The Dandy-Guru as Theater Director in the *Nāṭyaśāstra*

It is a remarkable fact overlooked by scholars of theater in India that the figures of the *viṭa* or dandy-guru of the courtesan and the theater director almost completely overlapped in the *Nāṭyaśāstra*: the *viṭa* was seen to possess all the skills of a theater director necessary to stage a play. This is significant because the director—perhaps even more than the playwright—was a central figure in the domain of theater in ancient India. Bharata, the author of the *Nāṭyaśāstra,* was himself primarily a director. In other words, it was primarily as a director that Bharata approached the art of theater in the *Nāṭyaśāstra*. Just as the figures of the actress and actor in the theater of love were historically anchored in the figures of the courtesan and her patron-consort, so the figure of the director was anchored in the historical figure of the dandy-guru.

The *Nāṭyaśāstra* leaves a clue regarding the historical origins of the theater director. While offering a brief portrait of the historical figure of the *viṭa*, or the dandy as the guru of the courtesan, the *Nāṭyaśāstra* says: "Possessing all the qualities that a director (*sūtradhāra*) is to have with regard to the theatrical production, the dandy-guru of the courtesan (*viṭa*) should be an expert in dealing with courtesans (*veśyopacāra*), sweet, impartial, a poet, proficient in the meaning of the *śāstras* and in the knowledge of the courtesans (*vaiśikeṣu*), capable of seeing the pros and cons of any argument, and eloquent and clever."[4] Notice that the *Nāṭyaśāstra* does not say the dandy-guru was, in fact, a director by profession; only that he had all the skills of a director to institute a theatrical performance. How did the dandy-guru come to have all these skills? Since he was not a director by profession, something about the very nature of his existence must have given the dandy-guru the skills of a theater director. In other words, it was perhaps as a dandy-guru that he became a director.

In the list of qualifications that one must possess to be a good director, the *Nāṭyaśāstra* also includes expertise in dealings with courtesans (*veśyopacāra*) and *ars erotica* (*kāmatantra*).[5] That the director must be expert in *ars erotica* is entirely understandable, given that theater as reflected in the *Nāṭyaśāstra* was primarily and for the most part a theater of love. Since sex was not to be represented on stage, by *ars erotica* the *Nāṭyaśāstra* does not mean the art of sex, but rather the art of love. However, two more questions remain to be answered: why did a director need to be an expert in dealing with courtesans and how did he acquire this expertise?

The answer to both these questions lies in the fact that *ars erotica* was still perhaps largely an oral tradition, and unlike a textual discourse, an oral discourse could not be separated from the figure in which it was anchored. An intimate relation with courtesans was imperative precisely because *ars erotica*, over which a theater director needed to have mastery, was not yet a textual tradition in the period before the second century CE and could not be learned from a text or by attending an academic institution. As *ars erotica* was still closely and intimately tied to its origins in the courtesan, one needed to be an expert in dealings with courtesans to be an expert in *ars erotica*. One could not have become an expert in *ars erotica* without also becoming involved with courtesans in an erotic relationship. In other words, before one could become a theater director by profession, one had to have had a long experience of apprenticeship as a dandy-consort to a courtesan (*vaiśika*, *nāyaka*). A theater director was likely to have been a former dandy-consort of a courtesan who had now become a *viṭa*, or dandy-guru. In what follows, I explore the nature of the *viṭa*'s extensive knowledge on erotics and the process by which he came to acquire it.

The Dandy-Guru in the *Bhāṇas* and the Discourse of Pleasure

The most important of the historical-literary sources that give a vivid portrayal of the figure of the *viṭa* or dandy-guru are, as mentioned above, the four oldest extant *bhāṇas*, or the *Caturbhāṇī*.[6] These *bhāṇas* are one-act plays in which the dandy-guru narrates to the audience his experiences in and around the courtesans' quarters, which he visits as part of his daily routine. In these *bhāṇas*, the dandy-guru—ever alert, excited, and impatient to move on—takes the audience with him on a journey through the courtesans' quarters and lets them in on his encounters with various figures, primarily courtesans, but also their patrons, lovers, mothers, and maids. He lets the audience in on his conversations with his interlocutors and also on his thoughts and feelings about what he sees and whom he meets.

Even though these *bhāṇas* are often presented as one-act monologue plays, strictly speaking they are not monologues at all, if the term monologue is meant to refer to speaking alone or speaking to oneself. The *bhāṇas* may appear to be monologues because it is one individual, the *viṭa* or dandy-guru, also the central character in the play, who presents these dialogues on stage. Also, the impression that the *bhāṇa* is a monologue is strengthened by the fact that the dandy-guru reproduces the conversations from his own perspective. However, a close look at the *bhāṇas* makes it clear that they are entirely made up of dialogues between two separate individuals, the dandy-guru most often being one of them. The narrative moves forward with the help of the dialogues in the form of conversations that the dandy-guru has with his numerous interlocutors on his way to or within the courtesans' quarters. On stage the dandy-guru takes on the roles of his interlocutors and delivers their dialogues himself.

The reason that the dialogical form of these *bhāṇas* is so important is because it is precisely this form that sets them apart from the *Nāṭyaśāstra* and the *Kāmasūtra* as two foundational texts in their fields. If one can use a loose analogy, the relationship between the *bhāṇas* and the more systematic and theoretical elaboration on the subject of pleasure in the *Nāṭyaśāstra* and the *Kāmasūtra* is somewhat similar to the relationship between the dialogues of Plato and the more systematic and academic exposition of philosophy in the works of Aristotle. And just as Plato's dialogues are embedded in the sociohistorical context and figures in which philosophy came to find its form, the *bhāṇas* also offer a vivid glimpse into the exact context and the social-historical figures in whom the discourse of pleasure—both erotic and aesthetic—came to be constituted.

It is not a mere coincidence that the *viṭa* is the leading figure in the *bhāṇas*. There is an essential historical connection between the figure of the dandy-guru and the content of these four *bhāṇas*. Literally, the word *bhāṇa* means "speech." But in this case it means specifically the speech of the dandy-guru. Of all the genres of plays, the *bhāṇas* are the only ones that are exclusively grounded in one historical figure. The overdetermining factor in the *bhāṇas* as a genre of plays is the figure of the dandy-guru, which cannot be replaced by any other character. The *bhāṇas* are not only about the dandy-guru but also about the world as seen, heard, and generally experienced by him. The narrative is born at the point of contact between the dandy-guru and the world. The other characters appear in the play only as they are refracted by his figure. While the dandy-guru speaks for himself on stage, the other characters in the play acquire a voice only through him. The dandy-guru has the final say, the ultimate judgment on the other characters in the play. In other words, what we see in the *bhāṇas* is the dandy-guru's experience and view of the world.

It is not too much to think that the *viṭa* is, in fact, the author of the *bhāṇas*. Given that the dandy-guru was not a common household figure, it would have been extremely difficult, perhaps impossible, for any author to put himself in the shoes of the dandy-guru and see the world from his eyes. And the success of the author as a playwright of the *bhāṇas* depended entirely on how well he could see the world with the eyes of the dandy-guru. What would have rendered an imitation of the dandy-guru even more difficult was that these plays were based on an intimate knowledge of courtesans that he had accumulated over the decades. The countless experiences with courtesans that had shaped the ethos and thoughts of the dandy-guru over many years would have been impossible for anyone else to reconstruct with the help of imagination. Moreover, the *bhāṇa* being a realistic genre, a rare phenomenon in ancient India, knowledge of the subject played a far more important role in its composition than imagination. There is therefore a likely identity between the dandy-guru and the author of the *bhāṇas*. The discursive identity of the dandy-guru and the author is clearly evident in one of the *bhāṇas*, the *Pādatāḍitaka*, in which the director introduces the play by stating that it was written by Śyāmilaka.[7] What is significant is that in the same *bhāṇa* the director also starts the play by presenting Śyāmilaka, a "baldheaded leader of the dandy-gurus (*viṭas*)" presiding over a large assembly of dandy-gurus that had met to resolve an urgent matter of concern relating to a complaint received from a Brahmin, customer of a courtesan, who accused her of insulting him.[8] The director presents Śyāmilaka as announcing the issue to be discussed in the assembly with the striking of a gong. It cannot be a mere coincidence that the author of this *bhāṇa* shares his name with the leader of the dandy-gurus in his own work. There is a clear intent in the *bhāṇa* to establish the identity of the author as a leading figure in the community of *viṭas*. The question for us is not whether the real individual known as Śyāmilaka was both the author of the *bhāṇa* and also a dandy-guru at the same time. What is more important is that even if the author was not really a dandy-guru himself, he found it entirely in the logic of things that he could have been one.

Not unlike many other texts from ancient India, there is uncertainty about the exact dates of these *bhāṇas*. There has been considerable debate on this subject.[9] As important as the precise dating of these *bhāṇas* may be in itself, this issue is not exactly central to my concerns here for various reasons. First of all, one needs to make a distinction between the *bhāṇas* as a genre of plays and the four extant *bhāṇas* that I am going to focus on. In including the *bhāṇa* as one of the ten established types of play, the *Nāṭyaśāstra* clearly acknowledged that the *bhāṇa* long preceded its own composition and compilation. It is significant that the *Nāṭyaśāstra* points out that what it has to say about the *bhāṇa* is entirely in accordance with the well-established tradition. This reference to tradition reveals that the *bhāṇas* had been long in existence before the *Nāṭyaśāstra* itself came to be composed. As for the four *bhāṇas* that I discuss, they are increasingly recognized as having been composed during the Gupta period, which puts them approximately within the same chronological range as the *Kāmasūtra* and the *Nāṭyaśāstra*. My focus is more on the *bhāṇas* as a genre than on the subtle variations and differences between them. In any case, when it comes to the *bhāṇas* the common themes they deal with are of far more importance than these rather superficial differences.

Another reason why a precise dating is not critical for my purposes is that I approach the *bhāṇas* from the perspective of the historical figure of the dandy-guru, the narrator and protagonist in the *bhāṇas*. There would have been no *bhāṇas* without this figure of the dandy-guru being already present. In other words, just as the *bhāṇas* precede the composition of the *Nāṭyaśāstra*, so too the origin and evolution of the figure of the dandy-guru also preceded the *bhāṇas* as a literary-theatrical form of discourse. Indeed his figure may well have preceded the *bhāṇas* by centuries because the *bhāṇa* as a genre appears to be the culmination of his long evolution. Both the *Nāṭyaśāstra* and the *Kāmasūtra* not only directly mention the dandy-guru but also put him in a critical position. A historical figure as complex and accomplished as the dandy-guru would have taken centuries to develop.

The Dandy-Guru as the Old Dandy-Consort

In order to understand the nature and origin of the discourse of erotic pleasure in the figure of the *viṭa* or dandy-guru, one must first grasp the precise nature of his relationship with the courtesan. After all, the discourse of erotic pleasure developed by the dandy-guru was not an exercise in theory, but was directly grounded in the figure of the courtesan. What was it about the nature of this relationship that allowed him to construct a discourse of erotic pleasure with her at its center? After all, as I discussed in the last two chapters, it was the figure of the dandy-consort (*vaiśika*, *nāyaka*) that emerged as the male counterpart of the courtesan and, as such, appeared closest to her. Given his closeness and intimacy, why did the figure of the dandy-consort not emerge as the historical medium through whom the discourse of erotics came to be articulated? Also, how exactly was the dandy-guru related to the dandy-consort of the courtesan?

In the *Kāmasūtra* the dandy-guru is described as a married man who lived with his family and earned his living as a teacher-adviser to courtesans and as a companion to the city dandy (*nāgaraka*).[10] Although the word *nāgaraka*, literally translated, means a "man of the city," this man was none other, as I discuss in the next chapter, than what the *Nāṭyaśāstra* called the dandy-consort of the courtesan (*vaiśika*). In the *bhāṇas*, in contrast, the male companions of courtesans were simply referred to as *kāmījana*, or pleasure seekers.[11] If the *Kāmasūtra* gave the same historical figure a new name, that was because of its larger social vision of the city based on art that required an agent. From the *Kāmasūtra*'s account, the dandy-guru seems equally close to both the courtesan and her patron-consort. Given his closeness to both, he functioned as the bridge between them and so was in an ideal position to know them intimately and understand the nature of their relationship.

In the *bhāṇas*, the dandy-guru is typically an old man. Not all dandy-gurus, it seems, were comfortable with their old age. Sometimes the dandy-gurus in the *bhāṇas* seem reluctant to acknowledge their advancing age and try various means to hide it to continue to look young.[12] They would often dye their hair or try to cover their baldness.[13] This made them vulnerable to ridicule from fellow dandy-gurus who did not miss an opportunity to make fun of them.[14] In general, however, it appears that the dandy-guru had left his years of pursuing sexual-erotic pleasure behind him or else it was no longer a very important part of his daily routine as a teacher-adviser to courtesans.

Also, the dandy-guru is invariably shown to be an extremely poor man who can barely manage to make ends meet for himself and his family. Indeed, his poverty seems to be one of his defining characteristics. And of course, without the money one could not expect to enter into an erotic relationship with a courtesan. In other words, the near absence of sexual-erotic relationships between dandy-gurus and courtesans may also have been, at least partly, a function of the former's poverty. According to the *Kāmasūtra*, having spent all his wealth, the dandy-guru had come to depend for his livelihood on courtesans and the city dandy. It should be noted that in making this observation, the *Kāmasūtra* did not have an individual dandy-guru in view, but the dandy-guru as a type, as a social-historical figure. It appears, therefore, that dandy-gurus usually came from a rich background but went on to lose their wealth, perhaps due to their lifestyle.

The *Nāṭyaśāstra* also confirms this impression of the dandy-guru as a wealthy man who had fallen on bad times. As I discussed earlier, the *Nāṭyaśāstra* attached a long list of accomplishments to the figure of the dandy-guru: mastery of *śāstras* as the highest genre of knowledge in major fields such as Brahmanical law (*dharma*) and political power (*artha*), eloquence, good judgment in intellectual arguments, skills as a poet, and cultivated speech and manners. These accomplishments must have required long years of learning and cultivation, which could only have been possible if the dandy-guru had an upper-class origin and upbringing. This description of the dandy-guru raises three questions: how did the dandy-guru lose his wealth and enter such a state of destitution? Also, of all the options available to him to make a living as a poor man, why did he choose to become a teacher-adviser to the courtesan and her dandy-consort? After all, this choice of a job would have been considered an unlikely one for someone who had experienced social respectability as a young man. And finally, how did he acquire the skill to become a bridge between the courtesan and her patron?

The dandy-guru's job as the link between the courtesan and her patron must have required an immense amount of knowledge and deep familiarity with courtesans' lives and the lives of their patrons. This was not theoretical-textual knowledge that the dandy-guru could have acquired from books or from academic institutions. The figure of the dandy-guru, after all, had emerged long before the composition and compilation of the *Kāmasūtra*, which could have been of some help. In other words, direct experience was the only way for the dandy-guru to acquire the knowledge required to do the job for his patrons in pursuit of erotic pleasure. That would suggest a long and deep association and intimacy with courtesans and their patrons. In other words, one would have been in a position to become a teacher-adviser to courtesans as an old man only if one had also spent one's years as a young man in their company. Although there were many ways to be associated with courtesans, the best and most important way for a young man to develop a deep and intimate connection with a courtesan was to be her lover-consort. This is particularly likely because the dandy-guru had been wealthy as a young man and it would also explain how he came to lose his wealth: he squandered his money on courtesans in pursuit of sexual-erotic pleasure.

This figure of the dandy-guru, it turns out, was none other than what the *Nāṭyaśāstra* identified as *vaiśika* and the *Kāmasūtra* as *nāyaka,* or the dandy-consort of the courtesan. With old age, it was this figure of the young lover-consort of the courtesan that morphed into the figure of the teacher-adviser to courtesans (*viṭa*).[15] That would also explain how he came to acquire the intimate knowledge of courtesans and their patrons that would enable him to work as a teacher-adviser to them. The courtesans and their patrons were typically young and needed the help of someone experienced in this field to help them. It would then appear that the lover-consort of the courtesan and the dandy-guru were not two different individuals, but two stages of the same individual in his association with courtesans.

There is an excellent example in one of the *bhāṇas* of the slow morphing of the figure of the *vaiśika* into that of the *viṭa.*[16] Viśvālaka is introduced as a man who had lost all his wealth in the course of his long association with courtesans.[17] Although not young any more, he still lived with an aging courtesan who found it difficult to get new patrons.[18] Viśvālaka, in other words, represents the figure of the dandy-consort of the courtesan. The dandy-guru in the *bhāṇa* seems to be extremely familiar with, and fond of, Viśvālaka, who, in turn, sees the dandy-guru as his teacher and holds him with the same kind of reverence that one would be expected to have for religious teachers. It is quite evident that Viśvālaka frequently sought out the dandy-guru's views on complex issues relating to different aspects of erotics and looked up to him as his role model. When the dandy-guru was about to take his leave after a conversation on various issues relating to erotics, Viśvālaka and his wife fell on his feet, both as a mark of their respect for him and as an effort to persuade him to stay and share more of his wisdom with them.[19] Viśvālaka, in other words, was an apprentice to the dandy-guru and was well on his way to becoming recognized as a *viṭa* himself.[20] The *viṭa* was thus a teacher not just to courtesans but also to former dandy-consorts of courtesans on the way to joining the ranks of the dandy-gurus.

The Dandy-Guru, the Courtesan, and the Sovereignty of Pleasure in the *Bhāṇas*

Experienced and wise in the ways of erotics, the dandy-guru, over time, thus came to be the teacher-adviser of the courtesan. And though it was indeed a source of his livelihood, the dandy's being was not exhausted by his job. The relationship between the courtesan and the dandy-guru was not transactional. Rather it was existential in nature. Even a casual reading of the *bhāṇas* reveals in stark terms that being a dandy-guru was an existential necessity—not a professional choice. Even though the dandy-guru as a relatively old man was mostly no longer in an erotic relationship with courtesans, it only seems to have added to the range and depth of his relationship with them. It is in the precise nature of this existential relationship between the dandy-guru and the courtesan that the clue to the origin of the discourses of erotics and theater lies buried.

Of all the social figures, the dandy-guru elevates the courtesan—not the king, as the *Nāṭyaśāstra* seems to do—in the most emphatic terms to the status of the sovereign figure in the discourse of erotic pleasure in the *bhāṇas*. It was in the *bhāṇas* that the discourse of erotic pleasure and the figure of the courtesan were joined together by the dandy-guru. It was also in the *bhāṇas* that the life of the courtesan became an object of minute observation, documentation, and reflection. Given that the *bhāṇa* as a genre preceded both the *Nāṭyaśāstra* and the *Kāmasūtra*, it was in the *bhāṇas* that the discursive sovereignty of erotic pleasure (*kāma*) as one of the trilogy—Brahmanical law (*dharma*) and political power (*artha*) being the other two—was announced much before those two iconic texts came to confirm it. Of the four *bhāṇas* two begin with elaborate invocations of the god of erotic pleasure, simply referred to as *kāma*.[21]

The sovereignty of *kāma*, or pleasure, and courtesans in the *bhāṇas* and the precise role of the dandy-guru in them come together in the opening scene of the *Pādatāḍitaka* in the words of the dandy-guru, who has just called an assembly of dandy-gurus to attention with the striking of a gong. The assembly is to discuss the complaint from a Brahmin who feels disrespected by a courtesan who had struck him on the head with her foot in the course of a love quarrel. Unfamiliar with the ways of love, the Brahmin brought his case to the assembly of the dandy-gurus seeking remedy. As if mocking the complainant and giving a hint of the nature of debate to follow, the leader of the assembly welcomes his fellow dandy-gurus assembled to discuss this apparently thorny but really hilarious complaint with these words: "Hail to the banner of the god of pleasure, the upraised foot [to strike the head of her lover in a mock erotic quarrel] of a coquettish woman adorned with an anklet, the foot that needs to be worshipped."[22] As the banner of the god of love or erotic pleasure (*kāma*), the raised foot of the woman, a courtesan, appears as a symbol of that god's sovereignty. It is the erotic equivalent of the upraised hand of a deity in a gesture of benediction to his devotee. It was because the courtesan emerged as the sovereign figure in the domain of erotics that her upraised foot ready to strike her lover came to be seen as the banner representing the sovereignty of the god of pleasure. Not surprisingly, unlike the Brahmin complainant who felt dishonored by it, the dandy-guru considered the same foot worthy of worship!

The dandy-guru was tied to the courtesan in the bond of what the *bhāṇas* call *autsukya*, or curiosity.[23] As the figure of the dandy-consort (*vaiśika*) mutated into that of the dandy-guru, his love and erotic passion for the courtesan was replaced by a deep and all-encompassing curiosity about her. Or, perhaps, it would be more accurate to say that an obsessive curiosity about everything related to courtesans emerged as the dandy-guru's new love. For the dandy-guru nothing that related to the courtesan was too small and insignificant to receive attention. Even the minutest and seemingly trivial details of her life held tantalizing clues into her character and her state of mind. Long before the emergence of erotic knowledge in the form of a discourse and texts, such as the *bhāṇas* and the *Kāmasūtra*, there was the erotic curiosity of the dandy-guru in whom knowledge came to be constituted as a form of love and erotic pleasure. The *bhāṇas* themselves as a genre of discourse are the product of a kind of intellectual curiosity that was indistinguishable from love.

The historical figure of the dandy-guru was tied to the courtesan in a bond that was more existential than professional. One of the *bhāṇas* offers a very interesting insight into the nature of the dandy-guru's relationship with the courtesan in his own words. Having been confined to his home for several days due to persistent rain, the desperate dandy-guru steps out the moment there is a break in the rain, breathlessly heading toward the courtesans' quarters. As soon as he gets the first sight of those quarters, the dandy-guru exclaims in excitement, "Life is back again."[24] So intimately intertwined was the dandy-guru's life with that of the courtesan that he felt alive only in her presence. Again, when he felt the touch of the cool winds coming in through the courtesans' quarters on his face, he could not help but remind himself that it came mixed with the breath of the courtesans.[25] It was as if the dandy-guru could only breathe the air already breathed by courtesans. Such was the existential knot that tied him to the courtesan.

Yet, it is important to keep in mind that the dandy-guru was not headed toward the courtesans' quarters in expectations, or even desire, of sexual pleasure—it was his curiosity (*autsukya*) that drove him. And as curiosity, it was his insatiable desire to see and know the courtesan, gain new insights into her character, and discover yet more gestures of love and seduction that drove him. Acutely aware of this curiosity that lay at the heart of his existence, the dandy-guru made a subtle distinction in the *bhāṇas* between two very different kinds of curiosity: that which exists for a reason, and that which has no discernible reason.[26] The dandy-guru also describes curiosity as a form of sickness: while the curiosity that exists for a reason is a disease that is curable, the one that survives without any reason is incurable.[27] The curiosity that exists for a reason, according to the dandy-guru, would cease to exist as soon as that reason was removed by its realization. In contrast, the curiosity that was without reason could not be cured and so could neither be satisfied nor ended in any other way. It would end only with the end of the life of the person who carried it, as if it were a terminal illness.

The dandy-guru's exposition of two kinds of curiosity is meant to apply to his own situation: Despite all the sweet words and protestations from his wife, the dandy-guru stepped out of the house as soon as the rain stopped, in a great hurry to get to the courtesans' quarters. His own curiosity is an incurable illness that will only end with his death—the insatiable curiosity that he carries toward the courtesan has no reason. His curiosity then is indistinguishable from his life—his curiosity is his life. Curiosity, in other words, is part of his very existence, not something external that can be realized with the acquisition of an object. It is a form of lifestyle to which his being is entirely given without any recourse. At the same time, the dandy-guru refers to his own curiosity as a form of sickness because it does not bring him either financial success or social recognition and, as such, could not be seen as a healthy curiosity. Indeed, the life of a dandy-guru is synonymous with failure—he is the very embodiment and icon of failure. His is not a useful and rewarding way of life. It is synonymous with wasting time without any care for his interests and the interest of his family.

Most of all, however, the dandy-guru's curiosity toward the courtesan was a form of sickness because it was love. Old as he was, the dandy-guru was still in love with the courtesan—only the nature of his love had changed. In the *bhāṇas* love is often referred to as a form of sickness.[28] Indeed, the dandy-guru often sees himself as playing the role of a doctor—a doctor of love—in his dealings with courtesans and their patrons. Given that the object of his obsessive curiosity was the courtesan and her life of erotic pursuits, the dandy-guru's curiosity was as erotic as it was intellectual. This was not a pursuit of knowledge in itself as a search for truth; it was a knowledge born out of love grounded in erotic pleasure. The discourse of erotic pleasure that is reflected in the *bhāṇas* was born of love, the love of a life of erotic pleasure, not truth.

In the *Dhūrtaviṭasaṁvāda* the dandy-guru declares that one does not have to be in a sexual relationship with a courtesan in order to enjoy her erotic qualities (*ramyān guṇān*); nor does one need any money for this.[29] Those who know the courtesans' ways of love (*jñyātopacāro janaḥ*) will be able to enjoy her erotic qualities without being in a relationship with her.[30] What the *bhāṇas* call erotic qualities (*ramyān guṇān*) and erotic ways (*upacāra*) include a complex set of erotic attitudes, physical attributes, skills, behavior, speech, actions, gaits, mannerisms, gestures, and expressions that reveal themselves in the course of an erotic relationship and are evident to someone with an eye for them. I would simply, if also somewhat vaguely, translate this complex set as a form of eroticism—the eroticism of the courtesan. What the dandy-guru claims then is, again, that one does not have to be in a sexual relationship with a courtesan to enjoy her eroticisms.

The dandy-guru was fond of claiming in the *bhāṇas* that he was "thousand-eyed" (*sahasrākṣa*).[31] Because of the dandy-guru's insatiable curiosity, his eagerness to watch and observe the erotic drama of the courtesans' lives unfold as they went about their pursuit of erotic pleasure, it was as if his entire being came to reside in his eyes and ears. He was ever curious; nothing escaped the all-encompassing vision of the dandy. From the postures of courtesans standing in the doorway or walking, talking, or looking at someone, the dandy was capable of constructing their erotic profiles, their sexual abilities and preferences.[32] From the sounds coming out of a closed house, the dandy could tell the sexual position of a couple.[33] When it came to the courtesans' affairs, the dandy-guru's was an all-seeing and all-knowing presence.

In one of the *bhāṇas*, *Padmaprābhṛtaka*, the dandy-guru, in the course of his daily wanderings through the courtesans' quarters, suddenly comes upon a young courtesan playing a ball game with her numerous maids. Riveted on this courtesan as she runs and hops around bouncing and catching the ball, his eyes capture in great detail and vividness her minutest and subtlest movements.[34] When the courtesan greets him saying that all this was in his service, he responds that seeing her alone was the greatest reward that he could hope for.[35] The intensity of his pleasure could be gauged from the fact that he describes seeing these scenes in the courtesans' quarters as ambrosia.[36]

In a remarkably revealing statement, the dandy-guru in one of the *bhāṇas* states that "just like the mind of the dandy-guru, this street goes to the courtesans' quarters."[37] His mind, that is to say his thought, is always directed toward the courtesan. The dandy-guru's mind does not turn back and reflect on itself. His thoughts, therefore, are not born out of his self-consciousness. Quite the opposite, in his consciousness it is the courtesan who resides as the sovereign figure. His thoughts are always about the courtesan, not in herself, but in the complex ways in which she is tied to the world of erotics around her. Indeed, it is in the consciousness of the dandy-guru that the complex life of the courtesan comes to be problematized as a discourse and a question of thought. It was as if in the consciousness of the dandy-guru it was the courtesan that came to find her self-consciousness, as if the two together constituted a single self or subjectivity. They were tied together as in a knot, in which both their beings were at stake. It is not surprising, therefore, that the only person to whom the dandy-guru—ever in a hurry to move on to other scenes and sights—said "remember me" while taking leave was a courtesan, as if that was the only favor the dandy-guru really sought or cared for.[38] In the memory—that is to say, thoughts—of the courtesan the dandy saw his own being at stake. The *bhāṇas* are both evidence and historical products of precisely this consciousness of the dandy-guru grounded in the figure of the courtesan. This is why the dandy-guru articulates his thoughts and impressions in the *bhāṇas* in the form of a dialogue, not as monologue or soliloquy.

From being a patron-lover as a young man, the dandy had turned into a teacher-adviser of courtesans. He was expected to teach courtesans *śāstra*, the genre of knowledge that lays out the basic principles of their lives.[39] Indeed, courtesans' mothers often requested the dandy-guru to teach their daughters *śāstra*.[40] If the dandy-guru was the teacher of *vaiśikaśāstra* to courtesans, it was because he was himself at the origin of this discourse.

Śabdakāma as Aesthetic Pleasure

The dandy-guru's relationship with the courtesan raises a few questions. What is the precise difference between the erotic pleasure of the dandy-consort (*vaiśika*), which was had by being in a sexual-erotic relationship with a courtesan, and the pleasure of the dandy-guru (*viṭa*), which could be had by simply watching and observing the courtesan in her pursuit of erotic love, without any sexual contact with her? What was the precise nature of the dandy-guru's pleasure in relation to the courtesan that was not sexual and yet erotic? What, after all, is left of erotics after its sexual content is lost? Finally, how can one understand the relationship between erotic knowledge and erotic pleasure?

In this regard, there occurs in the *bhānas* a very significant and revealing term—*śabdakāma*—that could offer an insight into the nature of pleasure associated with the dandy-guru. The term literally means "pleasure of words" and "desire for words."[41] Although the *bhāṇas* do not dwell on this term at length, it does appear to be a technical term, a concept of great significance. It could be argued that the emergence of a new discursive horizon within which the *bhāṇas* as a genre and later both the *Nāṭyaśāstra* and the *Kāmasūtra* came to be is named in this notion of *śabdakāma*, or word-pleasure/desire. The term word-pleasure/desire, however, does not refer to just any or all words, but rather to words of love and endearment. Also, in the context in which it occurs, the term does not refer just to words, but also includes all gestures and expressions in an erotic affair that are considered meaningful and as such can be rendered into words. In other words, *śabdakāma* includes not only what is heard but also what is seen.

This term *śabdakāma* was coined partly as a contrast to the experience of pleasure that was primarily focused on sex.[42] But even more importantly, it was coined to capture the discursive aspect of the erotic relationship and experience. Significantly, *śabdakāma* is contrasted with *dānakāma,* or the desire for gifts.[43] The desire for gifts refers to the courtesan's interest in acquiring gifts from her patron; it is related to the professional aspect of the courtesan's life. In making the observation that there may be many motivations in a courtesan's relationship with her patrons, the *bhāṇas* name *dānakāma* and *śabdakāma* as two of the many motivations that could go into the courtesan's erotic relationship. Behind the contrast between the desire for word-pleasure and the desire for gift lies hidden the contrast between the desire for love and the desire for money. In the context, the term word-pleasure/desire is simply used as a synonym for love.

However, in inventing the term *śabdakāma*, the *bhāṇas* also redefine the notion of love: this love is no longer anchored in an individual, a specific identity; love does not mean an absolute and abiding commitment to an individual. Nor does it mean an absolute commitment from a lover to oneself. In other words, the *bhāṇas* remove the aura of authenticity that the notion of love carries. Love in the *bhāṇas* means words, gestures, expressions, and acts of love exchanged between two individuals. The term word-pleasure can be used as a synonym for love only in a context in which love itself has morphed into a theater of love. It is only as a witness or spectator in a theater that one can look at love as word-pleasure. And since the *bhāṇas* are written from the perspective of the dandy-guru as witness and director in the theater of love between the courtesan and her patron, it is his view of love that is manifest in the term word-pleasure. It is evident here that it was the dandy-guru who was responsible for constructing the discourse of love as a discourse of theater. It is also evident at the same time that it was the relationship between the courtesan and her patron that constituted the real social-historical context in which the discourse of love emerged as the discourse of theater.

While the notion of word-pleasure as love contrasts with the notion of authentic love grounded in truth and identity, there is another contrast that is also assumed in the term: the contrast between word-pleasure as love and sexual pleasure. One way to understand the distinction between sexual pleasure and word-pleasure as the pleasure of love is to keep in mind the difference between the figures of the *gaṇikā* and an ordinary courtesan. In the case of an ordinary courtesan, sexual pleasure was exchanged for money. But as I discussed in chapter 3, in erotic relationships with the *gaṇikā* the event of sex could take place only within a narrative of erotic love; sexual pleasure thus could be had only in the context of word-pleasure as the pleasure of love. In a relationship with a *gaṇikā*, sexual pleasure is subordinated to *śabdakāma*, or word-pleasure.

This is precisely why the *gaṇikās'* training in sixty-four arts was so important. Indeed, art as such was part of the discourse of erotics. Art is the content in the domain of *śabdakāma* and becomes a medium of an erotic relationship. As I pointed out in the second chapter, just as in the *bhāṇas*, in the *Kāmasūtra* too, the event of sex was located within the discursive domain of erotics. That is what the *Kāmasūtra* means when it says that while animals engage in sex unthinkingly, human engage in it thoughtfully or thinkingly.[44] Recall also that it was precisely for this reason that the *Kāmasūtra* observed that animals are not driven to sex by the desire for sexual pleasure, but only by the necessity of their biological reproduction as a species. In contrast, the *Kāmasūtra* claimed, pleasure had become independent of the need for biological reproduction as a species amongst humans. In other words, it was precisely that which made erotic pleasure a matter of thoughtful pursuit that also made it an autonomous pursuit amongst humans.

Śabdakāma applies to both the courtesan and the dandy-guru. The only difference is that while in the courtesan word-pleasure is intimately and inseparably connected with sexual pleasure, in the dandy-guru word-pleasure comes into its own, in its relative autonomy. In one of the *bhāṇas*, the man who is declared to be the best of the dandy-gurus is described as someone whose "senses have weakened, but [who] still relishes conversations about love."[45] The *bhāṇa* then goes on to add that [sexual] potency is not important; it is the passion that matters because it is the [erotic] passion that delights, not sexual potency.[46]

It was as a man of *śabdakāma* that the dandy-guru became a poet, just as the *Nāṭyaśāstra* claimed. In the *bhāṇas*, the excited dandy strolling the streets of the courtesans' quarters frequently breaks out into moments of extempore versification at the sight of a beautiful courtesan, a sunset, the moon slowly rising on the horizon, a flight of birds, or the change of seasons.[47] As a poet the dandy-guru is not interested in nature as such, as it appears in all its untouched glory in the wild; he is interested in nature as it appears in the city, particularly in and around the courtesans' quarters, as part of an erotic landscape.

It is at this point that erotic pleasure becomes indistinguishable from aesthetic pleasure. Or to put it differently, it is at this point that erotic pleasure is transformed into aesthetic pleasure, and erotics into aesthetics. As "word-pleasure," *śabdakāma* is the most precise definition of aesthetics. In the dandy-guru, sexual-erotic pleasure subtly gives way to erotic-aesthetic pleasure as a relatively autonomous domain; sexual-erotic pleasure gives way to the pleasure of the discovery of erotics as a field of knowledge, because this pleasure of words is not possible without knowledge. It needs to be noted, however, that this knowledge is not grounded in truth, but rather in pleasure. It has no other purpose than the unique pleasure it offers.

As discussed in the last chapter, the figure of the dandy as a young man described by the *Nāṭyaśāstra* had two main aspects: erotic and aesthetic. Even as the dandy as a young man spent his years in sexual-erotic relationship with courtesans as their lover-consort, he was also at the same time an expert in a variety of fine arts and crafts. As the dandy grew older and his interest in sexual pleasure and erotic relations slowly faded, it was the intellectual and aesthetic aspects of erotics that emerged as the dominant and driving concerns in his life. His curiosity about the erotic affairs of courtesans was nothing other than an aesthetic mutation of his old sexual-erotic love. It was in this mutation that erotics also gave birth to aesthetics as an autonomous domain. The dandy-guru's pleasure was still erotic, but not sexual—it was erotic-aesthetic. His pleasure went hand in hand with his knowledge. The depth and intensity of his erotic-aesthetic pleasure depended on the depth and breadth of his knowledge of erotics and the figures in whom it was grounded.

From a Spectator to the Director of the Theater of Love

In the *bhāṇas*, the dandy-guru emerges as a relatively old man who is fascinated by the erotic affairs of young courtesans and their patrons. Having grown old, and no longer caught in the whirlwind of sexual pleasure, the dandy-guru as a spectator and connoisseur has gained some intellectual distance on the phenomenon of love. He now witnesses love as if it was a narrative unfolding on stage, with the courtesan and her lover-consort appearing as its main protagonists. It was in the eyes of this dandy-guru that the courtesan and her lover-consort began to appear as actor and actress. To the dandy the courtesans' quarter began to appear as a grand theater of love. As I discussed in the last chapter, the term *prakaraṇa*, the name of one of the two major genres of erotic-romantic plays, the popular romance, in the *Nāṭyaśāstra*, was used in the *bhāṇas* as a common everyday word to refer to real-life erotic-romantic affairs between a courtesan and her patron. If the popular romance emerged as a genre of plays, that was because it already appeared to be one in the eyes of the dandy-guru, to whom the courtesan's quarter appeared as a theater of love.

The erotic-aesthetic pleasure that the dandy-guru derived as the foremost connoisseur of love led to a slow but vast accumulation of knowledge on eroticism as a complex of erotic acts, manners, gestures, and expressions of courtesans and their lovers. As the leading connoisseur of the theater of love, the dandy-guru in the *bhāṇas* is defined by his deep and abiding obsession to watch, observe, and analyze those erotic affairs by breaking them down into their minutest components. To him even the most trivial gestures of courtesans and their patrons carried deep secrets to be deciphered. It was as a connoisseur of love that the dandy became a researcher, cataloguer, and archivist of the subtlest and most fleeting of the gestures and expressions of love. Long before the *Nāṭyaśāstra* and the *Kāmasūtra* carefully listed those gestures and expressions—a staggering number—the dandy carried them in his head as a living archive.[48]

On the basis of his vast knowledge of details, the dandy-guru was capable of constructing broad erotic profiles as types. Each erotic type had its own specific set of tastes and preferences. A single gesture could reveal the entire erotic profile of an individual to the dandy-guru. With his vast and intimate knowledge of the ways of love, the dandy-guru also became skilled at diagnosing and resolving problems in the domain of love and erotics. To him love began to appear as an art no different from the art of theater, which needed careful planning and execution. It was as a spectator that the dandy-guru had slowly acquired the skills of a director of the theater of love.

The dandy-guru made his living as an old man as a director in the theater of love. In the *bhāṇas* this is precisely what the dandy-guru did for those he called friends, who were at the same time his patrons. In a *bhāṇa* the word *kāmatantra-sūtradhāra*, meaning a director of *ars erotica*, is used to refer to the dandy-guru.[49] It was as if erotics were a kind of art that required the figure of the director. As a connoisseur of the theater of love, the dandy-guru also became a teacher and director in the art of love. As director, the dandy-guru became constitutive of this theater of love; he was no longer an outsider, a mere spectator. The dandy-guru came to be the teacher-adviser of the courtesan as a director in the field of *ars erotica*. And since *ars erotica* was at the center of the courtesan's being, the figure of the dandy was tied to her being in an existential relationship, not to one of her many skills.

That is why it is important to distinguish the dandy-guru from another figure of a teacher associated with the courtesan. Courtesans had two kinds of teachers: the dandy-guru (*viṭa*) and the teacher of specific skills (*ācārya*) in art. A regular teacher as *ācārya* was connected with one particular skill; for example, a painting teacher (*citrācārya*) or a teacher of a string instrument (*viṇācārya*).[50] For such a teacher (*ācārya*), teaching was a profession. In the figure of the dandy, on the other hand, all the individual skills came together as if into a whole, just as the skills related to different aspects of theater come together in the figure of the director. As already shown above, the dandy was an authority in *ars erotica* (*kāmatantra*), which included all the individual arts, such as music, dance, poetry, and acting.

The *Kāmasūtra,* as I have discussed in chapter 3, offers a vivid example of the precise manner in which the dandy-guru played the role of a director in the life of the courtesan. While addressing courtesans, the *Kāmasūtra* recommends that having located a suitable patron, the courtesan must "devise a plan for love" (*prītim yojayet*) under the guidance of the *viṭa*.[51] It is not a coincidence that among a variety of characters that lived off the courtesan, the *Kāmasūtra* chose the dandy-guru as someone with whom the courtesan must consult to devise a plan to make her potential patron fall in love with her. This was because of the *Kāmasūtra's* confidence in the dandy-guru's ability to quickly develop the erotic profile of her patron based on his interactions with him. Also, what comes out clearly in this instruction is that the figure of the dandy-guru is far closer to the courtesan than he is to her patron.

It is precisely in this moment that the theater of love is born. Love, for the dandy-guru, is not something one falls into in an unguarded moment as an act of complete spontaneity. Love becomes a subject of planning. In this situation, the dandy-guru is no longer a spectator to a theater of love unfolding in front of him, but rather a director staging a theater of love. The dandy-guru emerges as a technician in the art of love. To the dandy-guru, love is a project to be executed, directing the courtesan exactly as a director would direct an actress in theater. On the other hand, the same dandy-guru is also in touch with the potential patron-consort of the courtesan. Given that the dandy-guru had been a patron-consort of the courtesan early in his life, he understood the figure of the dandy-consort only too well.

It is not surprising that it was also part of the dandy-guru's duty to restrain a young courtesan when she seemed to be forgetting that hers must be a theater of love.[52] The dandy was there to remind her, not that love was only an illusion and as such must not be taken seriously, but rather that love must never be subordinated to an individual, to an identity—an act that would inevitably lead to marriage. In other words, it was the dandy's responsibility to make sure that love must never escape the domain of theater and pleasure, and so fall into the domain of Brahmanical law (*dharma*).

Śabdakāma as word-pleasure evolved in two related but separate directions: one led to the emergence of the discourse of erotics and the other to the discourse of theater. The *viṭa* constructed the discourse of sexual-erotic pleasure as *ars erotica* as the director in the real-life theater of love involving the courtesan and her patron-consort; this *ars erotica* was meant to facilitate his patron-students' pursuit of sexual-erotic pleasure. This *ars erotica* also involved the construction of a discourse of love as the foundation and primary condition for the pursuit of sexual-erotic pleasure. Although the dandy-guru was at its origin, *ars erotica* was constructed from the perspective of his patron-students, the courtesan and the dandy-consort, with sexual-erotic pleasure as its goal. However, he constructed the discourse of theater from his own perspective for the sake of theatric-aesthetic pleasure. It was in him that the sexual-erotic pleasure of his patron-students mutated into erotic-aesthetic pleasure; it was in him that the discourse of love found its autonomy from sexual pleasure. As I discussed in chapter 4, the relationship between the courtesan and her dandy-consort was already a form of erotic theater. Yet, in that theater sexual and aesthetic pleasure were inseparably bound together. Also, even though the dandy-consort of the courtesan appeared like an actor in a theater of love, he was too caught up in his erotic pursuit to see it as theater. The dandy-consort, therefore, was incapable of problematizing his own erotic affair in terms of theater. It was only after the transition of the dandy-consort into dandy-guru that the erotic affair between the courtesan and her patron began to appear as theater.

In the emergence of erotic theater there are two intimately related but also distinct relationships of pleasure that are involved: the relationship between the courtesan and the dandy-consort, on the one hand, and the relationship between the two and the dandy-guru, on the other. It is in the dandy-guru as the director and spectator that the erotic affair between the courtesan and the consort emerges as an erotic spectacle or theater. These two relations together constitute the origin of the discourse of theater in ancient India. Even as the relationship between the courtesan and the dandy-consort constitutes the content of this erotic theater, this theater would not have come into being as a discourse without the emergence of the figure of the dandy-guru as its foremost director and the first spectator.

The nature of the courtesan's complex and singular life as a form of theater brought forth the figure of the dandy-guru as a director. As the director in the life of the courtesan as a theater of love, the dandy-guru came to have the skills of a director on stage. It now becomes evident why in the *Nāṭyaśāstra* the two figures of the dandy-guru and the theater director overlap each other. It does not mean that all dandy-gurus were also at the same time directors by profession. It only means that the directors came from the ranks of dandy-gurus. That was how, in and through the old dandy-guru, erotics gave birth—subtly and almost imperceptibly—to theater-aesthetics. What is more, given that the dandy-guru was also a teacher and adviser to courtesans and their patron-consorts, this knowledge was also deployed back into producing sexual-erotic pleasure. In other words, in the historical moment of its origin, erotic knowledge was firmly grounded in pleasure: the erotic-aesthetic pleasure of the dandy-guru as spectator and director, and the sexual-erotic pleasure of his patrons.

The intertwining of the domains of erotics and theater has left an enduring legacy in the origin and evolution of aesthetics, particularly in the notion of aesthetic pleasure (*rasa*). Long after the advent of the *Nāṭyaśāstra*, the debate over the precise meaning of aesthetic pleasure was carried on for centuries and involved some of the greatest philosophers and literary theorists in Indian history. One of the many questions, for example, concerned the precise locus of aesthetic pleasure: did it reside in the characters in love stories or in the authors who wrote them, or in the actors who played them on stage, or in their readers? This imprecision and confusion in the notion of aesthetic pleasure has two sources. First, both in the *Kāmasūtra* and the *Nāṭyaśāstra* erotics and aesthetics extend into each other in ways that have not been fully appreciated. The second source of confusion has to do with the fact that the lives of the figures—the dandy-guru, the courtesan, the dandy-consort—in whom the notion of pleasure was historically grounded, straddled the domains of erotics and theater-aesthetics. The need to neatly delineate aesthetic pleasure in its purity and autonomy was a later problem that arose due to the slow dissociation of the discourse of love from erotics and from the courtesan as its sovereign figure. The discourse of love came to be reduced to the pages of a literary work; love was reduced to a text. Much of the later history of Indian aesthetics has been devoted to sorting out this confusion arising from the tangled historical origins of aesthetic pleasure.

The Birth of the Discourse of Erotics against *Dharma*

Once erotics emerged as a field of knowledge, even if only in a small but influential corner of society, it experienced what every new field of knowledge does—it slowly began to acquire a culture of intellectual debate and discussion. Soon there also emerged the need to define issues more precisely and to invent technical terms and categories. Moreover, as a newly emerging discourse, erotics inevitably came in conflict with the discourses already well-established and claiming hegemony, particularly the discourses of *dharma*, or Brahmanical law, and *mokṣa*, or spiritual liberation.[53] The dandy-guru as the founder of this new domain of discourse was compelled to rise to this challenge. The *bhāṇas* are the product of this intellectual challenge and the opportunity that came with it.

Inevitably the need to set up forums where ideas on the subject of erotics could be exchanged was felt. Differences and disputes began to emerge among the community of dandy-gurus on a variety of issues: Was sexual-erotic pleasure in the company of the courtesan worth the trouble if it meant risking the pleasure and happiness promised to a good man in heaven? Given that one could not trust a courtesan's love, was it wise to pursue pleasure with her? What was the difference between the experience of pleasure with the courtesan and pleasure with the wife? In seeking pleasure with a courtesan, was one not violating the Brahmanical law and hurting the institution of the family? It bears repeating that the *Nāṭyaśāstra* invested the figure of the dandy-guru with the ability to judge the pros and cons of an argument in an intellectual debate.

The figure of the old dandy as evident in the *bhāṇas* is marked by a boundless intellectual curiosity in all aspects of erotics. After spotting a patron of courtesans coming in his direction, the excited dandy-guru says to himself that he would like to read this fellow like a book.[54] In this statement the dandy-guru reveals a key to the very nature of his being. It also holds a clue to the historical moment in which the discourse of erotics was born. This comment shows that for the dandy-guru the the patron-consort of the courtesan was no longer just another man in love seeking erotic pleasure, but a book to be read or, indeed, deciphered, a puzzle to be solved. What is evident is an epistemological break that had taken place in the transition from the figure of the dandy-consort to the dandy-guru. It was precisely this break that allowed the dandy-guru to transform the dandy-consort as a figure of love into a book that also transformed erotic practice into a discourse. It was in this moment that *ars erotica* was born as a discourse.

To the old dandy-guru, no longer tethered to sexual pleasure but still very much part of the domain of erotics as the teacher-adviser to courtesans, a whole new discursive horizon opened up. All aspects of erotic practices emerged as discursive problems to the figure of the dandy-guru, problems that required a great deal of intellectual effort to be resolved. And since the courtesan was at the center of both erotics and theatrics, it ought not to come as a surprise that it was the dandy-guru who was at their discursive origins too. The dandy-guru emerged as a researcher, archivist, philosopher, and propagandist of erotics anchored in the figure of the courtesan.

The dandy-gurus often met in a variety of forums that mushroomed during that period to discuss issues relating to erotics. It was in these forums that love emerged as an object of knowledge, debate, and disputations. Love became an object that needed to be carefully observed, catalogued, categorized, and analyzed. The story of Viśvālaka as an apprentice to a dandy-guru offers an insight into one such forum, called *goṣṭhī* or salon. While talking to the dandy-guru, Viśvālaka refers to a *goṣṭhī* or literary salon in which a discussion on *ars erotica* had taken place recently. Since some of the issues raised in the salon had not yet been resolved to his satisfaction, Viśvālaka reports to the dandy his own views on the subject and pleads for his opinion. What is significant is that he takes the dandy-guru's pronouncements on the subject to be the proof or final word.[55] Viśvālaka, thereby, places the dandy-guru, and not a text, in the position of the ultimate authority on erotics. At this stage, the knowledge of erotics was still attached to the figure of the dandy-guru and had not yet separated into a text; *ars erotica* (*kāmatantra*), therefore, did not refer to a text, but to a domain of discourse and practice.

Since this discourse of erotics was grounded in the figure of the courtesan, in the process of developing this discourse the dandy-guru emerged as a spokesperson, an apologist, and, indeed, an ideologue for the courtesan in addition to being a mentor and personal guide to her. The *bhāṇas* are the historical evidence that the dandy-guru not only relentlessly battled all the social prejudices and phobias against courtesans; in the process he also constructed a discourse of erotic pleasure in which the courtesan had the pride of place, as if she ought to have been an indispensable part of any self-respecting society.

The nature of the grounding of the discourse of erotic pleasure in the figure of the courtesan is brought out dramatically in one of the accounts of a gathering called a *samāja*, or congress, of the dandy-gurus. It was the largest and grandest of all intellectual forums, where the dandy-gurus got together to fraternize and discuss the issues related to erotics. In one of the *bhāṇas* there is a vivid, dramatic account of one such congress of dandy-gurus sponsored by a very rich patron. This congress was called to attention with the striking of a gong:

> Here servants stand in the gateway holding silver jars filled with water for washing the feet [of the arriving guests]. The courtyard in front of the door is filled with thousands of chariots of the *viṭas* [dandy-gurus] who have assembled from everywhere. . . . For now here flowers of five colors thrown loosely in the air and are tied in branches. Incense is passed around. Lamps are lit. A word of welcome is spoken. A chariot is unfastened. Coquettish gestures can be seen. Songs are sung. Musical instruments are played. A hand is offered [in support]. Friendly words are spoken. Some warmly embrace one

> another. Others affectionately lend each other support. Some bow respectfully. Others touch the back of those who are bowed. Some move about with a frown. Others kiss one another on the head. Some stand around with coquettish gestures. Others sit down playfully. Some pass sandal around. Some rub on make-up. Some apply ointment. Others sprinkle themselves with powder. Coquettish women join in the joking of the *viṭas*. What is the use of many words?[56]

This account seems somewhat exaggerated, because it is difficult to imagine "thousands of dandy-gurus" arriving for this congress. The author of this *bhāṇa*, however, is simply trying to convey his impression of how large the gathering was. The chief of the dandy-gurus sponsored the congress. The women, present in significant numbers, were likely to have been courtesans.

The story that was to be discussed in this congress relates to a man who is kicked on the head by a courtesan in the course of a playful love quarrel. Being alien to the ways of erotic quarrels, this man takes great offense at the courtesan's act and begins to scold her. No amount of apologies from the alarmed courtesan, however, will suffice. He thus goes out in search of a proper remedy for the offense, while loudly proclaiming his status as a Brahmin, his expertise in grammar and logic—two disciplines assumed to be located at the opposite end of erotics—and his job as a writer of edicts for the king.[57] He is mischievously referred to an assembly of dandy-gurus to seek the right course of action. To the dandy-gurus, in contrast, receiving a kick on the head from a beautiful courtesan in the course of a love quarrel is, of course, the rarest and greatest of blessings. Not surprisingly, the assembly enjoys a session of uninhibited mirth at the expense of this pompous but hapless Brahmin—a man of *dharma*—caught in the upside-down world of erotic pleasure (*kāma*), a fool in the theater of love.

More than the Brahmin, however, it is the discourse of *dharma* and its denigration of women that is put to the sword in this *bhāṇa*. The *viṭa*'s defiant, mocking, and sarcastic utterances against the discourse of *dharma* and its promises of heaven and happiness were delivered in the streets and assemblies as part of a relentless battle he was fighting on behalf of erotics and its anchor, the courtesan.[58] Indeed it was the dandy-guru who delivered the first intellectual blows at the discourse of *dharma* and spiritual liberation (*mokṣa-nirvāṇa*) on behalf of the notion of sexual-erotic pleasure (*kāma*) and the figure of the courtesan. Erotic pleasures of this world were defended as far superior to anything promised in heaven.[59] The dandy-guru was the master in the discourse of sexual-erotic pleasure, and he had the same status in the domain of erotics that the Brahmin had in the domain of Brahmanical law.

Not surprisingly, it was in the figure of the dandy-guru that erotics emerged as a discourse.

It also needs to be noted that the aggrieved Brahmin was an expert in grammar and logic. Needless to say, the figure of the grammarian-logician seems to have been held in extreme contempt in the discourse of sexual-erotic pleasure. Is it just an accident that of all the social and intellectual figures available at the time, it is a man of grammar and logic that is made the public target of the dandy-guru's withering sarcasm? What made these twin figures stand out in the eyes of the dandy-guru? Since these two genres of knowledge were grounded in truth, the Brahmin as a grammarian-logician appears as a figure of truth in the *bhāṇa*. The Brahmin as a man of truth seemed to stand on the opposite side of a divide that separated the discourse of sexual-erotic pleasure from grammar and logic. This is, therefore, an important moment in the discourse of sexual-erotic pleasure. Recall that the notion of truth does not find a place in the trilogy of Brahmanical law (*dharma*), political power (*artha*), and pleasure (*kāma*). Yet truth was indeed part of the discourses of grammar and logic as two genres of knowledge that were not directly incorporated into the ontological complex of the trilogy. The derision and contempt masterfully exhibited toward the figure of the grammarian-logician is therefore directed primarily at the discourse of truth.

Also, what is starkly evident is the unsaid and subtle affinity between grammar and logic as the discourses of truth, on the one hand, and Brahmanical law and political power, on the other. Even as the Brahmin, the man at the receiving end of the dandy-gurus' contempt, was a figure of *dharma*, as a scribe responsible for writing edicts for the king he was also a figure of power (*artha*). In the *bhāṇas*, this figure of truth appears argumentative, quarrelsome, egotistical, and humorless. For him language is not a medium of expression—for example, the expression of love—but a medium of power and domination, a domain of law and authority. He is too focused on truth to see the poetic dimension of language. He uses language as a stick with which to beat and defeat his opponents. Proper and correct use of language shares its ethos with proper moral-legal behavior grounded in *dharma*; to the dandy-guru truth and correctness—grammatical, logical, moral, and legal—appear bound together by a secret affinity. The law of logic, grammar, and *dharma* share continuity with truth: truth as law and law as truth. For this man of grammar, a gesture, just like a word, has only one proper meaning: when the Brahmin was hit on the head in a gesture of erotic playfulness, all he could see was an immoral and improper act by a lowly courtesan to a great man of truth, law, and power; an erotic gesture appears not as an act of love, but an act of disrespect. If despite his contempt, the man of truth nevertheless came to the courtesan, that was because he wanted to receive sexual pleasure as a form of service in exchange for money, not as part of a discourse of love. Truth, just as in the works of Foucault, is located on the side of law (*dharma*) and power (*artha*).

Conclusion

It was through the *bhāṇas* that the *viṭa*, or dandy-guru, a seemingly marginal social figure, burst into the discursive world of ancient India. More importantly, through the figure of the dandy-guru, it was also the erotic discourse of *kāma* that forced its way into the discursive world that had been dominated by *dharma* and *artha*. There is a unique kind of literary imagination at work in these plays that consists of the ability to observe things closely and document them, not of imagining things that do not exist. They are realistic descriptions of an aspect of life in ancient India not seen elsewhere. But the reality that they describe is seen from the perspective of the dandy-guru grounded in erotic pleasure, or *kāma*, and the figure of the courtesan, not reality in itself accessible without interpretation. It is this perspective of *kāma* that opens up the discursive horizon, within which the *bhāṇas* as a new genre come to find a home. Through the figure of the dandy-guru there is a new discourse grounded in *kāma* that comes into being. The dominant interpretation of the *bhāṇas* as a genre of play has got in the way of seeing it more broadly as a new genre or domain of discourse.

Before the *viṭa* became the director and expert of love, he was the foremost spectator in the theater of love. All his knowledge, and other related skills, had their origins in him as a connoisseur of love, with the courtesan as the focus of his all-consuming curiosity and attention. Such was the dandy-guru's attachment to the object of his attention, the courtesan, that it was as if his being formed a circle with hers. The dandy-guru's was a derivative existence, a derivative life; his being was exhausted in witnessing the eroticisms of the courtesan. It was only from his existential orientation to the courtesan that the dandy-guru derived his own being. In turn he was the mirror in which the courtesan saw her own being captured as a discourse. It was as if she found her self-consciousness, grounded in erotic pleasure, in the consciousness of the dandy-guru. It was thus that the dandy-guru became the founder of the discourse of erotic pleasure.

The *bhāṇas*, as we have seen, are a dramatic account of a day in the life of the dandy-guru as the founder of the discourse of erotic pleasure. Together they constitute an archive that encompasses nothing short of the entire subjectivity of the dandy-guru, a subjectivity that was grounded in the figure of the courtesan. The *bhāṇas* give a vivid insight into not only what the dandy-guru thought, but also how he thought, and what he was. It is significant to note that in the *bhāṇas* thoughts on erotics have not yet separated themselves from the historical scenes and sites of their origins—erotics has not yet acquired the textual-theoretical form that it came to acquire in the *Kāmasūtra*. The dandy-guru, unlike a theoretician, could not separate himself from the scenes in which his thoughts formed as an activist, spokesperson, and teacher of erotics. In him, erotics was still bound to its historical roots in specific institutions and forums, such as salons (*goṣṭhī*), assemblies (*viṭasabhā*), congresses (*viṭa samāja*); in sites such as the marketplace and the streets in and around the courtesans' quarters; in figures such as the courtesan and her consort, and, of course, the dandy-guru himself. Not surprisingly, his consciousness as evident in the *bhāṇas* represented a cacophony of voices. That was the reason that the dandy-guru's thoughts unfolded in the form of dialogues in the *bhāṇas* and appeared as plays.

With the writing of the *Nāṭyaśāstra* and the *Kāmasūtra* within a century of each other, however, the discourses of erotics and theatrics acquired textual autonomy from the figure of the dandy-guru and his general historical-discursive context. They were no longer tied to the historical institutions, sites, scenes, and figures of their origin. It was as if the dandy-guru, having exhausted his being in these two founding texts of ancient Indian culture, walked into the sunset. In contrast to the *bhāṇas*, the works of the two Kashmiri authors Dāmodaragupta (eighth century CE) and Kṣemendra (eleventh century CE)—in some ways the two successor texts—which focused on the figure of the courtesan and other related themes, have the mother of the courtesan in the enunciative position, not the dandy-guru.[60] Evidently, by the eighth century the figure of the *viṭa* was no longer viable as the foremost anchor of the discourse of erotics. Indeed, the old figure of the dandy-guru was reduced to a mere pimp, a figure of scorn, living a furtive existence, just like his patron, the courtesan.

6

The City Dandy and the Vision of the City Based on Art

It is evident from our foregoing discussion that there is a deep discursive affinity and continuity between sexual-erotic pleasure and theatric-aesthetic pleasure in both the *Kāmasūtra* and the *Nāṭyaśāstra*. In the *Kāmasūtra* sexual-erotic pleasure and theatric-aesthetic pleasure were the private and public dimensions of one and the same lifestyle. Their affinity also reveals that they were complementary to each other, as if the private pursuit of sexual-erotic pleasure was not possible in the absence of the public discourse of aesthetic pleasure. Instead of being a sublimation of sexual pleasure, in the *Kāmasūtra* aesthetic pleasure was the ontological discursive precondition for sexual-erotic pleasure.

The continuity and complementarity between erotics and aesthetics are starkly evident in the figure of the *nāgaraka,* or the "city dandy," that the *Kāmasūtra* constructed as the male counterpart of the courtesan. This chapter focuses on the nature and origin of that figure as a new historical-discursive development in Indian culture. The emergence of this figure is symptomatic of a new strain in the evolution of premodern Indian society and culture, in which sexual-erotic pleasure and aesthetic pleasure constituted the private and public ends of a single continuum. Even though the city dandy was none other than the historical figure of the dandy-consort of the courtesan (*vaiśika*), the *Kāmasūtra* anchored the former figure as a connoisseur and patron of arts and artists, primarily in the public domain of aesthetic pleasure. If the *Kāmasūtra,* as the founding text of erotics, decided to anchor one of its two principal figures, the other being the courtesan, in aesthetic pleasure, then that was because the discourse of erotic pleasure was not possible in its absence. The *Kāmasūtra*'s concerns extended far beyond what in comparison appears to be its somewhat narrow focus on sexual-erotic pleasure. In anchoring the city in the dandy as the cornerstone of its discourse on erotics, the *Kāmasūtra* assumed a whole new vision of society based on art. In its view, for *ars erotica* to be possible, sexual-erotic practices needed to be anchored in a broader form of ethos grounded in art.

It is the popular understanding of sex as a purely sensual experience that comes in the way of precisely determining the meaning and significance of art and aesthetics in the discourse of erotics in the *Kāmasūtra*. What, however, sits silently at the core of this view of sex as an entirely sensual experience is the patriarchal discourse of power and virility that reduced women to their bodies as objects of pleasure. This perception of sex as a sensual experience reflects the history of man's access to the woman's body without a discourse of love. Not surprisingly, the discourse of art and aesthetics in the *Kāmasūtra* functioned primarily as a discourse of love. It was gender relations, particularly the status of women, which was really at stake in art and aesthetics as a discourse of love. The discourse of love introduces freedom for women and gender equality without using the political discourse of rights, indeed without ever using the word freedom. In the form of art and aesthetics, love functioned as a counter-discourse to Brahmanical law (*dharma*). In the discourse of art and aesthetics anchored in love, the *Kāmasūtra* sought to re-envision society and culture from the central perspective of gender relations. The real question, therefore, ought not to be the nature of aestheticization of sex in the *Kāmasūtra*, but rather the history of how it was de-aestheticized in the world outside it.

From the Dandy-Consort to the City Dandy: The Birth of Dandyism as Lifestyle

As I discussed in the third chapter, the *Kāmasūtra* found in the courtesan a sovereign figure in the domain of erotics, a figure in which pleasure attained its historical autonomy. The courtesan, however, could not constitute the entire discursive field of erotics by herself—she needed an erotic counterpart. The *Kāmasūtra*, therefore, sought to find a counterpart for the courtesan in order to construct a discourse of *ars erotica*. It was in search of this counterpart that the *Kāmasūtra* constructed the figure of the *nāgaraka*, which, if translated literally, means "a man of the city." But in the *Kāmasūtra* the word *nāgaraka* also carries the connotation of a distinct lifestyle of a man in the city. According to the *Kāmasūtra*, having entered the life of a householder and earned enough money, a man should settle into the "lifestyle (*vṛttam*) of a man of the city (*nāgaraka*)."[1] Since the *Kāmasūtra* uses the term *nāgaraka* to designate a lifestyle, and not merely the fact of living in a city, the term "man about town" may be a better translation.

There are, however, serious limitations even to this translation as "a man about town" because it only partially captures the real meaning of the term. It is difficult to fully understand the meaning and significance of the figure of the *nāgaraka* in the discourse of erotics unless we locate it in its precise discursive and historical context. As I will show, seen in light of this context, in the term *nāgaraka* the *Kāmasūtra* sought to discursively reconfigure the already existing historical figure of the dandy-consort of the courtesan. It was an attempt to discursively anchor the figure of the dandy, who was until now associated with the courtesan, in the city. I therefore translate the term *nāgaraka* as "city dandy."

As discussed in chapters 3 and 4, there was an actual historical figure called *nāyaka* in the *Kāmasūtra* and *vaiśika* in the *Nāṭyaśāstra*. Both these designations referred to the same historical figure of the dandy as the patron-consort of the courtesan in that period. Since the courtesan was the sovereign figure in the domain of erotics, her male counterpart—the dandy-consort—ought to have been the first choice for the *Kāmasūtra* when it searched for a male figure to anchor its discourse of erotics. Indeed, as I have also discussed in chapter 4, in one of the *bhāṇas* there appears a term, *vaiśika vṛtti*, which means "the lifestyle of [the dandy as] a patron-consort of the courtesan."[2] It is the closest equivalent to the *Kāmasūtra*'s "the lifestyle of a *nāgaraka*" (*nāgaraka vṛttam*). Evidently the term "lifestyle" (*vṛtti*) was used to designate the mode of being of the patron-consort of the courtesan. Also, the term was used in reference to a man who had failed in winning the love of a courtesan, as if he had failed in a test of his skill in the art of love. It appears, therefore, that the term *vaiśika vṛtti* also carried the additional meaning of "art of love." It also means that the male counterpart of the courtesan (*vaiśika*, *nāyaka*) was seen as a figure of love and a master in the art of love.

If we look a little more closely at the *Kāmasūtra* it becomes evident that behind the new designation of the *nāgaraka* is none other than the figure of the same dandy as the patron-consort of the courtesan. The *Kāmasūtra* has merely renamed the old dandy-consort of the courtesan as the "city dandy" (*nāgaraka*). The real historical identity of the city dandy as the patron-consort of the courtesan is most vividly revealed in the company he keeps as part of his daily routine. His companions are an assortment of the same cast of characters we have already encountered in the course of last three chapters: the dandy-guru (*viṭa*), the courtesan's art teacher (*pīṭhamarda*), and most of all, the courtesan herself.[3] As discussed in the last chapter, the dandy-guru was none other than the former patron-consort of the courtesan (*vaiśika*), who, having spent all his wealth and also grown old, had become more of a teacher and adviser to courtesans in their erotic pursuits. The *pīṭhamarda,* or art teacher, to courtesans and city dandies is described differently in the *Kāmasūtra,* as someone without a family and wealth. An expert in arts, this teacher appears to have come from another part of the country known for its art and famous artists.[4] The art teacher was entirely dependent for his living on courtesans and their patrons, the city dandies. The dandy-guru and the art teacher were an essential part of the city dandy's daily routine. The *Kāmasūtra* lists it as part of his everyday routine to check on them every afternoon, perhaps to schedule and plan the details for the rest of the day.[5] It was as if the two were the closest companions and ministers in the city dandy's own private court meant to manage and facilitate his erotic pursuits in the company of courtesans.

As is already evident from the discussion until now, the most important figure that looms large behind the city dandy is that of the courtesan herself. But the depth and diversity of the city-dandy's association with the courtesan went further still. The *Kāmasūtra* recommends the courtesan's presence and participation in most of the gatherings either hosted by the city dandy or attended by him. She was present in the literary salons (*goṣṭhīs*) organized by the city dandy, in which art and aesthetics constituted the main topics of conversation. What is also significant is that these literary salons were as likely to be hosted by courtesans, salons in which city dandies were invited as guests. Nor were the courtesans present in these salons as mute witnesses to intellectual exchanges between city dandies—they were active participants, sharing their own experiences and insights on the subject. Together with the city dandy's friends, courtesans were also invited to drinking parties held in the evening (*samāpānaka*).[6] Moreover, courtesans were once again an essential part of the city dandy's elaborate trips to gardens (*udyānagamana*), which included singing, dancing, and staging plays.[7] It appears that courtesans were an integral and important part of the city dandy's life, functioning as friends and companions. Their presence in the proximity of the city dandy reveals beyond any doubt the real historical identity of the city dandy as a patron-consort of the courtesan.

As we have also seen, the closest friends and associates of the city dandy were as close as he—perhaps even closer—to courtesans and worked as a bridge between the two. Indeed, as I discussed in the last chapter, it was in the dandy-guru that the courtesan found her mentor, spokesperson, and ideologue. The city dandy's friendship with the dandy-guru and the art teacher straddled both his erotic and aesthetic pursuits. The nature of friendship and intimacy between the city dandy, the dandy-guru (*viṭa*), and the art teacher (*pīṭhamarda*) is evident in the fact that the latter two accompanied the city dandy for much of the day as a matter of their daily routine. In the erotic routine of the city dandy with the courtesan as his partner, there was a long session of flirtation, music, singing, and dancing that preceded sex. The dandy-guru and the art teacher were part of this session, as singers, musicians, and friends.[8]

There is an interesting detail in the *Kāmasūtra* that reveals just how close and tightly knit this group of characters was: while addressing the city dandy, the *Kāmasūtra* suggests that if his erotic partner (*nāyikā*) got wet in the rain on her way to his house and lost her makeup then he or his companions should redo her makeup.[9] It is one thing for the city dandy to do his erotic partner's makeup, quite another for his male companions to do so. If this was at all possible without alarming the woman, that was perhaps for two reasons: first, the woman was likely to be a courtesan; any other woman would have found even the presence of the city dandy's male friends in such intimate moments awkward, let alone allowing them to do her makeup. Second, if the city dandy's erotic partner was indeed a courtesan, the dandy-guru and the art teacher were likely to be as familiar and intimate with her as they were with the city dandy. Given this long familiarity and intimacy, the courtesan alone would have had no hesitation in letting them do her makeup. It is also clear that the city dandy carried on much of his erotic affair—except sex—in the company of his friends. Involving as it did music, singing, and dancing, the city dandy's erotic existence appears like a carefully staged aesthetic affair, an event of theater. In this sequence, sex itself appears as the culmination of a private aesthetic affair. It is evident that erotics and aesthetics were seamlessly joined together in the life of the city dandy and all his closest companions. The only woman to be accomplished enough in both erotics and arts and bold enough to be a companion to the city dandy in his erotic pursuits in the company of his friends was the courtesan.

One question, however, still needs answering: if the city dandy was in fact the same figure as the dandy-consort, then why did the *Kāmasūtra* need a new designation of *nāgaraka* for this figure? For an answer to this question, the new designation has to be located in the intellectual and discursive complex of the trilogy—Brahmanical law (*dharma*), political power (*artha*), and sexual-erotic pleasure (*kāma*). As discussed in chapters 2 and 3, given that this trilogy converged on the same person and society, the question of reconciling the competition and conflict between its three constituents, while also securing discursive autonomy for pleasure, emerged as the central task for the *Kāmasūtra*. One way to manage the conflict within the trilogy was to set the three constituents in a hierarchical order. As the *Kāmasūtra* itself acknowledged, in this hierarchy Brahmanical law (*dharma*) occupied the top position, even as pleasure came at the bottom. This meant that pleasure found itself subordinated to Brahmanical law, a phenomenon that also resulted in the complete subordination of women and the exclusion of the discourse of love from the relationship between husbands and wives. It was under these circumstances that the *Kāmasūtra* declared the courtesan to be an exceptional figure in the domain of erotics—just as the king was in the domain of politics—a figure in whom pleasure could find autonomy.

For the autonomy of pleasure to be truly effective, however, the courtesan required a male counterpart for a sexual-erotic relationship. It would appear that the *Kāmasūtra* already had such a historical figure in the dandy-consort of the courtesan known by two interchangeable names: *nāyaka* and *vaiśika*. It was, however, one thing for a historical figure to be present, a very different thing for it to become a discursive figure within the domain of erotics. The *Kāmasūtra*'s task was to transform this historical figure into a discursive figure of sexual-erotic pleasure. Recall that even the courtesan—a familiar historical figure—was introduced into the discourse of pleasure only after creating a place for her within the logic of the broader discursive complex of the trilogy. Once again, the *Kāmasūtra* needed to construct a place for the historical figure of the dandy-consort of the courtesan within the discursive matrix of the trilogy. In making the choice of the courtesan as an exceptional figure in the domain of pleasure, it seemed that the *Kāmasūtra* had found a way to escape the hegemony of *dharma* as Brahmanical law. But now in search of a male counterpart of the courtesan, the *Kāmasūtra* found itself grappling once again with the same problem.

Unless they were part of the royal household or carried overt political ambitions, most men could afford not to engage in political power (*artha*) as one of the three members of the trilogy. But as a non-royal man belonging to a family, the courtesan's male counterpart could not claim any exception from the discourse of Brahmanical law (*dharma*) in which the institution of the family was grounded. He could not dedicate himself exclusively to pleasure (*kāma*) in complete disregard for Brahmanical law. He was therefore exposed to the simultaneous and contrary pulls of Brahmanical law and sexual-erotic pleasure. How would pleasure then find autonomy in a male figure? It was to solve this problem that the *Kāmasūtra*—in line with the broader Indian culture—developed a scheme of dividing life into multiple *āśramas,* or life-stages, each one dedicated—if only potentially—to one of the three ends.[10] The basic idea behind the notion of life-stages is to accommodate multiple unavoidable imperatives in a single life, while giving each one of them its relative autonomy.

The second chapter of the first book in the *Kāmasūtra* is dedicated to the question of pursuing the three ends in their relative autonomy while also maintaining concordance between them. According to the *Kāmasūtra*, "Having divided [the assumed life span] of one hundred years into [three] periods, a man should pursue the three ends [in such a way] that they are in concordance, not conflict, with each other."[11] Although the *Kāmasūtra* does not use the word *āśrama*, in dividing a person's life span into three periods, it nevertheless assumes the notion of life-stages (*āśrama*). The *Kāmasūtra* assigns the period of adolescence to receiving education; the years of youth are reserved for sexual-erotic pleasure; Brahmanical law (*dharma*) and spiritual liberation (*mokṣa*) are reserved for old age.[12] It then adds that having entered the life of a householder (*gārhsthya*) and accumulated enough wealth, one should take up the lifestyle of a city dandy (*nāgaraka*).

The act of entering the householder stage silently assumes getting married and starting a family. In other words, it was as a wealthy married man that one was to settle into the lifestyle of a city dandy, a lifestyle that involved deep and intimate association with courtesans. The *Kāmasūtra* found itself with no better choice. After all, there was a fundamental difference between the positions of a courtesan and her male counterpart. For the courtesan, the pursuit of pleasure and the pursuit of living coincided; her love and profession were two aspects of the same phenomenon. That was, however, not possible for her male counterpart. For the courtesan to be what she was her male patron had to have a considerable amount of wealth. He had to either earn it or inherit it from his family. In other words, the requirement of wealth made it inevitable that the male counterpart of a courtesan had to be a member, and possibly the head, of a family. Unlike the courtesan, who was located outside the family, her male counterpart would by definition come under the discourse of Brahmanical law (*dharma*). As is evident, despite the ambiguity left by the *Kāmasūtra*, the city dandy carried a conflict at the heart of his existence: he was simultaneously anchored in the discourses of both *dharma* and *kāma*.

In the logic of the circumstances that drove the *Kāmasūtra* to identify the male figure of pleasure, one can glimpse the reason for its choice of the term *nāgaraka*, or "man of the city." Having constructed discursively a life-stage for pleasure, the *Kāmasūtra* had the choice to keep the old historical name of *vaiśika*, meaning "the patron-consort of the courtesan," just as it had found it. In this term, however, the dandy was overtly anchored in the figure of the courtesan. Given the discursive context, this may have been seen as a direct attack on the discourse of Brahmanical law, and as such an extremely provocative gesture on the part of the *Kāmasūtra*. It may have been seen as a text that encouraged a young man to abandon his responsibilities as householder for the life of a lover-consort of courtesans. Directing a man to choose a life with a courtesan over one with a wife may have been seen as a direct assault on the institution of family. After all, the *Kāmasūtra* was a pedagogical, prescriptive text. As ever, the *Kāmasūtra* was very careful and strategic in its choice of the word "man of the city" (*nāgaraka*). Although in terms of its real content the term "man of the city" was the same as the "patron-consort of courtesans," the new name helped camouflage this content. What would have been provocative as "patron-consort of courtesans" became acceptable—or at least tolerable—as "man of the city."

The City Dandy as a Figure of Aesthetic Pleasure

There was another reason why the *Kāmasūtra* needed to anchor the figure of the dandy in the city: to project the city dandy primarily as a figure of aesthetic pleasure and anchor of the *Kāmasūtra's* vision of the city grounded in art.[13] It is important to note that all the forums, institutions, and events in which art was the central concern are discussed in the chapter on the city dandy. This shows how closely associated this figure was with art and aesthetics in the discourse of erotics constructed by the *Kāmasūtra*. Given that the city dandy is the same as the historical figure of the dandy-consort of the courtesan, this association with art is not really surprising. Recall the *Nāṭyaśāstra*'s definition of the patron-consort of the courtesan: he was intimately associated with courtesans and was also an expert in arts.[14] In other words, the patron-consort of courtesans had two dimensions: erotic and aesthetic. It appears that in the figure of the city dandy, the *Kāmasūtra* sought to split the aesthetic dimension from the erotic and anchor it in the city. The intention was to project the city dandy as a public figure in the domain of aesthetic pleasure. From its origin in the association with courtesans, this figure of the city dandy had come to play a major role in the cultural-aesthetic life of the city.

That the *Kāmasūtra's* expansive notion of sexual-erotic pleasure went far beyond just sex is most evident in its inclusion of two distinct sets of what it calls "sixty-four arts": sexual arts (*kāmātmaka*) and fine arts, crafts, and games. The third chapter of the first book in the *Kāmasūtra* starts with the declaration that just as one learns the constituent skills (*aṅgavidyā*) in the domains of political power (*artha*) and Brahmanical law (*dharma*), one also needs to learn the constituent skills of erotics (*kāma*). It then goes on to enumerate those sixty-four fine arts that include singing, dance, playing musical instruments, painting, staging plays, poetry. They also include other skills like dice games, talking to parrots, perfumery, gymnastics, making garlands, making beds, doing makeup, ability to conduct cockfights, dogfights, and ram fights.[15] As is evident, the sheer number and variety of arts and crafts one was expected to master in pursuit of erotic pleasure are staggering. Yet none of these sixty-four arts have anything directly to do with sex. Evidently the various arts and crafts not directly related to sex are nevertheless seen as constituent of the domain of erotics.[16] The *Kāmasūtra* promises to discuss the sixty-four sexual arts separately in the chapter on sex.[17] In this division of the arts into two separate but connected groups, the *Kāmasūtra* once again shows that the sexual and the aesthetic constituted two complementary aspects of the domain and discourse of erotic pleasure as a whole. Sex and sexual pleasure is only one end of the erotic continuum of which aesthetics and aesthetic pleasure constitute the other end.

It is significant that outside the specific chapter dedicated to the figure of the city dandy, the term *nāgaraka* is rarely used in the *Kāmasūtra*. Indeed, the chapters that discuss issues relating to erotics and sex rarely mention this word, as if it did not fit the function.[18] In the chapters that discuss sex or various other aspects of erotic affairs, the *Kāmasūtra* uses the terms *nāyaka*, or actor, for the male and *nāyikā*, or actress, for the female partner in an erotic affair. Indeed, the chapter after the one on the city dandy is focused on the figure of the *nāyaka* in pursuit of his erotic pleasure.[19] It was as if as soon as the pursuit of sexual-erotic pleasure began, a different logic and discourse silently took hold, replacing the figure of the city dandy imperceptibly by a pair of different figures: actor and actress. What this demonstrates is that the two figures—the *nāgaraka* and the *nāyaka*—were anchored in two different discursive planes serving two different functions.

The secret to the presence of the two different terms for what was a single historical figure lies in a subtle distinction that the *Kāmasūtra* makes between the private and individual pursuit of sexual-erotic pleasure and the public and social pursuit of aesthetic pleasure, suggesting that erotics and aesthetics were two subdomains of pleasure within the lifestyle of the city dandy. While discussing aesthetic pleasure, it is the figure of the city dandy that gets activated, but as soon as the discussion shifts to sexual and erotic pleasure, it is the figure of the actor that comes into play. Even as the city dandy pursued his sexual pleasure as an individual, the pursuit of aesthetic pleasure seemed to turn him into a leader of the city, a public figure.

As a figure of aesthetic pleasure, the city dandy hosted and participated in many different kinds of forums and gatherings related to art and aesthetics. One such forum was the literary salon (*goṣṭhī*). Described in the chapter in the *Kāmasūtra* on the city dandy, these salons were part of his regular routine.[20] The city dandy was not just a participant in them, but the organizer and host. Indeed, as a city dandy, it was his primary responsibility to organize these gatherings, meeting places for leading members of the society in the domain of art. The purpose of the salons was to have conversations about arts and aesthetics, and also to honor bright and popular artists. The *Kāmasūtra* directly instructs the city dandy to discuss subjects relating to poetry and arts in the *goṣṭhī*. The salon offered an occasion to collectively reflect on different kinds of arts, its nature, and significance. Given that these salons were not meant for performances, it is clear that the real purpose was to offer the accomplished artists an opportunity to talk about their experiences and skills, and in the process pass them on to the next generation. One can clearly see aesthetic categories coming into being during such discussions. These salons were also a way of disseminating knowledge and awareness of the nuances of arts to a larger audience.

The grounding of the city dandy in aesthetic pleasure, however, did not mean that the courtesan had receded from his life. On the contrary, she continued to be a major presence in his routine. Indeed, these literary salons were as likely to be hosted by a courtesan at her house as they were by a city dandy. The *Kāmasūtra* suggests that the salons should be organized either at a courtesan's house or at the house of another "equally qualified" person.[21] Courtesans' houses were the first choice to host *goṣṭhī*. In this instance, the courtesan is silently assumed to be the measure of an ideal host for such salons. Notice also the use of the word "qualified." By "qualified" the *Kāmasūtra* refers to the courtesan's credentials as a person of great learning and experience in the field of arts. It is clear that courtesans were present in these salons not for sexual reasons, but for their great ability to lead a conversation on matters of arts and aesthetics. Together with the city dandy, the courtesan as the embodiment of art was the most important anchor of the *goṣṭhī*. Given that these salons were either organized at the house of courtesans or in the houses of a city dandy in the presence of courtesans, it is apparent that rather than being seen as objects of popular revulsion, courtesans commanded considerable respect.

In these gatherings centered on art and aesthetics, the courtesan appears not in her predictable role as a sexual or erotic partner of the city dandy, but as a teacher and role model in the field of art and aesthetics. It is evident from these descriptions that the courtesan was seen as a major figure in the domain of aesthetics. In the *Kāmasūtra's* vision of the city based in art, the courtesan was just as important as the city dandy. Indeed, the courtesan was the source of the city dandy's skills in the field of art and aesthetics. After all, the *Kāmasūtra* does not recommend any specific set of training in art and aesthetics for an affluent male of the city as a necessary condition to take up the lifestyle of a city dandy—wealth was the only precondition. It was the courtesan that functioned as a teacher and role model to him; in the company of the courtesan the city dandy became a connoisseur of art and aesthetics. It was partly as a patron of art that the city dandy became a patron of the courtesan, the foremost practitioner of that art.

A New Vision of the City Grounded in Art

The *Kāmasūtra*'s understanding of art, however, is very different from the sense of art as a work of beauty or truth.[22] In the *Kāmasūtra*, art is anchored neither in beauty nor in truth, but rather in pleasure as play. Just as truth did not find a place in the trilogy, beauty too is missing from that list. As discussed in the last chapter, according to the *Nāṭyaśāstra*, art and aesthetics were squarely anchored in pleasure, not beauty. Just as in the *Kāmasūtra*, so too in the *Nāṭyaśāstra* truth and self were nothing more than instruments of theater as an event of aesthetic pleasure. What also comes out vividly in the *Kāmasūtra* is another dimension of art as a medium of relation and an event of *kriḍā*, or pleasure-play. The word *kriḍā* combines in it the meanings of both play and fun or pleasure. The words art (*kalā*) and play (*kriḍā*) often appear together as a pair, as if the two were in complete continuity with each other.[23] Indeed, even the *Nāṭyaśāstra* refers to theater as a form of play (*kriḍā*). It was as play that art became a medium of sexual-erotic relationship. It was as if the *Kāmasūtra* could not think of pleasure without also thinking of relations of pleasure as relations of play—both erotic and aesthetic.

The centrality of this notion of art as play in the *Kāmasūtra* is brought out by the fact that the chapter on the city dandy ends by reiterating the basic ethos of literary salons: "pleasure-play alone (*kriḍā mātra*) in harmony with the spirit of the society and people must be the ethos of the salon."[24] In "pleasure-play," the *Kāmasūtra* names the precise ethos and goal of art and aesthetics as a whole. The *Kāmasūtra* instructs the city dandy in emphatic words not to go to those gatherings where jealous and egotistical people only interested in criticizing others and winning arguments were present.[25] Such elements were sure to destroy the spirit of the gathering and subvert its core purpose. By reminding its readers of the fundamental spirit of these gatherings focused on art and literature, the *Kāmasūtra* emphasizes pleasure-play as the ground and end of art as a whole.

It is significant that art as play takes place between two or more individuals. Art in the *Kāmasūtra*, therefore, was not thought in terms of expression of an individual's feelings or thought, but in terms of the relationship of pleasure-play between the self and the other. Art consisted not in a genius producing great works, but as a medium of striking a relationship of pleasure-play with the other. Art in the *Kāmasūtra*, therefore, was not a solitary but a social pursuit. It was as play that art became a form and medium of socialization.

The notion of art as a medium of socialization needs to be located in the historical context of the city and its dominant ethos and logic of exchange, commerce, and power. Art as play suspended this logic and ethos of productive work and exchange as the hallmark of urban culture. In their pursuit of art and aesthetic pleasure, people met each other outside the context of exchange, forged personal bonds, and built institutions and organizations that were not bound by the logic of commerce. While the logic of commerce divided the city into individuals caught up in their isolated pursuits, the ethos of art as play came to play a major role in constructing the city as an undivided whole. The reason that art as a medium of socialization emerged as a major factor in the life of the city is that it was in cities that the force of commerce and its isolating and alienating implications were felt the greatest. In this light one can understand why the *Kāmasūtra* insisted on the city dandy accumulating enough wealth before setting out on the path of dandyism. It was as if the ethos that anchored the city dandy and the one that accompanied amassing wealth were altogether incompatible, and as such could not be maintained at the same time. The figure of the city dandy, not surprisingly, is that of a squanderer, not an accumulator of wealth.

As a medium of socialization art helped forge personal relations and build institutions and organizations evident in the many forums focused on arts and aesthetics that the city dandy either hosted or attended. The series of club-like forums the city dandy was involved in culminated in *samājas*, the largest festival of arts open to all. The *samāja* was a monthly, even fortnightly, festival of arts at a Sarasvatī temple in which city dandies played a leading role.[26] Sarasvatī was the goddess of learning, particularly the arts, and as such was nonsectarian in nature. Piety and aesthetics came together in the figure of this goddess. Hers was a popular festival open to the entire city; there was absolutely no hint of anyone being excluded from this festival. A whole set of different forms of art—music, dance, theater—were performed on this occasion.[27] Since theater itself was inclusive of major art forms, such as music, dance, and singing, it perhaps occupied the pride of place.

The festivities at the art festival went on for several nights with participants visiting from other cities. The *Kāmasūtra* instructs the city dandy to request particularly talented visiting artists to stay longer in the city and to perform on subsequent nights.[28] Apart from the amount of financial resources that such a venture required, the level of mobilization, coordination, and commitment of voluntary service from people needed to make this arts festival a success must have been considerable. This fortnightly mobilization at a massive scale would have had to become part of everyday culture and institutionalized in order for it to be sustained over a long period of time. For a considerable part of urban society, particularly amongst the youth, organizing such festivals may well have been their primary form of socialization. The fact that these events were organized at local temples makes it evident that they had become part of the permanent structure of the city and had become highly institutionalized. From the *Kāmasūtra*, it appears that certain individuals were also permanently appointed at the temple for the purpose of managing such festivals.[29]

While reminding the city dandy of his core duty and responsibility as the leading organizer of the *samāja*, the *Kāmasūtra* uses the term *gaṇa-dharma*, or "social ethics." The term "social ethics" (*gaṇa dharma*) reveals the core ethos that anchored the figure of the city dandy.[30] Although the notion of social ethics is not directly problematized, its significance is evident from the context of its use. The context in which the term appears involves guest artists from outside the city who had been invited to perform during the festival. Given his responsibilities as a host of this festival, the city dandy was perhaps also responsible for inviting these visiting artists to perform on such occasions. The city dandy's *gaṇa-dharma* consisted in offering respect, honor, and financial support to these artists. These concerns regarding the well-being of the artists suggest that for a significant number of them art was more a passion than a profession. They may not have been earning enough from these performances to make a living, and therefore depended on the kindness and generosity of city dandies as patrons and promoters of art.

Given the nature of this festival, it seems that theater was primarily a social, not commercial, affair. When art becomes a commercial venture, a division of labor is created between the producers and the consumers of art. When art, on the other hand, functions as a social affair, the society itself as a whole is the producer of that art. Moreover, in producing the work of art, society itself becomes a work—a product, if you will—of art. The society, which was otherwise dispersed in families, castes, and ethnicities, nevertheless became one during this festival of art. It was in the event of *samāja* that the society found itself to be a whole, a unity. It was in the medium of art that the society came to constitute itself. In the process, art emerged as one of the foundations of the society, particularly of the city. Because the society's own being was at stake in art, the notion of social ethics (*gaṇa-dharma*) comes up precisely in the context of the event of the largest festival of arts (*samāja*).[31]

The play *Mṛcchakaṭika*, or *The Little Clay Cart*, by Śudraka, comes closest to portraying the character of a dandy-consort as a city dandy. Although married, Carudatta falls in love with a wealthy courtesan called Vasantsena. Brahmin by caste and a businessman by profession, Carudatta was a typical city dandy who lost all his wealth as a patron of art, artists, and courtesans. Throughout the play he laments his poverty and inability to play a patron. When a thief makes a perfect round hole in the brick wall of his house and steals precious gems, Carudatta regrets only half-jokingly not having more for the thief to steal.[32] The perfect round hole in the wall suggested to Carudatta that the thief may have been an artist who had fallen on bad times and was perhaps forced to steal for survival. Carudatta's self-image appears to be that of a patron of art and artists.

When the *Kāmasūtra* expresses its concern for the artists, this concern is ultimately anchored in the concern for art itself. After all, this ethics was intended to make sure that *samāja* as a festival of arts was held successfully and in the right spirit. The real content of this social ethics, therefore, was art. Under the leadership of the city dandy, the *Kāmasūtra*'s was an attempt to build a city on the basis of art. Behind the *Kāmasūtra*'s modest and humble façade lay a comprehensive vision of society anchored in erotic-aesthetic pleasure (*kāma*). This ethics that anchored the figure of the city dandy was the commitment toward making aesthetics the foundation of the city. It was the city dandy's aesthetic pursuit that transformed him into a leader of the city. Thus, when the *Kāmasūtra* changes the designation of the dandy from patron-consort of the courtesan (*vaiśika*) to the city dandy (*nāgaraka*), it does two things: it partly reflects the already changed and considerably expanded function of the dandy in the life of the city, but it also makes the city dandy—together with the courtesan—the primary bearer of its vision of the city anchored in art.

One also needs to keep in view the historical context of the emergence of the city dandy as the leading male figure in the *Kāmasūtra* grounded in aesthetic pleasure. After a period of well over half a millennium of rapid and profound changes in all spheres of life—political, economic, social, religious, and cultural—in the third century CE, when the *Kāmasūtra* was most likely composed and compiled, Indian society and culture found itself in a period of consolidation. This was also true of cities: after centuries of rapid growth, which started in about the sixth century BCE, cities were beginning to develop a coherent urban culture and ethos of their own, and they were in search of a discourse that could give them a systematic form in thought. These cities were still trying to find an identity, a principle that would turn them into more than a collection of individuals pursuing their own economic interests. Both the *Kāmasūtra* and the *Nāṭyaśāstra* appeared as an answer to that search. A city or a society, after all, could be based on different things: state, religion, morality, law, and caste. Two broad visions claiming to offer a comprehensive foundation to society acquired prominence in the centuries preceding the *Kāmasūtra*: the discourse of political power (*artha*), anchored in the institution of the state and the figure of the king, and the discourse of-Brahmanical law (*dharma*), anchored in the division and hierarchy of castes and the figure of the Brahmin. Although the discourse of political power continued to exert immense influence, the period in which the *Kāmasūtra* came to be written witnessed the rapid ascendance of the Brahmanical vision of *dharma* based on caste identity. But the hold of caste as an organizing framework of life in the city seems not to have been sufficiently strong to offer the city a firm ground. This was perhaps due to the dominance in the city of an economy based on money, a historical force that could not be contained within the discourse of caste identity. Recall that the *Kāmasūtra* does not make caste identity a factor in the life of a city dandy; substantial reserves of money alone mattered. In the play *The Little Clay Cart,* Carudatta, the hero, is a Brahmin by caste but a businessman by profession.

The significance of the city in the origin of the discourse of sexual-erotic pleasure stands in stark relief when one considers the figure of an aspiring dandy in the village, to whom the *Kāmasūtra* dedicates only two sutras.[33] As soon as the *Kāmasūtra* turns to addressing this dandy, caste makes its appearance. The same *Kāmasūtra* that does not discuss the caste identity of the city dandy suggests to the village dandy to assemble a group of like-minded individuals from his own caste to form a salon.[34] In this suggestion the *Kāmasūtra* seems to assume *dharma* to be the dominant discourse in the village. It also appears that there were no women in the village salons of these aspiring dandies because the *Kāmasūtra* does not bring up courtesans or other women at all in those two sutras. Since the presence of courtesans in cities assumed a developed money-based economy, their absence in villages is understandable. Strict enforcement of caste rules also may have played a role in keeping women out of public forums. The absence of women meant that the sexual-erotic dimension was almost entirely missing in the lives of the dandies in the village. Instead, the *Kāmasūtra* instructs them to talk about city dandies in their gatherings for their own edification. This advice assumes that the leading city dandies were figures well known far beyond the city limits. In other words, the lives of city dandies and the courtesans as their companions were received as works of oral literature of love and care for the arts in the forums of village dandies. The severely limited resources of an aspiring dandy in the village reveals that in the absence of rich and powerful cities a discourse of sexual-erotic pleasure as reflected in the *Kāmasūtra* would have been impossible.

If the *Kāmasūtra* chose the "city dandy" to be the new designation of the old dandy-consort of the courtesan, then that was because in the figure of the city dandy two destinies met: the destiny of the city, as an emergent form of social life in search of an organizing principle in tune with its needs and ethos, and the status of erotic-aesthetic pleasure. The *Kāmasūtra* developed the discursive profile of the city dandy as a patron of art and artists. In fact, the patronage of arts and artists emerged as the city dandy's primary form of social ethics. The city dandy was the bearer and embodiment of this social ethics as care of art and artists, and indeed he was reconfigured by the *Kāmasūtra* in order to carry it out. The fact that the city dandy was expected to have a considerable amount of wealth before setting out on the path of dandyism was partly because of this expectation of patronage of arts and artists. It was as a patron of arts and artists that the city dandy emerged as one of the leaders of the city. In the care of art and artists as the ethics of the city dandy, it was the nature of the city itself that came to be determined. There has been so much emphasis in existing scholarship on the Brahmanical discourse of *dharma*, the discourse of power, and the various religious discourses based on notion of spiritual liberation that it has gone almost unnoticed that the *Kāmasūtra*, together with the *Nāṭyaśāstra*, also offered a comprehensive counter-vision anchored in art as a foundation of society.

The union of the social and the aesthetic was neither a matter of simple coincidence nor the *Kāmasūtra*'s own innovation. The *Kāmasūtra* as a text was part of a powerful movement in classical Indian culture seeking to construct an erotic-aesthetic discourse of pleasure (*kāma*) as a counter to the discourse of *dharma*. About a century before the *Kāmasūtra*, the *Nāṭyaśāstra* had already taken the first major step in this direction. Indeed, the *Kāmasūtra* was carrying on and consolidating a legacy it inherited from the *Nāṭyaśāstra*. The *Nāṭyaśāstra* and the *Kāmasūtra* are twin discourses that carry the same social and cultural ethos and vision. In light of the *Kāmasūtra's* notion of social ethics (*gaṇa dharma*) anchored in art, it is significant that in its origin narrative the *Nāṭyaśāstra* presented its own birth as a treatise on theater as an answer to an ethical crisis that threatened the cohesion and stability of society. Bharata, the author of the *Nāṭyaśāstra*, tells those eager to learn about the origin of the art of theater: "Then there was ascendance of vulgarity [*grāmyadharma*] . . . people came under the sway of sensuality and greed; they became afflicted with jealousy and anger . . . [then] the gods with the great Indra as their leader, came to Brahma and said, 'We want an object of play (*krīḍanīyaka*), which must be audible and visible [that is to say, theater]. Since the four existing Vedas cannot be heard by Śūdras [the lowest caste], be pleased to create the fifth Veda for all castes (*varṇas*).'"[35]

The fifth Veda that Brahma is implored to create is none other than the *Nāṭyaśāstra* itself. This citation reveals in the starkest way the measure of significance attached to art and aesthetics as a founding principle of society. It is remarkable that the gods did not ask Brahmā for a new avatar of god, or a new code of law, a better king, or a more powerful state, but rather for theater as a form of art, an object of play (*krīḍanīyaka*) to become the anchor of a society threatened by signs of moral degeneration reflected in the rise in greed, avarice, and sensual pleasure. This origin story of the *Nāṭyaśāstra* follows the exact pattern of the narrative associated with the coming of the new avatar of god each time ethics comes under serious threat, except that it is the *Nāṭyaśāstra* as a treatise on theater that appears in place of god. Art is offered as an anchor to the counter-discourse of ethics against the existing discourse of Brahmanical law (*dharma*) based in the division and hierarchy of castes.[36] The vision of the *Kāmasūtra* of the city based in art needs to be located within this broader historical-discursive context.[37]

Erotics and Aesthetics: The Nature of Continuity and Complementarity

It should be pointed out that the *Kāmasūtra* was not attempting to create a vision of a utopian society; it did not describe a society as it ideally ought to be. On the contrary, it was an aspect of the existing historical society that found its self-consciousness in the text of the *Kāmasūtra*. The vision and the discourse articulated in the *Kāmasūtra* are anchored in concrete historical practices. Indeed, this text is one of the most important historical documents opening up a window on everyday life in major ancient Indian cities.[38] The *Kāmasūtra* sought to construct a comprehensive vision of a society on the basis of existing institutions, ideas, practices, and figures that together offered a vision of the society counter to the one described in the *Mānava Dharmaśāstra*. After all, the *Kāmasūtra* was not a revolutionary discourse determined to constitute a new society on new principles. It is what could be called a pedagogical text.

Historically, the figure of the city dandy was derived from the figure of the courtesan. In his dual commitment to erotics and aesthetics, he mirrors the dual aspect of the courtesan. Apart from her erotic persona, the courtesan also had the public persona of an exemplary figure in the field of art. Just as in the domain of erotics, the courtesan was also the sovereign figure in the domain of art and aesthetics. It was as an artist that the courtesan, according to the *Kāmasūtra*, became a role model.[39] Even though the designation of city dandy seems to deterritorialize the figure of the dandy from the courtesan and territorialize it on the city, this ought not to be seen solely as an attempt on the part of the *Kāmasūtra* to hide the dandy's historical origins. The new name is also a sign that the discourse and practice of art and aesthetics that had its historical origin in the figure of the courtesan was beginning to radiate out to the larger society and gradually shape the city's identity. In the figure of the city dandy and the vision of the society anchored in art, the *Kāmasūtra* only sought to consolidate the historical achievements of the courtesan in the fields of both sexual-erotic and aesthetic pleasure. The city dandy was nothing but a new historical agent that carried forward what had its origin in the figure of the courtesan. In her life the courtesan offered the city and society new cultural and intellectual resources that she alone had to found a new discourse.

Why should the *Kāmasūtra* as a founding text on erotics be so committed to a vision of the city anchored in art and aesthetics? It is important to note that almost universally, an opposition is assumed between sex as a purely sensual experience and art as an intellectual-aesthetic experience. What is also assumed is that aesthetics has to do with works of art—a text of poetry, a painting, a sculpture, a melody—and its experience at a personal level, as if a sexual-erotic relationship of love could not belong to the domain of aesthetics. It was because women were reduced to nothing more than bodies that sex itself came to be seen as a purely sensual experience.[40] As shown in chapter 2, it was the discourse of Brahmanical law (*dharma*) in ancient India that put the woman's body at the disposal of man, even as it excluded the discourse of love as the anchor of the relationship between the husband and the wife.[41] This discourse had reduced women to being silent objects of pleasure. The husband spoke to his wife only in the language of command. There was no need for this man of patriarchy and virility to sing plaintively or dance amorously, let alone fall on the woman's feet as a gesture of supplication, as recommended by the dandy-guru in the *bhāṇas*.[42] After all, it was the woman's duty to serve her husband in the matter of sex, just as she had served him in every other aspect of his life.

Although Foucault problematized sex as a discursive phenomenon in the context of *scientia sexualis*, in the view of the *Kāmasūtra*, sex is always already a discursive phenomenon—there is no sex in itself. When the discourse and relationship of love are absent—as they were in the discourse of *dharma*—it does not mean that sex takes place in a discursive vacuum. What silently takes its place is the discourse of power evident in virility. When sex does not take place under the discourse of love, it occurs under the patriarchal discourse of power and virility. While the husband-wife relationship under the discourse of *dharma* constituted one discursive universe, the relationship between the courtesan and the dandy anchored in the discourse of love constituted another. Both of them involved sex, yet the discursive context was vastly different: while the former occurred under the discourse of power, the latter happened under the discourse of love.

As discussed in chapter 2, the *Kāmasūtra* states that, unlike animals, man approaches sex thoughtfully or "thinkingly." That is to say, discursively; it is in and through discourse that sexual pleasure becomes possible amongst humans. Sex, in other words, is a discursive event and experience. It was to refer to this discursive aspect of the erotic relationship and pleasure that the dandy-guru in the *bhāṇas* used the word *śabdakāma,* or "pleasure and love of the word."[43] This "pleasure of the word" is nothing but the pleasure of discourse. There is no sexual pleasure without discursive pleasure. This discourse, on the other hand, is none other than the discourse of love. The *Kāmasūtra* referred to precisely the same thing in the notion of *ābhimānika sukha,* or "pleasure of the mind-self."[44] According to the *Kāmasūtra*, only when sensual pleasure is injected with the pleasure of the mind-self that real erotic pleasure is born. This pleasure of the mind-self is the discursive pleasure of love that anchors the partners in an erotic relationship. The *Kāmasūtra* developed this notion precisely to counter the widespread belief at the time that sex was purely a sensual event and experience. Recall that the erotic routine of moon gazing (*candrikā-sevana*), which consisted of nothing more than a couple in love together gazing at the starry night while exchanging stories about the planets and constellations, was capable of generating pleasure of the highest intensity without involving sex at all. In this event it is impossible to distinguish erotic from aesthetic experience.

The public pedagogy in art and aesthetics as evident in the *Kāmasūtra* was a medium and instrument of devirilizing patriarchal masculinity. Once aesthetics as a discursive relationship of love is established between men and women, women are no longer simply regarded as being "bodies." In the discourse of love, women become subjects and objects of love. Recall that in the period preceding the writing of the *Kāmasūtra* women were excluded from the discourses of both political power (*artha*) and Brahmanical law (*dharma*). Those two discourses were not available to them in their communication with men. It was the hegemonic dominance of those two discourses—particularly Brahmanical law—that reduced women to being listeners and thus set up the relationship of obedience and command between her and her husband. Under these historical and discursive circumstances, the only discourse that could set up a channel of communication between men and women was that of love—the erotic-aesthetic discourse of love. It is for this reason that the *Kāmasūtra* insists on husbands establishing a discursive relationship of love with their newly wedded wives before proceeding to sex.[45] It also adds that a woman begins to hate sex and her husband, and men in general, if he engages in sex with her before establishing a discursive relationship of love.[46]

It is evident that in aesthetics as a discourse of love, it was the nature and fate of gender relations that hung in the balance. There is a freedom and equality of women inherent to the discourse of love. In a society in which under the ascendant and hegemonic discourse of *dharma* the discourse of love was slowly receding as an anchor to the relationship between men and women, theater, together with other forms of art, played a critical role in keeping that discourse alive in public space. Recall that Indian theater at the time, and for a long time to come, was synonymous with the theater of love, as if love was the only narrative worthy of being staged. As the *Nāṭyaśāstra* states, this theater of love as a public spectacle was watched not only by couples in love but also by fathers and sons, husbands and wives, mothers and daughters-in-law together. It is impossible to exaggerate the pedagogical value of this theater of love in the relations between men and women. This theater, and the arts in general, functioned as a public archive of the complex world of erotics: subtle but critical gestures, postures, attitudes, expressions, utterances, and acts of love.

It is in this historical and discursive context that we need to locate the reasons why the *Kāmasūtra* anchored its main male figure in the complex and demanding world of aesthetic pleasure; why a figure supposedly constructed as a model of erotic pleasure nevertheless had to devote a considerable part of his time and largesse to aesthetic pursuits. In the view of the *Kāmasūtra*, for *ars erotica* to be possible, a culture and society must also seek to anchor itself in art. Since no culture can ground itself in art and aesthetics entirely—given the presence of relations of power—it must seek to construct it as a counter-vision and discourse. The possibility of *ars erotica* in a culture, in other words, cannot be separated from the possibility of a vision of society based on art. *Ars erotica* as reflected in the *Kāmasūtra*, therefore, is nothing more than an extension into the field of erotic pleasure, a vision of a society founded on art. It was only as part of a larger vision of a society based on art that the domain of sexual-erotic practices came to acquire *ars erotica* in the form of the *Kāmasūtra*. It was with this vision in view that the *Kāmasūtra* constructed the figure of the city dandy as its main historical agent. If the *Kāmasūtra* invested the city dandy with duties that were primarily aesthetic in nature that was because it understood that it was in aesthetics that its own being as a discourse of erotics was at stake.

Conclusion

In the *Kāmasūtra*, the private pursuit of erotic pleasure and the public pursuit of aesthetic pleasure were two sides of one and the same phenomenon. In Indian culture the two ends of this erotic-aesthetic pleasure became reflected in the twin texts of the *Kāmasūtra* and the *Nāṭyaśāstra*. Sexual-erotic pleasure could be pursued only in conjunction with the pursuit of aesthetic pleasure. *Ars erotica* as a discourse was possible only in a culture that could project art and aesthetics as the core organizing principle of society. *Ars erotica*, as articulated in the *Kāmasūtra*, was an extension of this aesthetic vision of society based on art into the domain of sexual-erotic practices. It is not surprising, therefore, that even though historically the *Nāṭyaśāstra* had its origin in the sexual-erotic practices involving the courtesan and her patron-consort, discursively it preceded the *Kāmasūtra*—the founding text on erotics—as the primary carrier of this aesthetic vision by about a century.

Erotic pleasure is often regarded as a selfish, private, and furtive pursuit that begins and ends with sex. It is taken for granted, therefore, that let alone claiming to be the foundation of a society, erotic pleasure cannot generate a public discourse of its own.[47] Not surprisingly, it is often thought that of the three ends, only political power (*artha*) and Brahmanical law (*dharma*) offered a larger discourse and vision of society, while erotic pleasure (*kāma*) got lost in narrow pursuits. Nothing could be farther from the truth. The *Kāmasūtra* clearly has embedded within it a larger vision of a society anchored in erotic-aesthetic pleasure. Both the *Kāmasūtra* and the *Nāṭyaśāstra* offer this vision as a counter to the other two major visions offered—first, by the *Arthaśāstra* of a society anchored in the institution of the state and the figure of the king, and second, by the *Mānava Dharmaśāstra* of a society anchored in the division and hierarchy of castes and in the figure of the Brahmin. Art and aesthetics in Indian culture in the period of the *Nāṭyaśāstra* and the *Kāmasūtra* functioned as a public discourse of love, and complementing *artha* and *dharma*, constituted the third ontological domain.[48]

Centuries later, in Rājaśekhara's allegorical retelling of the original story of the birth of theater in the *Nāṭyaśāstra*, a geographical-territorial dimension was added to this vision of a society based in art.[49] A ninth-century court poet in central India, Rājaśekhara tells the story of the origin of literature as a love story between Poetry Man, the son of Sarasvatī, the goddess of speech, and Poetics Woman, the daughter of the goddess Umā, Śiva's wife. Dejected at not being allowed to accompany his mother to heaven for a meeting with the god Brahmā, Poetry Man left his home. Poetics Woman followed him as he wandered through different regions—east, north, west, and south—

of India because her love alone could bring him back. Seeking to win his love, she performed on stage in a style unique to each of the four regions, first elaborated in the *Nāṭyaśāstra*. When she finally unveiled the irresistible erotic-romantic style (*kaiśikī*)—at the heart of the *Nāṭyaśāstra* and the classical Sanskrit theater—in the south, Poetry Man fell in love and married her, and they returned home to the snowy mountains of the Himalayas. But their real home, Rājaśekhara added, was in the imagination of poets.

Rājaśekhara's love story was far more than a mere ruse to enumerate the major regions of India and their literary styles. In this story the political map of India is redrawn as a literary map of a country grounded in art. It is mapped out on the geography of India in a way that the four major regions, each home to a unique literary style, become the waystations in a circular journey of love; this love story that ends in the marriage of Poetry Man and Poetics Woman also ties the four regions of the country together into a knot. Unity of India in this story is envisioned as a unity of multiple literary styles grounded together in aesthetic pleasure, as if in the unity of literature it was also the nature and unity of the country that was at stake. After all, it was not a mere coincidence that it was as a poet that Rājaśekhara became a geographer of India.

Rājaśekhara's was a far more ambitious project than is often realized: it was to ground the state itself in aesthetic pleasure. He addresses the king as "king-poet" as if it was not enough for the king to be a great patron or a connoisseur of art and poetry; the king had to become a poet himself.[50] The same chapter that describes the daily routine of the poet also describes the routine of a king, as if they were one and the same. Rājaśekhara goes further still: he wants to found a society of poets, which is to say, a society grounded in poetry and aesthetic pleasure. He says, "The king-poet should establish a society (*samāja*) of poets."[51] As if to remove any doubts that by society he meant more than merely a club of poets, Rājaśekhara adds in the very next sentence, "When the king is a poet, the whole world (*sarvo lokaḥ*) becomes a poet."[52] It was not to become a better or more powerful ruler that the king needed to become a poet, but to be a role model for his subjects. Literature is not meant to be a means, but the ground and highest telos of the state to found a society grounded in aesthetic pleasure. It was an attempt to subordinate political power to the discourse of aesthetic pleasure. This was not an instance of putting literature and aesthetics in the service of the state, but exactly the opposite: putting state in the service of literature grounded in aesthetic pleasure. Only a little over a century later, near where Rājaśekhara had lived, reigned perhaps the greatest of such king-poets, Bhoja. For a king, the amount of writings—both literary and theoretical—he has left behind is astonishing in its originality, encyclopaedic range, and erudition.

Rājaśekhara's vision was not his alone; it was the culmination of a process that had been in the making for over half a millennium; here we see the movement set off by the *Nāṭyaśastra* and the *Kāmasūtra* find its full expression. Nor should it be seen as a royal project in its origin: long before the royal court became its custodian and trustee, this project had its origin in the trinity of the courtesan, the dandy-guru, and the city dandy. But the evolution and culmination of this vision of a society based on erotic-aesthetic pleasure was also marked by a break: the aesthetics-poetics of love parts way from the erotics of love. Bhoja's work is called *Śṛṅgāraprakāśa*, or "Light on Erotic Passion"; it could also be simply translated as Light on Love.[53] The poet of love has replaced the triumvirate of the courtesan, the city dandy, and the dandy-guru, and sexual-erotic relations of love have been replaced by the love in the imagination of the poet. Rājasekhara, in fact, added a chapter on the daily routine of a poet with an eye on the *Kāmasūtra*'s chapter on the daily routine of the city dandy.[54] The courtesan and the dandy-guru were still present in the royal court of Rājasekhara, but they sat behind the royal poet, far away from the bustling streets of the city, pale shadows of their old selves.[55]

7

Foucault and the *Kāmasūtra*: Parting Ways

Legend has it that Śaṅkara, the great eighth-century renunciate monk-philosopher and follower of the path of spiritual liberation, once offered a discourse on erotics when challenged by one of his interlocutors.[1] The cannabis-smoking *sadhus* whom we encountered in our discussion on Foucault in chapter 1 credit the same Śaṅkara for establishing their orders, into which they are still initiated as wandering celibate renunciates. While on a long campaign for an intellectual-spiritual conquest of India, one of Śaṅkara's female interlocutors challenged him to enlighten her on the subject of erotics. Caught by surprise at this unexpected turn of events, the celibate philosopher risked losing the debate if he failed to rise to the challenge. The ascetic pleaded for some time. He then left his own body in the care of his disciples and entered the body of a just-deceased king. In the body of the now newly revived king Śaṅkara went on to experience all aspects of sexual-erotic life. Having thus acquired the knowledge of the ways of sexual-erotic pleasure Śaṅkara returned to his interlocutor to offer his discourse on erotics and won the debate.

What we see hidden in this legend is an exact reproduction of the logic and structure of the historical origin of *ars erotica* as theater in India. It was not as himself that Śaṅkara experienced sexual-erotic pleasure-love, but as another person. Nor was his marriage as a king a true marriage, but only a theater of marriage. He was not the real husband; he only played one. The idea was not to become a husband as a step to becoming a father, the course laid out for men in the discourse of Brahmanical law, but only to experience both love and pleasure. His marriage was grounded in pleasure-love, not *dharma*. Śaṅkara's erotic detour was thus a theater of both identity and truth in the service of sexual-erotic pleasure, exactly as Foucault had surmised *ars erotica* to be when he contrasted it with *scientia sexualis,* grounded in truth and self. This legend reveals exactly what the investigations into the historical origins of the *Kāmasūtra* and the *Nāṭyaśāstra* also have: the inseparability of the discourses of sexual-erotic pleasure and the theater of love.

Sigmund Freud, the founder of psychoanalysis as a discourse of what Foucault called *scientia sexualis,* once observed that an extramarital sexual affair could prevent the onset of a looming neurosis in a married but unhappy woman long before psychoanalysis would need to step in with a cure. Recall that together with the courtesan, the wife as an adulteress was one of the actresses in the theater of pleasure-love in the *Kāmasūtra.* It is as if erotics grounded in pleasure-love and psychoanalysis grounded in truth and self were alternative ways of dealing with the same problem of neurosis.[2] On their parts, both the *Kāmasūtra* and the *Nāṭyaśāstra* also acknowledged a link between love and madness in listing it (madness) as one of the ten stages of love.[3] Here love and pleasure, until now inseparable in the *Kāmasūtra,* part ways. Madness, after all, is a stage of love, not pleasure; indeed, madness is precisely the absence of pleasure. In the absence of the other to whom it is directed and in whom it would have found its fulfillment as sexual-erotic pleasure, this love begins a long and lonely journey that passes through many waystations before arriving at madness, and then terminating in death as the final stage. Madness is the absence of the other as a figure of love. For both the *Kāmasūtra* and the *Nāṭyaśāstra,* the history of madness is a part of the history of love. In not calling madness an illness, the *Kāmasūtra* reveals an important aspect of *ars erotica.* To call madness illness, after all, would have amounted to declaring love itself to be an illness, an absence of health, as if love were a medical problem.

But that is precisely what Freud did: in treating madness as an illness, Freud reduced love—love for the other—to an illness. What cure did Freud offer for this illness? Once again, the answer to this question from the perspective of the *Kāmasūtra* and the *Nāṭyaśāstra* is inescapable: Freud offered truth and self-love, or truth as self-love, as a cure. In search for a cure to madness, Freud substituted the otherness of another person to whom one's love is directed by the otherness of one's unconscious. With this substitution the question of love for another person is transformed into the question of the truth of one's desire hiding in one's own unconscious, as if in love one is related to one's own unconscious, that is to say, with oneself. The endless search for the truth of one's desire in the unconscious is at the heart of that economy of self-love. The erotic problem of the seduction of the other becomes the medical-scientific problem of the search for truth within one's own self. Even as psychoanalysis holds out the hope to liberate one from one's dependence on the other and someday lift oneself up by one's own bootstraps, this bottomless and labyrinthine unconscious grounded in truth and the reflexive self is just another version of Foucault's prison, self as prison.

But love as the cornerstone of erotics in the *Kāmasūtra* is also missing from Foucault's reflections on *ars erotica*. One major difference between Foucault and the *Kāmasūtra* is in their choices of the primary figures and relationships of sexual-erotic pleasure. These differences are just as profound and revealing as their similarities. While the *Kāmasūtra* declared the courtesan to be the sovereign figure in the domain of erotics, Foucault chose the stranger. The *Kāmasūtra* grounded sexual-erotic pleasure in the discourse and relationship of love. The relationship between strangers, however, is a chance encounter that is exhausted by the event of pleasure. Not surprisingly, the discourse and relationship of love beyond the event of pleasure is missing in Foucault. Is the rise of the stranger as the primary figure of sexual-erotic pleasure in Foucault merely a matter of personal choice, or is it a major historical development symptomatic of the age we live in? Is it possible that what we encounter in Foucault's stranger as the exemplary figure of pleasure is a herald of the death of love both as a discourse and as a relationship? Was the historian of the death of man also the prophet of the death of love?

Despite the difference, a reading of the *Kāmasūtra* as presented in this book makes it evident that Foucault's thoughts on *ars erotica* are profoundly insightful in anticipating the fundamental fault lines that determined the nature and origin of the discourse of erotics in ancient India. His decision to problematize both *ars erotica* and *scientia sexualis* in terms of a conflict over legislative sovereignty between truth and identity, on the one hand, and sexual-erotic pleasure, on the other, seems to be at the very heart of the *Kāmasūtra*. Foucault's insight that the presence or absence of *ars erotica* in a culture is not a matter of chance but reflects the deepest undercurrents of a culture's relation with knowledge formation also seems to be absolutely correct.

Yet, Foucault in his later life seems to have developed misgivings about his earlier contrast of *ars erotica* and *scientia sexualis* as one of the starting points of his original research agenda. In one of his interviews Foucault offers a clue. Responding to a question relating to *ars erotica*, Foucault, somewhat surprisingly, said,

> One of the numerous points where I was wrong in that book was what I said about this *ars erotica*. I should have opposed our science of sex to a contrasting practice in our own culture. The Greeks and Romans did not have any *ars erotica* to be compared with the Chinese *ars erotica* (or at least it was not

> something very important in their culture). They had a *techne tou biou* [art of life] in which the economy of pleasure played a very large role. In this "art of life" the notion of exercising perfect mastery over oneself soon became the main issue. And the Christian hermeneutics of the self constituted a new elaboration of this *techne*.[4]

Notice that Foucault did not say that the facts or concepts behind his contrast were wrong, but rather that the choice of contrast was wrong. The alternative vision of sexual practice as a critical anchor to his project, he clearly felt now, ought to have been located in the West. From Foucault's comments one may be led to think that the issue was limited to the choice of the contrast and had nothing to do with the nature and content of the project itself, as if the change in the choice of the contrast would have left the project itself untouched. However, as we have already discussed, *ars erotica* was more than just a simple case of contrast; it anchored the critical perspective—particularly the notion of pleasure as the sovereign principle—of his entire project. Foucault's history of sexuality project, therefore, would not have survived in its original form if Foucault changed the contrast.[5]

In fact, Foucault's position on the subject of *ars erotica* and pleasure had already changed at least three years before he made these comments in 1983. Not surprisingly, there took place a dramatic about-turn in Foucault's research agenda that became evident with the second and third volumes of *The History of Sexuality,* called *The Use of Pleasure* and *The Care of the Self*.[6] Even as the much-anticipated volumes of the history of sexuality seemed to get indefinitely delayed, there were clear indications from his lectures and interviews beginning in 1980 that his project was beginning to go through a radical and surprising reorientation, indeed reversal.[7] It was evident that Foucault had dropped pleasure as his critical ground, even as he transformed his project, all too abruptly, into a history of the practices of truth and self. From being a target of his critical-historical investigations, the twin notions of truth and self had become the guiding principles and the horizon of his own research.

What is also evident is the changed style of Foucault's prose that emerged in the last two volumes: it was still analytical, but deliberately and unrelentingly descriptive, without any signs of the critical tenor and fervor of old. The reason, however, is the same: insofar as pleasure in *ars erotica* was the very ground of his critique of the science of sexuality, once he decided to abandon it, Foucault in effect dropped his critical ground. In the last two volumes, he could still make it appear as if it were the history of sexuality, but as is all too apparent, he could not make it critical. Much of the drama so characteristic of Foucault's unrivaled prose in his earlier works, with its roots in the clash of contrasting perspectives, disappeared. In his final writings, Foucault's perspective is, even if not entirely identical to, largely in conformity with the perspective of his sources.[8]

In an interview given in January 1984, a few months before his death, Foucault offered, with striking candor and forthrightness, further insight into the precise nature and intellectual context of the reversal in the direction of his research. When asked about issues relating to truth and power, he stated,

> After all, why truth? Why are we concerned with truth, and more so than with the care of the self? And why must the care of the self occur only through the concern for truth? I think we are touching on a fundamental question here, what I would call *the* question for the West: How did it come about that all of western culture began to revolve around this obligation of truth that has taken a lot of different forms? Things being as they are, nothing so far has shown that it is possible to define a strategy outside of this concern. It is within the field of the obligation of truth that it is possible to move about in one way or another, sometimes against effects of domination that may be linked to structures of truth or institutions entrusted with truth.[9]

It would be difficult to find a passage as candid as this in Foucault's writings or interviews after the turn. In these few lines Foucault reveals, if only indirectly, in the starkest terms the real reasons behind the reversal in his research agenda that saw the emergence of truth and self as the sovereign categories. Foucault had often explained the change in the direction of his research in methodological and programmatic terms, as if what was at stake was nothing more than the gradual maturing and evolution of a large and complex intellectual project like the history of sexuality spanning a period of over two millennia.[10] There is no such attempt here. It is quite evident that in the turn much more than simply methodological and programmatic issues were at stake. This realization that finding a position of exteriority to truth and self may not be possible or perhaps even desirable was the watershed moment in Foucault's life as a historian-philosopher. It divides Foucault's intellectual evolution into two parts: the earlier period that was anchored in the search for an exteriority to truth and self and the later period that sought to find a ground within truth and self.

Notice also that Foucault still seems to suggest that in an ideal world one would have access to a position of exteriority to truth. He was thus at the same time acknowledging that that had indeed been the direction in which much of his own research had proceeded until then. Whether one agreed with Foucault's conclusion about the possibility of finding an exteriority to truth—and its derivative self—or not, one would have to acknowledge that the notion of pleasure as a sovereign principle in *ars erotica* constituted precisely such an exteriority, and indeed was the very ground of Foucault's critical approach to the history of sexuality. The very existence of *ars erotica* as an autonomous discourse was a proof that such a strategy was indeed possible. After all, it was in his quest to find a point of exteriority to truth as the dominant intellectual concern in the West that Foucault had chanced upon *ars erotica* in nonwestern cultures.

The helplessness evident in the citation above seems to suggest that Foucault, after years of struggle, decided to reconcile with the principles of truth and self as the ground of western culture. It shows that having abandoned the search for exteriority to these founding principles in pleasure, Foucault was fully committed to finding a new intellectual ground for himself within this long and varied history of truth and self. He still seemed committed to opposing certain traditions of truth and self—for example, metaphysics.[11] Only now it had to be opposed in the name of truth and self, another truth and self, of course, but truth and self nonetheless, not pleasure.[12] Pleasure as an event and experience of desubjectivation, death of the self, as the critical anchor of Foucault's research was a distant memory.

On the surface it may appear as if the theme of the practices of self, central in Foucault's later works, is the continuation of the old theme of inventing identities for the purpose of pleasure. But these two instances of inventing or constructing a self could not be more different. While the first takes place under the legislative sovereignty of pleasure, the second takes place under the sovereignty of truth and self. That is what explains the appearance of reflexivity in Foucault's description of the practices of self as self's work on itself.[13] This reflexivity is symptomatic of the interiority and sovereignty that the notion of self had acquired in late Foucault.[14] The same reflexivity and interiority appears in how Foucault describes the activity of thought: "What is philosophy today—philosophical activity, I mean—if it is not the critical work that thought brings to bear on itself?"[15] Not surprisingly, Foucault locates the nature of his own intellectual exertions directly in the ancient philosophical tradition of *askesis* as "an exercise of oneself in the activity of thought."[16]

Is it any surprise then that Foucault in his last years began to identify himself as a philosopher, not as a historian? If Foucault, trained as a philosopher, had nevertheless found himself doing history for much of his life, then that was because of his underlying intellectual drive to find an exteriority to philosophy—anchored in truth and self—in history.[17] Late in his life he increasingly began to characterize his works as those of a philosopher, and indeed he defended the right—modest though it was—of philosophy to look after its own business.[18] Foucault's retreat to the notion of self and truth was, therefore, also at the same time a retreat into the interiority of philosophy as distinct from history.

It has become a well-known fact that after radically revising his original project on the history of sexuality, Foucault in his last years moved his research agenda in the direction of aesthetics, or, what he called, aesthetics of existence.[19] Yet Foucault's journey from *ars erotica* to aesthetics of existence did not constitute a continuum, but rather was marked by a break, a break that saw pleasure imperceptibly recede as the sovereign category, giving way to the return of truth and self. In Foucault's version of the aesthetics of existence, art and aesthetics became a medium of the self's relation with itself. Art was no longer a medium of desubjectivation as death of the self.

Not surprisingly then, there is a vast difference between the *Kāmasūtra*'s and Foucault's notions of the aesthetics of existence: unlike in later Foucault, in the *Kāmasūtra* the aesthetics of existence was neither anchored in one's relation with oneself nor in one's relations with truth. Exactly the opposite of later Foucault, in the *Kāmasūtra* art and aesthetics functioned as a medium of relationship with the other, a medium of socialization, not a medium of self-reflection. Neither of the *Kāmasūtra's* two primary figures of pleasure—the courtesan and the dandy—was anchored in the care of the self. Since he was ever busy organizing the next literary salon or festival of arts, or enjoying the company of his friends and his beloved, it would be difficult to think of the city dandy of Pāṭalīputra—the earliest imperial city in India—sitting by himself, let alone sitting in front of a mirror, watching and admiring his own reflection as a work of art, as Baudelaire described the Parisian dandy as doing.[20]

The difference between the ancient Indian and the Parisian dandies parallels the difference between early and later Foucault: while the Indian dandy, like early Foucault, was anchored in pleasure, the Parisian dandy of Baudelaire, like later Foucault, was anchored in the self. For the Parisian dandy, art was a medium of self-reflection.[21] For the Indian dandy, art was a medium of relationship with the other, a form of play and socialization. That was also why, even as Foucault seemed to retreat from the collective to the individual in his notion of the aesthetics of existence, the *Kāmasūtra*, as evident in the figure of the city dandy, went on to offer art and aesthetics as the ground of the city.

Notes

Introduction

1. Devadatta Shastri, ed., *Kāmasūtra of Vātsyāyana, with the Commentary of Yaśodhara* (Varanasi: Chaukhambha Sanskrit Sansthan, 1964). Also, see Wendy Doniger and Sudhir Kakar, *Vātsyāyana Kāmasūtra: A New, Complete Translation of the Sanskrit Text* (New York: Oxford University Press, 2002).

2. Doniger and Kakar, *Vātsyāyana Kāmasūtra*. Apart from the introduction to her translation of the *Kāmasūtra*, Wendy Doniger has also published a number of other articles in recent years on various topics in the *Kāmasūtra*: see "The *Kāmasūtra*: It Isn't All about Sex," *Kenyon Review* 25, no. 1 (2003): 18–37; "On Translating the *Kāmasūtra*: A Gurudaskhina for Daniel H. H. Ingalls," *Journal of Indian Philosophy* 29, nos. 1–2 (2001): 81–94. Also, see Laura Desmond, "The Pleasure Is Mine: The Changing Subject of Erotic Science," *Journal of Indian Philosophy* 39 (2011): 15–39; Kumkum Roy, "Unraveling the *Kāmasūtra*," in *The Power of Gender and the Gender of Power: Explorations in Early Indian History* (New Delhi: Oxford University Press, 2010), 324–42.

3. Michel Foucault, *The History of Sexuality: An Introduction*, vol. 1 of *The History of Sexuality*, trans. Robert Hurley (New York: Vintage Books, 1990), 57.

4. "The rallying point for the counterattack against the deployment of sexuality ought not to be sex-desire, but bodies and pleasures." Foucault, *History of Sexuality: An Introduction*, 157.

5. Richard Shusterman has been an exception to this general trend. He also makes a very perceptive comparison of Chinese and Indic historical sources on the subject of *ars erotica*. See Richard Schusterman, "Asian *Ars Erotica* and the Question of Sexual Aesthetics," *Journal of Aesthetics and Art Criticism* 65, no. 1 (2007): 55–68.

6. After he touched on the subject in his first volume, Foucault never really got back to this topic of *ars erotica* in any of his published work. When he did focus on the subject of pleasure later, in the second and third volumes of *History of Sexuality*, Foucault's position was no longer the same. So these later reflections in the last two volumes, though revealing in other ways, were no longer in direct continuity with his observations on *ars erotica* and pleasure in the first volume. Most of Foucault's insightful observations on pleasure came in numerous interviews he gave in the wake of the publication of the first volume. See Michel Foucault, "The Gay Science," *Critical Inquiry* 37, no. 3 (Spring 2011): 385–403, and "An Ethics of Pleasure," in *Foucault Live: Collected Interviews, 1961–1984*, ed., Sylvere Lotringer, trans., Lysa Hochroth and John Johnson (New York, Semiotext [E]), 371–81.

7. Michel Foucault, *Discipline and Punish: The Birth of the Prison*, trans. Alan Sheridan (New York: Vintage Books, 1995).

8. "This is why, in a way that is, at the moment, absolutely sketchy *[en pointille]* and for which I have as yet no content, I was putting forward, if you will, the theme of pleasure. Which seems to me to escape the medical and naturalist connotations and which have the notions of sexuality built into them. After all, there is no 'abnormal pleasure,' there is no pathology of pleasure." Michel Foucault, "The Gay Science," 388.

9. The word *kāma* means both desire and pleasure. As I discuss later in this Introduction, as a member of the *trivarga*, or trilogy, of *dharma*, *artha*, and *kāma*, it carries the primary meaning of pleasure.

10. Foucault, *The History of Sexuality: An Introduction*, 57.

11. When I use the term "Indian culture," I do not mean it as a simple unity. Rather, I use this term in the sense of a complex whole which carries discursive conflicts and contradictions at its heart: for example, the conflict between *kāma,* or pleasure, and *dharma*, or Brahmanical law, a theme central to this book.

12. Indeed, the *Kāmasūtra* locates itself within this discursive universe very directly and self-consciously. In fact, that is the very first thing it does in the book. The first three chapters of the first book are dedicated to it. The *Kāmasūtra* uses the word *trivarga*, or set of three, that leaves out spiritual liberation as the fourth end. There is a subtle but important difference between the notions of *trivarga* and *puruṣārtha*. My purpose here, however, is limited to pointing out how knowledge is anchored in one of the ends—irrespective of where they are a set of three or a set of four—and as such is not anchored in truth. That is why as important as the difference is, its discussion here is not germane. *Kāmasūtra*, 1.1–3.

13. What the *Kāmasūtra* calls the triple set later came to be more popularly known as *puruṣārthas*, or the primary ends of man. As *puruṣārtha*, however, the ends are four in number—hence, also the name *caturavarga*, or "the set of four"—and include, apart from the three already mentioned, *mokṣa* (or spiritual liberation) as the fourth member. Even though the *Kāmasūtra* does not mention *mokṣa* as one of the ends in its opening sutra, it seems to be aware of the fact that it was widely seen as such. See *Kāmasūtra*, 1.2.4. The notion of four primary ends was so pervasive in ancient Indian culture that Sheldon Pollock calls it the Indian "common sense." Pollock thinks of the *puruṣārtha* as "one of the primary *geschichtliche Grundbegriffe*," or "historical core concepts," in the "ideal-typical template of Indian culture" that took on the "character of common sense." There are subtle and important differences in the naming of the ends as *trivarga* and *puruṣārthas*. However, given that I intend to touch only on the broadest of their aspects in a brief way, those subtle nuances are not directly relevant here. Sheldon Pollock, *The Ends of Man at the End of Premodernity* (Amsterdam: Royal Netherlands Academy of Arts and Sciences, 2005), 10. Arvind Sharma, similarly, sees the *puruṣārthas* as the "fundamental building blocks of Hindu axiology." Arvind Sharma, *The Puruṣārtha: A Study in Hindu Axiology* (East Lansing: Asian Studies Center, Michigan State University, 1982), 40. Also, see Donald R. Davis Jr., "Being Hindu or Being Human: A Reappraisal of the *Puruṣārthas,*" *International Journal of Hindu Studies* 8, nos. 1/3 (January 2004): 1–27; Sharma, *The Puruṣārthas*; Charles Malmoud, "On the Rhetoric and Semantics of *Puruṣārthas*," in T. N. Madan, ed., *Way of Life: King, Householder, Renouncer, Essays in Honour of Louis Dumont* (Delhi: Vikas, 1982), 33–54; P. Nagaraja Rao, *The Four Values in Indian Philosophy and Culture: A Study of the Puruṣārthas* (Mysore: University of Mysore, 1970); Rajendra Prasad, "The Theory of *Puruṣārthas*: Revaluation and Reconstruction," *Journal of Indian Philosophy* 9, no. 1 (1981): 49–76.

14. Patrick Olivelle, *Manu's Code of Law: A Critical Edition and Translation of the Mānava-*

Dharmaśāstra (New York: Oxford University Press, 2005), and *King, Governance, and Law in Ancient India: Kautilya's Arthaśāstra* (New York: Oxford University Press, 2013); R. P. Kangle, ed., *Kautilya: Arthaśāstra* (Bombay: University of Bombay, 1965); *Brahmasūtra: With a Commentary by Bhaskarācārya*, ed. Vindhyesvari Prasada Dvivedin (Benares: Chowkhamba Sanskrit Book Depot, 1903).

15. See Martin Heidegger, *Being and Time* (New York: State University of New York Press, Revised Edition, 2010).

16. Both the *Arthaśāstra* and the *Kāmasūtra* are aware of this potential conflict and the need to overcome it. *Arthaśāstra*, 3.7.3; *Kāmasūtra*, 1.2.1.

17. *Kāmasūtra*, 1.2.18.

18. Probably more than any other text in Indian history, Manu's *Dharmaśāstra* has determined the western understanding and perception of Indian society and culture. See Olivelle, *Manu's Code of Law*. The notion of *dharma* is one of the most complex in all of Indic intellectual history. See Patrick Olivelle, ed., *Dharma: Studies in Its Semantic, Cultural and Religious History* (Delhi: Motilal Banarsidass Publishers, 2009).

19. For works on women and the *Mānava Dharmaśāstra*, see Roy, *The Power of Gender and the Gender of Power*; Patrick Olivelle, "Rhetoric and Reality: Women's Agency in the *Dharmaśāstra*," in *Encounters with the Word: Essays to Honour Aloysius Pieris S.J.*, ed. Robert Crusz, Marshal Fernando, Asanga Tilakaratne (Colombo: Ecumenical Institute for Study and Dialogue, 2004), 489–505; Stephanie Jamison, "Women 'Between the Empires' and 'Between the Lines,'" in Patrick Olivelle, ed., *Between the Empires: Society in India 300 BCE to 400 CE* (New York: Oxford University Press, 2006), 191–214; R. M. Das, *Women in Manu and His Seven Commentators* (Varanasi: Kanchana Publications, 1962); Prabhati Mukherjee, "Widowhood and Niyoga in the Arthasastra and Manusmrti," *Our Heritage* 11, no. 1 (1963): 1–11; Deepali Bhargave. *Manu Smriti: A Sociological Analysis* (Jaipur: Rawat Publications, 1989). Also, see James B. Nelson and Sandra P. Longfellow, eds., *Sexuality and the Sacred: Studies on the Impact of Religious Teachings on Women* (Geneva: WCC Publications, 1990).

20. For discussions on the question of the historical and cultural construction of gender and sexuality, see Joan Scott, "Gender: A Useful Category of Historical Analysis," *American Historical Review* 19, no. 5 (1985): 1053–75, and "The Evidence of Experience." *Critical Inquiry* 17, no. 4 (1991): 58–68. Also, see Joanne Meyerowitz, "A History of 'Gender,'" in *AHR Forum*: "Revisiting 'Gender: A Useful Category of Historical Analysis,'" *American Historical Review* 113, no. 5 (2008): 1346–56; Jeffrey Weeks, *Sexuality and Its Discontents: Meanings, Myths, and Modern Sexualities* (London: Routledge & Kegan Paul, 1985); Denise Riley, "Am I That Name?" in *Feminism and the Category of "Women" in History* (London: Macmillan, 1988); Catherine A. MacKinnon, "Does Sexuality Have a History," *Michigan Quarterly Review* 30 (1991); S. Ortner, S. and H. Whitehead, eds., *Sexual Meanings: The Cultural Construction of Gender and Sexuality* (Cambridge: Cambridge University Press, 1981); Judith Butler, "Contingent Foundations: Feminism and the Question of Postmodernism," in *Feminists Theorize the Political*, ed. Judith Butler and Joan W. Scott (New York: Routledge, 1992), and *Gender Trouble: Feminism and the Subversion of Identity* (New York: Routledge, 1990); Gayle Rubin, "Thinking Sex: Notes for a Radical Theory of the Politics of Sexuality," in *Pleasure and Danger: Exploring Female Sexuality*, ed. Carole S. Vance (Boston: Routledge, 1984), 267–319. For an excellent introduction to the historiography on gender, see Susan Kingsley Kent, *Gender and History* (New York: Palgrave Macmillan, 2012).

21. Even as scholars of gender such as Judith Butler have problematized the self-evident nature of gender identity while exposing it as nothing more than a historical and cultural construction anchored in relations and practices of power, what is also evident about this scholar-

ship is that it rarely seeks to go beyond the discourse of identity as such. In contrast, Foucault's own reflections on sexuality and identity were anchored in pleasure that constituted an exteriority to power. Even as I expose gender identity and gender relations as historically constructed, I also approach them from the perspective of pleasure that exceeds the discourse of identity. For some of the best discussions on gender, particularly as it related to the question of identity and its historical construction anchored in power, see Judith Butler, *Gender Trouble: Feminism and the Subversion of Identity* (New York: Routledge, 2006). Also, see her *Undoing Gender* (New York: Routledge, 2004) and *Bodies That Matter: On the Discursive Limits of Sex* (New York: Routledge, 2011).

22. One of the interesting, and perhaps surprising, features of the *Kāmasūtra* is the near absence of any serious engagement with homoeroticism, though it is not absent as a detail. On the basis of the details available in the *Kāmasūtra*, it is difficult to tell the nature and status of its occurrence in the society at the time beyond the fact that it did exist. It is not possible here to delve into the phenomenon of homoeroticism in ancient India. It is, however, important to locate its precise place in the *Kāmasūtra*. Given the *Kāmasūtra's* approach in locating sexual-erotic pleasure beyond the need for reproduction, homoeroticism may appear to be a very relevant subject; homoeroticism, after all, is unburdened by the concerns about reproduction. What then explains the absence of a serious engagement with the subject of homoeroticism? In the search for an answer to this question, it is important to keep in mind that the *Kāmasūtra* ought not be seen as a theoretical or philosophical text that was bound only by the intellectual limitations of its author. On the contrary, it was bound by the limitations of the sources of its historical origin. This absence of homoeroticism as a major theme should not be attributed to the possible moral inhibitions of the author of the *Kāmasūtra*. In reality, whenever sexual practices related to homoeroticism come up, as it does in chapter 9 of book 2, the *Kāmasūtra* does not betray any signs of moral concern or judgment at all. It describes those practices as entirely normal ways of pursuing pleasure. Indeed, the *Kāmasūtra* designates the men who engaged in homoerotic pursuits as belonging to what it called "third nature" (*tṛtīyā prakṛti*). This term clearly suggests that the *Kāmasūtra* saw homoerotic sexual practices to be just as natural as those engaged in by the members of the other two "natures."

The term is all the more significant because it was by no means a generic designation used universally in ancient India. On the contrary, the medical texts in ancient India put men who engaged in homoeroticism under exactly the opposite category of *vikṛti*, or "distortion" and "deviation," that is to say, unnatural. The designation of homoeroticism as unnatural was a logical extension of the approach of medical literature that was grounded in the central concern relating to biological reproduction, more precisely embryology. In this approach, any sexual activity that could not result in reproduction fell under the category of unnatural. Since homoeroticism did not involve reproduction, it came to be termed unnatural. This was precisely the historical-intellectual context in which the *Kāmasūtra* decided to locate sexual-erotic practices in pleasure. In grounding itself in the notion of pleasure, therefore, the *Kāmasūtra* launched a counter-discourse not only to *dharma* but also to medical discourse. In an otherwise very valuable article on "queerness in classical Indian medicine," Sweet and Zwilling bundle the approach to homoeroticism in the *Kāmasūtra* with that of the medical treatises, as if there were a complete continuity between the two. The main burden of the article is to show that, contrary to Foucault's claim that homosexuality was the result of a medicalization of sexual behavior and practices that was characteristic of the West alone, it occurred in a nonwestern culture like India too. The authors come to this conclusion on the basis of their study of the two major medical treatises from the first two centuries CE, the *Carakasaṃhitā* and the *Suśrutasaṃhitā*. Nothing could be further from the truth; the approaches of the *Kāmasūtra* and the medical texts were exactly the opposite of each other. Remarkably, even as the authors note the term "third nature" as used in the *Kāmasūtra*, they do not quite draw out its far-reaching significance. The reason for this oversight on the part of these authors is their general approach, which views ancient Indian culture as a simple unity. However, as I have already discussed, culture in ancient India was a complex phenomenon that carried conflicting discursive formations at its heart. See Michael J. Sweet and Leonard Zwilling, "The First Medicalization: The Taxonomy and Etiology of Queerness in Classical Indian Medicine," *Journal of the History of Sexuality* 3, no. 4 (April 1993): 590–607; Vaidya Jādavaji Trikāmji Achārya, ed., *The Carakasaṃhitā of Agniveśa revised by Caraka and Dridhabala with the Ayurveda-Dīpika Commentary of Cakrapānidatta* (1941; rpt. New Delhi, 1981); Vaidya Jādavaji Trikāmji Achārya and Nārāyan Rām Achārya, eds., *Suśrutasaṃhitā of Suśruta* (Varanasi, 1980). For homoeroticism in the *Kāmasūtra*, see *Kāmasūtra*, 2.9.

23. Chapter 6 in the *Kāmasūtra* is dedicated exclusively to the affairs of the courtesan. Some relevant works on courtesans in ancient India are Ludwik Sternbach, *Gaṇikā-vrtta-sammṃgrahah: Or Texts on Courtezans in Classical Sanskrit* (Hoshiarpur: Visheshvarananda Vedic Research Institute, 1953), and "Legal Position of Prostitutes According to Kautilya's *Arthaśāstra*," *Journal of the American Oriental Society* 71, no. 1 (January–March 1951): 25–60; Sukumari Bhattacharji, "Prostitution in Ancient India," *Social Scientist* 15, no. 2 (February 1987): 32–61; Kumkum Roy, "Re-presenting the Courtesanal Tradition: An Exploration of Early Historical Texts," in *The Power of Gender and the Gender of Power*, 111–31; Monika Saxena, "Ganikas in Early India," *Social Scientist* 34, no. 11/12 (November–December 2006): 2–17; S. N. Sinha, N. K. Basu, and Rita Sil, *History of Marriage and Prostitution: Vedas to Vātsyāyana* (New Delhi: Khama Publishers, 1992); Moti Chandra, *The World of Courtesans* (Delhi: Vikas Publishing House, 1973); Santosh Kumar Mukherji, *Prostitution in India* (New Delhi: Inter India Publications, 1986; reprint). For a very insightful account and analysis of courtesans in modern India, see Veena Talwar Oldenburg, "Lifestyle as Resistance: The Case of the Courtesans of Lucknow, India," *Feminist Studies* 16, no. 2 (Summer 1990): 259–87.

24. The *Kāmasūtra* does not raise the issue of caste while dealing with the figure of the courtesan, in terms of either her own identity or the identity of her patrons.

25. *Nāṭyaśāstra*, 25.1.

26. I am aware that the figure of the dandy was complex in Europe, with many aspects brought out by scholars. But, in deploying the term in this book, I broadly follow Baudelaire. I also discuss the differences between the Parisian dandy and the dandy in ancient Indian cities in some detail in the postscript. See Baudelaire, *The Painter of Modern Life and Other Essays*, trans., Jonathan Mayne (London: Phaidon, 1964), 26–29.

27. *Kāmasūtra*, 1.5.3.

28. *Kāmasūtra*, 6.1.1.

29. M. Ghosh, ed., *The Nāṭyaśāstra*, ascribed to Bharata Muni, Sanskrit text, vol. 1 (Calcutta: Manisha Granthalaya, 1967), and *The Nāṭyaśāstra*, ascribed to Bharata Muni, Sanskrit text, vol. 2 (Calcutta: Bibliotheca Indica 272 A, 1956). For a general introduction, see Kapila Vatsyayan, *Bharata, The Nāṭyaśāstra* (New Delhi: Sahitya Akademi, 1996). For the theory of aesthetics developed first in the *Nāṭyaśāstra*, see Sheldon Pollock, "What Was Bhatta Nāyaka Saying: The Hermeneutical Transformation of Indian Aesthetics," in *Epic and Argument in Sanskrit Literary History: Essays in Honor of Robert P. Goldman* (Delhi: Manohar, 2010), 143–84; Sheldon Pollock, "The Social Aesthetic and Sanskrit Literary Theory," *Journal of Indian Philosophy* 29, nos. 1–2 (2001): 197–229; Edwin Gerow, "Abhinavagupta's Aesthetics as a Speculative Paradigm," *Journal of the American Oriental Society* 114, no. 2 (April–June 1994): 186–208; J. L. Masson and

M. V. Patwardhan, *Santarasa and Abhinavagupta's Philosophy of Aesthetics* (Poona: Bhandarkar Oriental Research Institute, 1969); Raniero Gnoli, *The Aesthetic Experience According to Abhinavagupta* (Varanasi: Chowkhamba Sanskrit Series Office, 1968). For the impact of the philosophy of aesthetics developed by the *Nāṭyaśāstra* on the theology of devotional form of Hinduism, see David L. Haberman, *Acting as a Way of Salvation: A Study of Rāgānuga Bhakti Sādhana* (Oxford: Oxford University Press, 1988).

30. *Nāṭyaśāstra*, 7.6+.

31. *Nāṭyaśāstra*, 24.94–96.

32. It was nothing more than an itch, a purely sensual experience. *Kāmasūtra*, 2.1.11.

33. On the problems and possibilities of the intellectual history of premodern India, see Sheldon Pollock, "Is There an Indian Intellectual History? Introduction to 'Theory and Method in Indian Intellectual History,'" *Journal of Indian Philosophy* 36 (2008): 533–42; Sheldon Pollock, ed., *Forms of Knowledge in Early Modern Asia: Explorations in the Intellectual History of India and Tibet, 1500–1800* (Durham: Duke University Press, 2011), *The Ends of Man at the End of Premodernity* (Amsterdam: Royal Netherlands Academy of Arts and Sciences, 2005), "Comparison without Hegemony," in *The Benefit of Broad Horizons: Intellectual and Institutional Preconditions for a Global Social Science*, ed. Hans Joas and Barbro Klein (Leiden: Brill, 2010), 185–204. Also, see Jan E. M. Houben and Sheldon Pollock, "Theory and Method in Indian Intellectual History," *Journal of Indian Philosophy* 36 (2008): 531–32.

34. See Michel Foucault, *The Archaeology of Knowledge and the Discourse on Language*, trans. A. M. Sheridan Smith (London: Tavistock, 1972).

35. *Śṛṅgāra-Hata: A Collection of Four Sanskrit Bhāṇas*, critically edited and translated into Hindi by Dr. Motichandra and Dr. Vasudevasharan Agrawal (Bombay: Hindi Granth Ratnakar Private Limited, 1960).

36. See Jyoti Puri, "Concerning '*Kāmasūtras*': Challenging Narratives of History and Sexuality," *Signs* 27, no. 3 (Spring 2002): 632; Antonio Rocha, "*Scientia Sexualis* versus *Ars Erotica*: Foucault, van Gulik, Needham," *Studies in History and Philosophy of Biological and Biomedical Sciences* 42 (2011): 328–43.

37. Michel Foucault, *History of Madness*, ed. Jean Khalfa, trans. Jonathan Murphy and Jean Khalfa (New York: Routledge, 2006), xxx. Edward Said, *Orientalism* (New York: Vintage Books, 1979).

Chapter 1

1. *Kāmasūtra*, 2.1.38.

2. Michel Foucault, *Lectures on the Will to Know: Lectures at the College de France with Oedipal Knowledge* (New York: Palgrave Macmillan, 2013), 2.

3. *The History of Sexuality: An Introduction*, vol. 1 of *The History of Sexuality*, trans. Robert Hurley (New York: Vintage Books, 1990), 57.

4. "The rallying point for the counter attack against the deployment of sexuality ought not to be sex-desire, but bodies and pleasures." Foucault, *History of Sexuality: An Introduction*, 157.

5. Richard Shusterman has been an exception to this general trend. He also makes a very perceptive comparison of Chinese and Indian historical sources on the subject of *ars erotica*. See Richard Schusterman, "Asian *Ars Erotica* and the Question of Sexual Aesthetics," *Journal of Aesthetics and Art Criticism* 65, no. 1 (2007): 55–68.

6. "This is why, in a way that is, at the moment, absolutely sketchy *[en pointille]* and for which I have as yet no content, I was putting forward, if you will, the theme of pleasure. Which

seems to me to escape the medical and naturalist connotations and which have the notions of sexuality built into them. After all, there is no 'abnormal pleasure,' there is no pathology of pleasure." Michel Foucault, "The Gay Science," trans. Nicolae Morar and Daniel W. Smith, *Critical Inquiry* 37, no. 3 (Spring 2011): 385–403, 388.

7. Much of James Miller's biography of Foucault brings out this aspect. James Miller, *The Passion of Michel Foucault* (Cambridge, MA: Harvard University Press, 200). For Foucault's own observations on the significance of his personal experiences for his intellectual reflections, see pages 31–32 of Miller's book.

8. I will not touch upon the nature of truth and self in general, but only in the way and to the extent it concerns the nature of pleasure. See Foucault "The Gay Science." This interview has a number of observations on the nature of pleasure that give an insight into the precise intellectual context in which Foucault decided to make it a central category in his research on sexuality. Also, see Ladelle McWhorter, *Bodies and Pleasures: Foucault and the Politics of Sexual Normalization* (Bloomington: Indiana University Press, 1999); David M. Halperin, *Saint Foucault: Towards a Gay Hagiography* (New York: Oxford University Press, 1995), 85–97.

9. Foucault, *The History of Sexuality: An Introduction*, 157.

10. All these notions had their origins in various phases of Freud's intellectual evolution. The meanings of these critical terms also went through changes. To get a sense of the evolution of these notions over a long period of time, see Sigmund Freud, *The Freud Reader*, ed. Peter Gay (New York: W. W. Norton, 1989). For "anatomy is destiny," see Sigmund Freud, *Sexuality and the Psychology of Love* (New York: A Touchstone Book, 1997), 59. For the significance of anatomy, also see Sigmund Freud, *Three Essays on the Theory of Sexuality*, trans. James Strachey (Eastford, CT: Martino Fine Books, 2011).

11. For discussions on sexuality as a discursive phenomenon, see Judith Butler, *Bodies That Matter: On the Discursive Limits of Sex* (New York: Routledge, 2011); Jeffrey Weeks, *Sexuality and Its Discontents: Meanings, Myths, and Modern Sexualities* (London: Routledge & Kegan Paul, 1985); Denise Riley, *"Am I That Name?" Feminism and the Category of "Women" in History* (London: Macmillan, 1988); Catherine A. MacKinnon, "Does Sexuality Have a History," *Michigan Quarterly Review* 30 (1991, Winter), 1–11; S. Ortner, S. and H. Whitehead, eds., *Sexual Meanings: The Cultural Construction of Gender and Sexuality* (Cambridge: Cambridge University Press, 1981); Gayle Rubin, "Thinking Sex: Notes for a Radical Theory of the Politics of Sexuality," in *Pleasure and Danger: Exploring Female Sexuality*, ed. Carole S. Vance, 267–319 (Boston: Routledge, 1984).

12. Foucault, *The History of Sexuality: An Introduction*, 57–58.

13. See parts 1, 2, and 3 in Michel Foucault, *The History of Sexuality: An Introduction*, 1–74. Also, see "The History of Sexuality," in Michel Foucault, *Power/Knowledge: Selected Interviews and Other Writings, 1972–1977*, ed. Colin Gordon (New York: Pantheon Books, 1980), 183–93; "The Confession of the Flesh," in Foucault, *Power/Knowledge*, 194–228; "The End of the Monarchy of Sex," in Foucault, *Foucault Live: Interviews, 1961–1984*, ed. Sylvere Lotringer, trans. Lysa Hochroth and John Johnston (New York: Semiotext (E), 1996), 214–25.

14. For an exhaustive survey of the notion of pleasure in Plato and Aristotle, see J. C. B. Gosling and C. C. W. Taylor, *The Greeks on Pleasure* (Oxford: Clarendon Press, 1982).

15. Michel Foucault, *The Use of Pleasure* (New York: Vintage Books, 1990), 78–93, 229–46. For translation and general interpretations of Plato's dialogues on the question of eros, particularly the *Symposium* and the *Phaedrus*, see Alexander Nehmas and Paul Woodruff, trans., *Plato: Phaedrus* (Indianapolis: Hackett, 1995), and *Plato: Symposium* (Indianapolis: Hackett, 1989); K. J. Dover, *Plato's Symposium* (Cambridge: Cambridge University Press, 1980).

16. Foucault, *The Use of Pleasure*, 229–46. For a thorough discussion of *eros*, or love, and *philia*, or friendship, in Plato and Aristotle, see A. Price, *Love and Friendship in Plato and Aristotle* (Oxford: Clarendon Press, 1989).

17. *The Use of Pleasure*, 229–46. For *scientia sexualis* as a subtle form of *ars erotica*, see *History of Sexuality: An Introduction*, 70–72. For the notions of truth and eros in Foucault, see John Rajchman, *Truth and Eros: Foucault, Lacan, and the Question of Ethics* (New York: Routledge, 1991). For the *Symposium*, see *Plato: Complete Works*, ed. John M. Cooper, trans. Alexander Nehamas and Paul Woodruff (Indianapolis: Hackett Publishing Company, 1997), 457–505. Also, for the notion of eros in Plato's dialogues, particularly the *Symposium*, see D. C. Schindler, "Plato and the Problem of Love: On the Nature of Eros in the Symposium," *Apeiron: A Journal for Ancient Philosophy and Science* 40, no. 3 (Sept. 2007): 199–220; Frisbee Sheffield, *Plato's Symposium: The Ethics of Desire* (Oxford: Clarendon Press, 2006); David Roochnik, "The Erotics of Philosophical Discourse," *History of Philosophy Quarterly* 4, no. 2 (Apr., 1987): 117–29; D. C. Schindler, "Plato and the Problem of Love: On the Nature of Eros in the 'Symposium'" *Apeiron: A Journal for Ancient Philosophy and Science* 40, no. 3, (Sept., 2007): 199–220; Timothy E. Mahoney, "Is the Socratic Eros in the 'Symposium' Egoistic?" *Apeiron: A Journal of Ancient Philosophy and Science* 29, no. 1 (Mar., 1996): 1–18; David M. Halperin, "Plato and Erotic Reciprocity," *Classical Antiquity* 5, no. 1 (Apr., 1986): 60–80, and "Platonic Eros and What Men Call Love," *Ancient Philosophy* 5 (1985): 161–204.

18. Foucault, *The Use of Pleasure*, 242, 243.

19. When Foucault in the first volume of T*he History of Sexuality* called *scientia sexualis* grounded in truth a subtle form of *ars erotica* he could have as well been talking about Greek philosophy as it came to be articulated in the dialogues of Plato.

20. Foucault, *The History of Sexuality: An Introduction*, 71–72.

21. The notions of truth and self are umbilically tied together: both truth and self assume a certain reflexivity—the ability to turn back on themselves—that gives them interiority and autonomy. This reflexivity evident in the notion of thought thinking itself would not be possible without the self's ability to contemplate itself, as if in a mirror. The reflexivity of thought and self together constitute a unity; one is not possible in the absence of the other; the notions of truth and self-consciousness, therefore, go together. It is this reflexivity that offers both truth and self the interiority on the basis of which they can then claim autonomy from history, as if it were truth and self that make history, not the other way around. The two are, therefore, inseparable. It is for this reason that truth and self appear together in Foucault's works.

22. Michel Foucault, *Ethics: Subjectivity and Truth* (New York: New Press, 1997), 166.

23. Halperin, *Saint Foucault*, 86–87.

24. Foucault "The Gay Science," 399.

25. Michel Foucault, *Discipline and Punish*, trans. Alan Sheridan (New York: Vintage Books, 1995), 30. James Bernauer calls it "the single most important phrase in Foucault's writing." James Bernauer SJ in Michel Foucault, *Religion and Culture*, select. and ed. Jeremy Carrette (New York: Routledge, 1999), xiii.

26. This interview took place at Foucault's house on July 10, 1978. "The Gay Science," 400.

27. Foucault, "The Gay Science," 399–400. Since power operates in and through subjection, Foucault's claim amounts to saying that the event of pleasure exceeds the structures of power. Given how pervasive the structures of power appear in Foucault's works, the significance of pleasure as an event of de-subjection ought not to be underestimated. One could go so far as to argue that pleasure in its autonomy constituted an exteriority to power.

28. Foucault, "The Gay Science," 390.

29. As Foucault himself points out, it is not even accessible to heterosexual individuals. Foucault, "The Gay Science," 399.

30. Foucault, *The Use of Pleasure*, 25–32, 33–94, 185–226.

31. Foucault, *The Use of Pleasure,* 109–16.

32. Hubert L. Dreyfus and Paul Rabinow, *Michel Foucault: Beyond Structuralism and Hermeneutics* (Chicago: University of Chicago Press, 1983), 233.

33. David Halperin cited in James Davidson, "Dover, Foucault and Greek Homosexuality: Penetration and the Truth of Sex," *Past & Present*, no. 170 (Feb., 2001): 5.

34. Foucault, "The Gay Science," 389.

35. Cited in Halperin, *Saint Foucault,* 95.

36. Foucault, *The History of Sexuality: An Introduction*, 45.

37. See particularly the opening chapter, called "The Death of the Author." Miller, *Passion of Michel Foucault*, 13–36.

38. Foucault, "An Ethics of Pleasure," in *Foucault Live: Collected Interviews, 1961–1984*, ed. Sylvere Lotringer, trans. Lysa Hochroth and John Johnson (New York, Semiotext (E), 1996), 378.

39. "The philosophies that promise to teach us what to think about death or how to die bore me to tears." See "The Simplest of Pleasures" in *Foucault Live*, 296. How radically different this understanding and experience of death is should be evident as soon as one thinks of other major philosophical reflections on death. Death, for example, plays a major role in Heidegger's *Being and Time*. What is interesting is that in Heidegger self constitutes itself in the face of and in constant anticipation of its death. Indeed, formation of the self in the face of death functions as a measure and standard of authenticity of a self. In Foucault it is exactly the opposite: death is not a source of authentic self; it is a moment of loss of the self. Martin Heidegger, *Being and Time*, trans. John Macquarrie and Edward Robinson (San Francisco: HarperSanFrancisco, 1962), H.235–H.266.

40. Foucault, "An Ethics of Pleasure," in *Foucault Live: Collected Interviews, 1961–1984*, 378.

41. Any attempt to psychologically explain this motif in the life and works of Foucault would rob it of its intellectual value. James Miller, in many ways, does precisely that. Miller, *Passion of Michel Foucault.*

42. Derrida claims that Freud in his discovery of the death drive as going beyond the pleasure principle had left Foucault, who apparently was still stuck with pleasure, behind. For Derrida, Freud was not only at the origin of Foucault's insights about pleasure, he had also surpassed Foucault in going beyond pleasure in his discovery of the death drive. The very fact that Freud set up the notion of death drive against what he called the pleasure principle makes it evident that his notion of death drive could not be more different from, and was indeed just the opposite of, Foucault's. For Foucault the experience of death and the experience of pleasure coincide. Death and pleasure, in other words, were not the beyond of each other, as Freud, according to Derrida, thought. Jacques Derrida, "'To Do Justice to Freud': The History of Madness in the Age of Psychoanalysis," in *Foucault and His Interlocutors*, ed. Arnold I. Davidson (Chicago: University of Chicago Press, 1997), 57–96.

43. Foucault, "An Ethics of Pleasure," in *Foucault Live: Collected Interviews, 1961–1984*, 378.

44. Foucault, "The Simplest of Pleasures," in *Foucault Live: Collected Interviews, 1961–1984*, 296. In a 1981 interview Foucault once again makes similar comments. See "Passion According to Werner Schroeter," in *Foucault Live*, 318. To his biographer Miller this attraction toward death, the wish to turn death into an experience, of course appears as a scandal.

45. *Essential Works of Foucault: Power*, ed. James D. Faubion, trans. Robert Hurley et al., vol. 3 (New York: New Press, 2000), 247.

46. To an extent Miller structures his biography of Foucault as a response to this potential question. See Miller, *Passion of Michel Foucault*.

47. Miller, *Passion of Michel Foucault*, 245–52.

48. Miller, *Passion of Michel Foucault*, 251.

49. Miller calls it "epiphany." Miller, *Passion of Michel Foucault*, 252.

50. For a general reading on the subject of drugs, see Martin A. Lee and Bruce Shlain, *The Acid Dreams: The Complete Social History of LSD: The CIA, the Sixties, and Beyond* (New York: Grove Weidenfeld, 1992); Erika Dyck, *Psychedelic Psychiatry: LSD from Clinic to Campus* (Baltimore: Johns Hopkins University Press, 2008).

51. It is not clear, however, as to what exactly in this experience might have caused the change in Foucault's project on the history of sexuality. Miller, *Passion of Michel Foucault*, 252.

52. The similarities between sexual experience and the experience induced by the use of drugs had already been noted before Foucault. Timothy Leary too had already compared this experience with sexual pleasure. See Timothy Leary, Ralph Metzner, Richard Alpert, *The Psychedelic Experience: A Manual Based on the Tibetan Book of the Dead* (New York: Citadel Press, 1964); Timothy Leary, *Flashbacks: A Personal and Cultural History of an Era: An Autobiography* (Los Angeles: Jeremy P. Tarcher, 1990).

53. In some of his observations, Foucault did associate drugs with the experience of pleasure. For example: "Some drugs are really important for me because they are the mediation to those incredibly intense joys that I am looking for and that I am not able to experience, to afford by myself. . . . A pleasure must be something incredibly intense." Foucault, "An Ethics of Pleasure" in *Foucault Live*, 378.

54. The loss of the sense of the self as part of the experience induced by drugs was by no means an insight unique to Foucault. There were several authors—Aldous Huxley and Timothy Leary in particular—who dwelt on this issue at length. See Aldous Huxley, *The Doors of Perception & Heaven and Hell* (New York: Harper & Row, 1968); Leary, Metzner, and Alpert, *The Psychedelic Experience*. Also, see Leary, *Flashbacks*.

55. Aldous Huxley, *The Doors of Perception & Heaven and Hell* (New York: Thinking, 2011), 68.

56. See Aldous Huxley, *The Doors of Perception & Heaven and Hell*. The entire book is about how the experience of certain drugs opens a "door of perception in the wall."

57. Aldous Huxley, *Moksha*, ed. Michael Horowitz and Cynthia Palmer (Rochester, Vermont: Park Street Press, 1999), 9.

58. Foucault, *Religion and Culture*, 90.

59. This is a vast field with many aspects—scientific, psychiatric, sexual, literary, and spiritual—that has accumulated an immense amount of literature over the last several decades. Published in 1968, Tom Wolfe's *The Electric Kool-Aid Acid Test* offers perhaps the best account of the general ethos that accompanied this culture in America in the sixties. Tom Wolfe, *The Electric Kool-Aid Acid Test* (New York: Farrar, Straus & Giroux, 1968). Intellectually, Aldous Huxley (1894–1963) was one of the most important and influential early figures in this field. His book *The Doors of Perception*, published in 1956, described the experience of drugs in aesthetic and spiritual language. Another very important figure in this field was Timothy Leary (1920–96). In the description of his experiences with drugs, Leary deploys the language of both sexuality and spirituality. Albert Hofmann (1906–2008), the Swiss inventor of LSD and the first man to record his experiences of it, also describes it in the language of spirituality. Huxley, *The Doors of Perception*; Leary, Metzner, and Alpert, *The Psychedelic Experience*; Leary, *Flashbacks*; Albert Hofmann, *LSD, My Problem Child* (Los Angeles: Jeremy P. Tarcher, 1983). Also, see Peter H. Conners, *White Hand Society: The Psychedelic Partnership of Timothy Leary and Allen Gins-*

berg (San Francisco: City Lights Books, 2010); Don Lattin, *The Harvard Psychedelic Club: How Timothy Leary, Ram Dass, Huston Smith, and Andrew Weil Killed the Fifties and Ushered in a New Age for America* (New York: HarperOne, 2010); Robert Greenfield, *Timothy Leary: A Biography* (Orlando: Harcourt, 2006); Phillip Malcolm and Waller Thody, *Huxley: A Biographical Introduction* (New York: Scribner, 1973); Charles Mason Holmes, *Aldous Huxley and the Way to Reality* (Bloomington: Indiana University Press, 1970).

In literature, this cultural movement came to be known as the Beat Generation and consisted of figures such as the poet Allen Ginsberg (1926–97) and the novelists William S. Burroughs (1914–97) and Jack Kerouac (1922–69). For a detailed account of the nature of their contact with India and Indian culture, see Deborah Baker, *A Blue Hand: The Beats in India* (New York: Penguin Press, 2008). Also, see John Lardas Modern, *The Bop Apocalypse: The Religious Visions of Kerouac, Ginsberg, and Burroughs* (Urbana: University of Illinois Press, 2001); Steven Watson, *The Beat Generation: Visionaries, Rebels, and Hipsters, 1944–1960* (New York: Pantheon Books, 1995); Anne Waldman and Laura Wright, eds., *Beats at Naropa: An Anthology* (Minneapolis: Coffee House Press, 2009); Barry Miles, *The Beat Hotel: Ginsberg, Burroughs, and Corso in Paris, 1958–1963* (New York: Grove Press, 2000); Jonah Raskin, *Allen Ginsberg's Howl and the Making of the Beat Generation* (Berkeley: University of California Press, 2004); Timothy Miller, *The Hippies and American Value* (Knoxville: University of Tennessee Press, 1991).

60. Since a number of Indian traditions were based on the notions of spiritual liberation anchored in the event and experience of desubjectivation, they became a source of considerable curiosity. In *The Doors of Perception*, Huxley raises such issues as the nature of self and identity and often uses terms from Indian philosophy—particularly Buddhism and Vedanta—to articulate his experiences. For a while, the leading figures of the Beat Generation also got interested in different Indian intellectual and spiritual traditions. See Huxley, *The Doors of Perception*. For a detailed account of the nature of contact of the authors of the Beat Generation with India and Indian culture, see Baker, *A Blue Hand*. Also, see Rory MacLean, *Magic Bus: On the Hippie Trail from Istanbul to India* (New York: Penguin Books, 2008).

61. Philip Goldberg, *American Veda* (New York: Harmony Books, 2010), 158.

62. See Sadie Plant, *Writing on Drugs* (New York: Farrar, Straus & Giroux, 1999). Also, see Michel Foucault, "Theatrum Philosophicum," in *Language, Counter-Memory, Practice: Selected Essays and Interviews* (Ithaca, NY: Cornell University Press, 1980), 165–96. Also, see Natalie Zemon Davies, "Decentering History: Local Stories and Cultural Crossings in a Global World," *History and Theory* 50 (May 2011): 188–202.

63. See Plant, *Writing on Drugs*.

64. Foucault, *Religion and Culture*, 90.

65. Foucault, *History of Madness*, ed. Jean Khalfa, trans. Jonathan Murphy and Jean Khalfa (New York: Routledge, 2006).

66. Michel Foucault, *Language, Madness, Desire: On Literature* (Minneapolis: University of Minnesota, 2015), 25.

67. That is not to say that madness and pleasure were the same for Foucault, only that they both involved an event and experience of desubjectivation as their content.

68. See Foucault, *Language, Madness, Desire: On Literature*.

69. Unfortunately the radio broadcast in which Foucault talked about Henri Michaux under the theme of "artificially provoked madness" was not included in the volume. See Focualt, *Language, Madness, and Desire*, 6. Huxley also associated drugs with the experience of madness. See Huxley, *The Doors of Perception & Heaven and Hell*, 25–27.

70. Foucault thought of madness also as an event of revelation, an intellectual phenomenon.

That was the reason that, for him, names like Artaud, Nietzsche, Holderlin, and Nerval that are associated with madness stood as figures of knowledge. See particularly the appendix, "Madness, the Absence of an Oeuvre" in *History of Madness*, 541–49.

71. For *sadhus* in India, see Robert Lewis Gross, *The Sadhus of India: A Study of Hindu Asceticism* (Jaipur: Rawat Publications, 1992); G. S. Ghurye, with the collaboration of L. N. Chapekar, *Indian Sadhus* (Bombay: Popular Prakashan, 1964).

72. Not surprisingly, the act and idea of renunciation came to be associated with ritual suicide. See Patrick Olivelle, "Ritual Suicide and the Rite of Renunciation," in *Wiener Zeitschrift fur die Kunde Sudasiens* 22 (1978); 19–44.

73. In Indian traditions, ever since the days of the *Upaniṣads* and the birth of Buddhism, the act and life of renunciation have been anchored in the discourse of desubjectivation, known in Indian traditions as spiritual liberation—*mokṣa* in Upanisadic traditions and *nirvāṇa* in Buddhist. There were many variations with subtle differences between sects and traditions, but generally the notion of desubjectivation remained their general ground. See Patrick Olivelle, *The Samnyasa Upanisads: Hindu Scriptures on Asceticism and Renunciation* (New York: Oxford University Press, 1992); Eliot Deutsch, *Advaita Vedanta: A Philosophical Reconstruction* (Honolulu: University of Hawaii Press, 1980); *Upanisads*, trans. Patrick Olivelle (New York: Oxford University Press, 2008); Mark Siderits, *Buddhism as Philosophy: An Introduction* (Indianapolis: Hackett, 2007).

74. Patrick Levy, *Sadhus: Going beyond the Dreadlocks* (New Delhi: Fingerprint, 2015), 62.

75. Levy, *Sadhus*, 43.

76. For a comprehensive view of what *mokṣa* meant to Huxley, see Aldous Huxley, *Island: A Novel* (New York: Harperperennial, 1962). For "de-individualization," see Huxley, *The Doors of Perception & Heaven and Hell*, 68.

77. See Huxley, *Island*.

78. Huxley, *Island*, 195.

79. Huxley, *The Doors of Perception & Heaven and Hell*, 77.

80. What is also significant is that Friedrich Nietzsche—perhaps the most important philosopher and source of categories for Foucault—considered Schopenhauer to be his most important teacher. Dale Jacquette, *The Philosophy of Schopenhauer* (Ithaca, NY: McGill-Queen's University Press, 2005).

81. Rampuri, *Autobiography of a Sadhu: A Journey into Mystic India* (Rochester, VT: Destiny Books, 2010), 127.

82. Mādhvācārya, *Śrīmacchaṅkaradigvijayaḥ* (Śrīraṅgam: Śrīvaṇīvilāsamudraṇālayaḥ, 1972), 119–32. As for Śaṅkara being the founder of the order of sadhus, see Levy, *Sadhus*, 13.

83. *Kāmasūtra*, 7.2.57.

84. Foucault referred to madness as "the enigma of that Exteriority." Foucault, *History of Madness*, 541.

85. Foucault, *History of Madness*, xxx.

Chapter 2

1. See Antonio Rocha, "Scientia Sexualis versus Ars Erotica: Foucault, van Gulik, Needham," *Studies in History and Philosophy of Biological and Biomedical Sciences* 42 (2011): 328–343; Jyoti Puri, "Concerning 'Kāmasūtras': Challenging Narratives of History and Sexuality," *Signs* 27, no. 3 (2002): 632.

2. For general works on women in ancient India, see Stephanie W. Jamison, *Sacrificed Wife,*

Sacrificer's Wife: Women, Ritual, and Hospitality in Ancient India (New York: Oxford University Press, 1996); S. N. Sinha, N. K. Basu, and Rita Sil, *History of Marriage and Prostitution: Vedas to Vātsyāyana* (New Delhi: Khama Publishers, 1992); Laurie L. Patton, ed., *Jewels of Authority: Women and Textual Tradition in Hindu India* (Oxford: Oxford University Press, 2002); A. S. Altekar, *The Position of Women in Hindu Civilization* (New Delhi: Motilal Banarasidas, 1938); Wendy Doniger O'Flaherty, *Women, Androgynes, and Other Mythical Beasts* (Chicago: University of Chicago Press, 1980); Mildred Worth Pinkham, *Woman in the Sacred Scriptures of Hinduism* (New York: AMS Press, 1967); Saraswati Mishra, *Status of Indian Women* (New Delhi: Gyan Publishing House, 2002); Susan Wadley and Doranne Jacobson, *Women in India: Two Perspectives* (Delhi: Manohar, 1970).

3. For discussions on the question of gender and sexuality, see Joan Scott, "Gender: A Useful Category of Historical Analysis," *American Historical Review* 19, no.5 (1985): 1053–75, and "The Evidence of Experience," *Critical Inquiry* 17, no.4 (1991): 58–68. Also, see Joanne Meyerowitz, "A History of 'Gender,'" in *AHR Forum*: "Revisiting 'Gender: A Useful Category of Historical Analysis,'" *American Historical Review* 113, no.5 (2008): 1346–56; Jeffrey Weeks, *Sexuality and Its Discontents: Meanings, Myths, and Modern Sexualities* (London: Routledge & Kegan Paul, 1985); Denise Riley, *"Am I That Name?" Feminism and the Category of "Women" in History* (London: Macmillan, 1988); Catherine A. MacKinnon, "Does Sexuality Have a History," *Michigan Quarterly Review* 30 (1991); S. Ortner, S. and H. Whitehead, eds., *Sexual Meanings: The Cultural Construction of Gender and Sexuality* (Cambridge: Cambridge University Press, 1981); Judith Butler, "Contingent Foundations: Feminism and the Question of Postmodernism," in *Feminists Theorize the Political*, ed. Judith Butler and Joan W. Scott (New York: Routledge, 1992), and *Gender Trouble: Feminism and the Subversion of Identity* (New York: Routledge, 1990); Gayle Rubin, "Thinking Sex: Notes for a Radical Theory of the Politics of Sexuality," in *Pleasure and Danger: Exploring Female Sexuality*, ed. Carole S. Vance, 267–319 (Boston: Routledge, 1984).

4. *Manu's Code of Law: A Critical Edition and Translation of the Mānava-Dharmaśāstra*, ed. and trans. Patrick Olivelle (New York: Oxford University Press, 2005). I use Olivelle's translation of the *Mānava-Dharmaśāstra*, except in a few cases where I have slightly modified it for the consistency of my own terminology or to bring out certain nuances in the context of the discussion. I translate *dharma* as "Brahmanical law." In the word "Brahmanical" I also include the domain of religion-ritual in which the Brahmin and his notion of *dharma* as articulated in the *Mānava-Dharmaśāstra* was simultaneously grounded. In fact, in the *Mānava-Dharmaśāstra*, the domains of law, morality, religion, and ritual are parts of a single continuum. In the citations, however, I have kept Olivelle's translation of *dharma* as "Law."

5. As is well known, Foucault himself never focused on the history of gender relations in any extended way. It was Joan Scott who problematized the question about the history of gender relations in terms of Foucault's notion of subjectivity—gender as subjectivity—as a historically and discursively constructed phenomenon grounded in relations of power. See Scott, "Gender: A Useful Category of Historical Analysis," and "The Evidence of Experience." Also, see *AHR Forum*: "Revisiting 'Gender: A Useful Category of Historical Analysis.'"

6. For a perspective on the *Kāmasūtra*'s attitude toward the *Dharmaśāstra*, see Ludo Rocher, "The *Kāmasūtra*: Vatsyayana's Attitude toward Dharma and *Dharmaśāstra*," *Journal of the American Oriental Society* 105, no. 3 (1985): 521–29.

7. *Kāmasūtra*, 1.1–3. *The Kāmasūtra of Vātsyāyana, with the Commentary of Yaśodhara*, ed. Devadatta Shastri (Varanasi: Chaukhambha Sanskrit Sansthan, 1964).

8. *Kāmasūtra*, 1.1–3.

9. For a brief survey of the concept of *kāma* in Indian intellectual tradition, see Joanna Macy,

"The Dialectics of Desire," *Numen* 22, no. 2 (August 1975): 145–60. In a very perceptive observation, Doniger notes that "Sanskrit intermingles concepts of passion, love, and pleasure, which English tends to hold separate." See Wendy Doniger and Sudhir Kakar, *Vātsyāyana Kāmasūtra: A New, Complete Translation of the Sanskrit Text* (New York: Oxford University Press, 2002), lxiv.

10. *Kāmasūtra*, 2.10.9.

11. *Kāmasūtra*, 2.10.10.

12. *Kāmasūtra*, 3.2.19. The word used for desire in this instance is *icchā*.

13. Sigmund Freud, *The Freud Reader*, ed. Peter Gay (New York: W. W. Norton, 1989), 397.

14. *Kāmasūtra*, 1.1.1.

15. As if to remove any potential confusion in this regard, the *Kāmasūtra* in the very next sutra clarifies, "because of the nature of the subject matter." What the *Kāmasūtra* clearly means is that the three—*dharma*, *artha*, and *kāma*—are the major themes that it plans to focus on. See *Kāmasūtra*, 1.1.2.

16. Chapter 2 of book 1 in the *Kāmasūtra*, called *Trivargapratipattiprakaraṇam*, is devoted in its entirety to the question of *trivarga*. The *Kāmasūtra* also suggests to its readers to divide up the entire lifespan into three parts, each dedicated to one of the three members of the trilogy as three separate ends. Here the *Kāmasūtra* seems to have assumed that each of the three ends is best pursued during three different stages of life so that they are pursued as much as possible exclusively without coming into direct conflict with each other. See *Kāmasūtra*, 1.2. Since the history of the notion of trilogy (*trivarga*) is inextricably linked with the notion of *āśrama*, or life stages, in ancient India, Olivelle's book on the history of the *āśrama* system carries perhaps the most extended treatment of this topic. Patrick Olivelle, *The Āśrama System: The History and Hermeneutics of a Religious Institution* (New Delhi: Munshiram Manoharlal, 1993).

17. Even though the *Kāmasūtra* does not mention *mokṣa*, or spiritual liberation, as one of the ends in its opening sutra, it seems to be aware of the fact that it was widely seen as one of the ends. See *Kāmasūtra*, 1.2.4. The notion of four primary ends was so pervasive in ancient Indian culture that Sheldon Pollock calls it the Indian "common sense." Pollock thinks of the *puruṣārtha* as "one of the primary *geschichtliche Grundbegriffe*," or "historical core concepts," in the "ideal-typical template of Indian culture" that took on the "character of common sense." There are subtle and important differences in the naming of the ends as *trivarga* and *puruṣārthas*. However, given that I intend to touch only on the broadest of their aspects in a brief way, those subtle nuances are not directly relevant here. Sheldon Pollock, *The Ends of Man at the End of Premodernity* (Amsterdam: Royal Netherlands Academy of Arts and Sciences, 2005), 10. Arvind Sharma, similarly, sees the *puruṣārthas* as the "fundamental building blocks of Hindu axiology." Arvind Sharma, *The Puruṣārtha: A Study in Hindu Axiology* (East Lansing: Asian Studies Center, Michigan State University, 1982), 40. Also, see Donald R. Davis Jr., "Being Hindu or Being Human: A Reappraisal of the *Puruṣārthas*," *International Journal of Hindu Studies* 8, nos. 1/3 (Jan., 2004): 1–27; Arvind Sharma, *The Puruṣārthas: A Study in Hindu Axiology* (East Lansing: Asian Studies Center, Michigan State University, 1982); Charles Malmoud, "On the Rhetoric and Semantics of *Puruṣārthas*," in T. N. Madan, ed., *Way of Life: King, Householder, Renouncer, Essays in Honour of Louis Dumont* (Delhi: Vikas, 1982), 33–54; P. Nagaraja Rao, *The Four Values in Indian Philosophy and Culture: A Study of the Puruṣārthas* (Mysore: University of Mysore, 1970); Rajendra Prasad, "The Theory of *Puruṣārthas*: Revaluation and Reconstruction," *Journal of Indian Philosophy* 9, no. 1 (1981): 49–76.

18. Daya Krishna critiques the notion of the *puruṣārthas* for having no place for "any independent value to the life of the intellect" or "the independent life of reason." What he does not discuss is whether this omission is a simple failure, or if, in fact, it suggests a different under-

standing of knowledge, its origin and end. If there is no place for "the independent life of reason or intellect" in the discourse of the *puruṣārthas,* that is because it does not recognize reason and intellect to be independent to begin with. What Krishna also does not note is that the independent life of reason, as presented by Foucault, is precisely what western philosophy, with its origin in Greece, is grounded in. Daya Krishna, *Indian Philosophy: A Counter Perspective* (Delhi: Oxford University Press, 1991), 205.

19. See parts 1, 2, and 3 in Foucault, *The History of Sexuality: An Introduction*, 1–74. Also, see "The History of Sexuality," in Michel Foucault, *Power/Knowledge: Selected Interviews and Other Writings, 1972–1977*, ed. Colin Gordon (New York: Pantheon Books, 1980), 183–93.

20. The difference between Indian and western intellectual traditions has not been approached in a serious way from this angle. For some general issues relating to this difference between the two intellectual traditions, see J. N. Mohanty, "Are Indian and Western Philosophy Radically Different," in *Essays on Indian Philosophy: Traditional and Modern*, ed. Purushottama Bilimoria (Delhi: Oxford University Press, 1993), 312–30.

21. Indeed, the *Kāmasūtra* locates itself within this discursive context very directly and self-consciously. In fact, that is the very first thing it does in the book. The first three chapters of the first book are dedicated to it. See *Kāmasūtra*, 1.1–3.

22. See Michel Foucault, *Hermeneutics of the Subject: Lectures at the College de France, 1981–1982* (New York: Palgrave Macmillan, 2005), *The Government of Self and Others: Lectures at the College de France, 1982–1983* (New York: Palgrave Macmillan, 2010), and *The Courage of Truth: Lectures at College de France* (New York: Palgrave Macmillan, 2011). Also, see Timothy O'Leary, *Foucault: The Art of Ethics* (New York: Continuum, 2002); Thomas R. Flynn, "Truth and Subjectivation in the Later Foucault," *Journal of Philosophy* 82, no. 10 (Oct., 1985): 531–40.

23. Both the *Arthaśāstra* and the *Kāmasūtra* are aware of this potential conflict and the need to overcome it. *Arthaśāstra*, 3.7.3; *Kāmasūtra*, 1.2.1.

24. *Kāmasūtra*, 1.2. 17–18. Doniger and Kakar translate the word *parādhīnatva* as dependence and interpret the sutra to mean, "because a man and a woman depend upon one another in sex, it requires a method." Doniger and Kakar, *Vātsyāyana Kāmasūtra*, 9.

25. *Kāmasūtra*, 1.2.20.

26. *Kāmasūtra*, 1.2.20.

27. Sigmund Freud, *Sexuality and the Psychology of Love* (New York: A Touchstone Book, 1997), 59.

28. *Kāmasūtra*, 1.2.14.

29. *Kāmasūtra*, 1.2.20. Although the word *anāvṛt* here refers to the lack of freedom amongst women, it needs to be noted that in its other meaning as nudity it did not apply to women and men in the same way. For example, amongst Digamabara Jains, women, unlike men, could not pursue the goal for spiritual liberation because they could not go naked, a requirement in that sect for the monks, as if being clothed was an essential existential requirement for women in a way it was not for men. See Patrick Olivelle, *Ascetics and Brahmins: Studies in Ideologies and Institutions* (Firenze: Firenze University Press, 2006), 115. As we will see in more detail later in this chapter, the question of freedom and its absence comes up repeatedly every time the question of women's relations with men comes up. The term "freedom" should not be reduced to its dominant contemporary meaning as a legal and political right within a democratic polity based on individualism. It has to be remembered that this contemporary meaning of freedom is a very specific historical construction that does not—and must not—negate its occurrence in other historical contexts and cultures. The notion of freedom could occur in its different senses in varieties of historical contexts and cultures with specific senses that could only be determined

through a close historical investigation. For a discussion of this and other related issues, see Saba Mahmood, *Politics of Piety: Islamic Revival and the Feminist Subject* (Princeton, NJ: Princeton University Press, 2005).

30. *Kāmasūtra*, 2.8.39.

31. For *ratilālasā*, or desire for pleasure, see *Kāmasūtra*, 2.8.40.

32. The precise date of the *Mahabharata*'s composition is not exactly relevant for me here. My intention here is not to prove the textual-chronological relationship between the *Mahābhārata* and the *Mānava Dharmaśāstra*, but only to explore the meaning and discursive context of the term *anāvṛt* as unclothed and free. For a recent discussion of the questions relating to the date of the *Mahābhārata*, see Alf Hiltebeitel, *Dharma: Its Early History in Law, Religion, and Narrative* (New York: Oxford University Press, 2011). For a recent brief account of different approaches to the *Mahābhārata*, see Adam Bowles, *Dharma, Disorder and the Political in Ancient India: The Āpaddharmaparvan of the Mahābhārata* (Leiden: E. J. Brill, 2007).

33. For the status of women in the *Mahābhārata*, see Arti Dhand, *Woman as Fire, Woman as Sage: Sexual Ideology in the Mahābhārata* (New York: State University of New York Press, 2008); Shalini Shah, *The Making of Womanhood: Gender Relations in the "Mahābhārata"* (New Delhi: Manohar Publications. 1995); V. I. Kalyanov, "The Image of the Indian Woman in the *Mahābhārata*," *Annals of the Bhandarkar Oriental Research Institute* (1977–78): 161–72, Diamond Jubilee Volume; Shakambari Jayal, *The Status of Women in the Epics* (Delhi: Motilal Banarsidass, 1966); Hiltebeitel, *Dharma: Its Early History in Law, Religion, and Narrative*, 337–410, and "Draupadi's Garments," *Indo-Iranian Journal* 22 (1980): 97–112; Nancy Falk, "Draupadī and the Dharma," in *Beyond Androcentrism: New Essays on Women and Religion*, ed. Rita Gross, 89–114 (Missoula, MT: Scholars Press, 1977); Gregory Bailey, "Suffering in the *Mahābhārata*: Draupadī and Yudhiṣṭhira," in *Inde et Littératures: Études Reunies Par Marie-Claude Porcher*, 109–29 (Paris: École des Hautes Études en Science Sociale, 1983).

34. *Mahābhārata*, 1.113. 5–9. Interestingly, in the course of a discussion of women's agency in the *Dharmaśāstra* with respect to two categories of women, guarded and unguarded, Patrick Olivelle has also noted that this passage from the *Mahābhārata* may potentially be very significant. Patrick Olivelle, *Language, Text, and Society: Explorations in Ancient Indian Culture and Religion* (Firenze: Firenze University Press, 2005), 32, fn. 32.

35. The fact that the *Mahābhārata* puts the emergence of the discourse of *dharma* grounded in the subordination of women in historical perspective is in line with its major innovation to link the notion of *dharma* with the notions of time, such as *kalpa* and *yuga*. See chaps. 6 and 7 in Hiltebeitel, *Dharma: Its Early History in Law, Religion, and Narrative*, 243–336.

36. My observation applies only to this paragraph cited above. I do not claim that this was true of the *Mahābhārata* as a whole. On the contrary, scholars have argued that as a whole the *Mahābhārata* appears to be a Brahmanical intellectual response to the challenge posed by the rise of Buddhism and Jainism, on the one hand, and the Mauryan Empire (322 BCE–185 BCE), particularly under Emperor Aśoka (273 BCE–232 BCE), on the other. Despite its Brahminism, scholars agree that the *Mahābhārata* is too vast and complex to be reduced altogether to one perspective alone. Part of the reason is its narrative form, which inevitably brings different perspectives into contact and conflict, but also dialogue, with each other. For the *Mahābhārata* as a response to the Mauryan Empire, see James Fitzgerald, "Negotiating the Shape of 'Scripture': New Perspectives on the Development and Growth of the *Mahābhārata* between the Empires," in Olivelle, *Between the Empires*, 257–286. For the triumph of Brahminism in the *Mahābhārata*, particularly as it is reflected in the didactic parts of the text, also see Bowles, *Dharma, Disorder and the Political in Ancient India.*

37. *Mahābhārata*, 1.113.10–14. Also, see Patrick Olivelle, "Young Śvetaketu: A Literary Study of an Upaniṣadic Story," *Journal of the American Oriental Society* 119, no. 1 (Jan.–Mar., 1999): 46–70.

38. *Mahābhārata*, 1.113.17–20. For a different reading of this passage, see Dhand, *Woman as Fire, Woman as Sage: Sexual Ideology in the Mahabharata*, 128–30.

39. See Patrick Olivelle, "Caste and Purity: A Study in the Language of the Dharma Literature," in Olivelle, *Language, Text, and Society*, 217–46; Louis Dumont, *Homo Hierarchicus: The Caste System and Its Implications*, trans. M. Sainsbury, L. Dumont, and B. Gulati (Chicago: University of Chicago Press, 1980); T. N. Madan, *Non-renunciation: Themes and Interpretations of Hindu Culture* (Delhi: Oxford University Press, 1988); Mary Douglas, *Purity and Danger: An Analysis of the Concepts of Pollution and Taboo* (London: ARK Paperbacks, 1984).

40. One of the distinguishing features of the *Mahābhārata* is that it introduced doubts, questions, ambivalence, and ambiguity in the discourse of *dharma*. Two recent works in particular that offer the depth and complexity of the discourse of *dharma* as articulated in the *Mahābhārata* are Bowles, *Dharma, Disorder and the Political in Ancient India;* and Hiltebeitel, *Dharma: Its Early History in Law, Religion, and Narrative*. Also, see James L. Fitzgerald, "Dharma and Its Translation in the *Mahābhārata*" in *Dharma: Studies in Its Semantic, Cultural and Religious History*, ed. Patrick Olivelle, 249–63 (Delhi: Motilal Banarsidass Publishers, 2009); *The Collected Essays of Bimal Krishna Matilal: Ethics and Epics*, ed. Jonardon Ganeri (New Delhi: Oxford University Press, 2002).

41. Patrick Olivelle, *Manu's Code of Law: A Critical Edition and Translation of the Mānava-Dharmaśāstra*. For a comprehensive but brief introduction to this book, see Olivelle's introduction in the same volume. Patrick Olivelle, ed., *Dharma: Studies in Semantic, Cultural and Religious History*; Richard W. Lariviere, ed., *Studies in Dharmaśāstra* (Calcutta: Firma KLM, 1984); P. V. Kane, *History of Dharmaśāstra* (Poona: Bhandarkar Oriental Research Institute, 1968).

The *Mānava Dharmaśāstra* emerged to be the most important source of Western knowledge about Indian society and culture. Probably more than any other text in Indian history, it has determined the modern understanding of Indian society and culture. It was the first major ancient Indian Sanskrit text that came to be translated into English was done by William Jones. It is this text and its elaboration of *dharma* based on caste that is at the root of the dominant understanding of Indian society. Caste came to be seen as the key to Indian society, past and present. Indeed, caste became the key to Indian consciousness as a whole. All other visions of Indian society and culture became buried under this vision of caste-based society constructed in the *Mānava Dharmaśāstra*. For the role the social framework of caste played in the making of modern India under the British Empire, see Nicholas B. Dirks, *Castes of Mind: Colonialism and the Making of Modern India* (Princeton: Princeton University Press, 2001).

42. Patrick Olivelle thinks that the *Mahābhārata* indeed drew upon the *Mānava Dharmaśāstra* for its reflections on the question of *dharma*. Olivelle, *Manu's Code of Law*, 23. The notion of *dharma* is one of the most complex in all of Indian intellectual history. See Olivelle, *Dharma: Studies in Its Semantic, Cultural and Religious History.*

43. For a discussion of the possible date of composition of the *Mānava Dharmaśāstra*, see Olivelle, *Manu's Code of Law*, 18–25.

44. P V. Kane's multivolume *History of Dharmaśāstra* is the most comprehensive account of the Brahmanical discourse of *dharma* as a whole. P. V. Kane, *History of Dharmaśāstra* (Poona: Bhandarkar Oriental Research Institute, 1968).

45. The discourse of *dharma* in the epics, for example, is extremely important. John Brockington, "The Concept of *Dharma* in the Ramayana," in Olivelle, *Dharma: Studies in Its Semantic,*

Cultural and Religious History, 233–48; James Fitzgerald, "Negotiating the Shape of 'Scripture,'" in Patrick Olivelle, ed., *Between the Empires: Society in India 300 BCE to 400 CE* (New York: Oxford University Press, 2006), 257–86. Bowles, *Dharma, Disorder and the Political in Ancient India*; L. Fitzgerald, "Dharma and Its Translation in the *Mahābhārata*," 249–63; *The Collected Essays of Bimal Krishna Matilal.*

46. Patrick Olivelle puts forward a comprehensive perspective on the historical origins of the Brahmanical discourse of *dharma*: "My hypothesis is that the emergence of the Dharmaśāstric literature, first in the form of prose sutras and then in metrical treatises beginning with Manu, was direct consequence of Buddhist and *Aśokan* reforms." Patrick Olivelle, "The Semantic History of Dharma: the Middle and the Late Vedic Period," in Patrick Olivelle, ed., *Dharma: Studies in Its Semantic, Cultural, and Religious History*, 83.

47. For a brief overview of Aśoka's discourse of *dharma* as reflected in his inscriptions, see Bowles, *Dharma, Disorder, and the Political in Ancient India*, 125–32; Hiltebeitel, *Dharma*, 35–50. Also, see Patrick Olivelle, Janice Leoshko, and Himanshu Prabha Ray, eds., *Reimagining Aśoka: Memory and History* (Delhi: Oxford University Press, 2012); Romila Thapar, *Aśoka and the Decline of the Mauryas* and *Early India: From the Origins to AD 1300* (New Delhi: Oxford University Press, 1960).

48. Bowles, *Dharma, Disorder and the Political in Ancient India*, 131.

49. Olivelle, *Manu's Code of Law*, 41. James Fitzgerald thinks that the character of Yudhisthira in the *Mahabharata* was constructed with an eye on Aśoka. Fitzgerald cited in Bowles, *Dharma, Disorder, and the Political in Ancient India*, 127.

50. *Kāmasūtra*, 1.2.7.

51. For works on women and the *Mānava Dharmaśāstra*, see Patrick Olivelle, "Rhetoric and Reality: Women's Agency in the *Dharmaśāstra*," in *Encounters with the Word: Essays to Honour Aloysius Pieris S.J.*, ed. Robert Crusz, Marshal Fernando, and Asanga Tilakaratne (Colombo: Ecumenical Institute for Study and Dialogue, 2004), 489–505; Stephanie Jamison, "Women 'Between the Empires' and 'Between the Lines,'" in Olivelle, *Between the Empires*, 191–214; R. M. Das, *Women in Manu and His Seven Commentators* (Varanasi: Kanchana Publications, 1962); Prabhati Mukherjee, "Widowhood and Niyoga in the Arthasastra and Manusmrti," *Our Heritage* 11, no. 1 (1963): 1–11; Deepali Bhargave, *Manu Smriti: A Sociological Analysis* (Jaipur: Rawat Publications, 1989). Also, see James B. Nelson and Sandra P. Longfellow, eds., *Sexuality and the Sacred: Studies on the Impact of Religious Teachings on Women* (Geneva: WCC Publications, 1990).

52. C. K. Chatterjee, *Studies in the Rites and Rituals of Hindu Marriage in Ancient* India (Calcutta: Sanskrit Pustak Bhandar, 1978); Jatindrabimal Chaudhuri, *The Position of Women in the Vedic Ritual* (London and Calcutta: Pracyavani Research Series, 1956).

53. *Mānava Dharmaśāstra*, 9:20–21. For a Freudian analysis of this, see Sudhir Kakar, *Intimate Relations*: *Exploring Indian Sexuality* (Chicago: University of Chicago Press, 1990), 18–19.

54. As noted by Olivelle, all commentators, except Medhātithi and Bhāruci, who are silent, have concluded that the statement is to be repeated by the son as an act of expiation on behalf of the mother. But notice that the *Mānava Dharmaśāstra* says that even when the wife contemplates something bad about her husband in her mind, this sentence needs to be repeated. Since it happens in the mind of the wife-mother, there is no way for either the husband or the son to know it unless she tells them. There is, however, no indication in the *Mānava Dharmaśāstra* that the wife is supposed to confess either to her husband or to her son any thoughts or desires of infidelity and sexual transgressions. This is suggested almost as a mantra of expiation for the transgression she has committed in her mind, an incident of transgression in thought and desire. Indeed, in the *Mānava Dharmaśāstra* there is a conception of two kinds of sins: public and

private or secret sin. Private sin may refer to those acts of transgression that occur in the realm of thought and desire. As will be argued later in this chapter, this is in complete continuity with the emergence of the self, or subjectivity—or desire located in the mind—as the new domain of power, and the theme that the wife needs to keep a check not only on her actions but also on her desires and thoughts. This expiation, therefore, is meant for the wife as part of the wife-mother's responsibility to control her mind and desire. See notes in Olivelle, *Mānava Dharmaśāstra*, 324, n. 9.20–21. For two kinds of sins, see *Mānava Dharmaśāstra*, 11.227.

55. *Mānava Dharmaśāstra*, 9.8–9.

56. Cited from *Pāraskara Gṛhyasūtra* 2.3.2, in Olivelle, "Amṛtā: Women and Indian Technologies of Immortality," *Journal of Indian Philosophy* 25 (1997): 432.

57. The father-son relationship as discussed here presents an interesting problem regarding the exact meaning of the terms "self," "identity," and "individual." Here I use the term "identity" in a very specific sense to account for the reflexivity evident in the relationship between the father and the son. When the father addresses his son as his self, he makes the son constitutive of his own selfhood. In this regard it is important to mention two very well-known authors—McKim Marriott and Louis Dumont—who have dealt with the problem of the individual, or rather its absence, in Indian culture. According to Marriott, Indian society has what he calls "dividuals," not individuals. These "dividuals" are what they are only in relationship with the others. One of the defining and constitutive characteristics of these "dividuals" is the absence of reflexivity in them. For Marriott, reflexivity is an essential constitutive aspect of the individual. Dumont, on the other hand, does not make this reflexivity the most important criterion of the individual, and designates the renouncer who has quit the world and lives by himself to be the only individual in Indian culture. See McKim Marriott, "Constructing an Indian Ethnosociology," in McKim Marriott, ed., *India through Hindu Categories* (New Delhi: Sage Publications, 1990), 19, and "Hindu Transactions: Diversity without Dualism," in B. Kapferer, ed., *Transaction and Meaning* (Philadelphia: ISHI Publications, 1976). Also, see Edwin Gerow, "India as a Philosophical Problem: McKim Marriott and the Comparative Enterprise India through Hindu Categories," *Journal of the American Society of Oriental Society* 120, no. 3 (Jul.–Sep. 2000): 410–429. Even though Marriott's notion of dividual has not found much resonance amongst historians of pre-modern India, in recent years Marilyn Strathner, a very influential anthropologist, has used it as one of her central categories. See the introduction in Marilyn Strathner, *The Gender of the Gift: Problems with Women and Problems with Society in Melanesia* (Berkeley: University of California Press, 1988). For the relevant works of Louis Dumont, see his *Homo Hierarchicus* and the two essays, "World Renunciation in Indian Religions" and "The Individual as an Impediment to Sociological Comparison and Indian History," in Louis Dumont, *Religion/ Politics and History in India: Collected Papers in Indian Sociology* (Paris: Mouton Publishers, 1970), 33–60, 133–50.

58. Here it needs to be pointed out that in the *Mānava Dharmaśāstra* there are multiple, parallel, but also intersecting notions of self. Together these multiple selves constitute a complex. "The one who makes this body act is called *ksetrajna*, 'the knower of the field'; the one who does the actions, on the other hand, the wise call Bhutatman, 'the elemental self.' Another inner self innate to all embodied beings bears the name *jīva*, 'individual self,' by whom are experienced all the pleasures and pains in succeeding births." *Mānava Dharmaśāstra* 12.12–13. It is not possible to engage this complex of multiple selves here. Olivelle has dealt with some of these issues relating to the notion of self. As he notes, "The coexistence of different notions of self and after-death states makes for a messy situation. Clarity is often achieved in such situations only at the expense of accuracy." To bring some clarity to this confusing situation Olivelle uses Michael Carrithers's distinction between self as *personne* and self as *moi*. Olivelle defines *personne* in the context of

ancient Indian society and culture as "the selfhood of an individual, especially of a married male, within the society of ancient India hierarchically ordered according to class and gender. . . . Self as *moi*, on the other hand, sees the individual as a unique and self-contained entity transcending temporary social relationships. This conception of the self emerged in India within the context of the rebirth ideology which sees social relationships as fleeting and ephemeral, not affecting the inner core of one's self." Olivelle, "Amṛtā," 443, 429.

59. *Mānava Dharmaśāstra*, 9.32–44.

60. *Mānava Dharmaśāstra*, 9.45.

61. *Mānava Dharmaśāstra*, 9.22.

62. *Mānava Dharmaśāstra*, 9.5–7.

63. Patrick Olivelle, *The Āśrama System: The History and Hermeneutics of a Religious Institution* (New Delhi: Munshiram Manoharlal, 1993), 185.

64. *Mānava Dharmaśāstra*, 9.2–3. I have modified Olivelle's translation slightly here. Similar statements also occur in 5.147–49.

65. Given the context, the word *asvatantra* suggests more than a simple instance of dependence of women on their husbands. Men were as much dependent on women, yet it would have been odd to use the same word to describe their relationship with their wives. It is not dependence, but a relationship of mastery and subjection that is assumed in this word.

66. *Mānava Dharmaśāstra*, 9.14–15.

67. *Kāmasūtra*, 5.

68. *Mānava Dharmaśāstra*, 9.10–12.

69. Olivelle also notes, "The dual strategy of guarding them both externally and socializing them to be on guard internally appears to be Manu's strategy for dealing with the unbridled sexuality he imputes to women." Patrick Olivelle, "Rhetoric and Reality: Women's Agency in the *Dharmaśāstras*," in Olivelle, *Language, Text, and Society*, 257.

70. See Patrick Olivelle, trans., *King, Governance, and Law in Ancient India: Kautilya's Arthaśāstra, A New Annotated Translation* (New York: Oxford University Press, 2013); Thomas R. Trautmann, *Kauṭilya and the Arthaśāstra: A Statistical Investigation of the Authorship and Evolution of the Text* (Leiden: E. J. Brill, 1971).

71. However, even as the *Mānava Dharmaśāstra* invented a new discourse of power, it did not reject the largely political discourse of power based on violence. Indeed, there are numerous instances where the *Mānava Dharmaśāstra* emphatically demands the most exemplary form of violence, particularly against the *Śūdras* if they are found to be in violation of law. However, it subordinated the discourse of power based on violence to the new discourse of power based on subjectivity, just as it subordinated the discourse of political power (*artha*) to the discourse of Brahmanical law (*dharma*), and the figure of the king to that of the Brahmin. In the process, the *Mānava Dharmaśāstra* reduced political power to pure violence as *danda* or punishment in its pithy and precise definition: "the king is punishment (*daṇḍa*)." The king was reduced to simply being an enforcer of Brahmanical law (*dharma*) enunciated by the Brahmin. Often violent punishment is more likely to be recommended if the culprit happened to be a *Śūdra,* who fell outside the ambit of the discourse of *dharma* as a discourse of subjectivity; in the discourse of *dharma* the *śūdra,* after all, did not have a self, and so violence was the preferred way of punishing him. Chapter 9 of the *Mānava Dharmaśāstra* is entirely dedicated to the elaboration of its conception of the nature and function of the king and the state. See Olivelle, *Manu's Code of Law*, chap. 9. For violent punishments, also see "Punishing in Public: Imposing Moral Self-Dominance in Normative Sanskrit Sources," in *Tradition, Veda, and Law: Studies on South Asian Classical Intellectual Traditions*, ed. Frederico Squarcini (Anthem Press: London, 2011), 153–71.

72. The historical-discursive context of Buddhism and Jainism as two non-Brahmanical religions was also one of the factors behind the appearance of the theme of *ahimsa* in the discourse of *dharma*. Long before its appearance in the Brahmanical discourse of *dharma, ahiṃsā* had already emerged as one of the most important themes in both Buddhism and Jainism. Also, the emperor Aśoka of the Mauryan dynasty in the third century BCE had made *ahimsa* one of the central subjects in his ambitious public campaign to spread civic morality amongst his subjects. The appearance of *ahimsa* in the Brahmanical discourse of *dharma*, therefore, was partly a strategic response to this discursive and historical context. See "The Ascetic and the Domestic in Brahmanical Religiosity," in Olivelle, *Ascetics and Brahmins: Studies in Ideologies and Institutions*, 38–40.

73. *Mānava Dharmaśāstra*, 10.3.

74. *Mānava Dharmaśāstra*, 5.27–56.

75. *Mānava Dharmaśāstra*, 11.31–33.

76. *Mānava Dharmaśāstra*, 11.34–35.

77. One way in which the discourse of *dharma* sought to claim primacy or hegemony over that of *artha* or state power was by assigning the defense and maintenance of *dharma* based on the caste system as the most important responsibility of the state or the king. The *Mānava Dharmaśāstra* has an entire chapter dedicated to the functioning of the state under the notion of *rāja-dharma*, or the duties of a king. See Olivelle, *Mānava Dharmaśāstra*, chap. 7. Indeed, in the following centuries the entire genre of *arthaśāstra* became absorbed and transformed into what eventually came to be known as *rajadharmaśāstra*. In other words, the *arthaśāstra* tradition nearly lost its status as a separate and autonomous discourse. Sheldon Pollock, *The Ends of Man at the End of Premodernity* (Amsterdam: Royal Netherlands Academy of Arts and Sciences, 2005), 12.

78. *Mānava Dharmaśāstra*, 2.2–5. There have been doubts about whether this passage really belongs in this chapter of the *Mānava Dharmaśāstra*. As Olivelle notes, it goes against the flow of the major themes discussed in the chapter. He therefore puts the passage under the designation of "excursus." Although he allows the possibility of this passage being a later interpolation, Olivelle also notes that he is not entirely certain about such a possibility. However, if we see this passage within the broader context of the *Mānava Dharmaśāstra*'s discourse of power grounded in subjectivity, rather than force, it not only seems to belong to the text, it may be one of the most important passages that offers an insight into the real nature of the discourse of *dharma* as a discourse of power. For Olivelle's comments on these verses, see Olivelle, *Manu's Code of Law*, 54. Hiltebeitel thinks that verses designated "excursus" in Olivelle's translation ought to be seen as moments when Manu took the discussion beyond the preceding legal tradition, and that in such instances he might have been drawing upon nonlegal sources. Hiltebeitel, *Dharma*, 20.

79. In this regard, the works of two scholars, Stephanie Jamison and Patrick Olivelle, hold particular importance. These two scholars have focused on the questions of agency and desire in the discourse of *dharma* in the *Dharmaśāstras* in ancient India. Olivelle's "lived reality of women" as opposed to how they "ought to be" and Stephanie Jamison's "reading between the lines" are ways to get past the direct and strident pronouncements on women in the *Dharmaśāstras*. It is in their efforts to get past these pronouncements, in which much of the scholarship on the subject has remained trapped, that both Olivelle and Jamison discovered the presence of agency and desire.

As Jamison and Olivelle have noted, the *Dharmaśāstra*'s approach to the question of women was marked by a "paradox," "a schizophrenic attitude": even as it acknowledged agency in women, it also at the same time sought to deprive them of all independence, that is to say, deprive them of that agency. According to Jamison, the question of will and desire in the instances of adultery or extramarital relationship become a critical factor in determining the culpability and the right punishment. Jamison also shows this paradox to be a new historical development, because it is missing in the discourse of *dharma* reflected in the *Dharmasūtras*, a series of texts that preceded the appearance of the *Mānava Dharmaśāstra*. Even as the *Dharmasūtras* denied women agency, they also at the same time offered them [women] comparatively more autonomy in their relationship with their husbands. Both Olivelle and Jamison offer the emergence of the nuns in Buddhism and Jainism as the historical context which may have provoked this paradoxical approach. The independence of the nuns was evident not only in that they had left their patriarchal families behind, but also in that they pursued spiritual liberation as their highest religious spiritual goal, a goal which had until then been assumed to be meant only for men. Even as the presence of nuns made it difficult for the *Dharmaśāstra* to deny women agency, it also presented a threat to the institution and discourse of patriarchy in which the discourse of *dharma* had come to be grounded.

See Stephanie Jamison, "Women 'Between the Empires' and 'Between the Lines,'" in Olivelle, *Between the Empires*, 191–214; Olivelle, "Rhetoric and Reality: Women's Agency in the *Dharmaśāstras*," in Olivelle, *Language, Text, and Society*, 247–60. Also, see Kumkum Roy, "Of Theras and Therīs: Visions of Liberation in Early Buddhist Tradition," in *The Power of Gender and the Gender of Power: Explorations in Early Indian History* (New Delhi: Oxford University Press, 2010), 17–37.

80. *Mānava Dharmaśāstra*, 2.1

81. *Mānava Dharmaśāstra*, 12.37. I have slightly modified Olivelle's translation of this verse: instead of "inner being," I have translated the word *ātmā* as "self," and instead of "seeks" I have translated the word *icchati* as "desires." For Goodness (*sattva*) as a mark of *dharma*, see *Mānava Dharmaśāstra*, 12.38.

82. *Mānava Dharmaśāstra*, 2.6. Olivelle also notes that the phrases "assented to by the heart" and "what is pleasing to oneself" go together. See Olivelle, *Manu's Code of Law*, 243, n. 2.2. As the word "root" suggests, the *Mānava Dharmaśāstra* recognized "pleasure of the self" as one of the sources of *dharma*.

83. *Mānava Dharmaśāstra*, 2.12.

84. *Mānava Dharmaśāstra*, 12.38. I have slightly modified the translation.

85. *Mānava Dharmaśāstra*, 12.40.

86. *Mānava Dharmaśāstra*, 12.73–80.

87. *Mānava Dharmaśāstra*, 2.88, 98–100. The verses cited here, which form part of a set of verses 2.88–100, have also been suspected to have been later interpolations. Just as the verses on desire, Olivelle puts these verses also under the designation of "excursus," meaning that they do not quite fit into the flow of the discussion. However, as Olivelle points out, there is no sure way of determining if these verses were interpolations. But if these verses are seen in conjunction with the verses on desire, a fuller and more coherent picture emerges. Indeed, these two sets of verses designated "excursus" by Olivelle are best seen together as an elaboration of the same theme in two steps: while the first set of verses establishes desire as the foundation of man's being, the second set lays out the mechanics of how desire can be controlled and cultivated.

88. Here too, one has to keep the historical-discursive context in mind. Asceticism had emerged as a major form of spiritual pursuit both in Buddhism and Jainism long before the *Mānava Dharmaśāstra* made it its own. Olivelle calls it the "domestication of asceticism," because what was meant to be part of a renouncer's spiritual pursuit was being introduced into the

life of a householder—a figure exactly the opposite of the renouncer. See Olivelle, *Ascetics and Brahmins*, 27–41.

89. *Mānava Dharmaśāstra*, 2.89–92.

90. *Mānava Dharmaśāstra*, 2.93–97.

91. *Mānava Dharmaśāstra*, 12.3–4.

92. *Mānava Dharmaśāstra*, 9.29–30.

93. *Mānava Dharmaśāstra*, 9.28.

94. *Mānava Dharmaśāstra*, 4.6.

95. P. V. Kane, *History of Dharmaśāstra*, vol. 2, part 1, 565.

96. *Mānava Dharmaśāstra*, 4.43–44.

97. *Mānava Dharmaśāstra*, 5.154, 155.

98. *Mānava Dharmaśāstra*, 9.18.

99. *Mānava Dharmaśāstra*, 2.67.

100. Olivelle rightly calls it the "theology of the woman" and observes that it came to be internalized by most women. What Olivelle calls internalization is precisely the process through which the subjectivity of the wife came to be born in ancient India. A. Feldhaus, who translated these verses by Bahina, adds that "Bahina identifies service to a husband as the duty of a woman, adherence to duty as the teaching of the Vedas, and disregard of the Vedas as the surest way to miss the ultimate goal." A. Feldhaus cited in Olivelle, *The Āśrama System*, 186–87.

101. See "Symposium" in *Plato: Complete Works*, ed. John M. Cooper; trans. Alexander Nehmas and Paul Woodruff (Indianapolis: Hackett Publishing Company, 1997), 208d–212c.

102. Foucault has dwelt extensively on this conflict and the ways to overcome it in Greek culture. According to Foucault, it was partly in the process of overcoming the desire for pleasure that the discourse of the "care of the self"—along with the discourse of "know thyself"—came about in Plato's dialogues. That was how, according to Foucault, the discourse of asceticism was born in ancient Greece. See Michel Foucault, *Hermeneutics of the Subject: Lectures at the College de France, 1981–1982*, *The Government of Self and Others: Lectures at the College de France, 1982–1983*, and *The Courage of Truth: Lectures at College de France*. Also, see chap. 1 of this book for a brief discussion of this issue as it is reflected in Foucault's works.

Chapter 3

1. Some relevant works on courtesans in ancient India are Ludwik Sternbach, *Gaṇikāvṛttasaṃgrahaḥ: Or, Texts on Courtesans in Classical Sanskrit* (Hoshiarpur: Visheshvarananda Vedic Research Institute, 1953), and "Legal Position of Prostitutes according to Kautilya's *Arthaśāstra*," *Journal of the American Oriental Society* 71, no. 1 (Jan.–March 1951): 25–60; Sukumari Bhattacharji, "Prostitution in Ancient India," *Social Scientist* 15, no. 2 (Feb. 1987): 32–61; Monika Saxena, "Ganikas in Early India," *Social Scientist* 34, nos. 11/12 (Nov.–Dec. 2006): 2–17; S. N. Sinha, N. K. Basu, and Rita Sil, *History of Marriage and Prostitution: Vedas to Vātsyāyana* (New Delhi: Khama Publishers, 1992); Moti Chandra, *The World of Courtesans* (Delhi: Vikas Publishing House, 1973); Santosh Kumar Mukherji, *Prostitution in India* (New Delhi: Inter India Publications, 1986 reprint). For a very insightful account and analysis of courtesans in modern India, see Veena Talwar Oldenburg, "Lifestyle as Resistance: The Case of the Courtesans of Lucknow, India," *Feminist Studies* 16, no. 2 (Summer 1990): 259–87.

2. Book 6 in the *Kāmasūtra* is dedicated exclusively to the affairs of the courtesan. Translations of the citations from the *Kāmasūtra* are my own. Damodar Lal Goswami, ed., *Kāmasūtra*

of Vātsyāyana, with the Commentary of Yashodhara (Varanasi: Chaukhambha Sanskrit Sansthan, 1912); Devadatta Shastri, ed., *Kāmasūtra of Vātsyāyana, with the Commentary of Yashodhara* (Varanasi: Chaukhambha Sanskrit Sansthan, 1964). For an English translation of the *Kāmasūtra*, see Wendy Doniger and Sudhir Kakar, *Vātsyāyana Kāmasūtra: A New, Complete Translation of the Sanskrit Text* (New York: Oxford University Press, 2002).

3. *Kāmasūtra,* 2.2.31.

4. *Kāmasūtra,* 2.4.6.

5. Dāmodaragupta, *Kuṭṭanī-Matam: A Didactic Poem Composed about A.D. 755–786,* with a new commentary *Rasa-Dīpikā* by Tanasukhram Manasukharam Tripathi (Varanasi: Krishnadas Academy, 1991), 385–90.

6. Dāmodaragupta, *Kuṭṭanī-Matam*, 387.

7. *Kāmasūtra,* 1.2.15. With the exception of Burton and Upadhyaya, most translators and commentators of the *Kāmasūtra* have translated the part about *veśyā,* or courtesans, to mean that just as for the king, so too for the courtesan *artha* as money or wealth has the primacy. This reading, however, involves a serious misunderstanding. Although the aphoristic brevity of the *Kāmasūtra* and the courtesan's obvious interest in making money from her patrons may seem to support this interpretation, the train of thought leading up to this point leaves no doubt that in the courtesan it is *kāma* or sexual-erotic pleasure that finds its primacy and autonomy. The most important thing to keep in mind is that this sutra is primarily about the trilogy and the relationship between its three constituents, not about the king and the courtesan; the king and the courtesan appear only as the leading representatives of the discourses of political power (*artha*) and sexual-erotic pleasure (*kāma*), respectively. It should be noted that the second chapter of the first book in which this sutra occurs is called *trivarga-pratipatti-prakarṇam* and as such is meant to focus on the trilogy. Note also how the cited passage ends with the concluding statement that "thus the discussion of the trilogy is complete," reminding the readers once again that it is the trilogy and the relationship between its three constituents that have been at stake throughout this exposition. So when the *Kāmasūtra* sets out to identify the exceptions to this general dictum of the primacy of the discourse of Brahmanical law (*dharma*), it still has the relationship between the three constituents of the trilogy in view; in exceptions it seeks to identify the instances in which *dharma* cedes its primacy, setting *artha* and *kāma* free. To conclude, what the *Kāmasūtra* claims is this: just as *dharma* cedes its primacy to *artha* in the figure of the king, it cedes its primacy to *kāma* in the figure of the courtesan. See S. C. Upadhyaya, *The Kāmasūtra: The Hindu Art of Love* (London: Watkins Publishing, 2004); Richard F. Burton, *Kāmasūtra of Vātsyāyana*, 64.

8. According to Ludwik Sternbach, in classical Sanskrit courtesans were compared with kings more than with any other social or political figure. The reason for this, from the citations collected by Sternbach, was the popular perception of their shared duplicity: the king was interested in power alone even as he made public professions of people's welfare. And courtesans were interested in nothing but money, even as they put up a show of love to their patrons. Sternbach, *Gaṇikāvṛttasaṃgrahaḥ*, 143.

9. *Kāmasūtra*, 6.3.

10. Sukumari Bhattacharji, "Prostitution in Ancient India," *Social Scientist* 15 (1987): 33.

11. G. P. Singh, *Republics, Kingdoms, Towns and Cities in Ancient India* (New Delhi: D. K. Printworld, 2003), 212–13.

12. Bhattacharji, "Prostitution in Ancient India," 33.

13. Bhattacharji, "Prostitution in Ancient India," 43–44.

14. Bhattacharji, "Prostitution in Ancient India," 56.

15. Csaba Dezső and Somadeva Vasudeva, eds. and trans., *The Quartet of Causeries by Śyāmalika, Vararuchi, Śūdraka & Īśvaradatta* (New York: New York University Press and the JJC Foundation, 2009), 332–33.

16. Based on his survey of the ancient and early medieval Indian sources in Sanskrit, Sternbach concluded that "the word *gaṇikā* always denotes the highest degree of prostitutes—a courtesan." See Sternbach, *Gaṇikāvṛttasaṃgrahaḥ*, 26.

17. Altekar refers to them as the "custodians of fine arts." See A. S. Altekar, *The Position of Women in Hindu Civilization* (New Delhi: Motilal Banarasidas, 1938), 181–82.

18. Bhattacharji, "Prostitution in Ancient India," 43.

19. Santosh Kumar Mukherji, *Prostitution in India* (New Delhi: Inter India Publications, 1986 reprint), 65–66.

20. *Kāmasūtra,* 1.3.17–18.

21. According to the *Arthaśāstra,* it was the duty of the state that employed *gaṇikās* to offer them education in the sixty-four arts. See Ludwik Sternbach, "Legal Position of Prostitutes according to Kautilya's *Arthaśāstra,*" *Journal of the American Oriental Society* 71, no. 1 (1951): 25–60, 35.

22. This was despite the fact that courtesans, including the *gaṇikā,* were denounced in strongest words by much of the didactic and *dharma* literature of ancient and early medieval India. After a wide-ranging survey of classical Sanskrit, Sternbach concludes that "courtesans [were] considered as the most condemnable creatures." Sternbach, "Legal Position of Prostitutes," 151. Bhattacharji also notes this dual attitude toward courtesans in ancient India. Bhattacharji, "Prostitution in Ancient India," 53, 55–56.

23. Patrick Olivelle, *King, Governance, and Law in Ancient India: Kautilya's Arthaśāstra* (New York: Oxford University Press, 2013); R. P. Kangle, *The Kautilya Arthaśāstra. Three Parts. University of Bombay Studies, Sanskrit, Prakrit and Pali, Nos. 1–3* (Bombay: University of Bombay, 1960–65).

24. For a comprehensive study of the legal status of courtesans and the state of prostitution in the *Arthaśāstra,* see Sternbach, "Legal Position of Prostitutes."

25. It should be noted, however, that the *Arthaśāstra* is the only text from ancient India to use the word *gaṇikā* exclusively to describe those courtesans who were also state servants. See Sternbach, "Legal Position of Prostitutes," 35. Given that the *Arthaśāstra* was a formal treatise on statecraft, it is possible that the references to *gaṇikā* were part of Kautilya's vision of what a state ought to do with the *gaṇikās* in its territory, not a description of what they really did. Even so, there is no doubt that the *Arthaśāstra* assumed *gaṇikās* to be the most accomplished and the very best kind of courtesans.

26. Sternbach, "Legal Position of Prostitutes," 25.

27. *Kāmasūtra,* 1.5.

28. *Kāmasūtra,* 1.5.3.

29. *Kāmasūtra,* 1.5.3.

30. *Kāmasūtra,* 3.3.

31. *Kāmasūtra,* 3.5.29–30.

32. *Kāmasūtra,* 5.

33. *Kāmasūtra,* 1.4.3.

34. *Kāmasūtra,* 5.1.10.

35. *Kāmasūtra,* 4.2.31–35.

36. *Kāmasūtra*, 4.2.31–54

37. *Kāmasūtra*, 4.2.44.

38. *Kāmasūtra*, 4.2.42, 44.

39. *Kāmasūtra*, 1.5.6. Doniger and Kakar translate *punarbhū* as "second-hand woman." Doniger and Kakar, *Vātsyāyana Kāmasūtra*, 100.

40. *Quartet of Causeries*, 327.

41. *Kāmasūtra*, 1.5.2.

42. *Kāmasūtra*, 6.1–6.

43. *Kāmasūtra*, 6.2.3–8.

44. Based on his collection of aphorisms from classical Sanskrit in which courtesans are compared with actresses, Sternbach concludes: "Courtesans' behavior is very often compared with acting, and courtesans are compared with actresses or stage managers. And so, courtesans, like actresses, exhibit affection to gain money and pretend affection, love, anger, etc., or use theatrical postures, or, since they have been trained on the stage, change their voices, or act like stage-managers. Both courtesans and actors are also known to cause disorder." See Sternbach, *Gaṇikāvṛttasaṃgrahaḥ*, 145.

45. Ludo Rocher, "The *Kāmasūtra*: Vatsyayana's Attitude toward Dharma and *Dharmaśāstra*," *Journal of the American Oriental Society* 105, no. 3 (1985): 526.

46. *Kāmasūtra*, 6.2.60–61.

47. *Quartet of Causeries*, 175.

48. Bhattacharji, "Prostitution in Ancient India," 33.

49. Sternbach, "Legal Position of Prostitutes," 54–56.

50. *Kāmasūtra*, 6.1.21.

51. *Kāmasūtra*, 6.1.22–24.

52. *Kāmasūtra*, 6.1.25–29.

53. *Kāmasūtra*, 6.2.1.

54. *Kāmasūtra*, 6.2.63.

55. *Kāmasūtra*, 6.2.67–71.

56. *Kāmasūtra*, 6.2.72.

57. *Kāmasūtra*, 6.2.22.

58. *Kāmasūtra*, 6.2.44.

59. Even though others joined the rank of *gaṇikā*, it was preferable to have the daughters of *gaṇikās* carry on the legacy. According to the *Arthaśāstra*, the laws of inheritance in the case of *gaṇikās* followed the maternal line. Either the *gaṇikā's* daughter, sister, or mother inherited her property at her death, not her son. In this regard, a statement from the *Kut-t-animata*, a much later text dealing with the lives of courtesans, is very revealing: "Only daughters are praiseworthy; shame upon those who rejoice in the birth of a son." This shows just how different the status of the daughters was amongst courtesans from the rest of the society, where sons were seen as the anchors of the family. See Sternbach, "Legal Position of Prostitutes," 31, 40.

60. According to Bhattacharji, even as some of these sons "without any social identity" might have received training as musicians and actors for the stage, others not so fortunate "lived in a brothel until they could eke out a livelihood for themselves. . . . [They] were looked upon as waste products, like slag in a factory." Bhattacharji, "Prostitution in Ancient India," 45.

61. *Kāmasūtra*, 6.2.58.

62. *Kāmasūtra*, 6.2.59.

63. *Kāmasūtra*, 1.5.28.

64. Sigmund Freud, *The Psychology of Love*, trans. Shaun Whiteside with an introduction by Jeri Johnson (New York: Penguin Books, 2007), 245–47, 241–61.

Chapter 4

1. *Nāṭyaśāstram: The Nāṭyaśāstra of Bharatamuni, Text, Commentary of Abhinavabhāratī by Abhinavaguptācārya*, trans. M. Ghosh, ed. Pushpendra Kumar (Delhi: New Bharatiya Book Corporation, 2006). Henceforth, this text will be referred to as *Nāṭyaśāstra*. I use M. Ghosh's translations of the verses of the *Nāṭyaśāstra*, except in some places where I have had to modify them slightly for the reasons of consistency of my own terminology, and also to emphasize contextual and conceptual nuances of some of the more important terms.

2. While a few historians have suggested that theater migrated from Greece to India, particularly in the wake of Alexander's invasion of India in the fourth century BCE, this perspective has few followers today. This theory of Greek origins was first put forward by Albrecht Weber in 1852 and later elaborated by Ernst Windrisch in 1882. See Steven F. Walker, "The Invention of Theater: Recontextualizing the Vexing Question," *Comparative Literature* 56, no.1 (Winter 2004): 1–22. Also, see S. A. Srinivasan, *On the Composition of the Nāṭyaśāstra* (Reinbek: Verlag für Orientalistische Fachpublikationen, 1980). After the early arguments over the influence of Greek drama on Indic theater, much of the scholarship on the question of the origin of theater has remained focused on Vedic and non-Vedic rituals. My argument contests one of the central assumptions underlying the work of historians of ancient Indian theater: that it has its origin in religious rituals, Vedic and non-Vedic. The investigation into the origins of theater in Vedic rituals is most thoroughly carried out in F. B. J. Kuiper's *Varuṇa and Vidūṣaka: On the Origin of the Sanskrit Drama* (Amsterdam: Royal Netherlands Academy, 1979). Natalia Lidova traces the origin of theater in non-Vedic temple rituals known as *puja* in *Drama and Ritual in Early Hinduism* (Delhi: Motilal Banarsidass Publishers, 1994).

For a general ritual and literary context to the origin of theater, see A. Berriedale Keith, *The Sanskrit Drama in Its Origin, Development, Theory and Practice* (London: Oxford University Press, reprinted 1959). Keith also discusses the issue of Greek influence on theater in India briefly in this book. Though the question of Greek influence seems to have largely receded as a major scholarly concern, it has not completely disappeared. Also, see Anupa Pandey, *The Nāṭyaśāstra Tradition and Ancient Indian Society* (Jodhpur: Kusumanjali, 1993); R. K. Yajnik, *The Indian Theatre: Its Origins and Its Later Developments under European Influence with Special Reference to Western India* (London: George Allen & Unwin, 1933).

3. A detailed critical discussion of the historiography on the origins of theater in classical India is unnecessary, primarily because my perspective and how I problematize the question of origin are starkly different from the ones available in the existing scholarship. First of all, it is important to distinguish between an investigation into the origins of theater as such and an investigation into the origins of classical Sanskrit theater as reflected in the core of the *Nāṭyaśāstra*. I do not focus on the origin of theater as such, but rather on classical Sanskrit theater. Until now the practice has been to search for the origin of theater as such and then assume that classical theater evolved out of it. There has rarely been an effort to identify the stages through which theater evolved to its classical form. In the absence of a line of evolution connecting the earliest to the classical, it would not be an exaggeration to say that the origins of classical theater has not even been attempted. Part of the reason is that most scholars have tried to follow the lead offered by the *Nāṭyaśāstra* itself regarding its origin. Even though the *Nāṭyaśāstra* elaborates the classical

Sanskrit theater and aesthetics in most of its pages, in its origin narrative it locates the origin of theater in Vedic tradition. Another argument the scholars have made about pursuing the origin of theater in the direction of the Vedas is the presence of Vedic rituals in the *pūrvaraṅga,* or the preliminaries that are supposed to be performed before the start of the play. A theatrical performance as it ought to be ideally staged according to the *Nāṭyaśāstra* takes place in two steps. The first step, called *pūrvaraṅga,* or preliminaries, consists of a very brief set of rituals that takes place before the staging of the actual play. The second step consists of the staging of the play itself. The plays themselves consist of the two dominant types: *nāṭaka,* or royal romance, and *prakaraṇa,* or popular romance. Thematically and narratively these two steps are altogether separate and unrelated; there is absolutely no continuity between the Vedic rituals and the erotic-romantic plays. In other words, an investigation into the preliminaries tells us nothing about the nature or the origins of the plays themselves.

Indeed, F. B. J. Kuiper, who has pursued this line of enquiry most thoroughly, himself admits that there is no way to either work one's way up from the origins of theater in rituals to "classical drama"—that is to say, popular and royal romance—or, conversely, back from "classical drama" to its origins in Vedic rituals. In other words, what is offered as a history of the origin of theater is in fact the history of the origin of the ritual preliminaries (*pūrvaraṅga*). If Kuiper is still able to offer what amounts to be a history of the ritual preliminaries as the history of theater, that is because he, despite his acknowledgment of the complete absence of any evidence, simply assumes that classical drama must have come as the next stage in the historical evolution of the preliminaries as the original form of theater in ancient India. What should be evident is that the history of the origin of theater as reflected in the classical Sanskrit drama and most of the *Nāṭyaśāstra* has not yet been precisely problematized. See Kuiper's *Varuṇa and Vidūṣaka: On the Origin of the Sanskrit Drama*, 239.

4. For a general introduction, see Kapila Vatsyayan, *Bharata, The Nātyaśāstra* (New Delhi: Sahitya Akademi, 1996). Also, see Pandey, *The Nāṭyaśāstra Tradition.* For the theory of aesthetics developed first in the *Nāṭyaśāstra*, see Sheldon Pollock, "What Was Bhatta Nāyaka Saying: The Hermeneutical Transformation of Indian Aesthetics," in *Epic and Argument in Sanskrit Literary History: Essays in Honor of Robert P. Goldman,* ed. Sheldon Pollock, 143–84 (Delhi: Manohar, 2010); Sheldon Pollock, "The Social Aesthetic and Sanskrit Literary Theory" *Journal of Indian Philosophy* 29, nos. 1–2 (2001): 197–229.

5. See Edwin Gerow, "Abhinavagupta's Aesthetics as a Speculative Paradigm," *Journal of the American Oriental Society* 114, no. 2 (Apr.–June, 1994): 186–208; J. L. Masson and M. V. Patwardhan, *Śāntarasa and Abhinavagupta's Philosophy of Aesthetics* (Poona: Bhandarkar Oriental Research Institute, 1969); Raniero Gnoli, *The Aesthetic Experience according to Abhinavagupta* (Varanasi: Chowkhamba Sanskrit Series Office, 1968).

6. For the impact of the philosophy of aesthetics developed by the *Nāṭyaśāstra* on the theology of devotional form of Hinduism, see David L. Haberman, *Acting as a Way of Salvation: A Study of Rāgānuga Bhakti Sādhana* (Oxford: Oxford University Press, 1988).

7. See Devesh Soneji, *Unfinished Gestures: Devadasis, Moemory, and Modernity in South Asia* (Chicago: University of Chicago Press, 2012); Leslie C. Orr, *Donors, Devotees, and Daughters of God: Temple Women in Medieval Tamilnadu* (New York: Oxford University Press, 2000); Sasakiya C. Kersenboom, *Nityasumangali: Devadasi Tradition in South India* (New Delhi: Motilala Banarsidass, 2011).

8. P. V. Kane, *History of Sanskrit Poetics* (Delhi: Motilal Banarsidass Publishers, 1971), 22.

9. *Nāṭyaśāstra*, 1.17–18.

10. Alf Hiltebeitel, "Nahusa in the Skies: A Human King of Heavens," *History of Religions* 16, no. 4 (1977): 329–50.

11. *Nāṭyaśāstra*, 36.55.

12. *Nāṭyaśāstra*, 24.154.

13. *Nāṭyaśāstra*, 35.39.

14. Krishnakanta Handique, *Apsaras in Indian Literature and the Legend of Urvaśī and Purūravas* (New Delhi: Decent Books, 2001); Babu Ram Yadava, *Evolution of Urvaśī* (Aligarh: Vijñāna Prakāśana, 1986); Ramdhari Singh Dinkar, *Dinkar's Urvashi (A Saga of Human Love and Vedanta)*, trans. from the original Hindi by Krishna Kumar Vidyarthi (New Delhi: Siddharth Publications, 1994).

15. *The Rig Veda*, trans. Ralph T. H. Griffith, 10.95 (Lexington, KY: Forgottenbooks, 2008).

16. The story in the *Ṛgveda* is somewhat confusing. But later in the dialogue when Urvaśī does leave Purūravas, she promises to leave the son behind with him.

17. *Ṛgveda*, 10.95.2.

18. *Ṛgveda*, 10.95.14.

19. *Ṛgveda*, 10.95.18.

20. Handique, *Apsaras in Indian Literature*.

21. Kālidāsa, *The Vikramorvaśīyam*, critically edited by H. D. Velandar (New Delhi: Sahitya Akademi, 1961).

22. *Nāṭyaśāstra*, 36.61–62.

23. *Nāṭyaśāstra*, 1.79.

24. *Nāṭyaśāstra*, 1.106.

25. *Nāṭyaśāstra*, 1.44–45.

26. *Nāṭyaśāstra*, 22.47. Having given the definition, the *Nāṭyaśāstra* goes on to delineate different kinds of this style. See *Nāṭyaśāstra*, 22.48–53.

27. *Nāṭyaśāstra*, 1.44.

28. There are complex philosophical issues at stake in the nature and production of aesthetic pleasure, which I will not discuss here.

29. *Nāṭyaśāstra*, 24.97.

30. *Nāṭyaśāstra*, 1.46.

31. *Nāṭyaśāstra*, 35.47.

32. *Nāṭyaśāstra*, 35.47–55.

33. *Nāṭyaśāstra*, 35.55–56.

34. *Nāṭyaśāstra*, 35.54.

35. *Nāṭyaśāstra*, 35.49–50.

36. *Nāṭyaśāstra*, 35.37, 49, 52.

37. *Nāṭyaśāstra*, 35.38.

38. *Nāṭyaśāstra*, 35.37.

39. *Nāṭyaśāstra*, 35.39.

40. *Nāṭyaśāstra*, 1.46–47.

41. *Nāṭyaśāstra*, 36.70.

42. *Nāṭyaśāstra*, 35.40–41.

43. *Nāṭyaśāstra*, 36.51.

44. The *nāṭaka* and the *prakaraṇa* are by far the most important of the ten also because they include within them all the styles and thus allow for the full expression of all the different ele-

ments of drama as described in the *Nāṭyaśāstra*. *Nāṭyaśāstra*, 20.7. For an exhaustive exposition of the ten different types of plays, see *Nāṭyaśāstra*, 20.

45. *Nāṭyaśāstra*, 20.8–9.

46. For the definition of the *nāṭaka*, see *Nāṭyaśāstra*, 20.10–12; for the *prakaraṇa*, see *Nāṭyaśāstra*, 20.48–56.

47. *Nāṭyaśāstra*, 24.148–49.

48. *Nāṭyaśāstra*, 20.48.

49. *Nāṭyaśāstra*, 20.52.

50. *Nāṭyaśāstra*, 20.53.

51. *Nāṭyaśāstra*, 20.54–56.

52. *Nāṭyaśāstra*, 20.54–56.

53. *Padmaprābhṛtakam*, 41.1–2. See *Śṛṅgāra-Hāṭa: A Collection of Four Sanskrit Bhāṇas, One-Actor Plays, Viz., Padmaprābhṛtaka, Dhūrta-viṭa-saṁvāda, Ubhayābhisārikā and Pādatāḍitakam*, critically edited and translated into Hindi by Dr. Motichandra and Dr. Vasudevasharan Agrawal (Bombay: Hindi Granth Ratnakar, 1960).

54. *Padmaprābhṛtakam*, 33.18.

55. There is at least one instance in which the term *nāṭaka* also appears in the same *bhāṇa* in a similar context. When one of the acquaintances narrates his sexual encounter with one of the maids of a courtesan, the dandy-guru exclaims that "a *nāṭaka* has just taken place without the drums." Here the word *nāṭaka* is used in the same sense as the word *prakaraṇa* as reference to an erotic affair or episode. *Padmaprābhṛtakam*, 22.2.

56. See *Padmaprābhṛtakam*, 35.18; 38.24.

57. *Nāṭyaśāstra*, 25.1.

58. *Nāṭyaśāstra*, 25.2.

59. *Nāṭyaśāstra*, 20.51, 53.

60. Csaba Dezső and Somadeva Vasudeva, eds. and trans., *The Quartet of Causeries by Śyāmalika, Vararuchi, Śūdraka & Īśvaradatta* (New York: New York University Press and the JJC Foundation, 2009), 4.155.

61. *Nāṭyaśāstra*, 24.148–149.

62. While anticipating the subject of discussion in the next chapter, the last verse of chapter 24 says, "The etiquette with regard to [the women] outside will be explained in [the chapter] on courtesans." In light of this verse the title of the next chapter—chapter 25—should be *veśyopacāra*, or "dealings with courtesans." The term "women outside the family," in other words, was just a euphemism for courtesans. See *Nāṭyaśāstra*, 24.328.

63. *Kāmasūtra*, 1.4.3.

64. *Nāṭyaśāstra*, 6.45+.

65. *Nāṭyaśāstra*, 24.191, 201, 205; 25.38, 62, 65.

66. Śūdraka, *Padmaprābhṛtakam*, in *Śṛṅgāra-Hata: A Collection of Four Sanskrit Bhāṇas*, critically edited and translated into Hindi by Dr. Motichandra and Dr. Vasudevasharan Agrawal (Bombay: Hindi Granth Ratnakar, 1960), 11.9.

67. *Kāmasūtra*, 1.4.1.

68. I broadly follow Baudelaire's characterization of the dandy. But given the complexity of this figure, there have been numerous works focusing on different aspects of it in the European context. It is not relevant for me here to go into those aspects in any detail. The classic account of the dandy in European history is Ellen Moers, *The Dandy: Brummell to Beerbohm* (New York: Viking Press, 1960). Two literary figures who made the figure of the dandy important were Charles Baudelaire and Oscar Wilde. See Charles Baudelaire, *Baudelaire as a Literary Critic: Se-*

lected Essays Introduced and Translated by Louis Boe Hyslop and Francis E. Hyslop, Jr. (University Park: Pennsylvania State University Press, 1964); Walter Benjamin, *Charles Baudelaire: A Lyric Poet in the Era of High Capitalism*, trans. Harry Zohn (London: Verso, 1983); Oscar Wilde, *The Picture of Dorian Gray and Other Writings*, 1891 (New York: Bantam. Reprint, 1982). Other works include James Eli Adams, *Dandies and Desert Saints: Styles of Victorian Masculinity* (Ithaca, NY: Cornell University Press, 1995); Elisa Glick, "The Dialectics of Dandyism," *Cultural Critique* 48 (2001): 129–63.

69. I will discuss this aspect in more detail in chap. 6.

70. See Moers, *The Dandy: Brummell to Beerbohm.*

71. "Dandyism is a mysterious institution . . . it is of great antiquity, Caesar, Catiline and Alcibiades providing us with dazzling examples; and very widespread, Chateaubriand having found it in the forests and by the lakes of the New World." Charles Baudelaire, *The Painter of Modern Life and Other Essays*, trans. Jonathan Mayne (London: Phaidon, 1964), 26.

72. Baudelaire, *The Painter of Modern Life*, 26–29.

73. The *Kāmasūtra* discusses the figure of the "city dandy," or *nāgaraka,* and his everyday routine in great detail. See *Kāmasūtra*, 1.4.

74. I will discuss this aspect of the figure of the dandy in the next two chapters.

75. Given that the *Kāmasūtra*'s term *nāgaraka* is often translated as "man about town," it is interesting that in the very first line of her book on the dandy, Moers notes the equivalence between the figure of man about town and the dandy. Moers, *The Dandy: Brummell to Beerbohm*, 11.

76. Bhāsa, *Cārudattam* (Varanasi: Chaukhamba Sanskrit Sansthan, 1997).

77. Heinrich Luders, *Fragments of Buddhist Drama*, trans. Arati Mitra (Calcutta: Sanskrit College, 1994), 6, 9.

78. Luders, *Fragments of Buddhist Drama*, 21.

79. *Padmaprābhṛtakam*, 31.18–20, in *Śṛṅgāra-Hata: A Collection of Four Sanskrit Bhānas*, critically edited and translated into Hindi by Dr. Motichandra and Dr. Vasudevasharan Agrawal (Bombay: Hindi Granth Ratnakar, 1960).

80. It is not surprising, therefore, that those scholars who have approached *kaiśikī* exclusively as a theatrical style have run into insoluble contradictions. There is a tension between the historical and the theatrical meanings of this notion. Historically, *kaiśikī* as *vṛtti* referred to a form of erotic lifestyle, but as a category of theater it also came to refer to a theatrical style. Two separate meanings of the word *vṛtti,* thus, run into each other in the term *kaiśikī vṛtti.* To use the *Nāṭyaśāstra*'s own terms, *kaiśikī vṛtti* came to be grounded in two conventions at the same time: popular conventions, or *lokadharmī,* and theatrical conventions, or *nāṭyadharmī.* All the problems arise when these two sets of conventions—popular and theatrical—converge on the same notion. Here is an example: acknowledging that the *kaiśikī* as a theatrical style does not fit the other styles, Dr. V. Raghavan comments, "Bharata himself did not know what that name meant or how the graceful situations came to be called by that name. Words like *kaiśikī* became *ruḍhis* (conventions) and even while Bharata wrote, many things were forgotten." Dr. V. Raghavan, *Sanskrit Drama: Its Aesthetics and Production* (Mr. R. Kalidas: Madras, 1993), 270–271; 269.

81. *Nāṭyaśāstra*, 20.10–12.

82. *Nāṭyaśāstra*, 24.154.

83. Kālidāsa, *The Vikramorvaśīyam.*

84. *Nāṭyaśāstra*, 24.261.

85. *Nāṭyaśāstra*, 24.321.

86. *Nāṭyaśāstra*, 24.327.

87. *Nāṭyaśāstra*, 24.321.

88. *Nāṭyaśāstra*, 24.323.

89. *Nāṭyaśāstra*, 24.322.

90. *Nāṭyaśāstra*, 24.324–325.

91. *Nāṭyaśāstra*, 24.326.

92. *Nāṭyaśāstra*, 34.31–34.

93. *Nāṭyaśāstra*, 34.48–51.

94. *Nāṭyaśāstra*, 35.81–83.

95. See Patrick Olivelle, *King, Governance, and Law in Ancient India: Kautilya's Arthaśāstra* (New York: Oxford University Press, 2013), 2.27–28.

96. *Nāṭyaśāstra*, 34.78.

97. The discussion of the nature and production of aesthetic pleasure is concentrated primarily in chaps. 6 and 7 of the *Nāṭyaśāstra*. The discussion of the nature of erotic pleasure, on the other hand, is carried out mainly in chap. 24.

98. With 318 verses, chap. 24 is the longest in the *Nāṭyaśāstra*. A detailed account of the discussion of all the topics relating to erotics in this chapter is neither possible nor directly relevant here. So I will briefly touch on some of the most important themes. Also, the number of topics in common between the *Kāmasūtra* and the *Nāṭyaśāstra* are too numerous for all of them to be included here. I will list here only the relatively more important of them. For the definition of pleasure, see the *Nāṭyaśāstra*, 95–98. For the status of pleasure (*kāma*) in the triset, see the *Nāṭyaśāstra*, 24.94–95. For a discussion of the relationship between the mind and the sense organs, see the *Nāṭyaśāstra*, 24.86–87. In naming women after animals while enumerating their different erotic types, the *Nāṭyaśāstra*, unlike the *Kāmasūtra*, does so not on the basis of the sizes and shapes of their sexual organs but on their general physical and psychological attributes. See the *Nāṭyaśāstra*, 24.99–145. The *Nāṭyaśāstra*'s description of the *nāyikās*, or heroines, differs both in number and in substance from the *Kāmasūtra*. For example, in contrast to the *Kāmasūtra*, which has four different types of heroines, there are eight in the *Nāṭyaśāstra*. Also, while the *Kāmasūtra* designates four social figures—the unmarried woman, the remarried woman, another man's wife, and the courtesan—as the primary heroines, the *Nāṭyaśāstra* names the heroines after different states of a woman in an erotic affair. For eight types of *nāyikās*, see the *Nāṭyaśāstra*, 24.210–219. For the signs of love, see the *Nāṭyaśāstra*, 24.159–167. For the ten stages of a maiden's love, see the *Nāṭyaśāstra*, 24.168–197. The *Nāṭyaśāstra* also offers its own version of the *Kāmasūtra's nāgaraka*, or city dandy, in the figure of the *vaiśika*, or the dandy-consort of the courtesan. I will argue in the last chapter that the figures of the dandy-consort of the courtesan and the city dandy were historically identical. See the *Nāṭyaśāstra*, 25.1–8. As is obvious from this discussion, the figure of the courtesan is present all through the *Nāṭyaśāstra*. Although the *Nāṭyaśāstra* does not quite discuss it in detail, the figure of "another man's wife" (*paradāra*) is present as "*mandakulastrī*," or the wayward wife. See the *Nāṭyaśāstra*, 20.53.

99. *Nāṭyaśāstra*, 24.147.

100. *Nāṭyaśāstra*, 24.98.

101. *Nāṭyaśāstra*, 24.95.

102. *Nāṭyaśāstra*, 7.6+.

103. E. Powys Mathers, *Eastern Love: English Versions*, vol. 1 (New York: Horace Liveright, 1930), 74.

104. Aristotle, *Metaphysics*. (*The Complete Works of Aristotle*, ed. Jonathan Barnes, vol. 2 [Princeton, NJ: Princeton University Press, 1995; sixth printing, with corrections], 1588).

Chapter 5

1. See Michel Foucault, *The Archaeology of Knowledge and the Discourse on Language*, trans. A. M. Sheridan Smith (London: Tavistock, 1972).

2. Scholars have translated the term *viṭa* as pimp, parasite, pander, and libertine. See, for example, Csaba Dezső and Somadeva Vasudeva, eds. and trans., *The Quartet of Causeries by Śyāmalika, Vararuci, Śūdraka & Īśvaradatta* (New York: New York University Press and the JJC Foundation, 2009), xvii.

3. See *Śṛṅgāra-Hāta: A Collection of Four Sanskrit Bhānas, One-Actor Plays, Viz., Padmaprābhṛtak, Dhūrtaviṭasaṁvāda, Ubhayābhisārikā and Pādatāḍitaka*, critically edited and translated into Hindi by Dr. Motichandra and Dr. Vasudevasharan Agrawal (Bombay: Hindi Granth Ratnakar, 1960). Translation of the citations from the *bhāṇas* are my own, unless mentioned otherwise. For the English translation, see Dezső and Vasudeva, eds. and trans., *The Quartet of Causeries*. See *Pādatāḍitaka of Śyāmilaka*, 2 parts. Part 1: G. H. Schokker, ed. (The Hague: Mouton & Co., 1966); part 2: trans. G. H. Schokker and P. J. Worsley (Dordrecht: D. Reidel Publishing Company, 1976).

4. *Nāṭyaśāstram: The Nāṭyaśāstra of Bharatamuni, Text, Commentary of Abhinavabhārati by Abhinavaguptācarya*, trans. M. Ghosh, ed. Pushpendra Kumar (Delhi: New Bharatiya Book Corp., 2006), 35.76–77.

5. *Nāṭyaśāstram*, 35.66–73.

6. See *Śṛṅgāra-Hāta: A Collection of Four Sanskrit Bhāṇas*; for the English translation, see Dezső and Vasudeva, *The Quartet of Causeries*.

7. *Pādatāḍitaka*, 1.

8. *Pādatāḍitaka*, 5.4–6.

9. With regard to the precise period of their origin, Manmohan Ghosh has placed the *bhāṇas* in the fourth and third centuries BCE. T. Venkatacharya, on the basis of his readings of some references to the terms of theater in the play, places Vararuci's *Ubhayābhisārikā* before the *Nāṭyaśāstra*, which is generally dated to the second century CE. See Manmohan Ghosh, *Glimpses of Sexual Life in Nanda-Maurya India*, part 1 (translation) and part 2 (text) (Calcutta: Manish Granthalaya, 1975); T. Venkatacharya, "The Significance of the Title *Ubhayābhisārikā* and the Date of the Play," *Journal of the American Oriental Society* 88, no. 2 (April–June 1968): 350–52. Also, see S. K. De, "A Note on the Sanskrit Monologue Plays (*Bhāṇas*), with Special Reference to the *Caturbhāṇis*," *Journal of the Royal Asiatic Society of Great Britain and Ireland*, no. 1 (Jan. 1926): 63–90. And see *Pādatāḍitaka of Śyāmilaka*. In the discussions on the chronology of the *bhāṇas*, what has not been given sufficient attention is the absence of any reference to the *Kāmasūtra* in them. Given that Dattaka is referred to a number of times as an authority on the ways of courtesans, it is extremely surprising that the *Kāmasūtra* is not mentioned at all. On the other hand, general discursive continuities with the *Kāmasūtra* are quite evident. Though there were some attempts to keep this genre alive, particularly in South India, it appears too artificial and contrived. For references to Dattaka, see *Dhūrtaviṭasaṁvāda*, 58.2; *Padmaprābhṛtaka*, 24d.

10. *Kāmasūtra*, 1.4.32.

11. *Dhūrtaviṭasaṁvāda*, 16.3; 67.14; *Ubhayābhisārikā*, 3.1; 34c; 34.4.

12. *Padmaprābhṛtaka*, 20.4–6.

13. *Padmaprābhṛtaka*, 21a.

14. *Padmaprābhṛtaka*, 20.4–21.4.

15. Edwin Gerow translates *viṭa* as "man about town," a term that has come to be associated

with the figure of the *nāgaraka*. Gerow seems to see the continuities between the two figures. See Edwin Gerow, "Sanskrit Dramatic Theory and Kalidasa's Play," in Barbara Stoler Miller, ed., *Theater of Memory: The Plays of Kalidasa* (New York: Columbia University Press, 1984), 50.

16. *Dhūrtaviṭasaṁvāda*, 27.5–71.1.

17. *Dhūrtaviṭasaṁvāda*, 27.6.

18. *Dhūrtaviṭasaṁvāda*, 27.7–9.

19. *Dhūrtaviṭasaṁvāda*, 70.6.

20. In another place, the dandy-guru is asked by a young man he runs into on the street if he would accept him [the young man] as his student. The word used is *śiṣyatva*, or studenthood. *Padmaprābhṛtaka*, 18.35; 19.6–7.

21. *Padmaprābhṛtaka*, 1a–2e; *Pādatāḍitaka*, 1.a–2.d.

22. *Pādatāḍitaka*, 7.a–d.

23. *Dhūrtaviṭasaṁvāda*, 6c; 6.1, 2; 8.1; *Padmaprābhṛtaka*, 38.14.

24. *Dhūrtaviṭasaṁvāda*, 15.1–2.

25. *Dhūrtaviṭasaṁvāda*, 16a–d.

26. *Dhūrtaviṭasaṁvāda*, 6.1.

27. *Dhūrtaviṭasaṁvāda*, 6.1–3.

28. *Padmaprābhṛtaka*, 6.9.

29. *Dhūrtaviṭasaṁvāda*, 9a–d.

30. *Dhūrtaviṭasaṁvāda*, 9d.

31. *Padmaprābhṛtaka*, 18.27.

32. *Padmaprābhṛtaka*, 51.5–53.d.

33. *Pādatāḍitaka*, 87.a–d.

34. *Padmaprābhṛtaka*, 29.12–15; 30a–16; 31a–e.

35. *Padmaprābhṛtaka*, 31.3–4.

36. *Padmaprābhṛtaka*, 30.3.

37. *Dhūrtaviṭasaṁvāda*, 14.2.

38. *Padmaprābhṛtaka*, 31.5.

39. *Ubhayābhisārikā*, 15.5.

40. *Ubhayābhisārikā*, 20.2.

41. *Pādatāḍitaka*, 10.6–8. My translation of the word *śabdakāma* differs from that of Schokker. Schokker translates *śabdakāma* as "longing for title." The reason for this translation is perhaps the context: this term occurs in the course of a conversation about a courtesan's affair with a man of some political weight—he drafts edicts for the king and is also the son of a high-ranking officer. According to Schokker, *śabdakāma* refers to the courtesan's longing for her patron's political power. The word "title" is perhaps used to refer to the symbolic value of political position or authority. Indeed, translating another sentence Schokker says that she is not really interested in the gifts (*dānakāma*) but in the title (*śabdakāma*).

However, a closer consideration of the immediate context in which the term appears reveals a different meaning. The individual at the center of the story in the *bhāṇa* is the same man who is directed to an assembly of the dandy-gurus to seek the right legal remedy for getting kicked on the head by a courtesan during a love quarrel. The same man, however, is also a grammarian, someone who knows the language very well and is supposedly good at using words. In the *bhāṇas* grammarians are considered to be some of the most unerotic-unromantic figures; they are often shown as a quarrelsome and egotistical bunch, constantly fighting over the rules of grammar. They take their grammar too seriously to be able to play with words and use it as a medium of love. In the context of this story the word *śabdakāma* is used by the dandy-guru as a pun: the courtesan has such a powerful desire to hear the sweet words of love that she gets into an erotic affair with a grammarian, a man of words and language, only to discover to her horror and alarm that the man of grammar was utterly alien to the ways of love. There is another very funny account of the dandy-guru's encounter with a grammarian, of Panini School, who has just come out of a fight with the Katantri School of grammarians. He loudly and defiantly complaints to the dandy-guru how he was set upon by them. See *Padmaprābhṛtaka*, 16.6–18.5. For Schokker's discussion of the term, see *Pādatāḍitaka of Śyāmilaka*, part 1, 152.

42. *Pādatāḍitaka*, 78.4, 6.

43. *Pādatāḍitaka*, 10.5–6.

44. Devadatta Shastri, ed., *Kāmasūtra of Vātsyāyana, with the Commentary of Yaśodhara* (Varanasi: Chaukhambha Sanskrit Sansthan, 1964), 1.2.20.

45. *Pādatāḍitaka*, 21b–c.

46. *Pādatāḍitaka*, 21d.

47. For example, see *Pādatāḍitaka*, 3–8.d.

48. See, in particular, chaps. 24 and 25 of the *Nāṭyaśāstra*. *Nāṭyaśāstra*, 24, 25.

49. *Padmaprābhṛtaka*, 6.10.

50. *Ubhayābhisārikā*, 31.2; *Pādatāḍitaka*, 69.15.

51. *Kāmasūtra*, 6.1.24.

52. *Ubhayābhisārikā*, 20.2.

53. It did not really come in conflict with the discourse of *artha* as political power because the state in ancient India did not really come in the way of erotic pleasure with the courtesan at its center. Indeed, as I discussed in chaps. 3 and 4, courtesans were employed in significant numbers in the royal harem in various capacities. They were offered instructions in various arts at the expense of the state.

54. *Padmaprābhṛtaka*, 18.15.

55. *Dhūrtaviṭasaṁvāda*, 29.10.

56. *Pādatāḍitaka of Śyāmilaka*, 117.12–39. I have used Schokker's translation of the passage.

57. For the dandy-guru's derisive comments on a grammarian he runs into on his way to the courtesans' quarters, see *Padmaprābhṛtaka*, 16.6–38, 17.1–21, 18.1–5. For logic and grammar in ancient India, see Bimal Krishna Matilal, *Epistemology, Logic, and Grammar in Indian Philosophical Analysis* (The Hague: Mouton and Co., 1971); Matilal, *The Character of Indian Logic* (Albany: State University of New York Press, 1998). Also, see Jonardon Ganeri, ed., *Indian Logic: A Reader* (Richmond: Curzon, 2001).

58. For the dandy-guru's views on heaven and its promises of happiness, see Īśvaradatta, *Dhūrtaviṭasaṁvāda*, 67.1–24, 68.a–d, 1–3.

59. *Dhūrtaviṭasaṁvāda*, 67.1–24.

60. Dāmodaragupta, *Kuṭṭanī-Matam: A Didactic Poem Composed about A.D. 755–786*, with a new commentary *Rasa-Dīpikā* by Tanasukhram Manasukharam Tripathi (Varanasi: Krishnadas Academy, 1991); Pandit Durgaprasad and Kasinath Pandurang Parab, eds., *The "Samayamātrkā" of* Kṣemendra (Bombay: Nirnaya-Sagara Press, 1888).

Chapter 6

1. *Kāmasūtra*, 1.2.1.

2. *Padmaprābhṛtaka* in *Śṛṅgāra-Hata: A Collection of Four Sanskrit Bhānas*, critically edited and translated into Hindi by Dr. Motichandra and Dr. Vasudevasharan Agrawal (Bombay: Hindi Granth Ratnakar, 1960), 11.9.

3. *Kāmasūtra*, 1.4.31–32.

4. *Kāmasūtra*, 1.4.31.

5. *Kāmasūtra*, 1.4.8.

6. *Kāmasūtra*, 1.4.22–23.

7. *Kāmasūtra*, 1.4.24–26.

8. *Kāmasūtra*, 1.4.10, 12.

9. *Kāmasūtra*, 1.4.13.

10. For an exhaustive account of the origin and evolution of the idea of *āśrama* or life-stages, see Patrick Olivelle, *Āśrama System: The History and Hermeneutics of a Religious Institution* (New York: Oxford University Press, 1993).

11. *Kāmasūtra*, 1.2.1.

12. *Kāmasūtra*, 1.2.2–4. It is interesting that even as the *Kāmasūtra* seems to have an understanding of life-stages, it does not quite follow what Olivelle calls its classical understanding. In contrast to the *Kāmasūtra*, in the classical version there are four stages: studenthood *brahmacarya*, householder *gārhsthya*, reclusive living *vānapratha*, and renunciation *saṃnyāsa*. Moreover, the *Kāmasūtra* pairs *dharma* and *mokṣa* together in the third stage. *Brahmacarya* became the very first period of life that is dedicated to the pursuit of knowledge while maintaining complete celibacy. The requirement of celibacy clearly shows that *kāma* was excluded in this period. That is to say pleasure and knowledge could not go together. See Olivelle, *Āśrama System*.

13. Although city dandies came from various groups, castes, and classes, including Brahmins, royal households, government officials, the largest number of them, it seems, came from the class of business people. See Shonaleeka Kaul, *Imagining the Urban: Sanskrit and the City in Early India* (New York: Seagull, 2011), 135–36.

14. *Nāṭyaśāstra*, 25.2.

15. *Kāmasūtra*, 1.3.15.

16. *Kāmasūtra*, 1.2.1.

17. *Kāmasūtra*, 1.3.16.

18. Twice the term "man of the city" has been used to simply mean city dwellers or men, not in the technical sense that this term otherwise carries. See *Kāmasūtra*, 2.9.31, 36.

19. *Kāmasūtra*, 1.5.

20. *Kāmasūtra*, 1.4.19.

21. *Kāmasūtra*, 1.4.19.

22. G. W. F. Hegel, *Aesthetics: Lectures on Fine Art*, 3 vols., trans. T. M. Knox (Oxford: Clarendon Press, 1975); Martin Heidegger, "The Origin of the Work of Art," in *Basic Writings from "Being and Time" (1927) to "The Task of Thinking" (1964)*, edited with general introduction by David Farrell Krell (New York: Harper Collins, 1993), 139–212.

23. *Kāmasūtra*, 1.4.8.

24. *Kāmasūtra*, 1.4.39.

25. *Kāmasūtra*, 1.4.38.

26. *Kāmasūtra*, 1.4.15.

27. *Kāmasūtra*, 1.4.16.

28. *Kāmasūtra*, 1.4.16.

29. *Kāmasūtra*, 1.4.15.

30. *Kāmasūtra*, 1.4.17.

31. Chakladar interprets the word *gaṇa* to mean "corporation" or "guild" and assumes that city dandies belonged to guilds. If the guild were indeed an important institution in the life of the city dandy, the *Kāmasūtra* would have said something about it. Haran Chandra Chakladar,

Social Life in Ancient India: Studies in Vātsyāyana's Kāmasūtra (Delhi: Bharatiya Publishing, 1976), 115, 116.

32. R. D. Karmakar, ed. and trans. *Mṛcchakaṭika of Śūdraka* (Poona: Aryabhushan Press, 1937), Act III.

33. *Kāmasūtra*, 1.4.36–37.

34. *Kāmasūtra*, 1.4.36.

35. *Nāṭyaśāstra*, 1.7–12.

36. It is ironic that historians until now have focused on the Vedic origins of the *Nāṭyaśāstra*, when, in fact, it was an attempt to break free from the Vedas. Not surprisingly, arts were seen with a great deal of suspicion and hostility in the *dharma* literature. According to Kane, "Gradually, orthodox opinion stiffened against actors, dancers, and signers in the times of the *Dharmasūtras* and early *Smṛtis*. *Apastamba Dharmasūtra* (I.1.3.11–12) prescribes that a student was not to see dancing and not to frequent *sabhās* [assemblies focused on art] and *samājas* [public festivals of art]. Manu (II.178) provides that a student was to avoid dancing, singing, and instrumental music. Gautama (15.18) prescribes that those brāhmaṇas that practiced dancing, singing, playing on musical instruments and beating time were not to be invited to a dinner in honor of gods or Manes." What is evident is that the *dharma* tradition saw a threat in art and erotics. As I have already discussed, these assemblies and public festivals of art were at the heart of the *Kāmasūtra*. Notice that in advocating their boycott, this also at the same time acknowledges that there may have been Brahmins who did in fact engage in such activities. P. V. Kane, *History of Sanskrit Poetics* (Delhi: Motilal Banarsidass Publishers, 1971), 22.

37. In recent years two perspectives have emerged to approach literary-aesthetic culture in ancient India: while one seeks to ground aesthetics and literature in the royal court, the other locates it in the city. The best example of the first approach is Pollock's *The Language of the Gods*. The best example of the second approach grounded in the city is Shonaleeka Kaul's *Imagining the Urban*. Through a study of major literary works in Sanskrit of the first millennium, she comes to this conclusion: "Does the evidence suggest any single overarching characterization which we could describe as the *kāvya's* ultimate vision of the city? The answer is yes, and I designate that characterization *kāma* culture—the city as the center of an ethic of pleasure." Kaul, *Imagining the Urban*, 195; Sheldon Pollock, *The Language of the Gods in the World of Men: Sanskrit, Culture, and Power in Premodern India* (Berkeley: University of California Press, 2006).

38. See Chakladar, *Social Life in Ancient India*.

39. *Kāmasūtra*, 1.3.17–18.

40. The *Kāmasūtra* took this widespread perception of sexual experience as being entirely sensual very seriously and tried to refute it in an extended discussion on the topic. See *Kāmasūtra*, 2.1.9–38.

41. I have discussed this topic extensively in chap. 2.

42. Much of the *Pādatāḍitaka* is dedicated to the story of a man who gets kicked in his head by a courtesan during a love quarrel and seeks proper remedy. He becomes a target of ridicule in the assembly of dandy-gurus. See *Pādatāḍitaka of Śyāmilaka*, 2 Parts. Part I, G. H. Schokker, ed. (The Hague: Mouton & Co., 1966), 125–47.

43. *Pādatāḍitaka of Śyāmilaka*, 10.6–8.

44. *Kāmasūtra*, 1.2.12.

45. The entire second chapter of book 3 is dedicated to this topic. See *Kāmasūtra*, 3.2.

46. *Kāmasūtra*, 3.2.6, 35.

47. My use of the terms private and public is contextual, not conceptual. It is meant to characterize the distinction that is assumed in the life of the city dandy.

48. Historians have only recently begun to tell the story of the deep association in premodern Indian culture of the state with art and aesthetics. The most important work in this regard is Sheldon Pollock's *The Language of the Gods*. In deciding to tell the story of *rājya*, or the state, and *kāvya*, or literature, together, Pollock reveals just how much was at stake for the state in literature. It was as if in literature or *kāvya* it were the state's own existence that was at stake. Until then, *dharma* as a discourse both of caste and rituals had served as the privileged, indeed dominant, vantage point to tell the history of Indic world. In decisively breaking away from this old and entrenched paradigm, Pollock's book inaugurated a new era in the understanding of Indian culture.

49. *Kāvyamimāṃsa of Rājaśekhara*, ed. Ganga Sagar Rai (Varanasi: Chowkhamba Vidyabhawan, 1964), 12–22.

50. *Kāvyamimāṃsa*, 118.

51. *Kāvyamimāṃsa*, 118.

52. *Kāvyamimāṃsa*, 118.

53. *Śṛṅgāraprakāśa of Bhoja*, ed. V. Raghavan (Cambridge, MA: Harvard University Press, 1998).

54. *Kāvyamimāṃsa*, 109–20.

55. *Kāvyamimāṃsa*, 119.

Chapter 7

1. Mādhvācārya, *Śrīmacchaṅkaradigvijayaḥ* (Śrīraṅgam: Śrīvaṇīvilāsamudraṇālayaḥ, 1972), 119–32.

2. Sigmund Freud, *Sexuality and the Psychology of Love*, with an introduction by Philip Rieff (New York: Simon & Schuster, Touchtone edition, 1997), 23.

3. *Kāmasūtra*, 5.1.4-5; *Nāṭyaśāstra*, 24.168–197.

4. Hubert L. Dreyfus and Paul Rabinow, *Michel Foucault: Beyond Structuralism and Hermeneutics* (Chicago: University of Chicago Press, 1983), 234–35.

5. As Foucault clearly stated, "The study of the problematization of sexual behavior in antiquity could be regarded as a chapter—one of the first chapters—of that general history of the 'techniques of the self.'" That is to say, history of sexuality became a part of the general history of the techniques and practices of the self. Michel Foucault, *The Use of Pleasure*, vol. 2 of *The History of Sexuality*, trans. Robert Hurley (New York: Vintage Books, 1990), 11. The abandonment of the history of sexuality, however, is most evident in his collection of lectures beginning in 1980, delivered at the Collège de France. These lectures have only remotely anything to do with the history of sexuality.

6. Foucault, *The Use of Pleasure*; Michel Foucault, *The Care of the Self*, vol. 3 of *The History of Sexuality*, trans. Robert Hurley (New York: Vintage Books, 1988).

7. One of the earliest indications of the dramatic change in Foucault's agenda came in his lectures in the United States in the fall of 1980. In these lectures Foucault also offers an explanation for how he came to reorient his research. See Michel Foucault, "About the Beginning of the Hermeneutics of the Self: Two Lectures at Dartmouth," *Political Theory* 21, no. 2 (May 1993): 198–227. Also, long before the second and third volumes of the *History of Sexuality* came out, this turn in his research agenda was evident to the auditors of his lectures at the Collège de France. The lectures give a detailed and unprecedented insight into the nature and process of this turn as it was articulated in stages. See *Hermeneutics of the Subject: Lectures at the College de France, 1981–1982* (New York: Palgrave Macmillan, 2005); *The Government of Self and Others: Lectures*

at the College de France, 1982–1983 (New York: Palgrave Macmillan, 2010); *The Courage of Truth: Lectures at College de France* (New York: Palgrave Macmillan, 2011). Also, see Timothy O'Leary, *Foucault: The Art of Ethics* (New York: Continuum, 2002); Thomas R. Flynn, "Truth and Subjectivation in the Later Foucault," *Journal of Philosophy* 82, no. 10 (Oct. 1985): 531–40.

8. Even as Foucault showed little interest in the metaphysical speculations of the ancient philosophers, particularly Plato, he takes up the theme of the practices of truth and self as if his main purpose was to retrieve—rather than critique—this tradition by way of its history. It was as if in his Greek sources Foucault was looking for a model, or at least the fragments of it, of a new form of life. Not surprisingly, therefore, Foucault locates the nature of his own intellectual exertions directly in the ancient philosophical tradition of *askesis* as "an exercise of oneself in the activity of thought." Foucault, *The Use of Pleasure*, 9. On the nature and significance of *askesis* for Foucault, see Edward F. McGushin, *Foucault's Askesis: An Introduction to the Philosophical Life* (Evanston, IL: Northwestern University Press, 2007).

9. Michel Foucault, *Foucault Live: Collected Interviews, 1961–1984* (New York: Semiotext (E), 1996), 444.

10. "Three domains of genealogy are possible. First, an historical ontology of ourselves in relation to truth through which we constitute ourselves as subjects of knowledge; second, an historical ontology of ourselves in relation to a field of power through which we constitute ourselves as subjects acting on others; third, an historical ontology in relation to ethics through which we constitute ourselves as moral agents." Dreyfus and Rabinow, *Michel Foucault: Beyond Structuralism and Hermeneutics*, 237. As is only too evident, by dividing them neatly into three domains, Foucault makes it appear as if what was at stake in the turn is nothing more than shifting the focus from the domain of power to the domains of the practices of truth and self. The fact, however, is that the relationship between power and truth was not symmetrical in Foucault's works, and as such their positions could not be simply switched. Given the precise nature of the notion of power in his earlier works, Foucault cannot reduce it [power] to one of the many domains without seriously modifying, if not altogether abandoning, it. But that is exactly what Foucault's later realignment that elevates truth and self into autonomous domains requires. Foucault, of course, tries to reconcile what seems like incompatible positions in programmatic and methodological terms. But as is obvious, there is more than methodology that is at stake in this recalibration of concerns and categories. Although we cannot go into it here, looked at closely what appears to be a neat division into three ontological domains is actually riddled with deep contradictions. Foucault, *The Use of Pleasure*, 3–7. For a more programmatic context to the turn, see Michel Foucault, *The Politics of Truth*, ed. Sylvere Lotringer and Lysa Hochroth (Los Angeles: Semiotext (E), 1997).

11. See the long note at the end of *The Courage of the Truth*, 338–40.

12. Difficult, if not impossible, though it was under the changed circumstances, Foucault tried to maintain his opposition to truth and self as a discourse of identity. For example, Foucault opposes the notion of the practices of truth as *parrhesia*, or "the courage of truth," against what could be termed the metaphysics of truth. See especially the note at the end of *The Courage of Truth* that contains what Foucault had on the manuscript but did not have the time to read it out in his last lecture before his death. The very last lines of the manuscript reassert Foucault's commitment to the otherness of truth: "But what I would like to stress in conclusion is this: there is no establishment of the truth without an essential position of otherness; the truth is never the same; there can be truth only in the form of the other world and the other life." But as is also evident, this "otherness" or difference had to be accommodated within the general horizon of truth, that is to say, within the horizon of western intellectual traditions. *The Courage*

of Truth, 340. Foucault also opposes the less-talked-about Socratic injunction of the "care of the self" against the better-known "know thyself." Foucault pitched this care of the self as a form of subjectivization as aesthetics of existence against subjection as an exercise in power. *Hermeneutics of the Subject*, 1–24. While talking about his own motivations behind his works in his last years, Foucault says: "It was a philosophical exercise. The object was to learn to what extent the effort to think one's own history can free thought from what it silently thinks, and so enable it to think differently." *The Use of Pleasure*, 9. Even as he comes very close to the classical tradition grounded in identity in the characterization of his work or vocation as thought thinking itself, Foucault nevertheless insists that the goal is to become different.

13. See Foucault, *Hermeneutics of the Subject*.

14. Foucault in fact uses the word "interiority" in the sense of individuality of citizens in ancient Greece. Foucault, *The Use of Pleasure*, 78–79.

15. Foucault, *The Use of Pleasure*, 8–9.

16. Foucault, *The Use of Pleasure*, 9. Leo Bersani also noted the sudden appearance of the old figure of "the philosopher as someone capable of thinking himself out of his own thought." Leo Bersani, "Pedagogy and Pederasty," *Raritan* 5, no. 1 (Summer 1985): 20.

17. Less than a decade before this surprising turn how eloquently and fiercely Foucault had attacked philosophy's sovereign claim to interiority while anchoring himself firmly in history as a domain exterior to philosophy. See particularly Appendix III, "Reply to Derrida," in Michel Foucault, *History of Madness*, ed. Jean Khalfa, trans. Jonathan Murphy and Jean Khalfa (New York: Routledge, 2006), 575–90. Also, see "The Thought of the Outside," in *The Essential Foucault: Selections from Essential Works of Foucault, 1954–1984*, ed. Paul Rabinow and Nikolas Rose (New York: New Press, 2003). For a general discussion on Foucault as a historian and philosopher, see Clare O'Farrell, *Foucault: Historian or Philosopher?* (London: Macmillan, 1989); John Rajchman, *Michel Foucault: The Freedom of Philosophy* (New York: Columbia University Press, 1985).

18. Foucault categorically states that "the studies that follow . . . are not the work of a historian. . . . It was a philosophical exercise." He then goes on to add, "There is always something ludicrous in philosophical discourse when it tries, from the outside, to dictate to others, to tell them where their truth is and how to find it. . . . But it is entitled to explore what might be changed, in its own thought, through the practice of a knowledge that is foreign to it." Foucault, *The Use of Pleasure*, 9.

19. See Foucault, "An Aesthetics of Existence," in *Foucault Live: Collected Interviews 1961–1984*, ed. Sylvere Lotringer, trans., Lysa Hochroth and John Johnston (New York: Semiotext (E), 1996), 450–54.

20. Baudelaire anchors the figure of the dandy in what he calls "the cult of the self": "What is this unofficial institution which has formed so haughty and exclusive a sect? It is first and foremost the burning need to create for oneself a personal originality, bounded only by the limits of the proprieties. It is a kind of cult of the self which can nevertheless survive the pursuit of a happiness to be found in someone else—in woman, for example; which can survive all that goes by in the name of illusions." Charles Baudelaire, *The Painter of Modern Life and Other Essays*, trans. Jonathan Mayne (London: Phaidon, 1964), 27.

21. For Foucault's comments on Charles Baudelaire and his understanding of modernity and the figure of the dandy, see "What Is Enlightenment?" in *The Essential Foucault: Selections from the Essential Works of Foucault, 1954–1984*, ed., Paul Rabinow and Nikolas Rose (New York: New Press, 2003), 49–51.

Bibliography

Primary Sources

ANCIENT INDIAN TEXTS AND TRANSLATIONS

Arthaśāstra

Olivelle, Patrick, trans. *King, Governance, and Law in Ancient India: Kautilya's Arthaśāstra*. New York: Oxford University Press, 2013.

Shamasastry, R., trans., and V. Narain, ed. *Kautiliya Arthaśāstra (Sanskrit Text with English Translation and an Exhaustive Introduction)*. Vol. II: Books V–XV. Delhi: Chaukhamba Sanskrit Pratisthan, 2005.

Brahmasūtra

Dvivedin, Vindhyesvari Prasada, ed. *Brahmasūtra: With a Commentary by Bhaskaracarya*. Benares: Chowkhamba Sanskrit Book Depot, 1903.

Caturbhāṇī

Dezső, Csaba, and Somadeva Vasudeva, eds. and trans. *The Quartet of Causeries by Śyāmalika, Vararuchi, Śūdraka & Īśvaradatta*. New York: New York University Press and the JJC Foundation, 2009.

Ghosh, Manomohan, ed. and trans. *Glimpses of Sexual Life in Nanda-Maurya India: Translation of the Caturbhāṇī Together with a Critical Edition of the Text*. Calcutta: Manisha Granthalaya, 1975.

Pādatāḍitaka of Śyāmilaka, 2 parts. Part I, edited by G. H. Schokker. The Hague: Mouton & CO., 1966; Part II, trans. G. H. Schokker and P. J. Worsley. Dordrecht: D. Reidel Publishing, 1976.

Śṛṅgāra-Hāta: A Collection of Four Sanskrit Bhāṇas, One-Actor Plays, Viz., Padmaprābhṛtaka, Dhūrta-viṭa-saṁvāda, Ubhayābhisārikā and Pādatāḍitakam. Critically edited and translated into Hindi by Dr. Motichandra and Dr. Vasudevasharan Agrawal. Bombay: Hindi Granth Ratnakar, 1960.

Vaidya Jādavaji Trikāmji Achārya, ed. *The Carakasaṃhitā of Agniveśa revised by Caraka and Dridhabala with the Ayurveda-Dipika Commentary by Chakrapānidatta*. Bombay: Nirnaya Sagar Press, 1941.

Daśarūpaka

Daśarūpaka of Dhanaṃjaya, with the Avaloka of Dhanika, and the Subcommentary of Bhaṭṭa Nṛsiṃha, ed. T. Venkatacharya. Madras: Adyar Library and Research Centre, 1969.

Dhvanyāloka

Ingalls, D., J. M. Masson, and M. V. Patwardhan, trans. *The Dhvanyāloka of Ānandavardhana with the Locana of Abhinavagupta*. Cambridge, MA: Harvard University Press, 1990.

Shastra, Pattabhirama, ed. *Dhvanyāloka of Ānandavardhana, with the Commentary of Abhinavagupta*. Varanasi: Chowkambha Sanskrit Series Office, 1940.

Gaṇikā-vṛtta-saṁgrahah

Sternbach, Ludwik, ed. *Gaṇikā-vṛtta-saṁgrahah: or, Texts on Courtezans in Classical Sanskrit*. Hoshiarpur: Visheshvarananda Vedic Research Institute, 1953.

Kāmasūtra

Burton, Richard F., trans. *The Kāmasūtra of Vātsyāyana: The Classic Hindu Treatise on Love and Social Conduct*. New York: E. P. Dutton, 1962.

Doniger, Wendy, and Sudhir Kakar, eds. *Vātsyāyana Kāmasūtra: A New, Complete Translation of the Sanskrit Text*. New York: Oxford University Press, 2002.

Lal Goswami, Damodar, ed. *Kāmasūtra of Vātsyāyana, with the Commentary of Yashodhara*. Varanasi: Chaukhambha Sanskrit Sansthan, 1912.

Shastri, Devadatta, ed. *Kāmasūtra of Vātsyāyana, with the Commentary of Yaśodhara*. Varanasi: Chaukhambha Sanskrit Sansthan, 1964.

Kāmakuñjalata

Sastri, D., ed. *Kāmakuñjalatā: A Collection of Rare Works on Kāmaśāstra*. Varanasi: Chowkhambha Sanskrit Series Office, 1967.

Kāvyamimāṃsa

Ganga Sagar Rai, ed. *Kāvyamimāṃsa of Rājaśekhara*. Varanasi: Chowkhamba Vidyabhawan, 1964.

Kuṭṭanī-Matam

Bedi, B. P. L., and Alexander von Humboldt, trans. *The Art of the Temptress: Translation of the 1200-Year-Old Sanskrit Classic, The Kuttni Mahatmyam of Damodar Gupta*. Bombay: Pearl Books, 1968.

Damodaragupta, *Kuṭṭanī-Matam or Shambhali-Matam: A Didactic Poem Composed about A.D. 755–786, with a new commentary Rasa-Dipika by Tanasukhram Manasukharam Tripathi*. Varanasi: Krishnadas Academy, 1991.

Mahābhārata

Sukthankar, V. S., and S. K. Belvalkar, eds. *Mahābhāratam*. Poona: Bhandarkar Oriental Research Institute, 1961.

Van Buitenen, J. A. B., trans. *The Mahābhārata*. 3 vols. Chicago: University of Chicago Press, 1973–78.

Mānavadharmaśāstra

Doniger, Wendy, and Brian Smith, trans. *The Laws of Manu*. New York: Penguin, 1991.

Jolly, J., ed. *Mānava Dharma-śāstra*. London: Trübner, 1887.

Olivelle, Patrick, ed. and trans. *Manu's Code of Law: A Critical Edition and Translation of the Mānava-Dharmaśāstra*. New York: Oxford University Press, 2005.

Mṛcchakaṭika

Karmakar, R. D., ed. and trans. *Mṛcchakaṭika of Śūdraka*. Poona: Aryabhushan Press, 1937.

Van Buitenen, J. A. B. *Two Plays of Ancient India: The Little Clay Cart; The Minister's Seal*. New York: Columbia University Press, 1968.

Nāṭyaśāstra

Ghosh, M., ed. *The Nāṭyaśāstra, ascribed to Bharatamuni*. 2 vols. Sanskrit text. Vol. I. Calcutta: Manisha Granthalaya, 1967; vol. II, Calcutta: Asiatic Society, 1956.

———, trans. *The Nāṭyaśāstra, ascribed to Bharatamuni*, Sanskrit text. Bibliotheca Indica, no. 272. 2 vols. Vol. I, Calcutta: Royal Asiatic Society of Bengal, 1950; vol. II, Calcutta: Asiatic Society, 1961.

Kumar, Pushpendra, ed. *The Nāṭyaśāstra of Bharatamuni: Text, Commentary of Abhinava Bhāratī by Abhinavaguptācārya and English Translation*, trans. M. M. Ghosh. Delhi: New Bharat Book Corporation, 2006.

Rasagaṅgādhara

Sastri, Mathuranath, ed. *Rasagaṅgādhara* of Jagannātha Paṇḍitarāja. Bombay: Nirnaya Sagar Press, 1947.

Ratirahasya

Comfort, Alex, trans. *The Koka Shastra*. London: George, Allen & Unwin, 1964.

———. *The Illustrated Koka Shastra: Erotic Indian Writings Based on the Kama Sutra*. London: Mitchell Beazley, 1997.

Sharma, Ramananda, ed. *Ratirahasyam of Kokkoka with the Dīpika Commentary of Kāncīnātha*. Varanasi: Krishnadas Academy, 1994.

Samayamātṛkā

Durgaprasad, Pandit, and Kasinath Pandurang Parab, eds. The *Samayamātrkā* of Kshemendra. Bombay: Nirnaya-sagara Press, 1888.

Śṛṅgāraprakāśa of Bhoja

Raghavan, V., ed., *Śṛṅgāraprakāśa of Bhoja*. Cambridge, MA: Harvard University Press, 1998.

Suśrutasaṃhitā

Achārya, Vaidya Jādavaji Trikāmji, and Nārāyan Rām Achārya, eds. *The Suśrutasaṃhitā of Suśruta*. Varanasi, 1980.

Upaniṣads

Radhakrishnan, S., ed. and trans. *The Principal Upaniṣads*. Atlantic Highlands, NJ: Humanities Press, 1992.

MICHEL FOUCAULT: WRITINGS AND INTERVIEWS

Foucault, Michel. *Language, Counter-Memory, Practice: Selected Essays and Interviews by Michel Foucault*. Ed. Donald F. Bouchard. Ithaca, NY: Cornell University Press, 1977.

———. *The History of Sexuality: An Introduction*, vol. 1 of *The History of Sexuality*. New York: Vintage, 1980.

———. *Power/Knowledge: Selected Interviews and Other Writings, 1972–1977*. Ed. Colin Gordon. New York: Pantheon Books, 1980.

———. *The Use of Pleasure*, vol. 2 of *The History of Sexuality*. New York: Vintage, 1985.

———. *Technologies of the Self: A Seminar with Michel Foucault*. Ed. Luther Martin. Amherst: University of Massachusetts Press, 1988.

———. *Discipline and Punish*. Trans. Alan Sheridan. New York: Vintage Books, 1995.

———. *Foucault Live: Collected Interviews, 1961–1984*. Ed. Sylvere Lotringer; trans. Lysa Hochroth and John Johnston. New York: Semiotext (E), 1996.

———. *Ethics, Subjectivity and Truth: The Essential Works of Foucault*, vol. 1. Ed. P. Rabinow. New York: New Press, 1997.

———. *The Politics of Truth*. Ed. Sylvère Lotringer and Lysa Hochroth. New York: Semiotext (E), 1997.

———. *Aesthetics, Method, and Epistemology: Essential Works of Foucault, 1945–1984*, vol. 2. Ed. J. D. Eribon. New York: New Press, 1998.

———. *Religion and Culture*. Sel. and ed. Jeremy Carrette. New York: Routledge, 1999.

———. *Essential Works of Foucault: Power.* Vol. 3. Ed. James Faubion, trans. Robert Hurley et al. New York: New Press, 2000.

———. "The Thought of the Outside." In *The Essential Foucault: Selections from Essential Works of Foucault, 1954–1984*, ed. Paul Rabinow and Nikolas Rose. New York: New Press, 2003.

———. *History of Madness*. Trans. J. Murphy and J. Khalfa. New York: Routledge, 2006.

———. *Death and the Labyrinth: The World of Raymond Roussel.* Trans. C. Ruas. London: Continuum, 2006.

———. *The Essential Foucault: Selections from Essential Works of Foucault, 1954–1984*. Ed. Paul Rabinow and Nikolas Rose. New York: New Press, 2003.

———. *The Birth of Biopolitics: Lectures at the College de France 1978–79*. Ed.Michel Senellart; trans. Graham Burchell. New York: Palgrave Macmillan, 2008.

———. "The Gay Science." *Critical Inquiry* 37, no. 3 (2011): 385–403.

———. *Lectures on the Will to Know: Lectures at the College de France with Oedipal Knowledge.* New York: Palgrave Macmillan, 2013.

———. *Language, Madness, Desire: On Literature.* Minneapolis: University of Minnesota, 2015.

Secondary Sources

Adams, James Eli. *Dandies and Desert Saints: Styles of Victorian Masculinity*. Ithaca, NY: Cornell University Press, 1995.

Agarwal, P. K. *The Unknown Kamasutras: Being an Anthology of the Ancientmost Love-Aphorisms of Seers of the Tradition and Its Exposition*. Varanasi: Prithivi Prakashan, 1983.

Ali, Daud. *Courtly Culture and Political Life in Early Medieval India*. Cambridge: Cambridge University Press, 2004.

Allan, D. J. *The Philosophy of Aristotle*. 2nd ed. Oxford: Oxford University Press, 1970.

Allen, A. *The Politics of Our Selves: Power, Autonomy and Gender in Contemporary Critical Theory*. New York: Columbia University Press, 2008.

Altekar, A. S. *The Position of Women in Hindu Civilization*. New Delhi: Motilal Banarasidas, 1938.

———. "The Ashrama System." *Professor Ghurye Felicitation Volume*. Ed. K. M. Kapadia. Bombay: Popular Book Depot, 1955.

Aristotle. *Metaphysics*. Vol. 2, *The Complete Works of Aristotle*, ed. Jonathan Barnes. Princeton, NJ: Princeton University Press, 1995.

———. *Nicomachean Ethics*. Trans. T. Irwin. Indianapolis: Hackett Publications, 1985.

Auboyer, Jeannine. *Daily Life in Ancient India: From 200 BC to 700 AD.* Trans. Simon Watson Taylor. London: Weidenfeld & Nicolson, 1961.

Babb, Lawrence A. "Marriage and Malevolence: The Uses of Sexual Opposition in a Hindu Pantheon." *Ethnology* 9, no. 2 (1970).

Bailey, Gregory. "Suffering in the Mahābhārata: Draupadī and Yudhiṣṭhira." In *Inde et Littératures: Études Reunies Par Marie-Claude Porcher*, 109–29. Paris: École des Hautes Études en Science Sociale, 1983.

Baker, Deborah. *A Blue Hand: The Beats in India*. New York: Penguin Press, 2008.

Banerjee, S. C. *Dharma-Sūtras: A Study in Their Origin and Development*. Calcutta: Punthi Pustak, 1962.

Banerjee, Sumanta. *Dangerous Outcast: The Prostitute in Nineteenth-Century Bengal*. New York: Seagull Books, 1998.

Banga, Indu, ed. *The City in Indian History: Urban Demography, Society, and Politics*. Columbia, MO: South Asia Publications, 1991.

Barbey d'Aurevilly, Jules. *Dandyism*. Trans. Douglas Ainslie. New York: PAJ, 1988.

Basu, Jyotirmayee. "The Role of *Aśramas* in the Life of Ancient Hindus." *Journal of Indian History* 42 (1964): 847–76.

Basu, N. K., and S. N. Sinha. *History of Prostitution in India*. New Delhi: Cosmo Publications, 1994.

Bataille, Georges. *Erotism: Death and Sensuality*. Trans. Mary Dalwood. San Francisco: City Lights Books, 1986.

Baudelaire, Charles. *Baudelaire as a Literary Critic: Selected Essays*. Introd. and trans. Louis Boe Hyslop and Francis E. Hyslop, Jr. University Park: Pennsylvania State University Press, 1964.

———. *Painter of Modern Life and Other Essays*. London: Phaidon, 1964.

Baudrillard, Jean. *America*. New York: Verso, 2010.

Baumer, Rachel van M., and James R. Brandon, eds. *Sanskrit Drama in Performance*. Honolulu: University of Hawaii, 1981.

Benjamin, Walter. *Illuminations*. Ed. Hannah Arendt; trans. Harry Zohn. New York: Schocken, 1969.

———. *Charles Baudelaire: A Lyric Poet in the Era of High Capitalism*. Trans. Harry Zohn. London: Verso, 1983.

———. *Reflections*. Trans. Edmund Jephcott. New York: Schocken, 1986.

———. *The Origin of German Tragic Drama*. Trans. John Osborne. London: Verso, 1998.

Bersani, Leo. "Pedagogy and Pederasty," *Raritan* 5, no. 1 (1985).

———. *Homos*. Cambridge, MA: Harvard University Press, 1995.

Bhargave, Deepali. *Manu Smriti: A Sociological Analysis*. Jaipur: Rawat Publications, 1989.

Bhāsa. *Cārudattam*. Varanasi: Chaukhamba Sanskrit Sansthan, 1997.

Bhattacharji, Sukumari. "Prostitution in Ancient India," *Social Scientist* 15, no. 2 (1987): 32–61.

Bhattacharya, Biswanath. *Sanskrit Drama and Dramaturgy*. Delhi: Sharada Publishing House, 1994.

Bhattacharya, Narendra Nath. *A History of Indian Erotic Literature*. Delhi: Munshiram Manoharlal, 1975.

Bilimoria, Purushottama, ed. *Essays on Indian Philosophy: Traditional and Modern*. Delhi: Oxford University Press, 1993.

Bowles, Adam. *Dharma, Disorder and the Political in Ancient India: The Āpaddharmaparvan of the Mahābhārata*. Leiden: E. J. Brill, 2007.

Bremmer, Jan, and Herman Roodenburg. *A Cultural History of Gesture: From Antiquity to the Present Day*. Cambridge: Polity/Blackwell, 1991.

Brockington, J. L. *The Sanskrit Epics*. Leiden: E. J. Brill, 1999.

Bryant, Edwin F. *The Yoga Sūtras of Patañjali: A New Edition, Translation and Commentary, with Insights from Traditional Commentators*. New York: North Point Press, 2009.

Butler, Judith. *Gender Trouble: Feminism and the Subversion of Identity*. New York: Routledge, 1990.

———. "Contingent Foundations: Feminism and the Question of Postmodernism." In *Feminists Theorize the Political*, ed. Judith Butler and Joan W. Scott. New York: Routledge, 1992.

———. *Undoing Gender*. New York: Routledge, 2004.

———. *Bodies That Matter: On the Discursive Limits of Sex*. New York: Routledge, 2011.

Butler, Judith, and Joan W. Scott. *Feminists Theorize the Political*. New York: Routledge, 1992.

Camus, Albert. *The Rebel: An Essay on Man in Revolt.* Trans. Anthony Bower. New York: Vintage Books, 1956.

Caputo, John, and Mark Yount. *Foucault and the Critique of Institutions.* University Park: Pennsylvania State University Press, 1993.

Chakladar, H. C. *Social Life in Ancient India: Studies in Vatsyayana's Kamasutra.* Calcutta: Greater India Society, 1929.

Chakrabarty, Dipesh. *Provincializing Europe: Postcolonial Thought and Historical Difference.* Princeton, NJ: Princeton University Press, 2000.

———. *Habitations of Modernity: Essays in the Wake of Subaltern Studies.* Chicago: University of Chicago Press, 2002.

Chakrabarty, Uma. "Whatever Happened to the Vedic Dāsi?" In *Recasting Women: Essays in Colonial History*, ed. Kumkum Sangari and Sudesh Vaid, 27–87. New Delhi: Kali for Women, 1989.

Chakrabarty, Uma, and Sangari Kumkum, eds. *From Myths to Markets: Essays on Gender.* Delhi: Manohar, IIAS, 1998.

Champakalakshmi, R. *Trade, Ideology, and Urbanization: South India, 300 BC to 1300 AD.* New Delhi: Oxford University Press, 1998.

Chandra, Moti. *The World of Courtesans.* Delhi: Vikas Publishing House, 1973.

Chartier, Roger. *Cultural History: Between Practice and Representation.* Trans. Lydia Cochrane. Ithaca, NY: Cornell University Press, 1988.

Chatterjee, C. K. *Studies in the Rites and Rituals of Hindu Marriage in Ancient India.* Calcutta: Sanskrit Pustak Bhandar, 1978.

Chattopadhyaya, Brajadulal. "The City in Early India: Perspectives from Texts." *Studies in History* 13, no. 2 (1997): 181–208.

Chattopadhyaya, Siddheswar. *Theater in Ancient India.* New Delhi: Manohar, 1993.

Chaudhuri, Jatindrabimal. *The Position of Women in the Vedic Ritual.* London and Calcutta: Pracyavani Research Series, 1956.

Clément, Catherine. *Syncope: The Philosophy of Rapture.* Trans. Sally O'Driscoll and Deirdre M. Mahoney. Minneapolis: University of Minnesota Press, 1994.

Cohen, D. *Law, Sexuality, and Society: The Enforcement of Morals in Classical Athens.* Cambridge: Cambridge University Press, 1991.

Cohen, Ed. *Talk on the Wilde Side: Toward a Genealogy of a Discourse on Male Sexualities.* New York: Routledge, 1993.

Connell, R. W. *Gender and Power: Society, the Person and Sexual Politics.* Stanford, CA: Stanford University Press, 1987.

Conners, Peter H. *White Hand Society: The Psychedelic Partnership of Timothy Leary and Allen Ginsberg.* San Francisco: City Lights Books, 2010.

Coward, Rosalind. *Female Desire: Women's Sexuality Today.* London: Paladin, 1984.

Curtain, Michael. "A Question of Manners: Status and Gender in Etiquette and Courtesy." *Journal of Modern History* 57 (1985): 395–423.

Dallapiccola, Anna Libera, ed. *Shastric Traditions in Indian Arts.* Stuttgart: Steiner, 1989.

Dandekar, R. N., ed. *The Mahābhārata Revisited.* New Delhi: Sahitya Akademi, 1990.

Daniélou, Alain. *The Hindu Temple: Deification of Eroticism.* Trans. Ken Hurry. Rochester, VT: Inner Traditions International, 2001.

Das, R. M. *Women in Manu and His Seven Commentators.* Varanasi: Kanchana Publications, 1962.

Das, Veena. "On Female Body and Sexuality." *Contributions to Indian Sociology* 21, no. 1 (1987): 57–66.

Dasgupta, Surendranath. *A History of Indian Philosophy*. 5 vols. Cambridge: Cambridge University Press, 1922.

Davidson, Arnold, ed. *Foucault and His Interlocutors*. Chicago: University of Chicago Press, 1997.

———. "Foucault, Psychoanalysis and Pleasure." In *The Emergence of Sexuality: Historical Epistemology and the Formation of Concepts,* ed. Arnold Davidson. Cambridge, MA: Harvard University Press, 2001.

Davidson, James. *Courtesans and Fishcakes: The Consuming Passions of Classical Athens*. London: St. Martin's Press, 1998.

———. "Dover, Foucault and Greek Homosexuality: Penetration and the Truth of Sex," *Past and Present*, no. 170 (2001): 3–51.

Davis, Natalie Z. "'Women's History' in Transition: The European Case." *Feminist Studies* 3 (1976): 83–103.

De, S. K. "A Note on the Sanskrit Monologue Plays (*Bhāna*), with Special Reference to the *Caturbhāni*." *Journal of the Royal Asiatic Society of Great Britain and Ireland*, no. 1 (Jan. 1926): 63–90.

———. *Ancient Indian Erotics and Erotic Literature*. Calcutta: Firma KLM, 1959.

———. *History of Sanskrit Poetics*. 2 vols. Calcutta: Firma KLM, 1968.

Deleuze, Gilles. *Foucault*. Trans. Sean Hand. Minneapolis: University of Minnesota Press, 1988.

———. *The Logic of Sense*. Translated by Mark Lester. New York: Columbia University Press, 1990.

———. *Two Regimes of Madness: Texts and Interviews 1975–1995*. Ed. David Lapoujade; trans. Ames Hodges and Mike Taormina. New York: Semiotext (E), 2007.

Deleuze, Gilles, and Félix Guattari. *Anti-Oedipus: Capitalism and Schizophrenia*. Trans. Robert Hurley, Mark Seem, and Helen R. Lane. Preface by Michel Foucault. Minneapolis: University of Minnesota Press, 1983.

Derrett, J. D. M. *Religion, Law and the State in India*. London: Faber, 1968.

Derrida, Jacques. *Writing and Difference*. Chicago: University of Chicago, 1978.

———. *Of Grammatology*. Baltimore: Johns Hopkins University Press, 1997.

———. '"To Do Justice to Freud': The History of Madness in the Age of Psychoanalysis." In *Foucault and His Interlocutors*, ed. Arnold Davidson, 57–96. Chicago: University of Chicago Press, 1997.

Detel, Wolfgang. *Foucault and Classical Antiquity: Power, Ethics, and Knowledge*. Cambridge: Cambridge University Press, 2005.

Dewey, J. *Art as Experience*. New York: Perigee Books, 1980.

Dhand, Arti. *Woman as Fire, Woman as Sage: Sexual Ideology in the Mahābhārata*. New York: State University of New York Press, 2008.

Diamond, Irene, and Lee Quinby. *Feminism and Foucault: Reflections on Resistance*. Boston: Northeastern University Press, 1988.

"Dinkar," Ram Dhari Singh. *Dinkar's Urvashi (A Saga of Human Love and Vedanta)*. Translated from original Hindi by Krishna Kumar Vidyarthi. New Delhi: Siddharth Publications, 1994.

Doniger, Wendy. *Asceticism and Eroticism in the Mythology of Śiva*. Oxford: Oxford University Press, 1973.

———. *Śiva, the Erotic Ascetic*. London: Oxford University Press, 1973.

——— (as O'Flaherty). *Women, Androgynes, and Other Mythical Beasts*. Chicago: University of Chicago Press, 1980.

———. "Begetting on Margin: Adultery and Surrogate Pseudomarriage in Hinduism." In *From the Margins of Hindu Marriage: Essays on Gender, Religion, and Culture*, ed. Lindsey Harlan and Paul B. Courtright, 160–83. New York: Oxford University Press, 1995.

———. *Splitting the Difference: Gender and Myth in Ancient Greece and India*. Chicago: University of Chicago Press, 1999.

———. "On Translating the Kāmasūtra: A Gurudaskhina for Daniel H. H. Ingalls." *Journal of Indian Philosophy* 29, nos. 1–2 (2001): 81–94.

———. "The *Kāmasūtra*: It Isn't All about Sex." *Kenyon Review* 25, no. 1 (2003): 18–37.

Dover, K. J. *Greek Homosexuality*. Cambridge, MA: Harvard University Press, 1978.

———. *Plato's Symposium*. Cambridge: Cambridge University Press, 1980.

Dreyfus, H. *Being-in-the-World: A Commentary on Heidegger's "Being and Time," Division I*. Cambridge, MA: MIT Press, 1991.

Dreyfus, Hubert L., and Paul Rabinow. *Michel Foucault: Beyond Structuralism and Hermeneutics*. Chicago: University of Chicago Press, 1983.

Dumont, L. *Homo Hierarchicus: The Caste System and Its Implications*. Trans. M. Sainsbury. Chicago: University of Chicago Press, 1970.

———. *Religion, Politics and History in India: Collected Papers in Indian Sociology*. Paris/The Hague: Mouton Publishers, 1970.

Dyck, Erika. *Psychedelic Psychiatry: LSD from Clinic to Campus*. Baltimore: Johns Hopkins University Press, 2008.

Eagleton, Terry. *The Ideology of the Aesthetic*. Oxford: Blackwell, 1990.

Erdosy, G. *Urbanization in Early Historic India*. BAR International Series 430. Oxford: B.A.R., 1988.

Eribon, Didier. *Michel Foucault*. Trans. Betsy Wing. Cambridge, MA: Harvard University Press, 1991.

Falk, Nancy. "Draupadī and the Dharma." In *Beyond Androcentrism: New Essays on Women and Religion*, ed. Rita Gross, 89–114. Missoula, MT: Scholars Press, 1977.

Feldman, Jessica. *Gender on the Divide: The Dandy in Modernist Literature*. Ithaca, NY: Cornell University Press, 1993.

Feldman, Martha, and Bonnies Gordon, eds. *The Courtesan's Arts: Cross-Cultural Perspectives*. Oxford: Oxford University Press, 2006.

Feuerstein, Georg. *The Philosophy of Classical Yoga*. New York: St. Martin's Press, 1980.

Fiser, Ivo. "The Kāmasūtra of Vātsyāyana: A Bibliographical Study." In *Lex et Litterae: Studies in Honour of Professor Oscar Botto*, ed. Siegfried Lienhard and Irma Piovano, 208–9. Torino: Edizioni dell'Orso, 1997.

Fitzgerald, James L. *Indian Erotics of the Oldest Period*. Praha: Universita Karlova, 1967.

———. "*Dharma* and Its Translation in the *Mahābhārata*." *Journal of Indian Philosophy* 32, no. 5 (Dec. 2004): 671–85.

Flax, Jane. "Postmodernism and Gender Relations in Feminist Theory," *Signs* 12, no. 4 (1987): 621–43.

Fraser, Nancy. *Unruly Practices: Power, Discourse and Gender in Contemporary Social Theory*. Minneapolis: University of Minnesota Press, 1989.

Freud, Sigmund. *The Freud Reader*. Ed. Peter Gay. New York: W. W. Norton, 1989.

———. *Sexuality and the Psychology of Love*. New York: A Touchstone Book, 1997.

———. *Beyond the Pleasure Principle*. Seattle, WA: Pacific Publishing Studio, 2010.

———. *Civilization and Its Discontents*. Trans. Joan Riviere. Mansfield Centre, CT: Martino Publishing, 2010.

———. Three Essays on the Theory of Sexuality. Trans. James Strachey. Eastford, CT: Martino Fine Books, 2011.

Ganeri, Jonardon, ed. *Indian Logic: A Reader*. Richmond: Curzon, 2001.

Ganguly, A. B. *Sixty-Four Arts in Ancient India*. New Delhi: English Book Store, 1962.

Gearhart, S. "Foucault's Response to Freud: Sado-Masochism and the Aestheticization of Power." *Style* 29 (1995): 389–403.

Geertz, Clifford. *Negara: The Theatre State in Nineteenth Century Bali*. Princeton, NJ: Princeton University Press, 1980.

Gerow, Edwin. "India as a Philosophical Problem: McKim Marriott and the Comparative Enterprise India through Hindu Categories," *Journal of the American Society of Oriental Society* 120, no. 3 (July–Sept. 2000): 410–29.

Gerow, Edwin, and Abhinavagupta. "Abhinavagupta's Aesthetics as a Speculative Paradigm." *Journal of the American Oriental Society* 114, no. 2 (1994): 186–208.

Ghosh, A. *The City in Early Historical India*. Simla: Indian Institute of Advanced Study, 1973.

Ghosh, N. N. *Early History of Kaushambi*. Allahabad: Allahabad Law Journal Press, 1935.

Ghurye, G. S. *Indian Sadhus*. Bombay: Popular Prakashan, 1964.

Gispert-Sauch, G., S.J. *Bliss in the Upaniṣads: An Analytical Study of the Origin and Growth of the Vedic Concept of Ānanda*. New Delhi: Oriental Publishers & Distributors, 1977.

Glick, Elisa. *The Dialectics of Dandyism*. Cultural Critique 48 (2001): 129–63.

Glucklich, Ariel. *Religious Jurisprudence in the Dharmaśāstra*. New York: Macmillan, 1988.

Gnoli, Raniero. *The Aesthetic Experience according to Abhinavagupta*. Varanasi: Chowkhamba Sanskrit Series Office, 1968.

Gode, P. K. *Studies in Indian Cultural History*. 3 vols. Hoshiarpur: Vishveshvaranand Indological Institute, 1960.

Godfrey, Sima. "The Dandy as Ironic Figure." *Substance* 11, no. 3 (1982): 21–33.

Goldman, R. P. "Fathers, Sons, Gurus: Oedipal Conflict in the Sanskrit Epics." *Journal of Indian Philosophy* 6 (1978): 325–92.

Goldstein, Jan. *Foucault and the Writing of History*. Cambridge, MA: Blackwell, 1994.

———. "Foucault among the Sociologists: The 'Disciplines' and the History of the Professions." *History and Theory* 23 (1984): 170–92.

Gonzales, Francisco J. *Plato and Heidegger: A Question of Dialogue*. University Park: Pennsylvania State University Press, 2009.

Goodwin, Robert. *The Playworld of Sanskrit Drama*. Delhi: Motilal Banarsidass, 1998.

Gosling, J. C. B. *Pleasure and Desire: The Case for Hedonism Reviewed*. Oxford: Clarendon Press, 1969.

Gosling, J. C. B., and C. C. W. Taylor. *The Greeks on Pleasure*. Oxford: Clarendon Press, 1982.

Grant, B. "Translating 'The' *Kāmasūtra*." *Third World Quarterly* 26, no. 3 (2005): 509–16.

Greenfield, Robert. *Timothy Leary: A Biography*. Orlando: Harcourt, 2006.

Grimes, John. *A Concise Dictionary of Indian Philosophy*. Albany: State University of New York Press, 1996.

Gross, Robert Lewis. *The Sadhus of India: A Study of Hindu Asceticism*. Jaipur and New Delhi: Rawat Publications, 1992.

Gupta, R. *Studies in nāyaka-nāyikā-bheda*. Varanasi: Chowkhamba Sanskrit Series Office, 1967.

Haberman, David L. *Acting as a Way of Salvation: A Study of Rāgānuga Bhakti Sādhana*. Oxford: Oxford University Press, 1988.

Habermas, Jurgen. *The Structural Transformation of the Public Sphere.* London: Polity Press, 1999.

Hadot, Pierre. *Philosophy as a Way of Life: Spiritual Exercises from Socrates to Foucault.* Ed. Arnold Davidson; trans. Michael Chase. Oxford: Blackwell, 1995.

Halbfass, Wilhelm. *On Being and What There Is: Classical Vaiśeṣika and the History of Indian Ontology.* Albany: State University of New York Press, 1992.

Halperin, David M. "Platonic Eros and What Men Call Love." *Ancient Philosophy* 5 (1985): 161–204.

———. "Plato and Erotic Reciprocity." *Classical Antiquity* 5, no. 1 (1986): 60–80.

———. *One Hundred Years of Homosexuality and Other Essays on Greek Love.* New York: Routledge, 1990.

———. *Saint Foucault: Towards a Gay Hagiography.* New York: Oxford University Press, 1995.

Halperin, David M., John J. Winkler, and Froma I. Zeitlin. *Before Sexuality: The Construction of Erotic Experience in the Ancient Greek World.* Princeton, NJ: Princeton University Press, 1990.

Hampiholi, Vishwanath K. *Kāmashastra in Classical Sanskrit Literature.* Delhi: Ajanta Publications, 1988.

Handique, Krishnakanta. *Apsaras in Indian Literature and the Legend of Urvaśī and Purūravas.* New Delhi: Decent Books, 2001.

Heesterman, J. C. "Householder and Renouncer." In *Way of Life: King, Householder, Renouncer: Essays in Honour of Louis Dumont*, ed. T. N. Madan, 251–71. Delhi: Vikas Publishing, 1982.

———. *The Inner Conflict of Tradition: Essays in Indian Ritual, Kingship, and Society.* Chicago: University of Chicago Press, 1985.

———. *The Broken World of Sacrifice: An Essay in Ancient Indian Ritual.* Chicago: University of Chicago Press, 1993.

Heidegger, Martin. *Being and Time.* Trans. John Macquarrie and Edward Robinson. San Francisco: Harper & Row, 1962.

———. *Identity and Difference.* Translated with an Introduction by Joan Stambaugh. Chicago: University of Chicago Press, 2002.

———. *Four Seminars.* Trans. Andrew Mitchell and François Raffoul. Bloomington: Indiana University Press, 2003.

———. *Being and Truth.* Trans. Gregory Fried and Richard Polt. Bloomington: Indiana University Press, 2010.

Hiltebeitel, Alf. "The *Mahābhārata* and Hindu Eschatology." *History of Religions* 12, no. 2 (1972): 95–135.

———. "Nahusa in the Skies: A Human King of Heavens." *History of Religions* 16, no. 4 (1977): 329–50.

———. "Draupadi's Garments." *Indo-Iranian Journal* 22 (1980): 97–112.

———. "Toward a Coherent Study of Hinduism." *Religious Studies Review* 9, no. 3 (1983): 206–12.

———. *Rethinking the Mahābhārata: A Reader's Guide to the Education of the Dharma King.* Chicago: University of Chicago Press, 2001.

———. *Dharma: Its Early History in Law, Religion, and Narrative.* New York: Oxford University Press, 2011.

Hiriyanna, M. *The Essentials of Indian Philosophy.* London: George Allen & Unwin, 1967.

Hocart, A. M. *Caste: A Comparative Study.* London: Methuen, 1950.

Hofmann, Albert. *LSD, My Problem Child.* Los Angeles: Jeremy P. Tarcher, 1983.

Holdheim, W. Wolfgang. "Auerbach's Mimesis: Aesthetics as Historical Understanding." *Clio* 10, no. 2 (1981): 143–54.

Holmes, Charles Mason. *Aldous Huxley and the Way to Reality.* Bloomington: Indiana University Press, 1970.

Horner, Isaline Blew. *Women under Primitive Buddhism: The Position of Laywomen and Almswomen in Early Buddhist Times Followed by a History of the "Order of Almswomen," Collected from Canonical and Post-Colonial Pali Literature and Commentaries with Notes and an Index.* Amsterdam: Philo Press, 1930.

Horowitz, Michael, and Cynthia Palmer, eds. *Moksha: Aldous Huxley's Classic Writings on Psychedelics and the Visionary Experience.* Rochester, VT: Park Street Press, 1999.

Huntington, Samuel P. *The Clash of Civilizations and the Remaking of the World Order.* New York: Touchstone, 1998.

Huxley, Aldous. *The Doors of Perception & Heaven and Hell.* New York: Harper & Row, 1968.

Hyland, Drew A., and John Panteleimon Manoussakis, eds. *Heidegger and the Greeks: Interpretive Essays.* Bloomington: Indiana University Press, 2006.

Inden, Ronald. "Lordship and Caste in Hindu Discourse." In *Indian Religion,* ed. Audrey Cantile and Richard Burghart. London: Curzon Press, 1985.

———. *Imagining India.* Oxford: Blackwell, 1990.

Irigaray, Luce. *The Sex Which Is Not One.* Trans. Catherine Porter and Carolyn Burke. Ithaca, NY: Cornell University Press, 1985.

Jacquette, Dale. *The Philosophy of Schopenhauer.* Ithaca, NY: McGill-Queen's University Press, 2005.

Jaini, P. S. *Gender and Salvation: Jaina Debates on the Spiritual Liberation of Women.* Berkeley: University of California Press, 1991.

Jamison, Stephanie W. *Sacrificed Wife Sacrificer's Wife: Women, Ritual, and Hospitality in Ancient India.* New York: Oxford University Press, 1996.

Jayal, Shakambari. *The Status of Women in the Epics.* Delhi: Motilal Banarsidass, 1966.

Jung, Patricia Beattie, Mary E. Hunt, and Radhika Balakrishnana, eds. *Good Sex: Feminist Perspectives from the World's Religions.* Newark, NJ: Rutgers University Press, 2001.

Kakar, Sudhir, and John Munder Ross. *Tales of Love, Sex, and Danger.* Oxford: Blackwell, 1986.

———. *Intimate Relations: Exploring Indian Sexuality.* Chicago: University of Chicago Press, 1990.

———. *The Ascetic of Desire: A Novel of the Kama Sutra.* New York: Overlook Press, 2000.

Kale, Pramod. *The Theatric Universe: A Study of the Nāṭyaśāstra.* Bombay: Popular Prakashan, 1974.

Kalyanov, V. I. "The Image of the Indian Woman in the *Mahābhārata.*" In *Annals of the Bhandarkar Oriental Research Institute,* 161–72. Diamond Jubilee Volume, 1977–78.

Kane, P. V. *History of Dharmaśāstra.* I.1 (1968), I.2 (1975), II. 1–2 (1974), III (1973), V.1 (1974), V.2 (1962). Poona: Bhandarkar Oriental Research Institute, 1962–75.

———. *History of Sanskrit Poetics.* Delhi: Motilal Banarsidass Publishers, 1971.

Kangle, R. P. *The Kautilya Arthaśāstra.* Three Parts. University of Bombay Studies, Sanskrit, Prakrit and Pali, nos. 1–3. Bombay: University of Bombay, 1960–65.

Kaul, Shonaleeka. "Women about Town: An Exploration of the Sanskrit Kāvya Tradition." *Studies in History* 22, no. 1 (2006): 59–76.

———. "Pleasure and Culture: Reading Urban Behaviour through Kāvya Archetypes." In *Ancient India: New Research,* ed. Upinder Singh and Nayanjot Lahiri. Delhi: Oxford University Press, 2009.

———. *Imagining the Urban: Sanskrit and the City in Early India*. New York: Seagull Books, 2011.

Keith, A. B. *The Religion and Philosophy of the Veda and Upanishads*. Cambridge, MA: Harvard University Press, 1925.

———. *A History of Sanskrit Literature*. Oxford: Oxford University Press, 1928.

———. *The Sanskrit Drama in Its Origin, Development, Theory and Practice*. London: Oxford University Press, 1964.

Kersenboom, Sasakiya C. *Nityasumangali: Devadasi Tradition in South India*. New Delhi: Motilala Banarsidass, 2011.

Kisiel, Theodore. *The Genesis of Heidegger's "Being and Time."* Berkeley: University of California Press, 1993.

Klostermaier, K. K. *A Survey of Hinduism*. Albany: State University of New York Press, 1989.

Konow, Sten. *The Indian Drama (The Sanskrit Drama)*. Calcutta: General Printers and Publishers, 1969.

Kosambi, D. D. *Culture and Civilization of Ancient India in Historical Outline*. Delhi: Vikas Publishing, 1965. Reprint 1975.

———. *Myth and Reality: Studies in the Formation of Indian Culture*. Bombay: Popular Book Depot, 1962.

Krishna, Daya. *Indian Philosophy: A Counter Perspective*. Delhi: Oxford University Press, 1991.

Kuiper, F. B. J. *Varuṇa and Vidūṣaka: On the Origin of the Sanskrit Drama*. Amsterdam: Royal Netherlands Academy, 1979.

Kumari, Ranjana. *Female Sexuality in Hinduism*. Delhi: Published for the Joint Women's Programme ISPCK, 1988.

Lacan, Jacques. *Female Sexuality: Jacques Lacan and the École Freudienne*. Ed. Juliet Mitchell and Josephine Rose; trans. Josephine Rose. New York: W. W. Norton, 1982.

———. *The Ethics of Psychoanalysis, 1959–1960: The Seminar of Jacques Lacan Book VII*. Ed. Jacques-Alain Miller; trans. Dennis Porter. New York: W. W. Norton, 1986.

Lal, Ananda. *The Oxford Companion to Indian Theatre*. New Delhi: Oxford University Press, 2004.

Laqueur, Thomas. *Making Sex: Body and Gender from the Greeks to Freud*. Cambridge, MA: Harvard University Press, 1990.

Lariviere, Richard W., ed. *Studies in Dharmaśāstra*. Calcutta: Firma KLM, 1984.

Larmour, D. H., J. Miller, P. Allen, and C. Platter, eds. *Rethinking Sexuality: Foucault and Classical Antiquity*. Princeton, NJ: Princeton University Press, 1998.

Larson, G. J. *Classical Samkya: An Interpretation of Its History and Meaning*. Delhi: Motilal Banarsidass, 1969.

Lattin, Don. *The Harvard Psychedelic Club: How Timothy Leary, Ram Dass, Huston Smith, and Andrew Weil Killed the Fifties and Ushered in a New Age for America*. New York: HarperOne, 2010.

Leary, Timothy. *Flashbacks: A Personal and Cultural History of an Era: An Autobiography*. Los Angeles: Jeremy P. Tarcher, 1990.

Leary, Timothy, Ralph Metzner, and Richard Alpert. *The Psychedelic Experience: A Manual Based on the Tibetan Book of the Dead*. New York: Citadel Press, 1964

Lee, Martin A., and Bruce Shlain. *The Acid Dreams: The Complete Social History of LSD: The CIA, the Sixties, and Beyond*. New York: Grove Weidenfeld, 1992.

Levine, Philippa. *Prostitution, Race, and Politics: Policing Venereal Disease in the British Empire*. New York: Routledge, 2003.

Levy, Patrick. *Sadhus: Going beyond the Dreadlocks*. New Delhi: Fingerprint, 2015.

Lidova, Natalia. *Drama and Ritual of Early Hinduism*. Delhi: Motilal Banarsidass, 1994.

Lingat, R. *The Classical Law of India*. Trans. J. D. M. Derrett. Berkeley: University of California Press, 1962.

Loos, Tamara. "Transnational Histories of Sexualities in Asia." *American Historical Review* 114, no. 5 (2009): 1309–24.

Luders, Heinrich. *Fragments of Buddhist Drama*. Trans. Arati Mitra. Calcutta: Sanskrit College, 1994.

Ludwig, Paul. *Eros and Polis*. Cambridge: Cambridge University Press, 2002.

Lynch, Owen. "The Social Construction of Emotion in India." In *Divine Passions: The Social Construction of Emotion in India*, ed. Owen Lynch, 3–34. Berkeley: University of California Press, 1990.

MacKinnon, Catherine A. "Does Sexuality Have a History?" *Michigan Quarterly Review* 30, no. 1 (1991): 1–11.

MacLean, Rory. *Magic Bus: On the Hippie Trail from Istanbul to India*. New York: Penguin Books, 2008.

Macy, Joanna. "The Dialectics of Desire." *Numen* 22, no. 2 (1975): 145–60.

Madan, T. N., ed. *Way of Life: King, Householder, Renouncer: Essays in Honour of Louis Dumont*. New Delhi: Vikas Publishing, 1982.

Mādhvācārya. *Śrīmacchaṅkaradigvijayaḥ* (Śrīraṅgam: Śrīvaṇīvilāsamudraṇālayaḥ, 1972).

Mahmood, Saba. *Politics of Piety: Islamic Revival and the Feminist Subject*. Princeton, NJ: Princeton University Press, 2005.

Mahoney, Timothy E. "Is the Socratic Eros in the 'Symposium' Egoistic?" *Apeiron: A Journal of Ancient Philosophy and Science* 29, no. 1 (1996): 1–18.

Majumdar, R. C. *Corporate Life in Ancient India*. Calcutta: Calcutta University, 1922.

Malamoud, Charles. "On the Rhetoric and Semantics of Puruṣārtha." In *Way of Life: King, Householder, Renouncer: Essays in Honour of Louis Dumont*, ed. T. N. Madan, 33–54. New Delhi: Vikas Publishing, 1982.

———. "Semantics and Rhetoric in the Hindu Hierarchy of the 'Aims of Man.'" In *Cooking the World: Ritual and Thought in Ancient India*, ed. C. Malamoud, 109–29. Delhi: Oxford University Press, 1987.

Malcolm, Phillip, and Waller Thody. *Huxley: A Biographical Introduction*. New York: Scribner, 1973.

Marcuse, Herbert. *Eros and Civilization*. Boston: Beacon Press, 1955.

Marglin, Frederique Apfell. "Female Sexuality in the Hindu World." In *Immaculate and Powerful*, ed. Clarissa W. Atkinson, Constance H. Buchanan, and Margaret R. Miles, 39–59. Boston: Beacon Press, 1985.

Marriott, McKim. "Hindu Transactions: Diversity without Dualism." In *Transaction and Meaning*, ed. B. Kapferer. Philadelphia: ISHI Publications, 1976.

———. "Constructing an Indian Ethnosociology." In *India through Hindu Categories*, ed. McKim Marriott. New Delhi: Sage Publications, 1990.

Martin, Biddy. "Feminism, Criticism, and Foucault." *New German Critique* 27 (1982): 3–30.

Masson, J. L., and M. V. Patwardhan. *Śāntarasa and Abhinavagupta's Philosophy of Aesthetics*. Poona: Bhandarkar Oriental Research Institute, 1969.

Mathers, E. Powys. *Eastern Love*. 3 vols. New York: Horace Liveright, 1930.

Matilal, Bimal Krishna. *Epistemology, Logic, and Grammar in Indian Philosophical Analysis*. The Hague: Mouton and Co., 1971.

———. *The Character of Indian Logic*. Albany: State University of New York Press, 1998.

McConnachie, James. *The Book of Love: In Search of the Kamasutra*. London: Atlantic Books, 2007.

McLure, L. K., and C. A. Faraone, eds. *Prostitutes and Courtesans in the Ancient World*. Madison: University of Wisconsin Press, 2006.

McWhorter, Ladelle. *Bodies and Pleasures: Foucault and the Politics of Sexual Normalization*. Bloomington: Indiana University Press, 1999.

Megill, Alan. "The Reception of Foucault by Historians." *Journal of the History of Ideas* 48 (1987): 117–41.

Menski, Werner F. "Marital Expectations as Dramatized in Hindu Marriage Rituals." In *Roles and Rituals for Hindu Women*, ed. Julia Leslie, 47–67. Delhi: Motilal Banarsidass, 1992.

Meyer, Johann Jakob. *Sexual Life in Ancient India*. New York: Barnes & Noble, 1953.

Meyerowitz, Joanne. "A History of 'Gender.'" In *AHR Forum*: "Revisiting 'Gender': A Useful Category of Historical Analysis," *American Historical Review* 113, no. 5 (2008): 1346–56.

Miles, Barry. *The Beat Hotel: Ginsberg, Burroughs, and Corso in Paris, 1958–1963*. New York: Grove Press, 2000.

Miller, Barbara Stoler, ed. *Theater of Memory: The Plays of Kalidasa*. New York: Columbia University Press, 1984.

———, ed. *The Powers of Art: Patronage in Indian Culture*. Delhi: Oxford University Press, 1992.

Miller, James. *The Passion of Michel Foucault*. Cambridge, MA: Harvard University Press, 1993.

Miller, Timothy. *The Hippies and American Value*. Knoxville: University of Tennessee Press, 1991.

Mishra, Saraswati. *Status of Indian Women*. New Delhi: Gyan Publishing, 2002.

Modern, John Lardas. *The Bop Apocalypse: The Religious Visions of Kerouac, Ginsberg, and Burroughs*. Urbana: University of Illinois Press, 2001.

Moers, Ellen. *The Dandy: Brummell to Beerbohm*. New York: Viking Press, 1960.

Mohanty, J. N. "Are Indian and Western Philosophy Radically Different?" In *Essays on Indian Philosophy: Traditional and Modern*, ed. Purushottama Bilimoria, 312–30. Delhi: Oxford University Press, 1993.

Mosse, George L. *The Image of Man: The Creation of Modern Masculinity*. New York: Oxford University Press, 1996.

Mukherjee, Mithi. *India in the Shadows of Empire: A Legal and Political History, 1774–1950*. New Delhi: Oxford University Press, 2010.

———. "Transcending Identity: Gandhi, Nonviolence, and the Pursuit of a 'Different' Freedom in Modern India." *American Historical Review* 115, no. 2 (2010): 453–73.

Mukherjee, Prabhati. "Widowhood and Niyoga in the Arthasastra and Manusmrti." *Our Heritage* 11, no. 1 (1963): 1–11.

Mukherji, Santosh Kumar. *Prostitution in India*. New Delhi: Inter India Publications, 1986. Reprint.

Nagaraja Rao, P. *The Four Values in Indian Philosophy and Culture: A Study of the Puruṣārthas*. Mysore: University of Mysore, 1970.

Nehamas, Alexander. *Nietzsche: Life as Literature*. Cambridge, MA: Harvard University Press, 1987.

———. *The Art of Living: Socratic Reflections from Plato to Foucault*. Berkeley: University of California Press, 1998.

Nelson, James B., and Sandra P. Longfellow, eds. *Sexuality and the Sacred: Studies on the Impact of Religious Teachings on Women*. Geneva: WCC Publications, 1990.

Nietzsche, F. *The Birth of Tragedy and the Case of Wagner*. Trans. W. Kaufman. New York: Random House, 1967.

———. *The Will to Power*. Trans. W. Kauffman and R. J. Hollingdale. New York: Vintage Books, 1968.

———. *Beyond Good and Evil*. Trans. R. J. Hollingdale. London: Penguin Books, 1973.

———. *The Gay Science*. Trans. W. Kaufmann. New York: Vintage Books, 1974.

———. *On the Genealogy of Morality*. Ed. K. Ansell-Pearson; trans. C. Diethe. Cambridge: Cambridge University Press, 1994.

Nilson, Herman. *Michel Foucault and the Games of Truth*. Trans. Rachel Clark. New York: St. Martin's Press, 1998.

Nussbaum, Martha. "Affections of the Greeks." *New York Times Book Review*, November 10, 1985, 13–14.

Nussbaum, Martha, and Juha Sihvola. *The Sleep of Reason: Erotic Experience and Sexual Ethics in Ancient Greece and Rome*. Chicago: University of Chicago Press, 2002.

O'Farrell, Clare. *Foucault: Historian or Philosopher?* London: Macmillan, 1989.

———. *Michel Foucault*. Thousand Oaks: Sage Publications, 2005.

O'Hanlon, Rosalind. "Issues of Masculinity in North Indian History: The Bangesh Nawabs of Furrukhabad." *Indian Journal of Gender Studies* 4, no. 1 (1997): 1–18.

Oldenburg, Veena Talwar. "Lifestyle as Resistance: The Case of the Courtesans of Lucknow, India." *Feminist Studies* 16, no. 2 (1990): 259–87.

Olivelle, Patrick. "Ritual Suicide and the Rite of Renunciation." *Wiener Zeitschrift fur die Künde Südasiens* 22 (1978): 19–44.

———. *Samnyasa Upanisads: Hindu Scriptures on Asceticism and Renunciation*. New York: Oxford University Press, 1992.

———. *The Aśrama System: The History and Hermeneutics of a Religious Institution*. New York: Oxford University Press, 1993.

———. "Amrta: Women and Indian Technologies of Immortality." *Journal of Indian Philosophy* 25 (1997): 427–49.

———."Orgasmic Rapture and Divine Ecstasy: The Semantic History of *Ānanda*." *Journal of Indian Philosophy* 25 (1997): 153–80.

———. "Caste and Purity: A Study in the Language of the Dharma Literature." *Contributions to Indian Sociology* 32, no. 2 (1998): 189–216.

———. *Dharmasūtras: The Law Codes of Āpastamba, Gautama, Baudhāyana, and Vasiṣṭha*. Delhi: Motilal Banarsidass, 2000.

———. *Language, Text, and Society: Explorations in Ancient Indian Culture and Religion*. Firenze: Firenze University Press, 2005.

———. *Between the Empires: Society in India, 300 BCE to 400 CE*. New York: Oxford University Press, 2006.

———, ed. *Dharma: Studies in Semantic, Cultural and Religious History*. Delhi: Motilal Banarsidass, 2009.

———. *Ascetics and Brahmins: Studies in Ideologies and Institutions*. New York: Anthem Press, 2011.

———. "Punishing in Public: Imposing Moral Self-Dominance in Normative Sanskrit Sources." In *Tradition, Veda, and Law: Studies on South Asian Classical Intellectual Traditions*, ed. Frederico Squarcini. London: Anthem Press, 2011.

Olivelle, Patrick, Janice Leoshko, and Himanshu Prabha Ray, eds. *Reimagining Aśoka: Memory and History*. Delhi: Oxford University Press, 2012.

Orsini, Francesca, ed. *Love in South Asia: A Cultural History*. Cambridge: Cambridge University Press, 2006.

Orr, Leslie C. *Donors, Devotees, and Daughters of God: Temple Women in Medieval Tamilnadu*. New York: Oxford University Press, 2000.

Ortner, S., and H. Whitehead, eds. *Sexual Meanings: The Cultural Construction of Gender and Sexuality*. Cambridge: Cambridge University Press, 1981.

Pandey, Anupa. *The Nāṭyaśāstra Tradition and Ancient Indian Society*. Jodhpur: Kusumanjali, 1993.

Paras, Eric. *Foucault 2.0: Beyond Power and Knowledge*. New York: Other Press, 2006.

Parrinder, Geoffrey. *Sex in the World's Religions*. New York: Oxford University Press, 1980.

Patton, Laurie L., ed. *Jewels of Authority: Women and Textual Tradition in Hindu India*. Oxford: Oxford University Press, 2002.

Pinkham, Mildred Worth. *Woman in the Sacred Scriptures of Hinduism*. New York: AMS Press, 1967.

Plant, Sadie. *Writing on Drugs*. New York: Farrar, Straus & Giroux, 1999.

Plato. *Symposium*. Trans. Alexander Nehmas and Paul Woodruff. Indianapolis: Hackett, 1989.

———. *Phaedrus*. Trans. Alexander Nehmas and Paul Woodruff. Indianapolis: Hackett, 1995.

Pollock, Sheldon. "The Theory of Practice and the Practice of Theory in Indian Intellectual History." *Journal of the American Oriental Society* 105, no. 3 (1985): 499–519.

———. "The Sanskrit Cosmopolis, 300–1300 CE: Transculturation, Vernacularization, and the Question of Ideology." In *Ideology and Status of Sanskrit: Contributions to the History of the Sanskrit Language*, ed. Jan E. M. Houben, 197–249. New York: E. J. Brill, 1996.

———. "The Cosmopolitan Vernacular." *Journal of Asian Studies* 57, no. 1 (1998): 6–37.

———. "The Social Aesthetic and Sanskrit Literary Theory." *Journal of Indian Philosophy* 29 (2001): 197–229.

———, ed. *Literary Cultures in History: Reconstructions from South Asia*. Berkeley: University of California Press, 2003.

———. *The Ends of Man at the End of Premodernity*. Amsterdam: Royal Netherlands Academy of Arts and Sciences, 2005.

———. *The Language of the Gods in the World of Men: Sanskrit, Culture, and Power in Premodern India*. Berkeley: University of California Press, 2006.

———. "Is There an Indian Intellectual History?" *Journal of Indian Philosophy* 26, nos. 5–6 (2008): 533–42.

———. "What Was Bhatta Nāyaka Saying: The Hermeneutical Transformation of Indian Aesthetics." In *Epic and Argument in Sanskrit Literary History: Essays in Honor of Robert P. Goldman*, ed. Sheldon Pollock, 143–84. Delhi: Manohar, 2010.

———. "Introduction." In *Forms of Knowledge in Early Modern Asia: Explorations in the Intellectual History of India and Tibet, 1500–1800*, ed, Sheldon Pollock. Durham, NC: Duke University Press, 2011.

———. "Vyakti and the History of Rasa." *Vimarsha, Journal of Rasthriya Sanskrit Sansthan (World Sanskrit Conference Special Issue)* 6 (2012): 232–53.

Porter, James I. "Foucault's Ascetic Ancients." *Phoenix* 59, no. 1/2 (2005): 121–32.

Potter, Karl H. *Presuppositions of India's Philosophies*. Englewood Cliffs, NJ: Prentice-Hall, 1963.

Prabhu, Avatar. *The Revised Kamasutra: A Novel*. Fairfield, IA: Sunstar Publishing, 1998.

Prasad, Rajendra. "The Theory of *Puruṣārthas*: Revaluation and Reconstruction." *Journal of Indian Philosophy* 9, no. 1 (1981): 49–76.

Price, A. *Love and Friendship in Plato and Aristotle*. Oxford: Clarendon Press, 1989.

Puri, Jyoti. "Concerning 'Kāmasūtras': Challenging Narratives of History and Sexuality." *Signs* 27, no. 3 (2002): 632.

Rai, Ram Kumar. *Encyclopedia of Indian Erotics*. Varanasi: Prachya Prakasan, Chowkhamba Sanskrit Series Office, 1981.

Rajchman, John. *Michel Foucault: The Freedom of Philosophy*. New York: Columbia University Press, 1985.

———. *Truth and Eros: Foucault, Lacan, and the Question of Ethics*. New York: Routledge, 1991.

Ramazanoglu, Caroline, ed. *Up against Foucault: Explorations of Some Tensions between Foucault and Feminism*. New York: Routledge, 1993.

Rampuri. *Autobiography of a Sadhu: A Journey into Mystic India*. Rochester, VT: Destiny Books, 2010.

Raskin, Jonah. *Allen Ginsberg's "Howl" and the Making of the Beat Generation*. Berkeley: University of California Press, 2004.

Rawson, Philip. *Erotic Art of India*. London: Thames & Hudson, 1977.

Ray, Amita. *Villages, Towns and Secular Buildings in Ancient India c. 150 B.C.–350 A.D.* Calcutta: Firma KLM, 1964.

Rhodes, James M. *Eros, Wisdom, and Silence: Plato's Erotic Dialogues*. Columbia and London: University of Missouri Press, 2003.

Riley, Denise. *"Am I That Name?": Feminism and the Category of "Women" in History*. London: Macmillan, 1988.

Rocha, Antonio. "Scientia Sexualis versus Ars Erotica: Foucault, van Gulik, Needham." *Studies in History and Philosophy of Biological and Biomedical Sciences* 42 (2011): 328–43.

Rocher, Ludo. "The *Kāmasūtra*: Vatsyayana's Attitude toward Dharma and *Dharmaśāstra*." *Journal of the American Oriental Society* 105, no. 3 (1985): 521–29.

Roochnik, David. "The Erotics of Philosophical Discourse" *History of Philosophy Quarterly* 4, no. 2 (1987): 117–29.

Roy, Kumkum, ed. "Unraveling the Kāmasūtra." In *A Question of Silence: The Sexual Economies of Modern India*, ed. M. E. John and J. Nair. Delhi: Kali for Women, 1998.

———. *Women in Early Indian Societies*. Delhi: Oxford University Press, 1999.

———. *The Power of Gender and the Gender of Power: Explorations in Early Indian History*. Delhi: Oxford University Press, 2010.

Rubin, Gayle. "Thinking Sex: Notes for a Radical Theory of the Politics of Sexuality." In *Pleasure and Danger: Exploring Female Sexuality*, ed. Carole S. Vance, 267–319. Boston: Routledge, 1984.

Said, Edward. *Orientalism*. New York: Vintage Books, 1979.

Sallis, John. *Platonic Legacies*. New York: State University of New York Press, 2004.

Santas, Gerasimos. *Plato and Freud: Two Theories of Love*. Oxford and New York: Basil Blackwell, 1988.

Sastry, Shama R. "A Note on the Supposed Identity of Vatsyayana and Kautilya." *Quarterly Journal of the Mythic Society* 7 (1917): 210–16.

Saxena, Monika. "Ganikas in Early India: Its Genesis and Dimensions." *Social Scientist* 34, nos. 11/12 (2006): 2–17.

Scharfe, Hartmut. *The State in Indian Tradition*. Leiden: E. J. Brill, 1989.

———. *Investigations in the Kautalya's Manual of Political Science*. Wiesbaden: Harrassowitz, 1993.

Schindler, D. C. "Plato and the Problem of Love: On the Nature of Eros in the Symposium." *Apeiron: A Journal for Ancient Philosophy and Science* 40, no. 3 (2007): 199–220.

Schmid, Susann. "Byron and Wilde: The Dandy in the Public Sphere." In *The Importance of Reinventing Oscar: Versions of Wilde during the Last 100 Years*, ed. Julie Hibbard et al., 81–90. Amsterdam: Rodopi, 2002.

Schusterman, Richard. "Asian Ars Erotica and the Question of Sexual Aesthetics." *Journal of Aesthetics and Art Criticism* 65, no. 1 (2007): 61.

———. *Body Consciousness: A Philosophy of Mindfulness and Somaesthetics*. New York: Cambridge University Press, 2008.

Scott, Joan W. "Gender: A Useful Category of Historical Analysis." *American Historical Review* 19, no. 5 (1985): 1053–75.

———. "The Evidence of Experience." *Critical Inquiry* 17, no. 4 (1991): 58–68.

———. "Experience." In *Feminists Theorize the Political*, ed. Judith Butler and Joan W. Scott, 22–40. New York: Routledge, 1992.

Sen, Ramendra Kumar. *A Brief Introduction to a Comparative Study of Greek and Indian Poetics and Aesthetics*. Calcutta: Sen. Ray & Co., 1954.

Shah, Shalini. *The Making of Womanhood: Gender Relations in the Mahābhārata*. New Delhi: Manohar Publications. 1995.

Sharma, Arvind, ed. *The Puruṣārtha: A Study in Hindu Axiology*. East Lansing: Asian Studies Center, Michigan State University, 1982.

———. *Essays on the Mahābhārata*. Leiden: E. J. Brill, 1991.

Sharma, Ram Sharan. *Sudras in Ancient India*. Delhi: Motilal Banarsidass, 1958.

———. *Material Culture and Social Formations in Ancient India*. Delhi: Macmillan, 1983.

———. *Urban Decay in India (c. 300–c. 1000)*. Delhi: Munshiram Manoharal, 1987.

Sheffield, Frisbee. *Plato's Symposium: The Ethics of Desire*. Oxford: Clarendon Press, 2006.

Shulman, David. *The King and the Clown in South Indian Myth and Poetry*. Princeton, NJ: Princeton University Press, 1985.

———. "Towards a Historical Poetics of the Sanskrit Epics." *International Folklore Review* 8 (1991): 9–17.

Siegal, Lee. *Fires of Love, Waters of Peace: Passion and Renunciation in Indian Culture*. Honolulu: University of Hawaii Press, 1983.

———. *Sacred and Profane Dimensions of Love in Indian Traditions as Exemplified in the "Gitagovinda" of Jayadeva*. Delhi: Oxford University Press, 1990.

———. *Love in a Dead Language: A Romance*. Chicago: University of Chicago Press, 1999.

Singh, G. P. *Republics, Kingdoms, Towns and Cities in Ancient India*. New Delhi: D. K. Printworld, 2003.

Sinha, Braj M. "*Arthaśāstra* Categories in the *Mahābhārata*: From Daṇḍaniti to Rājadharma." In *Essays on the Mahābhārata*, ed. Arvind Sharma, 369–83. Leiden: E. J. Brill, 1991.

Sinha, S. N., N. K. Basu, and Rita Sil. *History of Marriage and Prostitution: Vedas to Vātsyāyana*. New Delhi: Khama Publishers, 1992.

Smith, Bonnie G. *The Gender of History: Men, Women, and Historical Practice*. Cambridge, MA: Harvard University Press, 1998.

Smith, Brian K. *Classifying the Universe: The Ancient Indian Varna System and the Origins of Caste*. New York: Oxford University Press, 1994.

Smith, David. *The Dance of Śiva: Religion, Art and Poetry in South India*. Cambridge: Cambridge University Press, 1996.

Smith, Thomas Spence. "Aesthetiscism and Social Structure: Style and Social Network in the Dandy Life." *American Sociological Review* 39, no. 5 (1974): 725–43.

Snitow, Ann. *Powers of Desire: The Politics of Sexuality*. New York: Monthly Review Press, 1983.

Soneji, Devesh. *Unfinished Gestures: Devadasis, Moemory, and Modernity in South Asia.* Chicago: University of Chicago Press, 2012.

Srinivasan, Doris M. "Royalty's Courtesans and God's Mortal Wives: Keepers of Culture in Precolonial India." In *The Courtesan's Arts: Cross-Cultural Perspectives,* ed. Martha Feldman and Bonnie Gordon. Oxford: Oxford University Press, 2006.

Srinivasan, S. A. *On the Composition of the Nāṭyaśāstra.* Reinbek: Verlag für Orientalistische Fachpublikationen, 1980.

Sternbach, Ludwik. "Legal Position of Prostitutes according to Kautilya's Arthaśāstra." *Journal of the American Oriental Society* 71, no. 1 (1951): 25–60.

Stoler, Anne Laura. *Race and the Education of Desire: Foucault's History of Sexuality and the Colonial Order of Things.* Durham, NC: Duke University Press, 1995.

Strathner, Marilyn. *The Gender of the Gift: Problems with Women and Problems with Society in Melanesia.* Berkeley: University of California Press, 1988.

Strauss, Leo. *On Plato's Symposium.* Ed. Seth Benardete. Chicago: University of Chicago Press, 2001.

Sutherland, Sally. "Seduction, Counter-Seduction, and Sexual Role-Models: Bedroom Politics and the Indian Epics." *Journal of Indian Philosophy* 20 (1992): 243–51.

Sweet, Michael J., and Leonard Zwilling. "The First Medicalization: The Taxonomy and Etiology of Queerness in Classical Indian Medicine." *Journal of the History of Sexuality* 3, no. 4 (April 1993): 590–607.

Syrkin, A. Y. "Notes on the Kama Sutra." *Semiotica* 2 (1974).

Tarlekar, G. H. *Studies in the Nāṭyaśāstra.* Delhi: Motilal Banarsidass, 1975.

Thakur, Vijay Kumar. *Urbanization in Ancient India.* New Delhi: Abhinav Publication, 2003.

Thapar, R. *A History of India.* Harmondsworth: Penguin, 1966.

———. *Ancient Indian Social History: Some Interpretations.* New Delhi: Orient Longman, 1978.

———. *From Lineage to State: Social Formations in the Mid-First Millennium B.C. in the Ganga Valley.* Bombay: Oxford University Press, 1984.

———. *Interpreting Early India.* Delhi: Oxford University Press, 1992.

———. *Śakuntalā: Texts, Readings, Histories.* Delhi: Kali for Women, 1999.

———. *Early India: From the Origins to AD 1300.* Berkeley and Los Angeles: University of California Press, 2004.

Thornton, Bruce S. *Eros: The Myth of Ancient Greek Sexuality.* Boulder, CO: Westview Press, 1997.

Trautmann, Thomas R. *Kauṭilya and the Arthaśāstra: A Statistical Investigation of the Authorship and Evolution of the Text.* Leiden: E. J. Brill, 1971.

———. "Does India Have History? Does History Have India?" *Comparative Studies in Society and History* 54, no. 1 (2012): 174–205.

Upadhyaya, S. C. "Introduction." In *Kama Sutra of Vatsyayana,* trans. S. C. Upadhyaya. Bombay: Taraporevala, 1961.

———. *The Kāmasūtra: The Hindu Art of Love.* London: Watkins Publishing, 2004.

Urban, Hugh. *The Economics of Ecstasy.* New York: Oxford University Press, 2001.

Valverde, Mariana. *Sex, Power and Pleasure.* Toronto: Women's Press, 1985.

Van Buitenen, J. A. B. "*Ānanda*, or All Desires Fulfilled." *History of Religions* 19, no. 1 (Aug. 1979): 27–36.

Van Gulik, R. H. *Sexual Life in Ancient China: A Preliminary Survey of Chinese Sex and Society ca. 1500 B.C. till 1644 A.D.* Leiden: E. J. Brill, 2003.

Vanita, R. *Gender, Sex, and the City: Urdu Rekhti Poetry in India, 1780–1870*. New York: Palgrave Macmillan, 2012.

Vanita, R., and S. Kidwai. *Same-Sex Love in India: Readings from Literature and History*. Delhi: Macmillan, 2001.

Varadpande, M. L. *History of Indian Theatre: Lok Ranga Panorama of Indian Folk Theatre*. New Delhi: Abhinav Publications, 1992.

Varadpande, M. L., and Sunil Subhedar. *The Critique of Indian Theatre*. Atlantic Highlands, NJ: Humanities Press, 1982.

Vatsyayan, Kapila. *Traditional Indian Theatre: Multiple Streams*. New Delhi: National Book Trust, 1980.

———. *Bharata, The Nāṭyaśāstra*. New Delhi: Sahitya Akademi, 1996.

Venkatacharya, T. "The Significance of the Title Ubhayabhisarika and the Date of the Play." *Journal of the American Oriental Society* 88, no. 2 (April–June 1968): 350–52.

Wadley, Susan, and Doranne Jacobson. *Women in India: Two Perspectives*. Delhi: Manohar, 1970.

Waldman, Anne, and Laura Wright, eds. *Beats at Naropa: An Anthology*. Minneapolis: Coffee House Press, 2009.

Walker, Steven F. "The Invention of Theater: Recontextualizing the Vexing Question." *Comparative Literature* 56, no. 1 (Winter 2004): 1–22.

Warder, A. K. *Indian Kāvya Literature*. 5 vols. Delhi: Motilal Banarsidass, 1972.

Watson, Steven. *The Birth of the Beat Generation: Visionaries, Rebels, and Hipsters, 1944–1960*. New York: Pantheon Books, 1995.

Weeks, Jeffrey. *Sexuality and Its Discontents: Meanings, Myths, and Modern Sexualities*. London: Routledge & Kegan Paul, 1985.

———. *Sexuality*. London: Tavistock, 1986.

White, David Gordon. *Kiss of the Yogini: "Tantric Sex" in Its South Asian Contexts*. Chicago: University of Chicago Press, 2003.

Wilde, Oscar. *The Picture of Dorian Gray and Other Writings*. 1891. New York: Bantam. Reprint, 1982.

Wilhelm, Friedrich. "The Quotations in the Kāmasūtra of Vātsyāyana." *Indological Taurinensia* 7 (1979): 401–12.

Winkler, John J. *The Constraints of Desire: The Anthropology of Sex and Gender in Ancient Greece*. New York: Routledge, 1990.

Wojtilla, G. "Kāmaśāstra—a Short Report on Stand, Methods, and Tasks of Research." In *Trends in Indian Studies: Proceedings of the ESIS*, ed. J. Vace and J. Dvorak. Prague: Charles University Press, 1998.

Wolfe, Tom. *The Electric Kool-Aid Acid Test*. New York: Farrar, Straus & Giroux, 1968.

Yadava, Babu Ram. *Evolution of Urvaśī*. Aligarh: Vijñāna Prakāśana, 1986.

Yajnik, R. K. *The Indian Theatre: Its Origins and Its Later Developments under European Influence with Special Reference to Western India*. London: George Allen & Unwin, 1933.

Yeh, Catherine. *Shanghai Love: Courtesans, Intellectuals, and Entertainment Culture, 1850–1910*. Seattle: University of Washington Press, 2006.

Young, Serinity. *Courtesans and Tantric Consorts: Sexualities in Buddhist Narrative, Iconography, and Ritual*. New York: Routledge, 2004.

Zysk, Kenneth G. *Conjugal Love in India: Ratiśāstra and Ratiramaṇa*. Leiden: E. J. Brill, 2002.

Index

Abhijñāna Śākuntalam (royal romance play), 139
ābhimānika sukha (pleasure of the mind-self), 199
Abhinavagupta (philosopher), 114
abstinence, 78–80
ācārya (teacher), 144, 145, 171–72
actor (*nāyaka*), ix, 8–9, 13, 16, 94, 109–10, 134
actress (*nāyikā*)
  courtesan as, 16, 88, 94–100, 189
  courtesan-wife as, 9, 106–10
  use of term, ix, 8–9, 13, 16, 94, 134
  wife as, 99–100
adulteress, 7, 95, 96, 98–100, 110
adultery
  caste identity and, 63, 110
  as feticide, 63, 66
  paternity and, 63, 66–67
  physical confinement of women and, 71–73
  wife as adulteress, 7, 95, 96, 98–100, 110
  See also monogamy
aesthetic pleasure (*rasa*), 113, 121, 148, 174
aesthetics as the discourse of love, 10, 182, 200
aesthetics of existence, 210
afterlife, belief in the, 81, 84
ahiṃsā (nonviolence), 74, 231n72
Āmrapāli (Buddhist courtesan), 92
anāvṛt (being free and unfettered), 59, 225–26n29, 226n35
animals, 55, 57, 58, 199
annihilation of the individual, 44
anucārikā (maids in constant attendance), 143
apsaras (celestial maidens), 115, 124
Aristotle, 157
arranged marriage, 96
ars erotica (erotic arts)
  birth of, as theater of love, 9–11, 100–106, 132, 153, 170–74
  as a counter to the science of sexuality, x, xi, 1–2, 3, 18–19, 21–23, 23–27, 47–49, 53, 111–12, 198–99, 204–5, 207–10
  as field of knowledge, 174–79, 245n53
  grounding in sexual-erotic pleasure, 2, 152
  need for in ancient India, 50, 85–86, 180, 197–200
  as oral tradition, 156
  role of money in, 100–106
ars theatrica (art of theater)
  as discourse of erotic love, 10–11, 28, 119–22, 152, 153, 170–74
  founding of, 16–17, 115–19
  initial staging of (gods and demons), 9, 109, 120, 121–23, 151
  Kāmasūtra as, 9–10
  life transformed into, 104
  music and dance in, 113
  origin of, 237–38n3
  second staging (erotics) of, 119–25, 125–30, 135
art (*kalā*), 191–93, 196–97, 200
art festival (*samāja*), 192–93
artha (political power)
  and the discourse of *dharma*, 15–16, 51, 198
  discourse of political power, 4, 15, 74, 137
  and the discourse of virility, 31–32
  effect of absence of, 61
  in the *Kāmasūtra*'s trilogy, 53–55, 58–59, 89–91, 111
  king as central figure in, 87, 137, 138
  nonviolence and, 74
  over the self, 72–74
  S&M as acting out of power, 28
  subjectivity construction of, 15, 80–85
  subordination of women and, 10, 77, 80–85, 178–79

Arthaśāstra (political power text)
on courtesans, 93, 145–46
as founding text, 54–55, 87, 201
on political power, 4, 11, 15, 74, 137
artificial (*kṛtrim*) love, 101
art of life (*techne tou biou*), 207
art teacher (*pīṭhamarda*), 183, 184
Aśoka (Mauryan emperor), 65
āśramas (life stages), 186–88
assemblies (*viṭasabhā*), 180
asvatantra (subordination of women). *See under* women
ātman (the self, male), 68
autsukya (curiosity), 164–65, 166, 171, 174, 179
āviddha (violent/gods and demons) plays, 9, 109, 120, 122–23, 151
āyuktikās (women overseers), 143

Bahina Bai, 84–85
Baudelaire, Charles, 8, 134, 210, 250n20
bhakti (devotional form of Hinduism), 114
bhāṇas (one-act Sanskrit plays), 17, 98–99, 155, 157–59, 162–67, 179–80, 243n9
Bharata (sage)
identity of, 12–13, 153, 154
as theater director, 115–17, 119, 122–25, 139, 142, 155
Bhāsa (playwright), 134
bhoginī (concubines), 143
Bhoja (king-poet), 202–3
Brahmā (god of creation), 115, 119, 122–25, 135, 196–97
Brahmanical law. See *dharma*
Brahmasūtra, 4–5
Brahmin (priestly caste), 65, 74–75, 83
Butler, Judith, 213–14n21

Care of the Self (Foucault), 2–7
Cārudattam (play), 134
Caruso, P., 42–43, 45
caste
adultery and, 63, 110
the courtesan and, 16, 85, 86, 104–5, 116–19
discourse of dharma and, 6, 58, 62–64, 66–69, 110, 195
monogamy and, 61–64, 66–69, 71
patriarchy and, 63–64
ranking of, 65, 75, 97
subordination of women and, 80–85
See also identity
caturavarga (tetralogy), 4–5, 7
Caturbhāṇi (Quartet of *Bhāṇas*), 17, 92, 155
celestial maidens (*apsaras*), 115, 124
chief queen (*mahādevī*), 143
the city, as the origin of the discourse of sexual-erotic pleasure, 194–96
city dandy. *See* dandy
colonial politics, 14–15
concubines (*bhoginī*), 143
congresses (*viṭa samāja*), 180
constant insight (*jñyan*), 79
courtesan (*gaṇika*)
as an actress of love, 16, 88, 94–100, 189
in ancient Buddhist culture, 91, 92
in the *Arthaśāstra* (political power text), 93, 145–46
arts training of, 92–93, 144, 145, 150, 169, 171–72, 188–89
caste and, 7, 16, 85, 104–5, 116–19
celestial, 115–19, 124–29, 136, 139–42
as central figure in pleasure, 87–91, 114, 162–67, 177–78, 206, 234n8
charitable generosity of, 91
the city dandy and, 183–84, 190–91
in classical Indian culture, 12, 17, 92, 114–19, 151–52, 197–98
code of conduct of, 105
conflict between love and profession, 100–101, 103
the dandy-guru and, 105, 156–57, 160–62, 162–67, 171–72, 176–77, 179–80
dharma and, 89–91, 118–19
as discursive figure, 13, 14
dual attitude toward, 93, 235n22, 235n25
erotic theater as the core of her existence, 146–47, 150, 159–62
existential conflict between love and profession, 104–5, 236n44
Freud on, xi, 111–12, 151
as historical figure, 13–14, 16, 91–93
and the intimate associates of the city dandy, 184–85
mother figure, dandy-guru and, 105, 180
popular romance theater heroine, 125–29
profession (*vṛtti*) aspect of the courtesan-patron relationship, 100–106
rati (love-pleasure aspect of the courtesan-patron relationship), 100–106
role in erotics into theater transformation, ix, 1, 9, 16–17, 122–25, 126–29, 173
role in *Kāmasūtra of*, ix, 1, 7, 9, 11, 87–91, 92
role in *Nāṭyaśāstra* of, ix, 1, 140, 144–45
in the role of wife, 9, 106–10, 117–18
royal romance theater heroine, 125–29, 139–42, 142–47
as a servant of god, 114
in the service of the king, 145–47
sixty-four arts of, 92–93, 150, 169, 188–89
courtesan-wife (*ekacāriṇī*), 9, 106–10, 117–18
culture, 53
curiosity (*autsukya*), 164–66, 171, 174, 179

Dāmodaragupta (eighth century CE Kashmiri author), 89, 180
dānakāma (desire for gifts), 168
dandy
city dandy consort/patron (*nāgaraka*)
as actor, 189
in ancient Indian culture, 12, 18, 134, 181, 198, 210
art and social ethics role of, 191–96, 200
as audience for *Kāmasūtra*, 91
as central figure in aesthetic pleasure, 188–91
as central figure in sexual-erotic pleasure, 114, 182–83, 186–88
courtesan and, 183–84, 190–91
as dandy-consort in the *Nāṭyaśāstra* and, ix, 1, 8, 9, 16–17, 129–35, 159–62, 181–84, 186–88
erotic theater role of, 159–62, 173
as historical figure, 13–14, 181
as inspirational figure for village dandies, 195–96
intimate associates of, 184–85
Kāmasūtra and, ix, 1, 8, 9, 11, 51, 159–62, 181–88, 194–96
dandy-consort/patron (*vaiśika*)
as actor, 134, 135, 181–84, 186–88
as central figure in sexual-erotic pleasure, 114
dandy-city as historical figure of, 181
as historical figure, 13–14, 131–32
lifestyle of, 132, 133, 170
role in erotics into theater transformation, 8, 9, 16–17, 130–31
transitioning from customer to lover-consort, 7–8
dandy-guru (*viṭa*)
accomplishments and personal qualities of, 161, 164–67
as actor, 98–99
aesthetic pleasure and, 169–70
in ancient Indian culture, 12, 17–18, 134, 154–55
courtesan and, 156–57, 162–67, 171–72, 176–77, 179–80
courtesan, dandy-consort and, 160–62
courtesan, mother figure and, 105, 180
discourse of erotic pleasure and, 154–55, 157–59, 163–64, 173–79
erotic discussion forums and, 175–76
as erotic theater director, xi, 1, 8, 9, 16–17, 155–57, 159–62, 173–74, 179, 180
as erotic theater spectator, 170–74, 179
as the former dandy-consort, 160–62, 183–84
as guide to the courtesan, 107–8
Kāmasūtra and, ix, 1, 159–62, 180
Nāṭyaśāstra and, 8, 9, 16–17, 155–57, 159–62, 173–74, 179, 180
non-sexual erotic pleasure and, 167–70
as pimp, 180
as poet, 169
role in the *bhāṇas* and the discourse of pleasure, 157–59
darkness (*tamas*), 77
death, 35–37, 219n42
de-individualization, 42
dependence in human sexual relationships, 55–56
Derrida, Jacques, 219n42, 250n17
desire, 75–80
desubjectivation, 15, 17
as actual experience, 37–40, 42, 44
being and, 38
as critique and as actual experience, 37–40, 42, 44
death as, 36–37, 219n42
Foucault on, 15, 17, 23, 29–30, 35–37, 44, 82, 88, 89, 113, 149
identity loss as, 29–30, 38, 218n27
pleasure as, 15, 17, 23, 30, 35, 36–37, 38, 82, 88, 89, 113, 149
pleasure as event of, 26–34
spiritual liberation and, 48
devadāsī (humble servant of god), 114
devī (other queens), 143
devirilize, 18, 199
dharma (Brahmanical law)
arranged marriage in, 96
courtesan and, 89–91, 118–19
desire and, 75–80
different notions and traditions of, 65
discourse of, 4, 6, 10, 104
discourse on power, 15–16, 51, 198
erotic love as counter-discourse to, 10, 95–96, 158, 163–64, 174–79, 186, 195, 199–200
identity and, 28–29, 30, 51–59, 61–64, 64–66, 77, 87, 106, 118–19
in the *Kāmasūtra* trilogy, 53–55, 58–59, 89–91, 111, 149
nonviolence and, 74
patriarchal identity in, 6, 58, 66–69, 198–99
role of the king in, 87, 137, 138
sanātana dharma (eternal law), 60, 61, 64
subordination of pleasure to, 5–6, 15, 51–59, 72–74, 77, 87, 97, 198
"The Diet of Pleasures" (Foucault), 31
director of *ars erotica* (*kāmantantra-sūtradhāra*), 171
Discipline and Punish (Foucault), 2, 29
discourse
and chronology, 13

discursive figure, 186
difference between texts and, 12, 154
and the figure of the author, 153–54
Foucault on, 12
and historical figures, 12–13
oral discourse, 156
and the question of authorship, 12–13
theater as discourse of erotic love, 10–11, 28, 119–22, 152, 153, 170–74
dividual, 229n57
divyaveśyā (celestial courtesans), 115
domination, 31–32
drinking parties (*samāpānaka*), 184
drug use
in enlightenment, 39, 41–43, 45–46, 48
Foucault on, 39, 41–44, 47
Dumont, Louis, 229n57

ekacāriṇī (courtesan-wife), 106–10
eleven sense organs, 78–80, 82
enlightenment, 37–43
erotic-aesthetic pleasure (*śṛṅgāra rasa*), 121, 137, 148–50, 170–74
erotic arts. See *ars erotica*
erotic love as counter-discourse to *dharma* (Brahmanical law), 10, 95–96, 158, 163–64, 174–79, 199–200
erotic qualities (*ramyān guṇān*), 165–66
erotic-romantic style theater (*kaiśikī vṛtti*), 119–25, 125–30, 135, 151
eternal law (*sanātana dharma*), 60, 61, 64

family
discourse of *dharma* and, 6
patriarchal identity in, 61–64, 66–69, 85, 116–19
pre-patriarchal, 61–61
subordination of women in, 6–7, 15, 51, 59–62, 62–64, 67–73, 80–85, 97, 178–79, 198, 199–200
figure
in ancient Indian texts, 13
and category of thought, 13
city dandy as central figure in aesthetic pleasure, 188–91
city dandy as central figure in sexual-erotic pleasure, 114, 182–83, 186–88
courtesan as central figure in pleasure, 87–91, 114, 162–67, 177–78, 206, 234n8
courtesan as a discursive, 13, 14
courtesan as a historical, 91–93
difference between historical and discursive, 14, 186
and discourse, 12–13
historical, 12–13, 91–93, 181
in the *Kāmasūtra*, 7
private and public, 189
stranger as figure of pleasure, 29–30, 89, 101, 206
See also dandy-guru
Fitzgerald, James, 226n36, 228n49
Foucault, Michel
on the aesthetics of existence, 210
on the agency of sex, 23–24
on anniliation of the individual, 44, 46
on *ars erotica*, x, xi, 1–2, 3, 18–19, 21–23, 23–27, 47–49, 53, 111, 204–10, 211n6, 248n56
on the art of life, 207
charges of orientalism against, 14–15
on desubjectivation, 15, 17, 23, 29–30, 35–37, 44, 82, 88, 89, 113, 149
on desubjectivation as critique and as actual experience, 37–40, 42, 44
on drug use, 39, 41–44, 47
on Eastern culture in the West, 44, 47–48, 49
on enlightenment, 38–39
on erotic arts in the West, 3
gender relations and, 6
on Greek ethics of pleasure, 19, 26, 31
on identity, 28–29, 45–46
on illusion, 45
on madness, 14–15, 23, 44–45, 47, 49
as philosopher, 209–10, 250n18
on pleasure, 2, 7, 19, 22–23, 26, 31, 32–34, 35, 36–37, 37–42, 45, 85, 88, 207, 212n6, 216–17n6
on pleasure, truth, and identity, 103, 207–9
on pleasure, truth, and self, 209, 249–50n12
on pleasure, truth and sovereignty, 25–26
on power, 12, 21, 50
on sexuality and power, x, xi, 2, 31–32
on sexuality and truth, 24
on S&M, 28
on the stranger as figure of pleasure, 29–30, 89, 101, 206
on subjectivity, 21, 80–85, 115
on the subordination of sex to sexuality, 24
on three domains of genealogy/ontology, 249n10
on truth and identity, 2, 7
on truth and love, 26, 179, 205, 206
on truth and pleasure, 41
on truth and self, 10, 18–19, 21, 24, 249n8, 249n10
use of personal experience, 22
Freud, Sigmund
agency of sex and, 24
beyond the pleasure principle, 219n42
on the courtesan, xi, 111–12, 151
on the death drive, 219n42
on division between pleasure and love, xi, 52–53, 111–12
on division between sensuality and culture, x–xi, 27, 111–12

on humans as animals, 57
love as illness, 205
madness as illness, 205
patriarchy and, xi, 111
pleasure principle and death drive, 219n42
repression, sublimation, and, 24, 27, 52–53, 113
on truth and self-love, 205
See also *scientia sexualis*

gaṇa dharma (social ethics), 193, 196
gaṇika. See courtesan
gaṇikā-adhyakṣa (superintendent of courtesans), 93
garden parties (*udyānagamana*), 184
gārhsthya (householder), 187
gay bathhouse, 29
gender relations
in art and aesthetics as a discourse of love, 10, 182, 200
erotic arts and, 2, 11
female subordination and, xi, 6–7, 50, 80–85
Foucault and, 6
patriarchy and the *Kāmasūtra*, 15
as political relations of power, 85
power discourse in, 31–32
virility discourse in, 31–32
Ginsberg, Allen, 43
gods and demons plays (*āviddha*), 9, 109, 120, 122–23, 151
goodness (*sattva*), 77
goṣṭhi (salon), 176, 180, 184, 189–90
grammar, 177–79
grammarian
kicked on the head by courtesan, 163, 177–78, 244n41, 247n42
as the least erotic figure, 244n41
as a man of *dharma*, law, truth, and power, 177–79
Greek cultural immortality, 85
Greek ethics of pleasure, 19, 26, 31
guḍhākāra (secretiveness), 59

Halperin, David M., 32, 46
happiness, 149
harem. *See* royal harem
heaven, control of desire and attainment of, 80–81, 84
Heidegger, Martin, 5, 41, 219n39
Hiltebeitel, Alf, 226n35, 231n78
History of Madness (Foucault), 14–15, 23, 44, 49
History of Sexuality (Foucault), x, 21, 26, 30, 207
homoeroticism, 214–15n22
householder (*gārhsthya*), 187
husband
of a courtesan-wife, 106–10
dandy-patron consort in role of, 9
obedience to, 80–85, 87
rebirth of, in the son, 67–68, 85, 99, 117, 229n57, 229–30n58
with a remarried woman as his wife, 97–98
wife as obedient servant to, 80–85
See also son; wife
Huxley, Aldous, 42, 46

identity
adultery and, 63, 110
assumption of, 88
of child of a courtesan-wife, 108–9, 236n59–60
dharma and, 28–29, 30, 51–59, 61–64, 64–66, 77, 87, 106, 118–19
Foucault on, 28–29, 45–46
loss as desubjectivation, 29–30, 38
Mānava Dharmaśāstra on, 15–16, 50–51, 63–66, 66–69, 201
patriarchal, 61–64, 66–69, 85, 116–19
pleasure and, 3, 27–34, 51–59, 61–66, 71, 77, 85, 87, 95, 100–106, 204, 218n21
pre-patriarchal family and, 61–62
renunciation of, 45–46
subordination of, 2
truth and, 24
truth, pleasure, and, 102–3
use of, in pursuit of pleasure, 88, 102–3
of women, 6–7, 15, 16, 51, 67–69
See also caste
independence (*svādhīna*), 55
Island (Huxley), 46

Jamison, Stephanie, 231–32n79
jāyā (wife and mother), 67–68
jñyan (constant insight), 79

kaiśikī vṛtti (erotic-romantic style theater), 119–25, 125–30, 135, 151, 241n80
kalā (art), 191–93, 196–97, 200
Kālidāsa (playwright), 116–19, 139, 142–43, 147
kāma (erotic-aesthetic pleasure)
discourse of, 4, 154–55, 157–59, 163–64, 173–79
as framework for the king in the discourse of theater, 137
in the *Kāmasūtra* trilogy, 18, 53–55, 58, 111
in the *Nāṭṭyaśāstra*, 9–10, 148
subordination to *dharma*, 31–32, 51–59, 60, 77, 87
kāmācāravihārinī (a woman free to follow her desires), 60–61
kāmantantra-sūtradhāra (director of *ars erotica*), 171
kāma-śāstra (discourse of erotic-aesthetic pleasure), 4, 154–55, 157–59, 163–64, 173–79
Kāmasūtra (A Treatise on Pleasure)
on aesthetics of existence, 210

Kāmasūtra (*continued*)
in ancient classical Indian culture, 3–4, 211n11
in ancient Indian culture, ix, 21
arrival in the West of, x, 1
as ars theatrica, 9–10
on art and aesthetics in erotic relationship, 10–11, 85–86, 113, 149, 151, 153, 174, 181–82, 188–91
on art as a foundation of society, 196–97, 200, 201, 203, 247n37
on art as medium of socialization, 191–94, 198, 210
on art as pleasure-play, 191–97
on the city based on erotic-aesthetic pleasure, 18, 195–96
city dandy as arts patron in, ix, 1, 8, 9, 11, 51, 159–62, 181–88, 194–96
dandy-consort as actor in, 135, 181–84, 186–88
dandy-guru as theater director in, 159–62, 180
dharma and, 53–55, 58–59, 89–91, 111, 149
discourse of erotics and theater in, 12–14
on the discourse of love, 57, 153–55, 198
on the discourse of the trilogy, 57–58
on the distinctions between humans and animals, 56–57, 58, 199
as founding text, 54–55, 154, 157
on gender and patriarchy, 15
historical origins of, 11–12
as historical text, 94, 154, 197–200
as intellectual tradition, 21
on love, xi, 10, 11, 56, 57, 59, 96, 182, 205, 206
love based marriage in, 96
nature and origin of, 1, 5–6, 12–14, 20–21, 51–52
on pleasure, 2–3, 9, 88–91, 149, 151, 189–90, 199
on pleasure and the discourse of love, 34
the pleasure-wheel (*raticakra*) in, 34, 88–89
portrait of courtesans in, ix, 7, 9, 11, 87–91, 92
roles of women in, 6–9
on the sixty-four arts, 92–93, 150, 169, 188–89
as theater art, 9–10, 28, 94–111
on the *trivarga* (trilogy) of law, power, and pleasure, 4, 11, 53–55, 58–59, 89–91, 148, 163, 185–86, 212n12
vocabulary of, ix–x, 7–9
western knowledge systems view of, 3–4
kāmījana (pleasure seeker), 160
kanyā (young girl), 7, 95, 96
Kaul, Shonaleeka, 247n37
king
as central figure in *artha*, 87, 137, 138
courtesan in the service of, 145–47
as erotic hero, 140–42, 143
as focus of the royal romance, 125–26, 136–39
as king-poet, 202
power of, 75
as royal dandy, 138, 142–43
See also Bhoja
knowledge formation, 2, 3, 5
krama (sequence), 89
kriḍā (play), 191
kriḍā mātra (pleasure-play), 191
kṛtrim (artificial) love, 101
Kṣatriyas (warrior caste), 65
Kṣemendra (eleventh century CE Kashmiri author), 180
Kuiper, F. B. J., 238n3
kumārī (maidens), 143

Lamb, Charles, 47
Leary, Timothy, 42
Levy, Patrick, 46
life stages (*āśramas*), 186–88, 246n12
Light on Erotic Passion (*Śṛṅgāraprakāśa*), 203
The Little Clay Cart (*Mṛcchakaṭikam*), 126, 134, 193–94, 195
logic, 77–79, 244n41
logician. *See* grammarian
love
art and aesthetics anchored in, 10, 182, 200, 248n48
artificial, 101
of the dandy-guru for the courtesan, 165
death of, 206
defined, 168
discourse of, 10–11, 18, 28, 56, 57–58, 102–3, 119–22, 152, 153–55, 170–74, 182, 198, 199
Freud on, xi
Kāmasūtra on, xi, 10, 11, 56, 57, 59, 96, 182, 205, 206
language of, 167–70
obedient service substituted for, 84–85, 87, 99
planning for, 172
subordinated to pleasure, 102–3
truth and, 26, 102–3
love-pleasure (*rati*) aspect of the courtesan-patron relationship, 100–106
LSD, 43, 48

madness, 23, 35, 42, 44–45, 47
Mahābhārata (the epic)
on dharma and women, 64, 66
on the past without patriarchy, 16
on sexual fidelity, 62–63
on the son and the origin of monogamy, 62–64, 66–69
on women and freedom, 60–61, 62–63
on women and pleasure, 59–62, 116
on women and *sanātana dharma*, 60, 61, 64
mahādevī (chief queen), 143
mahattarās (matrons), 143

Mahmood, Saba, 225–26n29
maidens (*kumarī*), 143
maids in constant attendance (*anucārikā*), 143
man about town (*nāgaraka*), 132
Mānava Dharmaśāstra (Brahmanical law text)
  on abstinence, 78–80
  asceticism of, 78–79, 232–33n88
  on desire, 75–80, 231n78, 231–32n79
  on *dharma* and caste, 64, 227n41
  discourse of *dharma* within, 4, 6, 10, 104
  on the eleven sense organs, 78–80, 82
  as founding text, 4, 54–55
  on identity, 15–16, 50–51, 63–66, 66–69, 201
  on the law of monogamy, 62–63, 66–69
  as the most important source of knowledge about India, 227n41
  philosophy of, 6
  on power, 74–75, 80–85, 230n71, 231n77
  on subordinating and confining women, 69–73, 75–76, 82–83
  on violent punishment, 230n71
mandarasa (dull pleasure), 88
Manu (sage), 104
Marharishi Mahesh Yogi, 43
Marriott, McKim, 229n57
Mathers, E. Powys, 151–52
meditation, 43
men, 123–24
  See also husband
Michaux, Henri, 45
Miller, James, 35, 38, 39
mokṣa (spiritual liberation), 4, 46, 174, 177–78
mokṣa medicine, 46
monogamy, 61–64, 66–69, 71
the mother figure, 103–6, 109
Mṛcchakaṭikam (*The Little Clay Cart*), 126, 134, 193–94, 195

Nāgaraka. *See* city dandy, consort/patron
nagaraśobhinī (chief courtesan of the city), 92
Nahuṣa (earthly king in heaven), 115, 116, 117
Nārada (sage), 124
nartakī (dancers), 143
nāṭaka (royal romance theater), 125–29, 135–47
nāṭakiyā (actresses), 143–45
natural (*svabhāvikam*) love, 101
nāṭyadharmī (theatrical conventions), 241n80
Nāṭyaśāstra (A Treatise on Theater)
  aesthetic pleasure goal of, 9–10, 11, 17, 113, 149
  in ancient Indian culture, ix, 104, 114–19, 153, 237–38n3
  on art as a foundation of society, 196–97, 201, 203, 247n36
  on the *bhāṇas*, 159
  the celestial courtesan in, 115–19, 123–25, 139–43
  on the courtesan on stage, 144–45
  the dandy-consort in, 8, 9, 16–17, 129–35, 181–84, 186–88
  the dandy-guru in, 8, 9, 16–17, 155–57, 159–62, 173–74, 179, 180
  discourse of erotics and theater in, 12–14
  on the discourse of *kāma*, 18
  on erotic pleasure, 148–50, 151, 174
  as founding theater arts text, 115–19, 154, 157
  on happiness, 149
  historical origins of, 11–12
  on the internal/external divisions of the theater of love, 125–29, 131
  on love, 140, 205
  nature and origin of, 1, 12–14, 119–22
  on the participation of women in theater, 122–23, 124
  role in the discourse of theater, 153–55
  on romantic theater, 119–25, 129–30, 135
  the royal romance in, 125–29, 135–42
  sovereignty of erotic pleasure over *dharma in*, 149
  on the theater woman, 143–44
  on the *trivarga* (trilogy) of law, power, and pleasure, 148
  on violent (gods and demons) theater, 122–23
  women in the royal harem of the, 143–44, 146
nāyaka (actor), ix, 8–9, 13, 88, 114
nāyikā (actress), ix, 8–9, 13, 88, 95, 114
nonviolence, 74, 231n72

Olivelle, Patrick, 65, 69, 229–30n58, 230n69, 231n72, 231n79
oral discourse, 156
Orientalism (Said), 14
Orientalism and Foucault, 14–15

Pādatāḍitka (*bhāṇa* play), 158, 163–64, 177–78
Padmaprābhṛtaka (*bhāṇa*), 166
Pagal Baba (Mad Saint), 46
pākṣikī (another man's wife), 7, 95, 96
parādhīnatva (dependence/subordination), 55–56, 57–58
paricārikā (maids of special work), 143
parrhesia (courage of truth), 249n12
paternity, 63, 66–67
patriarchy
  caste and, 63–64
  the courtesan and, 16
  devirilizing, 199
  dharma and, 6, 58, 66–69, 198–99
  Freud and, xi, 111
  identity and, 61–64, 66–69, 85, 116–19
  subordination of women and, 6, 15, 59–62, 71, 182
perspective, 40–41
Phaedrus (Plato), 26

pīṭhamarda (art teacher), 183, 184
plan for love (*prītim yojayet*), 172
Plato, 26, 85, 157–58
play (*kriḍā*), 191
pleasure
  aesthetic, 9–10
  autonomy in, 7, 214–15n22
  courtesan as central figure in, 7, 87–91, 114, 149–52, 162–67, 177–78, 206
  death association of, 35–37, 219n39
  as desubjectivation, 15, 17, 23, 26–34, 30, 35, 36–37, 38, 82, 88, 89, 113, 149
  discourse of, and the dandy-guru, 154–55, 157–59, 163–64, 173–79
  dull, 88
  as an event of desubjectivation, 32–34
  as an event of enlightenment, 37–42
  Foucault on, 2, 19, 22–23, 24–25, 26, 31, 35–42, 45, 88
  identity and, 27–34, 30, 51–59, 61–64, 64–66, 77, 87, 95, 100–106, 204
  Kāmasūtra on, 2–3, 9, 57–58, 88–91, 149, 151, 189–90, 199
  knowledge and truth subordinated to, 177–79
  legislative sovereignty of, in ancient India, 3
  loss of sense of the self and, 30, 36–37, 38, 82, 89
  love subordinated to, 102–3
  of the mind-self, 199
  nature of, 35
  nonsubjective, 30
  obedient service substituted for, 84–85
  as ontic category, 5
  pleasure-power spiral, 34
  pursuit of, and identity assumption, 88
  raticakra (pleasure-wheel), 88–89
  and the remarried woman, 97–98
  repression and, xi, 27, 52–53, 113
  śabdakāma (word-pleasure/desire), 167–70, 172–73, 199
  scientia sexualis and, 25–26
  and the self, 23, 76–77
  the stranger as figure of, 29
  subjective, 30–31
  subordinated to identity, 3, 67–68, 71, 85
  subordinated to knowledge and truth, 3, 26–27, 85
  subordinated to power, 31–32, 51–59, 60, 77, 87
  and truth, 23, 24–27, 41, 54, 102–3
  truth and sovereignty, 162–67
  truth, self, and, 15, 110–11
  women and, 59–62, 70–71
  See also sexual-erotic pleasure
pleasure-play (*kriḍā*), 191
pleasure seeker (*kāmījana*), 160
pleasure-wheel (*raticakra*), 34, 88–89
Poetics Woman, 201–2
Poetry Man, 201–2
political power. See *artha*
Pollock, Sheldon, 212n13, 231n77, 247n37, 248n48
popular romance theater (*prakaraṇa*), 125–29, 129–35
pornography, x
prācchāditasvabhāva (veiled nature), 59
praharīs (ushers), 143
prajā (male offspring), 68
Prajāpati (Hindu deity), 70
prakaraṇa (popular romance theater)
  characters in, 130
  the courtesan role in, 125–29
  the dandy-consort role in, 129–35
  mutation into royal romance theater, 147
  origin of, 138
  in real-life erotic romance, 170–71
preṣanacārikā (maids for running errands), 143
prītim yojayet (plan for love), 172
psychedelic revolution, 41–43
psychedeliology, 42, 46
psychoanalysis, x–xi
punarbhū (remarried woman), 7, 95, 97
Purāṇas (ancient Indian culture text), 116
Purūravas (king), 116–19, 139, 147
puruṣa (full extent of man), 68
puruṣārthas (the ends of man), 4, 53, 224n17, 212n13
pūrvaraṅga, 238n3

rajas (vigor), 77
Rājaśekhara (ninth-century court poet), 201–3
rakṣa (to protect and guard), 69
Rāmāyaṇa (ancient Indian culture text), 116
Rampuri (sadhu), 48
ramyān guṇān (erotic qualities), 165–66
rasa (aesthetic pleasure), 17, 113, 121, 148, 174
rati (love-pleasure aspect of the courtesan-patron relationship), 100–106
raticakra (pleasure-wheel), 34, 88–89
ratilālasā (desire for pleasure), 59
ratim yojayet (love), 107
reincarnation, 80–81
remarried woman, 97–98
repression, xi, 27, 52–53, 113
Ṛgveda, 116
romantic theater, 119–25, 129–30, 135
royal dandy, 138, 142–43
royal harem, 72, 125, 135, 136, 142–47
royal romance theater (*nāṭaka*), 125–29, 135–42, 142–47

śabdakāma (word-pleasure/desire), 167–70, 172–73, 199, 244–45n41
sādhāraṇī (general woman), 106

sadhus (renunciate monks), 45–46
sahasrākṣa (thousand eyed), 166
Said, Edward, 14–15
Saint Foucault (Halperin), 46
salon (*goṣṭhi*), 176, 180, 184, 189–90
samāja (art festival), 192–93
sāmānyā (common woman), 106, 149–50
sāmānyaguṇayogena (universal emotion), 149
samāpānaka (drinking parties), 184
sanātana dharma (eternal law), 60, 61, 64
Śaṅkara (Indian philosopher), 48, 204–5
Sarasvatī (goddess of speech), 201
śāstra (sexual knowledge), 88–89, 156
sattva (goodness), 77
Schokker, G. H., 244–45n41
Schopenhauer, Arthur, 44, 47
scientia sexualis (science of sexuality)
  as a contrast to the erotic arts, x, xi, 1–2, 3, 10, 18–19, 21–23, 26–27, 53, 111–12, 204–10
  pleasure and, 25–26, 28
Scott, Joan, 223n5
secretiveness (*guḍhākāra*), 59
self
  cult of the self, 250n20
  immortality of, 67–68, 85
  loss of sense of and pleasure, 17, 27–34, 36–37, 38, 82, 89
  mastery of, 72–74, 80–85
  multiple selves in the *Mānava Dharmaśāstra*, 229n58
  pleasure of, 76–77
  pleasure, truth, and, 15, 23, 208–9
  and reflexivity, 218n21
  subordination of, 2
  truth, and self-love, 205
sex and sexuality, 2, 6, 23–24, 55–56, 56–57
sexual-erotic pleasure (*kāma*), 4, 5–6, 9–10, 18, 77
sexual-erotic pleasure discourse (*kāma-śāstra*), 4
sexual fidelity, 62–64, 66–69
  See also monogamy
sexual promiscuity and identity, 66–71, 85, 99, 117
śilpakārinī (craftswomen), 143
"Simplest of Pleasures" (Foucault), 37
sixty-four arts of the courtesan, 92–93, 150, 169, 188–89
social ethics (*gaṇa-dharma*), 193, 196
society, 193–97, 201–2, 202–3
Socrates, 26
son
  of the courtesan-wife, 108–9
  identity of, 61–62, 67, 228–29n54
  importance of, in patriarchal family, 61–62, 66–69
  and the origin of monogamy, 62–64, 66–69
  as rebirth of the father, 67–68, 85, 99, 117, 229n57, 229–30n58
spiritual liberation and desubjectivation, 43, 48, 221n60, 222n73
śṛṅgāra prakaraṇa (love affair), 129
Śṛṅgāraprakāśa (Light on Erotic Passion), 203
śṛṅgāra rasa (erotic-aesthetic pleasure), 121, 137, 148–50, 170–74
Sternbach, Ludwik, 93
sthāvirās (old dames), 143
sthāyinī (ordinary wives), 143
Story of Vikrama and Urvaśī (Kālidāsa), 116–19, 139, 142–43, 147
the stranger as figure of pleasure, 29–30, 89, 101
Strathner, Marilyn, 229n57
subjectivity and power, 15, 21, 80–85
sublimation, xi, 27
subordination
  Brahmanical law and, 15, 58–59
  gender relations and, 6–7, 213–14n21
  pleasure and truth, 3, 26–27
  sex to sexuality, 24
  of women (*asvatantra*), 6–7, 15, 51, 59–62, 62–64, 69–73, 75–76, 80–85, 97, 178–79, 182, 198, 199–200
Śūdraka (playwright), 134, 193–94
Śūdras (lowest caste), 65, 97
sukha (happiness), 149
sukumāra (erotic-aesthetic/romantic) plays, 122–23
superintendent of courtesans (*gaṇikā-adhyakṣa*), 93
śuśrūṣā (obedient service), 82–83
svabhāvikim (natural) love, 101
svādhīna (independence), 55
svāminī (highborn wives), 143
svātantrayam (freedom of the self), 68, 69, 70
Svātī (sage), 124
Śvetaketu, 62–63, 66
Sweet, Michael J., 214–15n22
Śyāmilka (*bhāṇa* playwright), 158–59
Symposium (Plato), 26, 85

tamas (darkness), 77
tapas (ascetic practices), 149
teacher of specific skills (*ācārya*), 171–72
techne tou biou (art of life), 207
theater arts. See *ars theatrica*
Three Essays on Love (Freud), xi
A Treatise on Pleasure. See *Kāmasūtra*
A Treatise on Theater. See *Nātyaśāstra*
trilogy-tetralogy discursive formations, 4–5, 7
trivarga (trilogy) of law, power, and pleasure, 4, 53–55, 58–59, 89–91, 148, 163, 185–86, 224n16, 234n7
tṛtīya prakṛti (third nature), 214n22

truth
  Foucault on, 24–25
  and identity in the discourse of love, 102–3
  ontic and ontological, 5, 41
  origin of, 5
  pleasure and, 3, 15, 23, 26–27, 38–42, 54, 85, 110–11, 208–9
  and reflexivity, 218n21
  and self-love, 205
  the self, pleasure, and, 15, 23, 204, 208–9
  subordination of, 2, 5, 178–79

Uddālaka, 62–63, 66
udyānagamana (garden parties), 184
Umā (Śiva's wife), 201
universal emotion (*sāmānyaguṇayogena*), 149
Upaniṣads (Sanskrit texts), 47
Urvaśī (celebrated celestial courtesan), 116–19, 139, 142–43, 147
Use of Pleasure (Foucault), 26, 30–31, 207
ushers (*praharīs*), 143

vaiśika. See dandy-consort/patron
vaiśika-śāsanam (courtesan's code of conduct), 105
vaiśikaśāstra (discourse on courtesan and her patron-consort), 132
Vaiśyas (business caste), 65
Vātsyāyana (philosopher), 12–13, 153, 154
Vedas and the Vedic period, 83–84, 91, 114, 115, 116, 197
veśyā (courtesan-actress). *See* courtesan
vigor (*rajas*), 77
Vikramōrvaśiyam (royal romance plays), 139
  See also royal romance theater
vikṛti (deformation of nature), 214n22
virility, 31–32, 199
Viśvālaka (apprentice to the dandy-guru), 162, 176
viṭa. See dandy-guru
viṭasabhā (assemblies), 180
viṭa samāja (congresses), 180
vivṛṇoti (true nature unveiled), 59
vṛtti (profession) aspect of the courtesan-patron relationship, 100–106

warrior caste (Kṣatriyas), 65
wife
  as adulteress, 7, 95, 96, 98–100, 110
  childlessness and autonomy of, 97–98
  constructing the subjectivity of, 71–73
  courtesan in role of, 9, 99–100, 106–10, 117–18
  exclusion from the *Kāmasūtra* of, 94–95
  identity lost in the figure of, 6–7, 15, 16, 51, 67–69, 105, 117–19
  as obedient servant, 80–85, 87, 99, 233n100
  See also husband; son
wife as mother (*jāyā*), 67–68
Will to Knowledge (Foucault), 34
women
  as adulteress, 7, 95, 96
  the courtesan, caste, and, 16
  dharma, power and, 6, 64, 66
  in erotic-aesthetic (romantic) theater, 122, 123, 124
  identity lost in the figure of the wife, 6–7, 15, 16, 51, 67–69
  kanyā (young girl), 7, 95, 96
  Mahābhārata on women and freedom, 60–61, 62–63
  Mahābhārata on women and pleasure, 59–62, 116
  as obedient servant, 80–85, 87, 99
  pākṣikī (another man's wife), 7, 95, 96
  participation of, in theater, 122–23, 124, 143–44
  physical confinement of, 71–73
  pleasure and, 59–62, 70–71
  punarbhū (remarried woman), 7, 95, 97–98
  roles of, in the *Kāmasūtra*, 6–9
  subordination of, 6–7, 15, 51, 59–62, 62–64, 69–73, 75–76, 80–85, 97, 178–79, 182, 198, 199–200
women overseers (*āyuktikās*), 143
word-pleasure/desire (*śabdakāma*), 167–70, 172–73, 199

young girl (*kanyā*), 7, 95, 96

Zwilling, Leonard, 214–15n22